BARRON'S
THE TRUSTED NAME IN TEST PREP

PSAT/NMSQT®
Study Guide
Premium
2025

Brian W. Stewart, M.Ed.
Founder and President
BWS Education Consulting, Inc.

Dedication

Dedicated to Caitlin, Andrew, and Eloise—without your love and support, this book would not have been possible. I would like to especially thank my mom, my dad, Andy, Pam, Hannah, Mitchell, Michal, Julia, and Lydia for their invaluable help with this undertaking. I am grateful to all the support from my publisher, especially Jennifer Goodenough and Angela Tartaro.

Thanks so much to all of my students over the years—I have learned far more from you than you have learned from me.

PSAT/NMSQT® is a registered trademark of the College Board and the National Merit Scholarship Corporation, which are not affiliated with Barron's and were not involved in the production of, and do not endorse, this product.

Published by Kaplan North America, LLC, d/b/a Barron's Educational Series
1515 W. Cypress Creek Road
Fort Lauderdale, FL 33309
www.barronseduc.com

ISBN: 978-1-5062-9246-5

10 9 8 7 6 5 4 3 2 1

Kaplan North America, LLC, d/b/a Barron's Educational Series print books are available at special quantity discounts to use for sales promotions, employee premiums, or educational purposes. For more information or to purchase books, please call the Simon & Schuster special sales department at 866-506-1949.

Table of Contents

MATH

ADAPTIVE PRACTICE TEST

APPENDIX

> Be sure to check out the over 200 Online PSAT Practice Questions that accompany this book to target your weak areas in the Digital PSAT format.

About the Author

Brian W. Stewart is the founder and president of BWS Education Consulting, Inc., a boutique tutoring and test preparation company based in Columbus, Ohio. Brian is a nationally recognized test preparation expert, having over 30,000 hours of direct instructional experience with a wide variety of learners from all over the world. He has earned perfect scores on many standardized tests, helped hundreds of students reach their college admissions goals, and presented on best tutoring practices at national conferences.

Brian has used his experience and expertise to write several best-selling books with Barron's, including *Barron's ACT* and *Barron's Digital SAT*. He is a former high school teacher and graduate of Princeton University (A.B.) and The Ohio State University (M.Ed.).

Brian resides in Columbus with his wife, two children, and an assortment of pets.

To learn more about Brian's online tutoring and group presentations, please visit www.bwseducationconsulting.com.

How to Use This Book

This book is designed to allow for highly targeted preparation for the Digital PSAT. Based on your previous PSAT test scores or the PSAT diagnostic test in this book, review the strategies and content knowledge that are most relevant to your needs. There are hundreds of drills that range in difficulty from easy to challenging so that you can achieve the very best results for your personal situation. What you find in the text is aligned with the information about the digital PSAT available in February of 2024. You should check information from the College Board for the latest updates.

Diagnostic Test

First, take the diagnostic test to gain an understanding of your strengths and weaknesses. It is a complete test with answer explanations and a question-type analysis guide, so you know what types of concepts need the most attention.

Review and Practice

The Reading, Writing, and Math sections each have:

- Proven test-taking strategies that allow you to customize your approach
- Extensive review of key concepts, particularly grammar and math knowledge
- Practice questions fully aligned with PSAT content
- Advanced practice drills for those students seeking National Merit recognition

Adaptive Practice Test

The final section of the book offers the opportunity to take a full-length PSAT adaptive practice test that includes all question types found on the actual PSAT for the Reading, Writing, and Math sections. Comprehensive answer explanations are provided for the questions.

Online Practice

In addition to the diagnostic test and adaptive test within this book, there are extensive targeted online drills that you can use to sharpen your weak areas. All questions include answer explanations. Further, there is a vocabulary resource available in the online practice if you need to improve your performance on word-in-context questions.

For Students

Every strategy and explanation is based on what I have found works best for students on the actual PSAT. No matter your personal goals and background knowledge, you will find practice drills and test-taking strategies that are geared toward your situation.

Best of luck,
Brian W. Stewart

For Teachers

While many students will like working through this book independently, others will maximize their learning when they have a great teacher or tutor as their guide. Help your students work smarter instead of simply working harder by utilizing the concept reviews and drills most appropriate for your students' needs. Also, you can coach your students on which test-taking strategies will be the best fit based on their past performance. I am hopeful that the skills that students develop from using this book will help them not just with the PSAT, but also with their academic coursework and future careers. If you have any suggestions for future editions, please reach out via the publisher.

Sincerely,

Brian W. Stewart

Introduction to the Digital PSAT/NMSQT

The PSAT is a preliminary SAT exam that is used both for assessing student academic progress and for determining eligibility for the National Merit Scholarship competition. Over 4,000,000 high school students take the PSAT or PSAT 10 each year. It is such a popular test because the PSAT helps students gauge their college readiness as well as prepare for the SAT exam. There are different PSAT exams, including PSAT 8/9, PSAT 10, and PSAT/NMSQT, which are typically based on a student's grade level.

What Does the PSAT Test Do?

The PSAT tests the skills and general knowledge you will need to be successful in college and beyond.

Reading Comprehension Skills

- Determining what you can infer from a reading passage
- Finding what evidence in a passage supports a claim
- Establishing the meaning of words in context
- Analyzing graphs as they relate to a reading passage

Writing Skills

- Knowledge of English grammar fundamentals (punctuation, subject-verb agreement, verb tense, etc.)
- Understanding how best to use notes to accomplish a specific task
- Awareness of proper use of transitions

Math Problem-Solving Skills

- Solving questions with an emphasis on Algebra 1 and Algebra 2 (just a handful of questions may relate to geometry and precalculus)
- Analyzing and problem-solving using charts and graphs
- Understanding and solving real-world applications

The digital PSAT has two Evidence-Based Reading and Writing modules (sections) and two Math modules. The test is **adaptive**—the second modules of both the Reading/Writing and the Math will change in difficulty based on how students do on the first modules of each type. Students who perform better on the first modules will have more challenging questions in the second modules, while students who do not perform as well will have easier questions in the second modules. Here is a summary of the format of the digital PSAT:

Digital PSAT Format

PSAT Module	Format
Reading and Writing One	32 Minutes, 27 Questions, Standard Difficulty
Reading and Writing Two	32 Minutes, 27 Questions, Adaptive Difficulty (easier or harder questions depending on how you did on the first Reading/Writing section)
Break—10 Minutes	
Math One	35 Minutes, 22 Questions, Standard Difficulty
Math Two	35 Minutes, 22 Questions, Adaptive Difficulty (easier or harder questions depending on how you did on the first Math section)

If you have previously taken or prepared for the paper-based version of the PSAT, here are some of the key differences between the older and current digital version of the PSAT:

Test Length

Old PSAT	Digital PSAT
▪ About three hours long, including breaks and administration ▪ 60 minutes for Reading ▪ 35 minutes Writing and Language ▪ 25 minutes for Non-Calculator Math ▪ 45 minutes for Calculator Math	▪ A little over two hours long; assesses the same skills as the longer PSAT by having an *adaptive* format ▪ Less time needed for test administration because students can download the testing app ahead of time

Test Format

Old PSAT	Digital PSAT
▪ One test form for all students on a particular test day ▪ Paper test booklets with scantron sheets for answers ▪ Can go back to questions within a section before time is called ▪ Students should bring their own watches and calculators—they are not provided. ▪ Can write on the test booklet ▪ Experimental questions (ones that don't count toward your score), if given, are in a section after the test.	▪ Different test questions for different students ▪ Taken on a laptop that students provide or that the test center makes available ▪ Can still go back and review questions. Questions can be flagged. ▪ Countdown clock and calculator built into the program, although students can still bring a watch and calculator if they would like. ▪ Can write on provided scrap paper ▪ A few experimental questions are incorporated into each test section.

Reading and Writing & Language

Old PSAT	Digital PSAT
▪ Reading passages are 500–750 words long and have 9–10 questions each. ▪ Reading genres include fiction, social science, historical documents, and natural science. ▪ Writing and Language passages are about 450 words long and have 11 questions each.	▪ Reading and Writing passages are no longer than 150 words. Each passage has just one question accompanying it. ▪ Has a greater variety of reading genres represented. Along with the existing PSAT reading genres, there will be humanities, drama, and poetry excerpts.

Math

Old PSAT	Digital PSAT
▪ Non-Calculator and Calculator sections ▪ Formula sheet provided at the beginning of the test section ▪ Students need to bring their own calculators.	▪ Calculator permitted throughout the test ▪ Formula sheet and digital Desmos™ calculator available in the program ▪ Word problems are typically more concise than they were before.

Why Has the College Board Made This Change to the PSAT?

- **Adaptive tests have a long track record of success.** The GRE and GMAT, both of which are used for graduate school admissions, are computer-based adaptive assessments. These tests are shorter than they would otherwise be since they adjust the difficulty of the questions based on student performance.
- **Students have become more comfortable with computer-based assessments.** With so many students learning remotely over the past few years, digital learning has become far more common.
- **The test should be easier to administer.** Testing administrators will not have to secure test booklets, and schools will not have to take nearly as much time out of the day to offer the PSAT.
- **Test security should be improved.** Since students will have different test questions, it is far more difficult to cheat. Also, it will be far less likely that a test security breach will lead to score cancellations.

What Should I Take to the Test?

Be certain to bring the following on test day:

- Pens or pencils you can use on the scrap paper.
- Your own laptop or tablet if you have one. (If you don't, can request one from College Board in advance.) If you want to use your own laptop or tablet for the PSAT, be sure to download the testing app ahead of time and make sure your device is fully charged.
- A permitted calculator (see *https://www.collegeboard.org/psat-nmsqt/approved-calculators* for a complete list). Although there is a Desmos calculator embedded in the testing program, you may prefer to use your own.
- A watch to monitor your pacing if you would prefer to not rely on the timer embedded in the testing program. (Be sure it doesn't make noise and cannot connect to the internet.)
- A photo ID. (If you are taking the exam at your own school, you will likely not need one.)
- An e-mail address, so colleges can contact you and you can access your scores online.
- A snack or drink for your break. Be sure you do not place these on your desk.
- Do NOT bring a cell phone. You don't want to risk it going off accidentally. Also, you won't be able to check it during a break.

What Should I Do in the Days Leading Up to the PSAT?

If the PSAT were a test for which you could cram, it would make sense to stay up late studying the night before. Since it is more of a critical thinking test, you need to be as relaxed and as well rested as possible to do your best. Here are some things you should do before the PSAT.

- Download the PSAT testing app ahead of time and familiarize yourself with the program. You can find the application at *https://bluebook.collegeboard.org/*. Don't let the day of the PSAT be the first time you use the computer-based format.
- Go to bed at a reasonable hour starting a week before the test. If you wait until the night before the test to get a good night's sleep, you may not be rested enough on test day. After all, calming down and relaxing the night before a major assessment can be extremely difficult.
- Know the test directions—you do not want to waste time reading the directions on each section. At a minimum, know that you SHOULD INCLUDE AN ANSWER for every question since there is no guessing penalty.
- Become comfortable with timing. Do at least some practice with timing so you will not work too quickly or too slowly on test day. Be aware that the timing on the second modules may be more challenging, as you may have a more difficult set of questions.
- Know your strategic approach ahead of time—this way you can devote your full attention to solving problems instead of experimenting with strategies during the test.

What Is a National Merit Scholarship and How Do I Qualify?

The National Merit Scholarship is a prestigious award administered by the National Merit Scholarship Corporation that recognizes students based on their academic merit, using PSAT scores as the principal eligibility factor. The scores are used to compute the selection index. Your section scores from the Reading/Writing and Math sections are taken to give you a selection index between 48 and 228. (Even though the Reading and Writing section comprises half of the PSAT, it makes up two-thirds of your selection index calculation.) Depending on which state you live in, a selection index in the 200s may qualify you for some type of National Merit recognition.

National Merit Scholarships range from single-payment $2,500 scholarships to college-sponsored scholarships that provide a full ride for tuition and room/board, plus a stipend for all four years of school. Out of the roughly 1.6 million high school juniors who take the PSAT/NMSQT, about 50,000 receive some sort of National Merit recognition, such as being named a Commended Scholar or a Semi-Finalist. Only about 7,500 students nationwide receive a National Merit Scholarship. In order to be a National Merit Scholar, you must typically perform in the top 0.5 percent of students. To learn more about the National Merit program, go to *www.nationalmerit.org*.

In addition to the National Merit Scholarship program, PSAT scores are now used to determine eligibility for other academic recognition programs. If you are African American, Hispanic American or Latino, or Indigenous, and/or live in a rural area, you may be eligible to apply for academic recognition by the College Board. You can go to *www.psat.org/recognition* and the appendix of this book for the latest information on these programs.

What Are the Requirements to Participate in the National Merit Scholarship Program?

- Take the PSAT/NMSQT no later than the third year of high school—typically this is the junior year for students who take the full four years to graduate.
- Be a high school student in the United States or its territories, or be a U.S. citizen or resident attending high school abroad.
- Be on track for high school graduation and college admission the fall after high school graduation.

What If I Miss the PSAT/NMSQT Because of an Emergency?

You or a school official should write to the National Merit Scholarship Corporation as soon as possible (at the latest, April 1 after the PSAT) to request information about alternate entry into the scholarship program. The mailing address is:

National Merit Scholarship Corporation
1560 Sherman Avenue, Suite 200
Evanston, IL 60201-4897
Go to *www.nationalmerit.org* for more details.

What About PSAT Accommodations and Extended Time?

If you are a student who has special learning needs and you have an IEP or 504 plan with your school, you may be eligible for accommodations on the PSAT. Some of the different types of accommodations offered include 50 percent or 100 percent extended time and extra breaks. Some students may qualify to take the PSAT in a paper-based format instead of a digital format. Applying for accommodations on the PSAT is easiest and fastest if you do so through your school. Keep in mind that you should allow at least seven weeks for the College Board to review your request. You can find more information about PSAT testing with accommodations at *https://accommodations.collegeboard.org/*.

What If English Is Not My Native Language?

The College Board offers testing options to students who have English language support in school and are considered to be *English learners* by the state or federal government. Students with English learner support may be able to use 50 percent extra time, an approved bilingual dictionary, and translated test directions. Unlike special needs accommodations, extended time for English learners is available only on the test date for which you register. Speak to your school counselor, ESL teacher, or administrator for help on PSAT English learner testing support.

What Is the PSAT 10? How Will This Book Help Me Prepare for It?

The PSAT 10 is the same test as the PSAT/NMSQT. Thus, if you would like to prepare for the PSAT 10, this book is exactly what you need. Although the tests themselves are identical, there are three important differences between the PSAT 10 and the PSAT/NMSQT.

- The PSAT 10 is offered in the spring, while the PSAT/NMSQT is offered in the fall.
- The PSAT 10 is for tenth-grade students, while the PSAT/NMSQT is for eleventh-grade students (although many freshmen and sophomores take the PSAT/NMSQT).
- The PSAT 10 will not enter students in the National Merit Scholarship competition, while juniors who take the PSAT/NMSQT can enter this competition. Students who take either exam will be considered for other scholarship programs through the Student Search Service.

If your school does not offer the PSAT 10 and you would like to try the PSAT as a tenth grader, talk to your guidance counselor about taking the PSAT/NMSQT in the fall of your tenth-grade year.

How Can I Manage My Test Anxiety?

With only one shot to perform well on the PSAT for National Merit consideration, taking the PSAT can be a stressful process. Being nervous is completely normal. Here are a few things to keep in mind if you find anxiety interfering with your ability to perform your best.

- When it comes to college admissions, how you perform on the actual SAT and/or ACT will be much more important than your PSAT performance. You will have many opportunities to take the SAT and/or ACT.
- Colleges will receive your scores only if you opt-in to the informational services.
- Mentally rehearse ahead of time to think about how you can best respond to the pressure of the PSAT. Are you someone who tends to rush through tests? Are you someone who tends to get stuck on questions? Knowing your tendencies will help you recognize if your thought process is off track, enabling you to make adjustments to your test-taking strategies for test day.
- Consider trying the Digital SAT before trying the Digital PSAT. The two tests have the same format and timing, so taking the Digital SAT before the Digital PSAT can be an excellent dress rehearsal.

Realize that if the PSAT doesn't go well even after quite a bit of preparation, you will have built skills that will help you on both the SAT and ACT since those two tests have questions very similar to much of what you will find on the PSAT.

How Can I Use This Book to Prepare?

This book allows you to focus on your areas of weakness. It also helps you customize your strategies and mindset depending on your situation. Not only can you spend your time practicing math, for example, but you can also spend your time practicing the types of math questions that are most challenging for you, be they algebra or data analysis. The practice exercises are designed to give you comprehensive coverage of all the types of questions and concepts you will face. If you work through everything in this book, it is unlikely that you will encounter surprises on test day.

If you are unsure what areas of the test are most difficult for you, start by taking the full-length PSAT diagnostic test. Evaluate your performance to see what types of passages and questions give you the most difficulty. Then review the strategies and materials from the different chapters to sharpen your skills. When you are done with the chapters, do more practice with the adaptive test at the end of the book. To really push yourself, try the advanced practice drills and online resources for additional questions.

If you wish to do even more long-term preparation, you should read a wide variety of well-written texts. At a minimum, install an e-reading app on your phone and use it to spend a few minutes each day reading, no matter where you are. If you want to go all out, seek the types of reading that you find most difficult. Read more material from those genres so that your weaknesses turn into strengths. Reading books will help improve your reading comprehension skills, your ability to pick up the meaning of vocabulary in context, and your feel for English grammar.

> **TIP**
>
> Remember that the strategy that works for one student may not work for another student. This book is designed to help you customize your strategy and practice.

What If I Have a Limited Amount of Time to Prepare?

Here are some suggested plans depending on how long you have to prepare.

- If you have one day, read through the strategies in the chapters for each test section: Reading, Writing, and Math. Look through the full-length diagnostic test to become familiar with the directions, time requirements, and structure of the PSAT. Try a few practice questions.
- If you have one week, take the full-length diagnostic test under timed conditions to determine your strengths and weaknesses. Then review the strategies in the chapters for each of the test sections. Target your areas of weakness based on the diagnostic test by working through selected review drills. The drills are broken down by categories, so it will be easy to pick out where you should focus.
- If you have one month, systematically work through everything in this book. The strategies, content review, drills, and practice tests will give you the best possible preparation to achieve a top score on the PSAT/NMSQT. Also, be sure to try the full-length PSAT practice in the College Board Bluebook application.

If you are a sophomore or freshman, you may want to take the PSAT when it is offered at your school even though it will not count toward National Merit consideration. The pressure of this actual test will prepare you for when it is most important for you to do well on the PSAT—in October of your junior year. The better prepared you are, the less nervous you will feel on test day.

Let's get to work!

> Be sure to check out the over 200 Online PSAT Practice Questions that accompany this book to target your weak areas in the Digital PSAT format.

Diagnostic Test

Diagnostic Test

A full-length PSAT diagnostic test is on the pages that follow. Allow a little over two hours of uninterrupted time to complete the entire test. Find a spot to take the test where you will not be distracted. You can take a ten-minute break after the two Reading and Writing modules and before the Math modules.

Note: On the following pages, there is an answer sheet you can use to write down your letter choices and math answers. Feel free to use the sheet to record your answers or simply circle and write down your answers in the test as you go.

Completing this diagnostic test will help you determine your PSAT strengths and weaknesses. Think about the following after you take the test.

- How are you with timing?
- Do you find certain types of reading questions to be challenging?
- Do particular reading texts and genres give you more difficulty than others?
- Do you need to review English grammar concepts?
- Do some types of writing questions give you more trouble than others?
- Do you need to review or learn some math concepts?
- What kinds of math questions are toughest for you?

After completing the test, review your answers with the "Diagnostic Test Analysis Guide" to determine what types of questions and concepts you most need to study.

Good luck!

ANSWER SHEET
Diagnostic Test

Reading and Writing Module 1

1. _____   10. _____   19. _____

2. _____   11. _____   20. _____

3. _____   12. _____   21. _____

4. _____   13. _____   22. _____

5. _____   14. _____   23. _____

6. _____   15. _____   24. _____

7. _____   16. _____   25. _____

8. _____   17. _____   26. _____

9. _____   18. _____   27. _____

ANSWER SHEET
Diagnostic Test

Reading and Writing Module 2

1. ____   10. ____   19. ____

2. ____   11. ____   20. ____

3. ____   12. ____   21. ____

4. ____   13. ____   22. ____

5. ____   14. ____   23. ____

6. ____   15. ____   24. ____

7. ____   16. ____   25. ____

8. ____   17. ____   26. ____

9. ____   18. ____   27. ____

ANSWER SHEET
Diagnostic Test

Math Module 1

1. _____   12. _____

2. _____   13. _____

3. _____   14. _____

4. _____   15. _____

5. _____   16. _____

6. _____   17. _____

7. _____   18. _____

8. _____   19. _____

9. _____   20. _____

10. _____   21. _____

11. _____   22. _____

ANSWER SHEET
Diagnostic Test

Math Module 2

1. ____   12. ____

2. ____   13. ____

3. ____   14. ____

4. ____   15. ____

5. ____   16. ____

6. ____   17. ____

7. ____   18. ____

8. ____   19. ____

9. ____   20. ____

10. ____   21. ____

11. ____   22. ____

Diagnostic Test

Section 1: Reading and Writing Module 1

32 MINUTES, 27 QUESTIONS

DIRECTIONS ⌄

You will be tested on a variety of important reading and writing skills. Each question has one or more passages, possibly including a graph or table. Carefully read each passage and question and choose the best answer to the question based on the passage(s).

Every question in this section is multiple-choice with four possible answers. Each question has only one best answer.

This cycle was broken by the unification of five Iroquois tribes in The Confederacy of Peace and Power. The confederacy was born from a Huron woman who had a dream that her son would be a prophet. She named him Deganawidah, or "the prophet." He preached to his people, but his words fell on deaf ears. Consequently, he left the Huron and traveled through the Iroquois spreading his message of peace. Within the Iroquois he <u>collected</u> many followers, including Hiawatha.

1

As used in the text, what does the word "collected" most nearly mean?

- Ⓐ Placated
- Ⓑ Composed
- Ⓒ Catalogued
- Ⓓ Gathered

To begin to understand the possibilities of time, we first need a brief introduction of spacetime. We're all familiar with our three-dimensional world, but we need to consider a fourth dimension as well—time. Time passes. Therefore, you can sit still in a chair not traveling in three dimensions, but traveling in spacetime. We think of time as <u>passing</u> forward.

2

As used in the text, what does the word "passing" most nearly mean?

- Ⓐ Living
- Ⓑ Moving
- Ⓒ Throwing
- Ⓓ Succeeding

1   MODULE 1   1

In science class, the two friends frantically mixed their chemical solutions together. They had failed to meet over the weekend and their assignment was nowhere close to being finished. When they received a failing grade, the teacher remarked that the _____ to their problem would come from adequate preparation.

3

Which choice completes the text with the most logical and precise word or phrase?

- (A) resolution
- (B) mixture
- (C) choice
- (D) origin

Employing slightly subtler brushstrokes than most of his counterparts, the artist focused his labors on capturing the tranquil, shore-side recreations of bourgeois vacationers. Around this time, it was becoming <u>fashionable</u> among the middle-class to possess commemorative depictions of the places one had traveled, and he managed to fill this niche masterfully.

4

As used in the text, what does the word "fashionable" most nearly mean?

- (A) Tailored
- (B) Popular
- (C) Leisurely
- (D) Economical

The stove and the oven remain to this day our most used cooking technologies, and innovations in the field of heating elements have frequently ameliorated the mechanism without much change to the principal design. The commercialization of natural gas in late 17th century England eventually gave cooks the ability to precisely _____ their cooking flame, as well as the convenience of instantaneous ignition. To this day, gas ranges are preferred by many professional chefs.

5

Which choice completes the text with the most logical and precise word or phrase?

- (A) annihilate
- (B) satisfy
- (C) craft
- (D) manipulate

Parthenogenesis is not limited to lizards and sharks, but is common in insects, crayfish, flatworms, snails, snakes, and even some birds. <u>The exception is mammals.</u> Although parthenogenesis can be artificially induced in a science laboratory, it is never known to have occurred in mammals naturally.

6

Which choice best states the function of the underlined sentence in the text as a whole?

- (A) To transition to a clarification
- (B) To define an unfamiliar term
- (C) To give ethical reasoning
- (D) To analyze an economic impact

MODULE 1

1 · 1

Text 1

We teach in schools that a presidential candidate must receive an absolute majority of the electoral college votes to win the presidential election, but we don't teach the mechanics of how a candidate actually receives these votes. A party's electors are chosen in a variety of ways, but they're typically reputable members of the party. When citizens cast a vote during the presidential election, they are actually voting for a particular party's electors to cast their votes for the presidential candidate to whom they have pledged.

Text 2

More than 200 years of complacency have left us with something resembling less a federal government than a yard sale of antiquated institutions, with none more dusty than the electoral college. Consider that it's theoretically possible to receive just eleven votes, have your opponent receive 200 million, and still win the election under the electoral college.

Social media in the workplace has gotten a bad rap; in many ways, it deserves it. But the role it can play—when embraced appropriately—in networking, collaboration, and retention proves that it isn't as simple as that. Like any new and rapidly changing technology, it will take time and adaptability for its advantages and pitfalls to be clear. The smart company will find it necessary to consider the implications social media presents for its future—is it really something that can just be ignored or banned altogether?

7

The relationship between the passages can best be described as which of the following statements?

Ⓐ Text 1 and Text 2 both cite political authority figures to make their cases.

Ⓑ Text 1 focuses more on voting technicalities while Text 2 focuses on historical context.

Ⓒ Text 1 presents more of a pious view of the founding of the United States than does Text 2.

Ⓓ Text 1 focuses more on political dishonesty while Text 2 focuses on economic repercussions.

8

Which of the following statements best expresses the main idea of the text?

Ⓐ Social media has already proven to be one of the most valuable workplace tools.

Ⓑ Social media should not be disregarded as a potentially valuable tool in the workplace.

Ⓒ The risks of social media are far too great to allow it in the workplace.

Ⓓ Employees should be able to decide for themselves how to best use social media while working.

1   MODULE 1   1

Though humans have likely marveled at the spectacle of Halley's Comet for thousands of years (the Talmudic astronomers of the first century describe a star that appears once every seventy years to wreak havoc on nautical navigation), it was little more than 300 years ago that Edmond Halley—a friend of Sir Isaac Newton's—used Newton's newly conceived laws of gravity to explain the motion and predict the periodicity of comets. Using these equations in tandem with historical records, Halley surmised that the comets observed in 1531 by German humanist Petrus Apianus, in 1607 by Johannes Kepler, and by himself and Newton in 1683 were one and the same. Moreover, he predicted its return for 1758.

9

The scientist Halley's relationship to the ideas of Newton most resembles the relationship between

(A) a musician who uses music theory to enable creative compositions.

(B) a politician who uses philosophical maxims to predict societal outcomes.

(C) a mathematician who uses scientific data to justify algebraic theories.

(D) an engineer who uses the laws of physics to build long-lasting constructions.

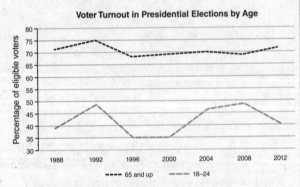

Voter Turnout in Presidential Elections by Age

---- 65 and up   --- 18–24

Source: 2012 U.S. Census Bureau: *http://www.census.gov/prod/2014pubs/p20–573.pdf*.

Many laypeople believe that the voter turnout rates between older and younger Americans are quite divergent. Often, however, the voter turnout rates between younger and older Americans are relatively close, as in the year _____

10

Which choice most effectively uses data from the table to complete the example?

(A) 1992.

(B) 2000.

(C) 2004.

(D) 2008.

1   MODULE 1   1

In the early 1990s, a scientist found an extremely large virus that infected an amoeba. The scientist noted that the size and composition of the virus's capsid outer coating was very similar to the protein structure of the nuclear membrane of a eukaryote, which is an organism with a clear nucleus. The scientist hypothesized that the modern cell nucleus may itself have originated from a similar viral infection.

11

Which finding, if true, would most support the scientist's hypothesis?

(A) Confirmation that the same virus has successfully reproduced in a new environment

(B) Experimental confirmation that the inner components of a virus are similar to those of a cell nucleus

(C) Observation of the destruction of a large virus by specially designed antiviral medication

(D) A scientific literature review that found other scientists investigating amoeba biology in recent decades

---

"Holy Sonnet 10" is an early 1600s poem by John Donne. In the poem, the speaker suggests that death is more of a random process than one of clear destiny: _____

12

Which quotation from "Holy Sonnet 10" most effectively illustrates the claim?

(A) "Death, be not proud, though some have called thee / Mighty and dreadful, for thou are not so;"

(B) "For those whom thou think'st [Death] dost overthrow / Die not, poor Death, nor yet canst thou kill me."

(C) "And soonest our best men with [Death] do go, / Rest of their bones, and soul's delivery."

(D) "[Death] art slave to fate, chance, kings, and desperate men, / And dost with poison, war, and sickness dwell,"

The text is adapted from the 1949 Geneva Conventions, which protects the human rights of those captured in war.

Until recent times war was ordinarily preceded by a regular diplomatic ceremonial. Before there was any resort to arms, there was a declaration of war by one of the opposing parties, followed by the inauguration of a state of war by both belligerents with all the legal consequences which that entailed, both in relation to nationals and in relation to enemy nationals and enemy property. Consequently, in those days, in theory, where war had not been declared, or the state of war had not been recognized by one of the parties for one reason or another, the applicability of the Convention might be contested. The danger arising in such cases is _____

13

Which choice most logically completes the text?

(A) unexpected.

(B) inconclusive.

(C) historical.

(D) obvious.

While we might think of the "cat video" as an invention of the twenty-first century, felines on film have been entertaining humans since the earliest days of cinema over a hundred years ago. Theories abound as to why we love to watch videos of cats, why we find these creatures so entertaining. Perhaps it is because the movements of a cat tend to be far less predictable than those of many other pets, such as dogs. After all, the cat is known for its fickle nature as a species, a fickleness that creates suspense in the viewer who wonders, "what will that cat do next?" Despite being the most common pet in the United States, _____

14

Which choice most logically completes the text?

(A) it is easy to know what a cat will want.

(B) cat behavior is anything but familiar to us.

(C) dogs have become increasingly popular among rural dwellers.

(D) other countries do not share the same love of felines.

In retrospect, I should _____ my bat a reprieve from the endless punishment; we should allow ourselves to rest, likewise.

15

Which choice completes the text so that it conforms to the conventions of Standard English?

(A) of given

(B) of give

(C) have given

(D) have give

MODULE 1

There are a variety of vital skills necessary for one to be a successful candidate for a job. At the top of the list are strong critical thinking skills and complex problem-solving, followed closely by problem sensitivity and deductive reasoning. _____ can be expected to have strengths in analyzing, evaluating, and interpreting highly complex data.

16

Which choice completes the text so that it conforms to the conventions of Standard English?

- (A) You
- (B) I
- (C) One
- (D) She

Today we can produce even very large sheets of glass of nearly uniform thickness using the *float glass* process invented by Sir Alastair Pilkington in the mid-1950s. As the name implies, this technique _____

17

Which choice completes the text so that it conforms to the conventions of Standard English?

- (A) involve floated molten glass on a bath of molten tin.
- (B) involve floating molted glass with a bath of molted tin.
- (C) involves floated molted glass on a bath of molted tin.
- (D) involves floating molten glass on a bath of molten tin.

Boiled down to its essence, the problem _____ to learn other languages I must speak other languages, but I rarely have the opportunity to do so.

18

Which choice completes the text so that it conforms to the conventions of Standard English?

- (A) is this:
- (B) is, this
- (C) is this
- (D) is this,

Once the body recognizes the attack, the inflammation process starts by increasing blood flow to the area and _____ white blood cells to help fight.

19

Which choice completes the text so that it conforms to the conventions of Standard English?

- (A) to sending
- (B) to send
- (C) sending
- (D) send

I don't think anyone would call me a world traveler. I have only been overseas twice. Everywhere I have traveled there _____ a trend—the ever-present difficulty of learning the new language.

20

Which choice completes the text so that it conforms to the conventions of Standard English?

- (A) has been
- (B) have been
- (C) will have been
- (D) be

When two people from different cities or countries meet, they have a topic that they can easily and freely _____ whose team is the best, they do agree that they love soccer.

21

Which choice completes the text so that it conforms to the conventions of Standard English?

- (A) discuss, even if they don't agree on
- (B) discuss; even if they don't agree on
- (C) discuss even if they don't agree on
- (D) discuss: even if they, don't agree on

Given how reading can benefit an individual, it is not surprising, then, that readers have positive effects on society. Those who read literature are more than twice as likely to volunteer or do charity work and more than three times as likely to go to museums, attend plays or concerts, and create art as those who do not. Good readers are even more likely to play sports, attend sporting events, or do outdoor activities. _____ criminals tend to have significantly worse reading skills than others.

22

Which choice completes the text with the most logical transition?

- (A) On the other hand,
- (B) Therefore,
- (C) Moreover,
- (D) Thus,

Luminescence is fundamentally distinct from the way we create light in incandescent light bulbs. Incandescence uses the super-heating of a filament to generate light by thermal radiation, and a lot of energy is wasted in the process. _____ less than 20% of luminescent light is created by thermal radiation, which has earned it the nickname "cold light."

23

Which choice completes the text with the most logical transition?

- (A) Additionally,
- (B) Moreover,
- (C) Consequently,
- (D) In contrast,

1   MODULE 1   1

When sweating or swimming, sunscreen products can be easily washed away. _____ a new application will not set the timer to zero: only time out of the sun will do that. What this means is that frequent applications (at least every two hours) and breaks from the sun are important.

24

Which choice completes the text with the most logical transition?

- (A) Subsequently,
- (B) Meanwhile,
- (C) To that end,
- (D) In addition,

Following their return to Spain in the late 1940s, Dali began drawing inspiration from his faith for his work. It was during this period of Dali's life that he produced *La Gare de Perpignan*, which contains several religious symbols and references. _____ there is the shadow of Christ on the cross bearing his thorny crown near the center of the painting.

25

Which choice completes the text with the most logical transition?

- (A) In contrast,
- (B) Surprisingly,
- (C) For instance,
- (D) As an example of what can be seen,

A student takes the following notes for her geography class:

- Two dimensional maps are imperfect in projecting three-dimensional surfaces, especially planetary surfaces like that of Earth.
- The Mercator projection is good for navigation because it makes it easy to distinguish between north and south.
- The Mercator projection is problematic in that it does not accurately show the surface area of countries.
- The Mercator projection makes the far northern and far southern countries appear to be much larger than they actually are.
- The Robinson projection shows all the surface of Earth connected together in one drawing.
- The Robinson projection distorts the size of the land masses close to the North and South Poles.

26

The student wants to emphasize a similarity between the Mercator and the Robinson projections. Which choice most effectively uses relevant information from the notes to accomplish this goal?

- (A) Both the Mercator and Robinson projections are equally useful for ship navigation.
- (B) Both the Mercator and Robinson projections inaccurately represent the surface areas of Earth.
- (C) Both the Mercator and Robinson projections are accurate in representing the surface area of Earth toward upper latitudes near the poles.
- (D) Neither the Mercator nor the Robinson projection can be drawn on a two-dimensional surface.

While researching a topic, a student has taken the following notes:

- Before the Incas and Aztecs, Teotihuacan flourished in what is today known as Mexico.
- Teotihuacan was a large city built in the Valley of Mexico and was at peak importance between 500 and 550 C.E.
- Teotihuacan is responsible for some of the most intact ruins and some of the most impressive pyramids in North America, including the Pyramid of the Sun and the Pyramid of the Moon.
- The city was the most important cultural center of Mesoamerica in its time and produced much of the art, music, and other culturally important concepts of the time.
- Teotihuacan eventually crumbled for reasons unknown; many archeologists suspect an uprising of the peasant class contributed to the demise of the once-great city.

27

The student wants to emphasize elements of Teotihuacan that are most likely still physically visible by people today. Which choice most effectively uses relevant information from the notes to accomplish this goal?

(A) Much of the culture in modern-day Latin American traces its influence to the concepts of the Inca.

(B) The large city of Teotihuacan was constructed over 1,500 years ago in the Valley of Mexico.

(C) Students today can still view the well-preserved Pyramid of the Sun and Pyramid of the Moon.

(D) Just as the civilization in Teotihuacan eventually deteriorated, our modern-day society is under the threat of class conflict.

Section 1: Reading and Writing Module 2

32 MINUTES, 27 QUESTIONS

Juan was surprised by what he heard but _____ the information as lies. He knew many of his peers were jealous of his success, but he doubted they would stoop so low.

1

Which choice completes the text with the most logical and precise word?

- (A) reduced
- (B) forgot
- (C) conceded
- (D) dismissed

When the speaker was done, the crowd rose and clapped vigorously. Yet, at the question and answer session, attentive spectators _____ several points—particularly that the speech's moral lesson came off as condescending and was generally unfounded.

2

Which choice completes the text with the most logical and precise word or phrase?

- (A) increased
- (B) elevated
- (C) put forward
- (D) nourished

At the turn of the nineteenth century, a prominent physicist stated that physics as a field of study was finished due to the belief that everything about the physical world had already been discovered. Newtonian Mechanics had held sway for over two hundred years and our understanding of the atom had not advanced much beyond the concepts of the ancient Greeks. The view of a static universe was the accepted <u>construct</u> and humanity's ignorance was a kind of simple bliss and arrogance.

3

As used in the text, what does the word "construct" most nearly mean?

- (A) Building
- (B) Observation
- (C) Theory
- (D) Astronomy

DIAGNOSTIC TEST

The following text is from Anatole France's 1912 French novel *The Gods Will Have Blood*.

The Citizeness Gamelin put the soup on the table, said the Benedicite, seated her son and her guest, and began to eat standing up, underlined{declining} the chair which Brotteaux offered her next to him, since, she said, she knew what courtesy required of her.

4

As used in the text, what does the word "declining" most nearly mean?

Ⓐ Repulsing

Ⓑ Decreasing

Ⓒ Turning down

Ⓓ Plummeting

Disinterested in a bleak future of more debt and less freedom, and wary of aligning themselves within partisanship, today's youth are doubtful of a government that promises few of the assurances it once pledged. Naturally, this trend is disquieting for a nation that depends on its voters and an interest in representation, both of which are in a state of deterioration. Yet, some may applaud the veer from partisanship—a phenomenon that has left more undone than accomplished. Still, if democracy is to survive, something must be done to align the cynical millennials with a system that desperately needs their interference.

5

What is the purpose of the underlined sentence in the text?

Ⓐ To state the thesis of the text

Ⓑ To give details about the pitfalls of partisanship

Ⓒ To acknowledge a contrasting viewpoint

Ⓓ To cite an expert point of view

The intrinsic difficulty of predicting a comet's greatness makes the consistency of Halley's visibility even more remarkable. Most great comets will pass near Earth only once every several thousand years, whereas Halley's does so on a cycle of about seventy-five years—making it the only great comet with the potential to appear twice in a human lifetime. With an eccentricity of 0.967, the orbit of Halley's Comet is extremely elliptical; at one end of its major axis Halley's is roughly the same distance from the sun as Pluto, whereas at the other it passes between the orbits of Mercury and Venus. The highly elliptic character of Halley's orbit means that, apart from having one of the highest velocities of any body in our solar system, it passes near Earth both during its approach and its return from the sun.

6

Which choice best states the main purpose of the text?

Ⓐ Discuss the physical definition of elliptical eccentricity

Ⓑ Provide scientific justification for the rarity of Halley's predictable visibility

Ⓒ Give historical evidence of human observation of Halley's velocity

Ⓓ Differentiate Halley's from other celestial bodies, such as planets and meteors

1 · MODULE 2 · 1

Text 1

One promising alternative fuel source is ethanol. This alternative fuel is made by fermenting crops such as wheat, corn, and sugarcane. One glucose molecule is broken down to form two ethanol molecules and two carbon dioxide molecules. Because it is made from organic matter, it is renewable—a big pro compared to oil. Another benefit is that it's domestically made, so we don't have to rely on other countries for it.

Text 2

Despite decades of apocalyptic forecasting of peak oil, petroleum output is as healthy as ever. In fact, petroleum companies are leaving the industry not because oil reserves are dwindling, but rather because oil production is so massive that demand is falling considerably.

7

The author of Text 1 would most likely state that the author of Text 2 needs to make what important clarification to the underlined statement in the text?

(A) To what extent this applies to just domestic petroleum production

(B) Whether the petroleum produced is organic and renewable

(C) If the petroleum production will generate greenhouse gases

(D) If the petroleum mentioned here will be more or less expensive than ethanol

Text 1

There is and must remain a standard by which good writing is measured and acknowledged. Take a moment to consider the alternative, and you'll surely come to agree with me. Without a standard, anything and everything could be considered *literature*. More so, it would change from person to person and place to place based solely on the rudimentary preference of varied individuals.

Text 2

Many will adore language that others detest, and some will gasp appreciatively at a metaphor that makes the masses vomit. And so I say, to each their own. What is thoughtful, good, and stirring is without impartiality, contingent not only on the reader but also on the reader's mood, location, and even on what the reader has recently read. Therefore, write what you will and read what you wish, and if you like it, then declare with authority that it is indeed exceptional.

8

Which option best expresses the overall relationship between the texts?

(A) Text 1 argues for the existence of literary objectivity, whereas Text 2 argues for the opposite.

(B) Text 1 asserts the primacy of reading literature, whereas Text 2 asserts that writing is the only gateway to understanding.

(C) Text 1 contends that good literature makes readers uncomfortable, whereas Text 2 contends that good literature is what is most popular.

(D) Text 1 focuses on the *great books*, whereas Text 2 focuses on excellence in poetic expression.

The following text is from Nathaniel Hawthorne's 1852 novel The Blithedale Romance.

I recognized no severe culture in Zenobia; her mind was full of weeds. It startled me, sometimes, in my state of moral as well as bodily faint-heartedness, to observe the hardihood of her philosophy. She made no scruple of oversetting all human institutions and scattering them as with a breeze from her fan. A female reformer, in her attacks upon society, has an instinctive sense of where the life lies, and is inclined to aim directly at that spot. Especially the relation between the sexes is naturally among the earliest to attract her notice. Zenobia was truly a magnificent woman.

9

Based on the text, what aspect of society is Zenobia most eager to reform?

(A) Xenophobic universities
(B) Widespread economic corruption
(C) Antiquated gender roles
(D) Environmental negligence

The following text is from Irina Petrov's 1917 work More than Many Sparrows.

Already that winter, [Kolya] had fed [the fire in the fireplace] half the books in his great grandfather's library. It had eaten up all the Napoleonic settees and tables that once adorned his ancestral home. He'd even offered it his mother's beloved mandolin, letting the strings on which she'd plucked his somber lullabies catch fire, snap, and turn to ash. He watched it happen, and felt nothing. Nothing, that is, but warm. It was winter, and sentimentality was not in season—nor had it been for many months. Besides, no one still living in the house knew how to play it.

10

What is a main idea of the text?

(A) The narrator's ancestral library must be preserved at all costs.
(B) Offerings to the gods may ward off misfortune.
(C) The narrator longs for the companionship of his deceased mother.
(D) The need for comfort overcomes familial nostalgia.

1   MODULE 2   1

Likelihood a Job Will Be Done by a Machine

Source: npr.org

With the advent of artificial intelligence technology, many sociologists are concerned about the possibility of workers being displaced from their careers. One sociologist argues that not every area of work will be equally affected: _____

11

Which choice most effectively uses data from the table to complete the example?

(A) GPS and automation will lead to bus drivers being obsolete.

(B) Careers with a high likelihood of a machine performing the job have poor employment outlooks.

(C) Historians are less likely to have their job performed by a machine than janitors are.

(D) More people are employed as umpires than any other profession.

I used to revel at my anxiety after turning in an assignment in my first years of my creative writing degree. One moment, I was quite sure that my work was genius. And another, I was the most dimwitted simpleton to ever put pen to paper. I had absolutely no idea whether my fiction would come back with an *A* or an *F* stamped on it—no clue how the professor might decide between the two. Often, I'd pull decent grades, but moan aloud when the instructor picked out my very favorite sentence— the one that was going to mark me the next Vonnegut or Kerouac—and crossed it out in red ink. *Rethink this* she'd scribble underneath. It took me two years and the onset of carpal tunnel to realize that there is no real way to know what's good, and that what's good is entirely subjective.

12

Which of the following, if true, would present the greatest challenge to the argument of the text?

(A) Some people adore Shakespeare, while others do not care for his work.

(B) Well-trained literary minds are able to use more sophisticated language to give their views on the quality of different texts.

(C) American book readership has steadily declined in the past three decades.

(D) The writer's academic evaluators graded in a hurried, haphazard way.

"Mabel Osborne" is a 1915 poem by Edgar Lee Masters, in which the narrator expresses her sorrow at being ignored by other people.

13

Which quotation from "Mabel Osborne" most effectively illustrates the claim?

(A) "But you do not ask for water. / You cannot speak!"

(B) "Everyone knows that you are dying of thirst, / Yet they do not bring water!"

(C) "Like this geranium which someone has planted over me,"

(D) "I who loved you, Spoon River, / And craved your love,"

Because DDT is no longer used, the approach to eliminating bedbugs must be multifaceted. Most poisons and bug bombs will not work as the bugs don't need to eat and the eggs won't be affected by sprays. The first step in the process is to reduce clutter in the home. These bugs like to live in small nooks and crannies; reducing clutter reduces their living space. Then, vacuum as many porous surfaces as possible to remove any active bugs. This won't be hugely helpful since regular vacuum cleaners can't fit into the small spaces where bedbugs choose to reside, but _____

14

Which choice most logically completes the text?

(A) it is a good preliminary step.

(B) it will provide a comprehensive solution.

(C) it is not worth the time and effort involved.

(D) bedbugs will be fully eradicated as a result.

The issues of both convenience and synchronous exposure in color photography were eventually solved by two professional, classical musicians— Leopold Mannes and Leopold Godowsky, Jr.— working recreationally for the Eastman Kodak Company. Together they designed a film that consisted of three separate emulsion layers mounted on a single flexible base, each of which captured and individually filtered the lens image. Their design was marketed by Kodak under the name *Kodachrome* and was the first system to make the use of color film widely available to lay photographers. With respect to their photographic research, Mannes and Godowsky can best be described as _____

15

Which choice most logically completes the text?

(A) serendipitous tinkerers.

(B) scholarly thinkers.

(C) scientific masterminds.

(D) musical prodigies.

1 MODULE 2 1

Tim, while appropriately interested in diagnosing and treating _____ problems with their teeth and gums, demonstrated real passion for repairing teeth and aiding in cosmetic dental concerns.

16

Which choice completes the text so that it conforms to the conventions of Standard English?

- (A) patients
- (B) patient's
- (C) patients'
- (D) those of patients

Apart from the drum, there is perhaps no instrument more widespread among the world's ancient cultures than the curious noisemaker known severally as the *bullroarer*, _____ *tundun*, or *whizzing-stick*.

17

Which choice completes the text so that it conforms to the conventions of Standard English?

- (A) rhombus',
- (B) *rhombus,*
- (C) rhombus's,
- (D) rhombus

Pitch modulation can be achieved by altering the speed of rotation, or the length of the cord. The capacity for pitch modulation has _____ to the idea that bullroarers could be used to communicate coded messages, with certain meanings attached to certain pitches.

18

Which choice completes the text so that it conforms to the conventions of Standard English?

- (A) lent credence
- (B) lended credibility
- (C) loaned credibility
- (D) lending credence

Not long after the Pinkertons surrendered, Pennsylvania Governor Robert Pattison authorized the militia to advance, and placed the town of Homestead under martial law. In the days that followed, steel production at the mill resumed with strikebreakers living on the _____ too dangerous for them to cross the picket.

19

Which choice completes the text so that it conforms to the conventions of Standard English?

- (A) mills grounds: it was still
- (B) mills' grounds—it was still
- (C) mill's grounds, it was still
- (D) mill's grounds; it was still

The tough competition and demanding prerequisites for the job market need not be deterrents. Leading journalism _____ students leave undergraduate programs with all the tools necessary for success.

20

Which choice completes the text so that it conforms to the conventions of Standard English?

(A) department's are ensuring that their

(B) departments' are ensuring that they're

(C) departments are ensuring there

(D) departments are ensuring that their

Allergens, pollution, bacteria, and sunlight—these are just some of the foreign objects that _____

21

Which choice completes the text so that it conforms to the conventions of Standard English?

(A) on a basis that is daily are attacking the human body.

(B) attacking the bodies of humans on a daily basis.

(C) attack the human body on a daily basis.

(D) attacks humans each and every day.

Marjorie, an immensely popular young woman, is plagued by Bernice, her dull cousin who fails to entertain _____ Marjorie's many social environments.

22

Which choice completes the text so that it conforms to the conventions of Standard English?

(A) or be entertained by

(B) and entertainment

(C) with the entertaining

(D) of the entertaining for

Nearly all tortoiseshell and calico cats are female. This is because the gene that dictates whether the cat's fur is orange or black is located on the X chromosome. Since male cats have XY chromosomes, they will usually only have one allele coding for either orange fur or black fur. Males would be calico or tortoiseshell if they had two X chromosomes along with a Y, _____ this is very rare.

23

Which choice completes the text with the most logical transition?

(A) so

(B) if

(C) but

(D) moreover

1 MODULE 2 1

The Depression arrived at a moment in time in which Sweden was particularly ripe for comprehensive reform; in hopes of stabilizing a rapidly declining economy, the Swedish people elected the Social Democratic Party to power in 1932. _____ contemporary socialist parties in Europe, Sweden's Social Democrats—rather than calling for the full socialization of private industry—made combating unemployment through bipartisan, interventionist legislation their main priority.

24

Which choice completes the text with the most logical transition?

(A) Also

(B) Unlike

(C) Consequently

(D) Therefore

For ten months while I was in high school, I lived with a host family in Germany. I attended tenth grade in a German upper school, traveled through northern Europe and, truth be told, learned a bit of German. _____ a German student traveling to the U.S., staying with a host family, and attending school for the same amount of time seems to learn significantly more English.

25

Which choice completes the text with the most logical transition?

(A) Therefore,

(B) However,

(C) Additionally,

(D) As a result,

While researching a topic, a student has taken the following notes:

- Humans are susceptible to infection by a variety of parasitic worms. These infections can be anywhere from a mild annoyance to life-threatening.
- Dracunculiasis, also known as guinea worm disease, starts when the host drinks water contaminated with the parasite.
- Incubation of the guinea worm can be a year and ends with a blister forming on the body. The blister becomes very painful as the parasite emerges. Hosts often put their body into water to ease the pain, which unfortunately stimulates the guinea worm to release larvae contaminating that water and perpetuating the cycle.
- To remove the guinea worm from the body, the worm is slowly wound around a stick or bit of gauze or fabric until the worm exits the body.

26

The student wants to emphasize the possible range of severity that could result from a parasitic worm infection. Which choice most effectively uses relevant information from the notes to accomplish this goal?

(A) Guinea worms are quite dangerous and should only be removed by a highly trained medical professional.

(B) The infection resulting from a parasitic worm can range from being mildly annoying to life-threatening.

(C) If you ingest contaminated water, you are more likely to contract a guinea worm infection.

(D) The self-perpetuating cycle of guinea worm disease has required very targeted programs and education to make guinea worm disease eradicated in many parts of the world.

While researching a topic, a student has taken the following notes:

- Land conservation and land preservation are two different concepts.
- Preservation focuses on keeping the land as it is as a sort of natural museum, unable to be used in any significant way by humanity. It preserves the nature as it is.
- Conservation focuses on keeping lands usable for anyone who might want to experience the outdoors. It allows people to use the land for recreation and ensures that cities and other human growth do not destroy natural areas.
- Teddy Roosevelt was one of the first proponents of conservationism in the United States. He started the National Parks System to ensure that generations of Americans could still see the wonders of the land.

27

The student wants to show a contrast between land preservation and land conservation. Which choice most effectively uses relevant information from the notes to accomplish this goal?

(A) Teddy Roosevelt was a major personality who inspired long-term investments in both land conservation and land preservation.

(B) Land conservation entails ensuring humans can use the land recreationally, while land preservation ignores this goal.

(C) While land preservation will cause existing human habitation to be removed, land conservation encourages urban development.

(D) Museumgoers are more likely to enjoy experiencing land in a similar way—therefore, the investment in national parks is worthwhile.

Section 2: Math Module 1

35 MINUTES, 22 QUESTIONS

- All expressions and variables use real numbers.
- All figures are drawn to scale.
- Every figure lies in a plane.
- The domain of given functions is the set of all real numbers for which the corresponding value of the function is real.

For **multiple-choice questions**, solve the problem and pick the correct answer from the provided choices. Each multiple-choice question has only one correct answer.

For **student-produced response questions**, solve each problem and enter your answer following these guidelines:

- If you find **more than one correct answer**, enter just one answer.
- You can enter up to five characters for a **positive** answer and up to six characters (this includes the negative sign) for a **negative** answer.
- If your answer is a **fraction** that does not fit in the given space, enter the decimal equivalent instead.
- If your answer is a **decimal** that does not fit in the given space, enter it by stopping at or rounding up at the fourth digit.
- If your answer is a mixed number $\left(\text{like } 4\frac{1}{2}\right)$, enter it as an improper fraction (9/2) or its decimal equivalent (4.5).
- Do not enter symbols like a comma, dollar sign, or percent sign.

Examples

Answer	Acceptable Entries	Unacceptable Entries That Will Receive Zero Credit
4.5	4.5 4.50 9/2	41/2 4 1/2
$\frac{8}{9}$	8/9 .8888 .8889 0.888 0.889	0.8 .88 0.88 0.89
$-\frac{1}{9}$	−1/9 −.1111 −0.111	−.11 −0.11

REFERENCE ∨

Radius of a circle $= r$

Area of a circle $= \pi r^2$

Circumference of a circle $= 2\pi r$

Area of a rectangle $=$ length $\times$ width $= lw$

Area of a triangle $= \frac{1}{2} \times$ base $\times$ height $= \frac{1}{2} bh$

Pythagorean theorem: $a^2 + b^2 = c^2$

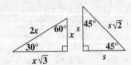

Special right triangles: 30-60-90 and 45-45-90

Volume of a box $=$ length $\times$ width $\times$ height $= lwh$

Volume of a cylinder $= \pi r^2 h$

Volume of a sphere $= \frac{4}{3}\pi r^3$

Volume of a cone $= \frac{1}{3}\pi r^2 h$

Volume of a pyramid $=$

$\frac{1}{3}$ length $\times$ width $\times$ height $= \frac{1}{3} lwh$

Key Facts:

- A circle has 360 degrees.
- There are 2π radians in a circle.
- There are 180 degrees in a triangle.

1

If $x^2 > y^2$, which statement must be correct?

(A) $x > y$

(B) $x < y$

(C) $x \neq y$

(D) $x^3 > y^3$

2

What is the product of x and y given the system of equations below?

$$4 + y = 32x$$
$$y = 2x + 2$$

(A) $\dfrac{6}{25}$

(B) $\dfrac{12}{25}$

(C) 12

(D) 15

3

Eloise is told by her doctor that she should try to average 9 hours of sleep a night, since that is what a typical teenager needs for optimal mental and physical health. If Eloise has been awake for 126 hours in a given week, how many additional hours of sleep should she have had in the entire week in order to follow her doctor's advice?

4

What are the values of a in this equation?

$$3a^2 - 27a - 108 = 0$$

(A) $-9, -3$

(B) $6, -4$

(C) $9, 6$

(D) $12, -3$

5

What is the difference between $7a^2 + 3ab - 8b$ and $-2a^2 + ab - 2b$?

- (A) $5a^2 + 4ab - 10b$
- (B) $9a^2 + 4ab - 8b$
- (C) $9a^2 + 2ab - 6b$
- (D) $7a + 3ab - 10$

6

If $2x + 3 = 4$, what is the value of $6x + 9$?

7

If a circle has a diameter of 8 centimeters, what is its circumference rounded to the nearest whole centimeter?

8

Allison is purchasing a new car that costs $25,000. She is trading in a used car that is worth $5,000, according to the dealer. The amount she pays for the new car is the new car price minus the amount she receives as a credit for the used car trade-in. If she has to pay 7% sales tax on the entire purchase, what expression would give the total amount she pays?

- (A) $0.07(25,000 - 5,000)$
- (B) $0.07(25,000) + 5,000$
- (C) $1.07(25,000 - 5,000)$
- (D) $1.7(25,000 + 5,000)$

2   MODULE 1   2

9

Which of the following operations could we perform on both sides of the inequality $-2x > 4$ in order to make it necessary to change the direction of the inequality sign while keeping x on the left-hand side of the inequality?

(A) Add 4

(B) Subtract 7

(C) Multiply by 12

(D) Divide by -2

10

The variables x and y have a linear relationship; the table below contains several corresponding x-y values for the line:

x	y
-1	-6
1	2
5	18
7	26

What is the equation of the line made up of x-y values?

(A) $y = 4x - 2$

(B) $y = 2x$

(C) $y = -2x + 4$

(D) $y = -4x + 2$

11

Maria currently has $10,000 in her retirement fund. She wants to see how much money she will have in her fund for several different years in the future, assuming that her portfolio has a steady annual growth rate of 10%. What function $f(n)$ would model the amount she should have in her portfolio in n years?

(A) $f(n) = 10,000^n$

(B) $f(n) = 10,000 \times 0.1^n$

(C) $f(n) = 10,000 \times 1.1^n$

(D) $f(n) = 10,000 \times 1.11^n$

12

A cylinder has a height of 4 feet and a diameter of 2 feet. What is the cylinder's volume in cubic feet?

(A) 3π

(B) 4π

(C) 8π

(D)   16

13

A convenience store has a *change bowl* on its counter in which there can be 5-cent nickels and/or 1-cent pennies. The store manager insists that whenever there is a dollar (100 cents) or more in the bowl, some change must be removed. What expression gives the range of P pennies and N nickels that could be in the change bowl at any given time without the cashier needing to remove any coins?

(A) $100P - N > 5$

(B) $6(P + N) < 100$

(C) $0.01P + 0.05N < 100$

(D) $P + 5N < 100$

14

The data are collected from a survey of 500 randomly selected people in the United States. The researcher asked participants their ages and the type of social media they use the most frequently: video sharing, photo sharing, text sharing, or none. The goal of the researcher was to determine the general characteristics of social media use by different age groups throughout the United States.

Type of Social Media Use by Numbers of People in Different Age Groups					
Age Group	Video Sharing	Photo Sharing	Text Sharing	No Social Media	Total
12–18	40	32	20	2	94
19–30	31	51	43	6	131
31–45	20	20	40	24	104
46–60	9	8	36	35	88
61–up	2	3	29	49	83

If one were to create a graph with age groupings (from younger to older) as the variable along the x-axis and percentage of group members who use video sharing (from smaller to larger) along the y-axis, what would be the relationship portrayed by the data?

(A) Positive correlation
(B) Negative correlation
(C) Equivalence
(D) Exponentially inverse

15

The variables m and n have a directly proportional relationship, given by the equation $m = kn$ where k is a constant of proportionality. When $m = 10$, $n = 2$. What will be the value of n if m is 38?

16

A parallelogram has one interior angle that measures 50 degrees. What is the measure of the largest interior angle of the parallelogram?

- Ⓐ   130 degrees
- Ⓑ   150 degrees
- Ⓒ   250 degrees
- Ⓓ   310 degrees

17

A new business uses a crowdfunding website to raise money for its expansion. The graph below plots the number of new investment pledges per week, collecting the data once at the end of each week after the crowdfunding has begun (for example, *Week 1* gives the total number of pledges at the very end of week 1).

A marketing professional defines the point at which something goes *viral* as the point at which the item shifts from linear to exponential growth. During what week does the value of the new investment pledges become viral?

- Ⓐ   2
- Ⓑ   3
- Ⓒ   6
- Ⓓ   10

2   MODULE 1   **2**

18

A dry cleaner has a computer program to determine the price it will charge an individual customer to clean a bag full of shirts (S) and pairs of pants (P). The total cost in dollars (C) is given by the following expression:

$$C = 10S + 6P + 5$$

What does the constant 5 most likely represent in the above expression?

- Ⓐ A set fee the cleaner assesses to do any amount of cleaning
- Ⓑ The cost to clean a shirt
- Ⓒ The cost to clean a pair of pants
- Ⓓ The total minimum cost to clean either one shirt or pair of pants

---

19

How many more kilograms (to the nearest hundredth) will a 2 cubic meter balloon that is filled with air weigh than an identical balloon that is filled with helium, given that helium has a density of $0.179 \frac{kg}{m^3}$ and air has a density of $1.2 \frac{kg}{m^3}$?

- Ⓐ 0.21
- Ⓑ 1.02
- Ⓒ 1.38
- Ⓓ 2.04

2   MODULE 1   **2**

20

A pretzel stand has fixed costs for the facility and cooking supplies of $500. The cost for the labor and supplies to cook one pretzel after the pretzel stand has been set up is $2 per pretzel. What is the graph of the cost function $c(x)$ given x pretzels?

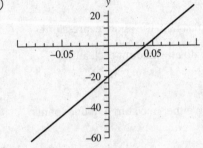

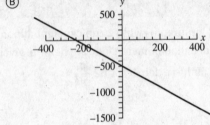

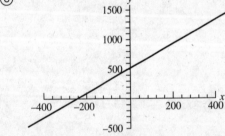

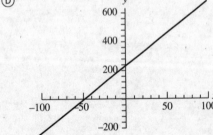

2

MODULE 1

2

21

In the equation $y = 2x^n$, in which x is an integer greater than 1, what is a possible value of n that will ensure that the expression has exponential growth?

- (A) 0
- (B) 1
- (C) 4
- (D) Not sufficient information

22

The function $f(x) = (x - 3)(x + 2)((x - 1)^2)$ will intersect the x-axis how many times?

Section 2: Math Module 2

35 MINUTES, 22 QUESTIONS

1

What are the values of y that satisfy these conditions?

$$x = y^2 - 3y + 1$$
$$2x = 10$$

- (A) -4 and 2
- (B) -1 and 4
- (C) 3 and 4
- (D) 6 and 10

2

When Andrew does his homework, he always takes 10 minutes to set up his desk and get totally ready to begin. Once he starts working, he is able to complete one homework problem every 5 minutes. Assuming that Andrew studies for over 10 minutes time, which of the following represents the total number of homework problems, p, Andrew is able to complete in m minutes?

- (A) $p = 5m + 10$
- (B) $p = 5m - 1$
- (C) $p = \frac{1}{5}(m - 10)$
- (D) $p = \frac{1}{10}(m - 5)$

3

How many solutions does the equation below have?

$$3x - 4y = 73$$

- (A) None
- (B) Exactly 1
- (C) Exactly 2
- (D) Infinite

4

$$\left(2x^2 + 4xy + 2y^2\right) \times \frac{1}{2x + 2y} =$$

(A) $y + x$

(B) $\dfrac{2x + 4y + 2}{x + y}$

(C) $2x + 4xy + 2y$

(D) 2

5

A professor will cancel his sociology class if the number of students in attendance is less than or equal to 10. Which of the following expressions would give the range of students S necessary for the professor to have class, given that S is a whole integer?

(A) $S < 10$

(B) $S > 10$

(C) $S \leq 10$

(D) $S \geq 10$

6

What is a possible value for x in the expression below?

$$-6 < \frac{8}{3}x < -\frac{1}{4}$$

(A) 8

(B) 1

(C) −2

(D) −5

7

A politician proposes a new federal tax bracket system for single taxpayers with the following tax rates for the given ranges of income:

Taxable Income Range	Tax Rate
$0 up to $9,000	15%
Greater than $9,000 up to $50,000	20%
Greater than $50,000	30%

If Julian has only $8,000 in taxable income, what is the total amount of federal tax he would pay under the proposed system?

(A) $400
(B) $800
(C) $1,200
(D) $1,600

8

If the line given by the equation $y = 4x + 7$ is reflected about the x-axis, what will be the graph of the resulting function?

(A)

(C)

(B)

(D)
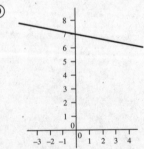

2   MODULE 2   2

9

What is (are) the solution(s) for x in this equation?

$$\frac{12}{\sqrt[3]{x}} = 4$$

Ⓐ   −3 and 81

Ⓑ   −27 and 27

Ⓒ   9 only

Ⓓ   27 only

10

How many solution(s) does this system of equations have?

$$m + 2n = 1$$
$$6n + 3m = 9$$

Ⓐ   None

Ⓑ   1

Ⓒ   2

Ⓓ   3

11

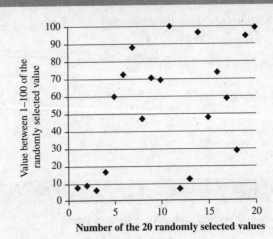

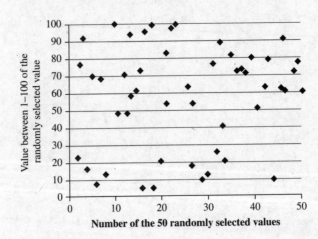

Suppose that the random selection process of numbers between 1 and 100 were conducted for a group of 100 values and a group of 1,000 values. After the selection process is completed, the range of each group is determined. What would most likely be closest to the difference between each group's range of values?

(A)   0

(B)   20

(C)   50

(D)   100

12

Which of these equations when combined into a set of equations with $4x = 2y - 6$ will result in no solutions to the set?

- (A) $y = x - 4$
- (B) $y = 2x + 10$
- (C) $y = 4x - 1$
- (D) $y = \frac{1}{4}x - 6$

13

The amount of money (A) in a bank account after a principal amount (P) is on deposit for t years at an annual interest rate r compounded n times per year is given by this equation:

$$A = P\left(1 + \frac{r}{n}\right)^{nt}$$

Suppose that a banker would like to determine how changes in these variables would cause the bank to pay *less* interest to its clients. Which of the variables—P, r, n, and t—if minimized, would cause less interest paid to clients?

- (A) P only
- (B) r and t only
- (C) n and t only
- (D) P, r, n, and t

14

In a certain right triangle, the sine of angle A is $\frac{5}{13}$ and the cosine of angle A is $\frac{12}{13}$. What is the ratio of the smallest side of the triangle to the median side of the triangle?

2   ◆ MODULE 2 ◆   2

15

If $x > 0$ and $x^2 + 10x = 11$, what is the value of $x + 5$?

_____

16

If a set of 20 different numbers has its smallest and largest values removed, how will that affect the standard deviation of the set?

(A)   It will increase.

(B)   It will decrease.

(C)   It will remain the same.

(D)   Not sufficient information.

17

Jay is purchasing gifts for his four friends' high school graduation. He has a budget of at most $150. He is purchasing a restaurant gift card of $25 for one friend, a tool set that costs $40 for another friend, and a $35 college sweatshirt for a third friend. For his fourth friend, he wants to see how many $0.25 quarters ($Q$) he can give for him to use for laundry money. What expression gives the range of quarters he can purchase given his budgetary restrictions?

(A) $1 \leq Q \leq 300$

(B) $1 \leq Q \leq 200$

(C) $10 \leq Q \leq 120$

(D) $40 \leq Q \leq 60$

18

What will happen to the graph of the function $f(x) = 4x^2 - 18$ if it is transformed into this function: $g(x) = 4(x - 2)^2 - 15$?

(A)   It will shift down 2 units and shift to the left 3 units.

(B)   It will shift up 3 units and shift to the right 2 units.

(C)   It will shift up 2 units and shift to the left 3 units.

(D)   It will shift down 3 units and shift to the right 2 units.

2 ◆ MODULE 2 ◆ 2

19

What is the surface area in square units of a right rectangular prism with edges of 2, 3, and 4 units?

20

Which of the following could be a value of x in this equation?

$$8x^2 = -16x - 2$$

I. $-1 - \dfrac{\sqrt{3}}{2}$

II. $\dfrac{1}{2}(-2 - \sqrt{6})$

III. $\dfrac{1}{2}(\sqrt{3} - 2)$

Ⓐ I only
Ⓑ II only
Ⓒ I and III only
Ⓓ II and III only

21

A botanist plants a small ivy plant and evaluates its growth function. She finds that at 2 months after planting, the plant is 5 inches tall; at 4 months after planting, the plant is 8 inches tall. Additionally, she has noticed that the plant has grown at a constant rate since its initial planting. Given this information, what was the plant's height in inches at the time it was planted?

22

An interior designer is selling wood flooring to be used by his client for a new room. The client has already purchased a set length of trim, which goes between the edge of the wood flooring and the wall. The trim is straight, and cannot be curved, yet it can be joined to make right angle corners. The client does not wish to purchase any more trim and would like to use all of his trim in building the new room. If the interior designer wants to maximize the amount of wood flooring that the client purchases, while satisfying the client's requirements, what should be the relationship between the length (L) and width (W) of the room's dimensions?

(A) $L = W$

(B) $L = 2W$

(C) $W = L^2$

(D) $L = W^3$

ANSWER KEY
Diagnostic Test

Reading and Writing Module 1

1. **D**	10. **D**	19. **C**
2. **B**	11. **B**	20. **A**
3. **A**	12. **D**	21. **B**
4. **B**	13. **D**	22. **A**
5. **D**	14. **B**	23. **D**
6. **A**	15. **C**	24. **D**
7. **B**	16. **C**	25. **C**
8. **B**	17. **D**	26. **B**
9. **B**	18. **A**	27. **C**

Reading and Writing Module 2

1. **D**	10. **D**	19. **D**
2. **C**	11. **C**	20. **D**
3. **C**	12. **D**	21. **C**
4. **C**	13. **B**	22. **A**
5. **C**	14. **A**	23. **C**
6. **B**	15. **A**	24. **B**
7. **A**	16. **C**	25. **B**
8. **A**	17. **B**	26. **B**
9. **C**	18. **A**	27. **B**

ANSWER KEY
Diagnostic Test

Math Module 1

1.	C	12.	B
2.	B	13.	D
3.	21	14.	B
4.	D	15.	7.6
5.	C	16.	A
6.	12	17.	C
7.	25	18.	A
8.	C	19.	D
9.	D	20.	C
10.	A	21.	C
11.	C	22.	3

Math Module 2

1.	B	12.	B
2.	C	13.	D
3.	D	14.	$\frac{5}{12}$ or 0.4166 or 0.4167
4.	A	15.	6
5.	B	16.	B
6.	C	17.	B
7.	C	18.	B
8.	A	19.	52
9.	D	20.	C
10.	A	21.	2
11.	A	22.	A

Diagnostic Test Analysis Guide

Use this guide to determine which skills you should focus on when you review the chapters. As you go through the test, circle the questions you missed. This will let you easily identify the areas in which you need to improve. The test questions that correspond to different skills are organized below.

Reading and Writing Module 1

Reading: Words in Context	1, 2, 3, 4, 5
Reading: Text Structure and Purpose	6
Reading: Cross-Text Connections	7
Reading: Central Ideas and Details	8, 9
Reading: Command of Evidence	10, 11, 12
Reading: Inferences	13, 14
Writing: Standard English Conventions	15, 16, 17, 18, 19, 20, 21
Writing: Expression of Ideas	22, 23, 24, 25, 26, 27

Reading and Writing Module 2

Reading: Words in Context	1, 2, 3, 4
Reading: Text Structure and Purpose	5, 6
Reading: Cross-Text Connections	7, 8
Reading: Central Ideas and Details	9, 10
Reading: Command of Evidence	11, 12, 13
Reading: Inferences	14, 15
Writing: Standard English Conventions	16, 17, 18, 19, 20, 21, 22
Writing: Expression of Ideas	23, 24, 25, 26, 27

Math Module 1

Algebra	2, 3, 5, 6, 9, 10, 13, 18
Problem-Solving and Data Analysis	8, 11, 14, 17
Advanced Math	1, 4, 15, 19, 20, 21, 22
Geometry and Trigonometry	7, 12, 16

Math Module 2

Algebra	2, 3, 5, 6, 10, 12, 17
Problem-Solving and Data Analysis	7, 11, 13, 16, 21
Advanced Math	1, 4, 8, 9, 15, 18, 20
Geometry and Trigonometry	14, 19, 22

Digital PSAT Scoring Chart

This will give you an approximation of the score you would earn on the Digital PSAT[1]. Tally the number of correct answers from the Reading and Writing section (out of 54) and the Math section (out of 44). Take the total for each of these and find the corresponding section score in the tables below.

Number of Correct Reading and Writing Questions (Out of 54)	Reading and Writing Test Score (Out of 760)	Number of Correct Reading and Writing Questions (Out of 54)	Reading and Writing Test Score (Out of 760)
0	160	28	490
1	170	29	500
2	180	30	510
3	190	31	520
4	200	32	530
5	210	33	540
6	220	34	550
7	230	35	560
8	240	36	570
9	250	37	580
10	260	38	590
11	270	39	600
12	290	40	610
13	300	41	620
14	310	42	630
15	320	43	640
16	340	44	650
17	350	45	660
18	360	46	670
19	370	47	680
20	390	48	690
21	400	49	700
22	420	50	710
23	430	51	720
24	450	52	730
25	460	53	750
26	470	54	760
27	480		

[1] Keep in mind that some of the questions on an actual PSAT test will be research questions that will not count toward your actual score. For the sake of simplicity, we are including possible research questions in your calculation.

Number of Correct Math Questions (Out of 44)	Math Section Score (Out of 760)
0	160
1	180
2	190
3	200
4	210
5	240
6	260
7	280
8	300
9	310
10	320
11	340
12	350
13	360
14	370
15	390
16	400
17	410
18	420
19	440
20	450
21	460
22	470

Number of Correct Math Questions (Out of 44)	Math Section Score (Out of 760)
23	480
24	490
25	500
26	510
27	520
28	530
29	540
30	550
31	560
32	570
33	580
34	590
35	610
36	620
37	640
38	650
39	660
40	680
41	710
42	730
43	750
44	760

Add the Reading and Writing section score and the Math section score to find your total PSAT Test score:

_____ Reading and Writing section score +

_____ Math section score =

_____ **Total PSAT Test score (between 320 and 1520)**

Approximate your testing percentiles (1st–99th) using this chart:

Total Score	Section Score	Total Percentile	Reading and Writing Percentile	Math Percentile
1520	760	99+	99+	99
1420	710	98	98	96
1320	660	94	94	91
1220	610	86	86	84
1120	560	74	73	75
1020	510	59	57	61
920	460	41	40	42
820	410	25	24	27
720	360	11	11	15
620	310	3	3	5
520	260	1	1	1
420	210	1	1	1
320	160	1	1	1

Scoring data based on information at *collegeboard.org*

Diagnostic Self-Assessment

Check any areas you feel you need to work on.

Reading

- ☐ Reading timing
- ☐ Overthinking Reading questions
- ☐ Not sure how to think through Reading questions
- ☐ Careless errors on Reading questions
- ☐ Other issues?

Writing

- ☐ Writing timing
- ☐ Writing grammar review
- ☐ Overthinking Writing questions
- ☐ Not sure how to think through Writing questions
- ☐ Careless errors on Writing questions
- ☐ Other issues?

Math

- ☐ Math timing
- ☐ Math formula and concept review
- ☐ Overthinking Math questions
- ☐ Not sure how to think through Math questions
- ☐ Careless errors on Math questions
- ☐ Other issues?

General

- ☐ Test anxiety and testing mindset issues?

Answer Explanations

Reading and Writing Module 1

1. **(D)** On the vocabulary questions, the wisest strategy is to insert each of the options into the text to determine the best choice in context. "Within the Iroquois, he *gathered* many followers" is the most sensible possibility, as seen in choice (D), since he is creating a group of people who follow him.

2. **(B)** *Passing* in this context means "going" or "progressing" because the sentence is expressing the nature of time. The best answer is *moving*, since it comes closest to meaning "going" or "progressing." It is not (A), *living*, because time is not a living thing, and is not described in this way—even metaphorically—in the surrounding sentences. It is not (C), because the type of movement that time undergoes is not a physical throw, but an abstract process. It is not (D), because although *succeeding* can mean "following," *passing* is describing an ongoing process, not a series of separate events.

3. **(A)** You can put your own synonym in here pretty easily. An "answer" or *resolution* to a problem is the intended meaning, so (A) works best. (B) refers to the first usage of *solution*, a mixture of liquids. (C) denotes an "option." (D) inaccurately signifies that the teacher is referencing the cause—a lack of preparation—rather than the solution, adequate preparation.

4. **(B)** *Fashionable* refers to the popularity of travelers placing paintings of their travel destinations in their homes. *Tailored* implies a level of customization that is not present in these works, *leisurely* refers more to the scenes of the paintings, and *economical* could apply to the practice of saving money by using more general scenes than customized ones, but the focus in these lines is on the increased interest in this practice.

5. **(D)** The idea expressed here is that natural gas gave cooks the ability to "control" or *manipulate* their cooking flames. It is not (A) because *annihilate* is to "destroy" something. It is not

(B) or (C) because *satisfy* and *craft* do not mean "control."

6. **(A)** The first part of the text makes a broad statement of parthenogenesis. The underlined sentence outlines an important exception to this, mammals, and transitions into a clarification about how parthenogenesis does not occur naturally in mammals. It is not (B) because this short sentence does not give a definition. It is not (C) or (D) because the focus is on science, not ethics and economics.

7. **(B)** Text 1 delves into the mechanics of how the electoral college works, while Text 2 puts the electoral college in the historical context of the past 200 years—all of this lines up with choice (B). It is not (A), because neither text cites political authority figures. It is not (C), because Text 1 does not address the founding of the United States. And it is not (D), because Text 2 does not address the economy.

8. **(B)** The text argues that the advantages of social media need to be considered in the workplace, so (B) is the correct choice. The author provides evidence of (A) to support the thesis, but it is not the thesis itself. (C) represents a general argument that the text questions. (D) is not discussed.

9. **(B)** Newton's theories gave Halley a general structure he could use to make better predictions about the behavior of comets. Out of the options, this is most similar to a politician who uses philosophical maxims to predict societal outcomes, since the philosophical maxims would give the theoretical structure that the politician would use to predict what would come next. It is not choice (A), because the musician is not making predictions. It is not (C), because the mathematician is using the data to create theories, whereas Halley was using the theory to make experimental predictions as to what the data would be. And it is not (D), because the engineer is not focused on making predictions about data but using established laws of physics for construction.

10. **(D)** The lines are closest to one another in 2008, so (D) is correct. The other choices provide years where the deviation between voters is greater than it is in 2008.

11. **(B)** *Experimental confirmation that the inner components of a virus are similar to those of a cell nucleus* would give further evidence that the modern cell nucleus originated from a viral infection. Choices (A), (C), and (D) would not relate to origin of the cell nucleus.

12. **(D)** By stating that death is a "slave to fate, chance," the poet suggests that death is more of a random process than one of clear destiny, in which the future would be more pre-determined. While the other options all mention death, they do not mention its randomness.

13. **(D)** The "cases" the text refers to in the final sentence are those in which due to confusion as to whether a war actually began, the applicability of the Geneva Convention would be "contested." Certain parties in the war may not consider respecting the human rights of those that they capture. This would therefore result in an *obvious* danger. The other options do not highlight the clear danger to combatants that such confusion would cause.

14. **(B)** The text describes cats as being entertaining, but "far less predictable" in their behavior than other pets and "fickle." The final sentence creates a contrast between how the cat is a very common pet—to complete that contrast, stating that cat behavior is unfamiliar would be logical. (A) is not supported because the cats are described as unpredictable. There is no evidence in the text to support choice (C). (D) is irrelevant to the focus of the text.

15. **(C)** In colloquial English, people use choice (A), but it ultimately is not correct usage. *Should have given* is the correct conjugation here. Remember that *should of, could of,* and *would of* are never correct verb usages. *Should have, could have,* and *would have* are the proper usages.

16. **(C)** Earlier in the text, the author uses "one." To be consistent with this pronoun use, use *one* in this instance as well. The other options would not match this pronoun usage.

17. **(D)** *Technique* is the singular subject, so the verb should be *involves*. (D) also uses the correct forms of *floating* and *molten* to describe the class—*molted* does not work as a word in this context—*molted* means for an animal to have shed its exterior coat. *Molten* means "liquified," which would be appropriate to describe hot glass. Choices (A) and (B) have plural verbs, and choice (C) uses *molted* instead of *molten*.

18. **(A)** "Boiled down to its essence, the problem is this" is an *independent clause,* meaning that it could be a full sentence on its own. It needs sufficient punctuation to separate it from what comes after. A colon would be best in this case because it acts as a lead-in to the second clause. Choice (A) is the correct answer. Choices (B) and (C) lack punctuation at the end of the independent clause. Choice (D) would be a comma splice.

19. **(C)** It is important to maintain parallelism within a clause. Notice how "increasing" is used first. It is necessary to maintain the gerund (-ing) form for the second action. *Sending* is the only option that appropriately maintains parallelism.

20. **(A)** The subject and verb must agree. In this case, the subject is "trend," which is a singular noun that will require a corresponding verb. Eliminate choices (B) and (D) for being plural verbs. Choice (C) incorrectly uses future perfect tense, whereas present is the desired tense. "There has been a trend" is the best answer.

21. **(B)** Recall that a semicolon is the best way to connect two independent clauses (two clauses that could otherwise be full, complete sentences). Choice (B) uses a semicolon effectively. Choice (A) is a comma splice. Choice (C) is a run-on sentence. Choice (D) is flawed in that it introduces an unnecessary comma.

22. **(A)** The best option here is a contrasting transition. Essentially, *good readers are active,* but *bad readers tend to end up as criminals.* A vast generalization, but that's the structure of the sentence. *On the other hand* is the only contrasting transition. *Therefore* and *thus* are cause-and-effect transitions. *Moreover* means "also."

23. **(D)** Choice (D) is the only option that demonstrates a contrast between the relatively wasteful process of incandescence and the far more efficient process of luminescence.

24. **(D)** This sentence provides an additional explanation that helps the reader understand how sunscreen is not a perfect solution in and of itself—responsible behavior, like taking breaks from the sun, is essential to sun safety. It is not choice (A) because this is not a subsequent, or next, event. It is not choice (B) because the previous and current sentences do not contrast with one another. And it is not choice (C) because the current sentence is not simply elaborating on the previous sentence but providing a new point.

25. **(C)** *For instance* provides a connection between the general statement made about the artwork in the previous sentence, followed by a specific example in the current sentence. Choices (A) and (B) do not provide this sort of transition, and choice (D) is too wordy.

26. **(B)** Both of these projections inaccurately display the area of surfaces of Earth, skewing the size based on where on Earth the section is found. The Mercator projection "does not accurately show the surface area of countries" and the Robinson projection "distorts the size of the land masses close to the North and South Poles." It is not (A), because the Mercator is likely more useful for ship navigation. It is not (C), because the projections are not accurate in displaying relative land area in latitudes close to the poles. It is not (D), because both projections can indeed be drawn on a two-dimensional surface.

27. **(C)** The student wants to emphasize what can be likely seen by people who want to see elements of Teotihuacan today. Since the Pyramid of the Sun and the Pyramid of the Moon are both well-preserved, they would be excellent elements of this past civilization that people today could visibly see. It is not choice (A) because this relates to the Inca, not to Teotihuacan. It is not (B) because this does not tell us what can physically be seen today. It is not (D) because this makes a general parallel between ancient and modern civilization.

Reading and Writing Module 2

1. **(D)** Here, *dismissed* means "discredited." (A) refers to a lower price. There is no suggestion that he has *forgotten* the information, as in (B). (C) means that he would "allow" this information to go forward, which is illogical.

2. **(C)** This line is referring to viewers who brought up, or presented, points that weakened the speaker's credibility. Therefore, the meaning is that they *put forward* several points. (A) would not refer to the act of expressing ideas. (B) is the definition for *raise* when it refers to lifting something up. (D) indicates bringing up and caring for someone, as a parent might raise a child. Make sure to read the sentence with the choices replacing the underlined portion if you are struggling between two answer choices.

3. **(C)** On vocabulary problems, if there is any uncertainty, it is best to plug the options into the text in place of the word. *Theory*, in this case, makes far more sense than *building, observation,* or *astronomy*. *Construct* isn't often used as a noun rather than as a verb, but when it is, its meaning is generally *an idea or a theory*.

4. **(C)** Gamelin politely refuses to sit in the chair that is offered to her, so she is best described as *turning down* the chair. *Repulsing* is too negative, and *decreasing* and *plummeting* generally relate to amounts of things.

5. **(C)** This sentence serves as the author's acknowledgment of a possible objection that would find a move away from partisanship a positive trend in American politics, so (C) is accurate. These lines show an opposing view, ruling out (A), and do not go into details as in (B). Finally, choice (D) is incorrect because the lines do not include a citation.

6. **(B)** The author uses this text to give scientific reasons, such as Halley's unusually elliptical orbit, as to why Halley's Comet is a uniquely observable comet. The other options do not give you the *primary* purpose of the text, just minor things that are mentioned.

7. **(A)** The underlined selection states that "petroleum output is as healthy as ever." Now, consider how the first author might respond. Choices (B), (C), and (D) are not variable: petroleum is not renewable, always generates greenhouse gases, and is less expensive than ethanol. (A) works because the first author would want to consider how much oil is available domestically since it impacts our self-sufficiency.

8. **(A)** The first text argues that literature is a term reserved for writing that is artistically superior and timeless, pursuing beauty, purpose, and meaning. The second text, on the other hand, postulates that standards of evaluation are illusory and biased. Therefore, (A) is the only option that captures the overall relationship between the two texts.

9. **(C)** Zenobia is most interested in the "relation between the sexes" when it comes to social reform, so she is most interested in reforming antiquated gender roles. There is no evidence that her primary reform objective is to change universities that are hostile toward foreigners (choice (A)), problems with economic fairness (choice (B)), or destruction of the environment (choice (D)).

10. **(D)** When answering questions like these, the challenge is recognizing the big picture idea of the text. You need to be able to fully understand the text and put the main idea of the text in your own words. In this text, the main idea is that Kolya is putting family heirlooms into a fire in order to keep warm in the bitter cold. Instead of prioritizing the sentimental value of these items, he is more interested in being comfortable in the harsh environment. Therefore, choice (D) makes the most sense since Kolya's need for comfort overcomes his familial nostalgia (sentimental longing). The incorrect choices will often trap you by presenting ideas that may represent small portions of the text, but do not accurately represent the text as a whole. Choice (A) states that the library must be preserved at all costs, which is inaccurate given that so many of the library books are being burned. Choice (B) incorrectly suggests that the narrator is making some sort of sacrifice to the gods; instead, he is simply trying

to stay warm. Choice (C) suggests that the narrator would like to be reunited with his deceased mother; while this may be true, there is no textual evidence to draw this conclusion, and this statement does not accurately represent the main idea of the text.

11. **(C)** Only use the evidence given. You cannot make conclusions about any employment outlooks, as in (A) and (B). Nor can you make assumptions about the number of people currently employed in these professions, as in (D). However, you can use the graph to show that janitorial jobs are more likely to be completed by machinery than historian jobs, making (C) correct.

12. **(D)** The author of Text 2 believes that the quality of writing is "entirely subjective," and bases this argument on inconsistent grading. So, choice (D) would rule out the evidence and undermine the author's argument. (A) would support the argument of the text. (B) and (C) don't affect the argument either way.

13. **(B)** This quotation most directly illustrates the sorrow at being ignored by other people, because even though the narrator is dying of thirst, no one brings her water. The other options do not effectively show the sorrow at being ignored by other people.

14. **(A)** The sentence notes that vacuuming won't be "hugely helpful," but it would be logical to state that it could be a *good preliminary step* that would do at least something useful. It is not choice (B) or (D) because the text does not suggest that vacuuming would result in complete elimination of the bedbugs. It is not choice (C) because the transition "but" leading into the underlined portion suggests that an acknowledgement of how the vacuuming can be helpful to some extent would be fitting here.

15. **(A)** The text describes Mannes and Godowsky as more casual tinkerers (as opposed to dedicated researchers) "working recreationally, "who had backgrounds in music rather than professional science. Thus, their discovery can best be described as *serendipitous*—i.e., a fortunate

finding by chance. The other options are all associated with focus in particular fields of study, which was not the case for Mannes and Godowsky with respect to their photographic research.

16. **(C)** A possessive is required that will express the idea of the problems of patients, where patients is plural. Choice (A) isn't possessive. Choice (D) incorrectly uses both *those of* and *patients*, which are illogical when combined. Choice (B) incorrectly expresses the problems of one patient. Choice (C) is the best answer.

17. **(B)** This is the only option parallel in use of italics and correct in use of the comma for a list. The other options either improperly use apostrophes or lack a comma.

18. **(A)** This is the only option that uses the correct present perfect tense. Choice (B) is past. Choice (C), *loaned*, is always incorrect. Choice (D) is in the progressive tense.

19. **(D)** The *mill* is singular, and it possesses the *grounds*. Also, there needs to be a clear separation between the two complete sentences, which the semicolon, but not a comma, can provide. Choice (A) provides no possession, choice (B) would be for plural mills, and choice (C) would cause a comma splice.

20. **(D)** This choice correctly does not have an apostrophe after *departments* because this word is functioning as the subject, not as a possessive adjective. Choices (A) and (B) incorrectly have apostrophes after *departments*. Choice (C) incorrectly uses *there*, which is used to indicate a place. Choice (D) correctly uses *their* to show possession.

21. **(C)** The subject is "foreign objects" which is a plural noun that requires a plural verb. Eliminate choice (A), as *basis that is daily* is an awkward way of saying "daily basis." Eliminate choice (D) for having a singular verb—*attacks*. Eliminate choice (B), as *that attacking* is inappropriate; *that attack*, as seen in choice (C), is preferable.

22. **(A)** The writer uses an interesting turn of phrase to state that Bernice does not listen to (entertain) or find amusing (be entertained by) Marjorie's social activities. Choice (B) does not work because a transitional word would be needed after *entertainment*. Choices (C) and (D) result in nonsensical meanings.

23. **(C)** This is the only option that provides a needed contrast between what could potentially cause males to be calico or tortoiseshell and the fact that such a possibility is quite rare.

24. **(B)** *Unlike* is the only option to show the necessary contrast between the view of the contemporary socialist parties that seek out full socialization of private industry and the more moderate Social Democrats who sought compromise.

25. **(B)** For transition questions, diagnose the relationship between this sentence and the preceding one. The author is arguing that, *even though* she learned some German, she didn't learn as much of the native language as a German student would learn of English in the United States. That *even though* is important, as it denotes a contrast between the two sentences. *However* is the only contrasting choice.

26. **(B)** Since the student wants to show the possible range of severity that could result from a parasitic worm infection, choice (B) is the most effective option. It outlines how an infected person could feel anything from mild annoyance to having potentially life-threatening consequences. The other options relate to infection, but do not discuss the possible range of severity.

27. **(B)** The notes state that land preservation does not factor in the potential use of the land by humans, while land conservation does factor in such use—this makes choice (B) the most logical option. Choices (A) and (D) do not draw a contrast, and choice (C) is inconsistent with the definitions of the ideas presented in the notes.

Math Module 1

1. **(C)** x and y could both either be negative or positive to make this true. Therefore, the only thing we can safely assume is that x and y are different. You can try this with sample values that make this expression true:

x	y	$x^2 > y^2$
−5	4	$25 > 16$
6	−1	$36 > 1$
3	0	$9 > 0$

2. **(B)** Solve for x and y by using substitution:

$$4 + y = 32x \text{ and } y = 2x + 2 \rightarrow$$

$$4 + (2x + 2) = 32x \rightarrow 6 = 30x \rightarrow x = \frac{1}{5} \rightarrow$$

Substitute $\frac{1}{5}$ in for x to solve for $y : y = 2 \times \frac{1}{5} + 2 = \frac{12}{5}$

Then, multiply x and y to solve for their product: $\frac{1}{5} \times \frac{12}{5} = \frac{12}{25}$

3. **(21)** In a typical week, Eloise should get $9 \times 7 = 63$ hours of sleep. We can see how much sleep she has gotten by subtracting the total hours she has been awake from the total hours in a week: $24 \times 7 - 126 = 42$. Then, we can calculate the additional hours of sleep she should get by subtracting how many hours she *actually* got (42) <u>from</u> the amount of sleep she *should have* gotten (63):

$$63 - 42 = 21 \text{ additional hours she should get}$$

4. **(D)** You could work backwards from the choices if you are so inclined. Algebraically, divide the expression by 3 to simplify:

$$3a^2 - 27a - 108 = 0 \rightarrow a^2 - 9a - 36 = 0 \rightarrow$$

Factor it: $(a - 12)(a + 3) = 0$

If $a = 12$, $(a - 12)$ is 0, making the entire expression equal to 0. Similarly, if $a = -3$, $(a + 3)$ is 0, making the entire expression equal to 0.

Therefore, the solutions are $12, -3$.

5. **(C)** The *difference* between two terms is the result when you subtract one term from another. Let us subtract one term from another—this is easiest to do if you place one term over the other so you

can easily match up common terms and carefully apply the negative sign:

$$\begin{array}{r} (7a^2 + 3ab - 8b) \\ - (-2a^2 + ab - 2b) \\ \hline 9a^2 + 2ab - 6b \end{array}$$

6. **(12)** Triple the given equation $2x + 3 = 4$ to give you the equation $6x + 9 = 12$:

$$2x + 3 = 4 \rightarrow 3 \bullet 2x + 3 \bullet 3 = 3 \bullet 4 \rightarrow 6x + 9 = 12$$

Alternatively, if you do not recognize this pattern, solve for x and plug the value into $6x + 9 = 12$ to see the value of the expression.

7. **(25)** Use the circumference formula, $2\pi r$, to solve for the circumference. Since the diameter is 8 centimeters, the radius will be half of this: 4 centimeters. Plug 4 into the circumference formula to solve for the circumference:

$$2\pi(4) = 8\pi = \approx 25.12$$

Round it to the nearest whole centimeter to get 25.

8. **(C)** The total price on which the sales tax will be applied is $25,000 - $5,000, since the new car is $25,000 and Allison receives $5,000 on the trade-in. To calculate the total after the sales tax is applied, take 100% of (25,000 − 5,000) and add 7% to it. Move the decimal point to the left two spots for each percentage: 100% becomes 1.00 and 7% becomes 0.07. So, multiply (25,000 − 5,000) by 1.07 to get the correct answer: 1.07(25,000 − 5,000).

9. **(D)** Multiplying or dividing an inequality by a negative number will change the direction of the inequality sign. The other operations mentioned will not do so. Here is how it would work with dividing the expression by −2:

$$-2x > 4 \rightarrow \frac{-2x}{-2} < \frac{4}{-2} \rightarrow x < -2$$

If you try some sample values that would work for x, such as −3 or −5, you will see that the inequality is true.

10. **(A)** Take the slope of the line using relatively simple points from the table, like (1, 2) and (5, 18):

$$\text{Slope} = \frac{Rise}{Run} = \frac{y_2 - y_1}{x_x - x_1} = \frac{18 - 2}{5 - 1} = \frac{16}{4} = 4$$

The only choice with a slope of 4 is (A).

11. **(C)** For each year she has the portfolio, it increases 10%. Therefore, the amount after one year of growth over the original amount at the beginning of that year will be 1.1 times the original amount. This process will repeat for each year she has the portfolio growing at this rate, making $f(n) = 10{,}000 \times 1.1^n$.

You can also see this using concrete numbers. If she starts with $10,000, after 1 year, she will have 10% interest added to the original amount:

$$10\% \text{ of } 10{,}000 = 0.1 \times 10{,}000 = 1{,}000$$

Then, you can add 1,000 to the original 10,000 to have $11,000 after the first year. Then, to see how much money she will have after two years, find 10% of this new total:

$$10\% \text{ of } 11{,}000 = 0.1 \times 11{,}000 = 1{,}100$$

Then, add this to the original 11,000 to find how much she will have in her account at the end of year 2:

$$11{,}000 + 1{,}100 = 12{,}100$$

The only option that fits these concrete numbers is choice (B).

12. **(B)** Use the provided formula for the volume of a cylinder:

$$V = \pi r^2 h$$

The height is 4 feet and the radius is half the diameter: 1 foot. Plug these values into the equation to solve for the cylinder's volume:

$$V = \pi r^2 h \rightarrow \pi(1^2)4 = 4\pi \text{ cubic feet}$$

13. **(D)** Each penny is 1 cent and each nickel is 5 cents. So, the total number of cents given by the total coins in the change bowl will be $P + 5N$. This needs to be less than 1 dollar total—i.e., 100 cents. This gives us the inequality $P + 5N < 100$ as our solution.

14. **(B)** As the age groups gradually increase in value (from 12 through 61+), the number of group members using video sharing steadily decreases (from 40 to 2). A negative correlation is defined as the relationship between two variables such that when one variable increases, the other variable decreases. So the relationship between age groups and percentage of group members using video sharing can best be described as a negative correlation.

A positive correlation is when the variables increase with one another. Equivalence simply means the variables are equal. An exponentially inverse relationship means that as one variable increases, the other decreases at an exponential rate. The decrease in video sharing is relatively steady, so the terms cannot be described as having an exponentially inverse relationship.

15. **(7.6)** Plug in the given values for m and n to determine what the value of the constant k is:

$$m = kn$$
$$10 = k \times 2$$
$$5 = k$$

Now, plug 38 in for m and 5 for k to get the value of n:

$$38 = 5n$$
$$7.6 = n$$

16. **(A)** A parallelogram has two sets of equivalent interior angle measures. Also, it is a quadrilateral that has a total interior angle measure of 360 degrees. Since one of the interior angles is 50 degrees, one of the other angles will also be 50 degrees. The other two angles will then add up to a total measure of $360 - 2(50) = 260$ degrees. Solve for the larger angle by dividing 260 by 2:

$$\frac{260}{2} = 130$$

17. **(C)** The slope of the function is steady and linear until around week 6, at which point it starts curving upwards exponentially. An exponential function is one that goes up at a rapidly increasing rate or goes down at a rapidly decreasing rate, as opposed to a steady, linear rate.

18. **(A)** No matter how many shirts or pants are cleaned, the cleaner has a $5 fee. The only logical explanation out of the given choices is that this is some kind of set fee. The cost to clean a shirt is 10, since it multiplies the shirt variable. The cost to clean a pair of pants is 6, since it multiplies the pants variable. And the total minimum cost to clean either one shirt or one pair of pants is 11, since it would be:

$$C = 10S + 6P + 5 \rightarrow C = 10 \times 0 + 6 \times 1 + 5 = 11$$

19. **(D)** The weight of the balloon itself is irrelevant since the balloon is identical in both situations. $1.2 - 0.179 = 1.021$ is the difference in density between the two balloons. Since you have a 2 cubic meter balloon, simply multiply 1.021 by 2 to give approximately 2.04.

20. **(C)** The fixed costs for the pretzel stand are $500, and the variable costs are $2. So, the cost function $c(x)$ given x pretzels is $c(x) = 2x + 500$. The graph of this function will therefore have a y-intercept of 500, and a slope of 2:

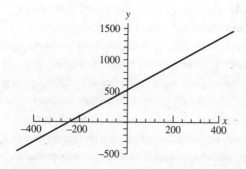

21. **(C)** A value of 4 for n will ensure that the expression has exponential growth since any power of 2 or greater will ensure exponential growth in the function. Anything raised to the 0 power simply equals 1. Anything raised to an exponent of 1 is simply itself. So choices (A) and (B) result in lines, not exponential functions.

22. **(3)** There are 3 values of the function where it will intersect the x-axis, which we can see by looking at the graph of the equation below:

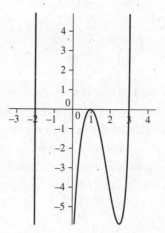

The values of 3, -2, and 1 are all zeros of the function.

You can perhaps more easily determine the zeros of the function if you recognize that the function is already factored:

$$f(x) = (x - 3)(x + 2)((x - 1)^2)$$

All you need to do is look at the values of x that would make the entire expression equal to zero. If $(x - 3) = 0$, or $(x + 2) = 0$, or $(x - 1) = 0$, the entire expression is equal to zero. Also, since $(x - 1)$ is squared, the $(x - 1)$ term repeats, so we will have only three zeros even though this will end up being a quartic equation (to the fourth power).

Math Module 2

1. **(B)** It is easiest to do substitution for x into the first equation.

$$2x = 10 \rightarrow x = 5$$

Substitute 5 into the first equation:

$$5 = y^2 - 3y + 1 \rightarrow y^2 - 3y - 4 = 0 \rightarrow$$

Factor it: $(y + 1)(y - 4) = 0$

Therefore, the solutions are -1 and 4.

2. **(C)** Whenever Andrew begins his study time, he always takes the 10 minutes of time to get set up. Then, he completes 1 problem every 5 minutes of

actual study. So, the number of minutes he takes to do p problems is $10 + 5p$. If we set up the equation for this, it is $m = 10 + 5p$. Then, if we solve for p, we will get the correct answer:

$$m = 10 + 5p \rightarrow m - 10 = 5p \rightarrow \frac{(m-10)}{5} = p$$
$$\rightarrow p = \frac{1}{5}(m-10)$$

3. **(D)** Since this is one equation with two variables, it will have infinite solutions. If we knew another line with which this equation intersected, the two equations would have a solution. To see how this equation has more than two solutions, try some sample values for x and y into the equation:

$$3x - 4y = 73$$

If x is 1, y is -17.5.

If x is 2, y is -16.75.

If x is 3, y is -16.

You can keep on going and you will find endless possibilities for x and y.

4. **(A)**

$$(2x^2 + 4xy + 2y^2) \times \frac{1}{2x + 2y} = \frac{2x^2 + 4xy + 2y^2}{2x + 2y} \rightarrow$$

$$\frac{x^2 + 2xy + y^2}{x + y} = \frac{(x+y)(x+y)}{(x+y)} = x + y = y + x$$

5. **(B)** The professor will cancel if there are 10 or fewer students in the class. So, there must be more than 10 students. Therefore, the answer is $S > 10$.

6. **(C)** What is a possible value for x in the expression below?

Take the original expression: $-6 < \frac{8}{3}x < -\frac{1}{4}$

Multiply everything by $\frac{3}{8}$ in order to get x by itself:

$$-\frac{9}{4} < x < -\frac{3}{32}$$

Make it easier by converting each fraction to a decimal so it is easier to determine what numbers would fall within this range. The fractions would convert to the following range expressed as decimals:

$$-2.25 < x < -0.09375$$

-2 is the only choice within this range.

7. **(C)** Since the amount of money he earns is only $8,000, it falls within the first tax bracket of 15%. Multiply 0.15 by $8,000 to find the total amount of tax on his income:

$$0.15 \times 8,000 = 1,200$$

8. **(A)** Take both the slope and the y-intercept and multiply them by -1 to get the reflection of the line. For $y = 4x + 7$ this will be the equation $y = -4x - 7$.

The general rule for a reflection of a function $f(x)$ across the x-axis is that the reflection is $-f(x)$.

9. **(D)** Solve for x as follows:

$$\frac{12}{\sqrt[3]{x}} = 4 \rightarrow 12 = 4\sqrt[3]{x} \rightarrow 3 = \sqrt[3]{x}$$
$$\hookrightarrow \text{Cube both sides} \rightarrow 27 = x$$

10. **(A)** $m + 2n = 1$ and $6n + 3m = 9$ are parallel lines that will not intersect, since they have the same slopes and different y-intercepts. Since they do not intersect at all, they will have no common solutions.

11. **(A)** The range is the difference between the maximum and minimum values in the set. With such large data sets, it is highly likely that both sets would have a wide range of large and small values, with both almost certainly having a value close to or at 1 and a value close to or at 100. So the range for both sets would be about 100. The difference between the ranges is calculated by subtracting one range from the other: $100 - 100 = 0$.

12. **(B)** We can begin by determining the slope of the line in the given equation by putting it in slope-intercept form ($y = mx + b$):

$$4x = 2y - 6 \rightarrow 2y = 4x + 6 \rightarrow y = 2x + 3$$

The line portrayed in choice (B), $y = 2x + 10$, is the only option that has the same slope of the line in the problem. This means that the two lines will never intersect and will have no common solutions since they are parallel to one another. Be mindful that this will only be true as long as the y-intercepts of the lines are different; if the y-intercepts are the same, then the lines will overlap.

13. **(D)** Minimizing all of the variables will decrease the amount of money in the account after a given period of time. While you could plug in a variety of sample values and test the impact of changing each variable on the overall amount of money in the account, this is easier to simply think through using common sense. If you start off with less money, have a lower interest rate, and have less frequent compounding of interest, there will be less money in the account.

14. $\left(\dfrac{5}{12}$ **or 0.4166 or 0.4167**$\right)$ The triangle as described looks like this:

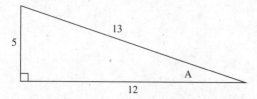

Given this sine and cosine, the triangle will be a multiple of the special right triangle, 5-12-13. The smallest side is 5 and the median side is 12, so the ratio of the smallest side of the triangle to the median side of the triangle is $\dfrac{5}{12}$.

Another way to think about it is that this is asking for what the tangent of angle A would be, which is the opposite side over the adjacent, giving you $\dfrac{5}{12}$.

15. **(6)** Look for a way to seamlessly make the original expression a variation on $x + 5$. Add 25 to both sides of the equation: $x^2 + 10x = 11$, and the result can be expressed as $(x + 5)^2 = 36$. Therefore, $x + 5 = 6$.

Alternatively, you could determine the value of x using the quadratic formula, $\dfrac{-b \pm \sqrt{b^2 - 4ac}}{2a}$, but this will be more labor-intensive than noticing the shortcut.

16. **(B)** The smaller the range of values in a data set, the lower the standard deviation will be. If the smallest and largest values are removed, this will decrease the range of values, therefore decreasing the standard deviation.

To be more precise, you can calculate standard deviation using this formula:

$$\text{Standard Deviation} = \sqrt{\text{Average of the squared distances of the data points from their mean}}$$

For example, the standard deviation of the set $\{1, 5, 6, 7, 10\}$ is approximately 3.3, while the standard deviation of the same set with the highest and lowest values removed $\{5, 6, 7\}$ would be 1. So, using this example, you can see that removing the smallest and largest values from the set will decrease the standard deviation of the set.

17. **(B)** After purchasing gifts for his other friends, Jay has $50 left. $50 has 200 quarters, so the range of what Jay can give his friend is between 1 and 200 quarters inclusive, which is expressed as $1 \leq Q \leq 200$.

18. **(B)** When you add a positive number to the y-value of a function, the function shifts up; when you subtract a number from its x-value, the function shifts to the right. This function has 3 added to its y-value and 2 subtracted from its x-value, so it will shift up 3 units and shift to the right 2 units.

19. **(52)** Each of the six faces of a right rectangular prism (a box) is a rectangle—you can calculate the area of a rectangle by multiplying its length by its width. So, for a right rectangular prism with edges of x, y, and z units, the surface area can be calculated as follows:

$$2xy + 2xz + 2yz$$

Plug in 2 for x, 3 for y, and 4 for z to calculate the total surface area:

$$2(2)(3) + 2(2)(4) + 2(3)(4) = 12 + 16 + 24 =$$
$$52 \ square\ units$$

20. **(C)** Which of the following could be a value of x in this equation?

$$8x^2 = -16x - 2$$
$$8x^2 + 16x = -2$$
$$x^2 + 2x = -\frac{1}{4}$$

Complete the square:

$$(x + 1)^2 = \frac{3}{4} \rightarrow x^2 + 2x + 1 =$$
$$\frac{3}{4} \rightarrow x^2 + 2x + \frac{1}{4} = 0$$

Use the quadratic equation to find the answers:

$$\frac{-b \pm \sqrt{b^2 - 4ac}}{2a} \rightarrow \frac{-2 \pm \sqrt{2^2 - 4 \cdot 1 \cdot \frac{1}{4}}}{2 \cdot 1}$$

$$= \frac{-2 \pm \sqrt{3}}{2 \cdot 1} = -1 \pm \frac{\sqrt{3}}{2}$$

Then, simplify the two ± solutions to see what they equal:

$$-1 + \frac{\sqrt{3}}{2} = \frac{-2}{2} + \frac{\sqrt{3}}{2} = \frac{1}{2}(\sqrt{3} - 2)$$

And $-1 - \frac{\sqrt{3}}{2}$.

21. **(2)** The plant increases 3 inches in height every 2 months. Simply backtrack 2 months from the time when it is 5 inches tall in order to see how tall it was when it was planted: $5 - 3 = 2$ inches.

22. **(A)** In order to maximize the area of the floor while minimizing the floor perimeter, a square floor would be the best choice. A square will always have at least as much and typically more area for a particular perimeter than a rectangle will of the same perimeter. Therefore, the length and width should be equivalent.

To see this, try using concrete numbers. If we have a square and a rectangle, each with a perimeter of 20 units, the length of each side for the square must be 5, and the lengths of the sides of the rectangle could be a wide range of possibilities, such as 2, 8, 2, 8. The area of the square with a side of 5 is $5^2 = 25$. The area of the rectangle is $2 \times 8 = 16$, which is much less than the area of the square. You can try this with other sample values for the rectangle's sides, but you will consistently find that having the sides equivalent will lead to the greatest possible area.

Reading

1

Reading

Reading for the Digital PSAT

The Digital PSAT Reading and Writing section combines both reading comprehension questions with grammar and editing questions to give you your total *Reading and Writing* score. How is this different from the old PSAT Reading format?

Old PSAT Reading	Digital PSAT Reading
■ Reading passages are 500–750 words long and have 10–11 questions each.	■ Reading and Writing passages are no longer than 150 words. Each passage has just one question accompanying it.
■ Reading genres include fiction, social science, historical documents, and natural science.	■ Has a greater variety of reading genres represented. With the current PSAT reading genres, there will be humanities, drama, and poetry excerpts.

The new Digital PSAT Reading and Writing section is structured as follows:

Reading and Writing Module One	32 Minutes, 27 Questions, Standard Difficulty
Reading and Writing Module Two	32 Minutes, 27 Questions, Adaptive Difficulty (easier or harder questions depending on how you did on the first Reading/Writing section)

- Out of the 54 total questions in the two modules, a little over half of them will likely be reading questions.
- Each reading question will have a small passage that accompanies it, ranging between 25 and 150 words. Some of the passages will also have a graph of some sort.
- 50 of the questions will count toward your score and four of the questions are *pre-test* questions that will not count but are used by the College Board to test future questions. *Do not worry about determining which questions are pre-test; just do your best on every question you encounter.*

This chapter contains:
- **15 Key strategies for success on PSAT Reading questions**
- **Question-specific strategies and practice** for the six types of PSAT Reading questions you will encounter:
  - **Information and Ideas**
    - *Central Ideas and Details*
    - *Command of Evidence*
    - *Inferences*
  - **Craft and Structure**
    - *Words in Context*
    - *Text Structure and Purpose*
    - *Cross-Text Connections*

Reading Strategies

1. Take your time.

A major shift in the digital PSAT is to make it an easier test to complete within the time constraints. Most test-takers will find that the PSAT Reading section is quite manageable to complete. Take approximately **70 seconds for each question** on the Reading and Writing section. To manage your time, utilize the countdown clock that is embedded in the testing program. Do be mindful that if you get the second, more difficult module on the reading, you may need to be more aware of your timing so you can finish all the questions.

You will likely do your best if you use the full amount of time to read the passages well, and think through the questions carefully. There is no prize for finishing the section early. In fact, if you find yourself finishing the Reading and Writing section with time to spare, you may want to try reading the more challenging texts a couple of times before attempting the questions. If you do have difficulty finishing the PSAT Reading, you can pick your battles by focusing on just those passages and questions that come to you most easily, and guessing on the questions you do not have time to attempt, since there is no guessing penalty.

2. Consider reading the questions before reading the passages.

Since each reading text has just one question that accompanies it, you may find it easier to focus on what you need to look for if you read the question before reading the text. This could be especially helpful on questions that ask you to focus on something more specific in the text: words in context, text structure and purpose, and command of evidence. On questions that involve determining the meaning of the passages in a more general way—central ideas and details, inferences, and cross-text connections—you may want to go ahead and read the passage before doing the questions.

3. Focus on the overall meaning of the text(s) as you read.

You should be able to restate the *gist* of what you have read—don't worry about memorizing details from the text. This is especially important for questions that ask about the general meaning or the primary function of the text. Sometimes there will be a brief note at the beginning of the text that will tell you the name of the author, the book, and the date—these pieces of information will help you preview the text, so be sure to read them. To help you stay focused as you ascertain the overall gist, use the provided scrap paper to take notes and briefly summarize the text in your own words.

4. Read actively, not passively.

Simply moving your eyes over the page is not enough to be sure that you understand what you are reading. What makes active reading and passive reading different?

Active Reading	Passive Reading
Paraphrase—You put the ideas of the text into your own words. You can state the main idea of what you read.	**No paraphrasing**—You get lost in the details and are unable to summarize what is happening.
Ask questions—You ask yourself questions about the text, such as, "Who is this character?" "What is going to happen next?" "What is the point of the text?"	**Don't ask questions**—Although you may be reading, you are not interacting with the text.
Focus on the task at hand—You think about the text, and if your mind wanders, you quickly refocus.	**Your mind is elsewhere**—You may look like you're reading but don't refocus when you become bored or distracted.

If you have trouble reading actively, what can you do to improve?

> ***FIND SOMETHING ABOUT THE TEXT THAT CAN INTEREST YOU:*** Reading actively is easy when the text is something you would read for pleasure. If the text is not on a topic you find particularly interesting, try to think of some connection you can make to the text from your schoolwork or life experiences. Suppose you had a text about human anatomy. Even if you haven't specifically studied the subject in school, you might be able to understand the concepts based on experiences you had going to the doctor or studying the biology of different animals.

> ***MAKE SURE YOU ARE WELL RESTED:*** It is more difficult to focus on reading when you are fatigued. Try your best to get about 8–9 hours of sleep on the nights leading up to the PSAT.

> ***RECOGNIZE WHICH PASSAGE TYPES ARE MORE CHALLENGING FOR YOU AND ALLOW MORE TIME ON THEM:*** Often, students find that older texts require more time to fully comprehend. Fiction texts may have flashbacks and metaphors that require a closer reading; some poetry selections may be over 200 years old, making some of the language antiquated. Experiment with reading the different text types so that you have a sense of which ones you can complete in less than 70 seconds and which may need more time.

5. Do not hesitate to skip and come back to questions.

You can flag questions in the testing program, making it easy to revisit the questions that you skipped. If you find yourself stuck on a question, come back to it so that you can allow your subconscious mind to process the possibilities. Once you come back to the question with fresh eyes, you will often surprise yourself at how well you can think through it at that point. Also, if you know that the reading questions are more difficult for you than the grammar questions in the same testing module, you could do the grammar questions first and save the reading questions for later. Recognize that you are in control of the order that you do things within the testing module, so do things in the order that best suits you.

6. Fully understand every part of the question.

A careless mistake in reading a question will likely lead to a wrong answer. Instead of quickly reading through the question, and then having to reread it, read it one time well. This will ensure that you not miss wording critical to understanding what the question is asking, such as *primary*, *purpose*, *suggest*, etc.

7. Do not look at the answer choices until you have an idea of what you are looking for.

On factual recall tests, checking out the answers before you have formulated an answer can help you narrow it down. With the critical thinking questions on the PSAT, in contrast, you will often find yourself misled by persuasive but ultimately incorrect answers. Take control of the questions and don't let them control you. Try your best to come up with an idea of the answer before actually looking at the answer choices. You can use the scrap paper to write down your thoughts before evaluating the choices.

8. Go back to the text as often as needed.

Most tests we take are closed-book—the PSAT Reading section is open-book. If you had an open-book test in school, you would surely use your textbook and notes to help you answer the questions. With the PSAT questions giving you key words and underlined selections, it makes sense to use the text whenever necessary.

9. The answers will be 100 percent correct or totally wrong.

A single word can contaminate an answer, making it completely wrong. When you narrow the choices down to two options, don't just look for the *best* answer—look for the *flawless* answer. Try to quickly debate with yourself the correctness or incorrectness of each answer, knowing that there is one that is definitely correct, and three that are definitely incorrect. The College Board has put a great deal of effort into creating the questions you will see on the PSAT, so you can safely assume they will be of the very highest quality.

10. Focus on meaning, not matching.

On ordinary school tests, we are often used to matching the choices with facts we recall from the assigned reading or the in-class lecture. On the PSAT, the fact that an answer has wording that matches parts of the passage text is no guarantee that it is correct. There is nothing wrong with picking an answer because it *does* have wording that is in the passage; just don't pick an answer *only because* it has matching wording. Be certain the overall meaning of an answer gives the correct idea.

11. Don't try to guess how you did.

Since the digital PSAT is adaptive, the later sections will change in difficulty depending on your performance on earlier sections. It will do no good to try to evaluate how difficult the later section questions are—you will waste time and energy that could be spent on figuring out the problems in front of you. Do your best to stay in the moment and not think back about how you performed on earlier sections. Moreover, be mindful that four of the Reading and Writing questions you encounter will be experimental and not scored—if a question seems a bit odd to you, do your best and don't dwell on it.

12. Practice with the testing application ahead of time.

You will be able to download the software that you will use on the actual digital PSAT—go to *collegeboard.org* for the latest details on how to do so. You can practice with this program on your own computer or on one at a library or school. Familiarize yourself with the software interface—the timer, the question-flagging feature, and the adaptive question style. The program will allow you to mark off answers you have eliminated and zoom in on the passages if you want to focus on part of the text. Since the passages are fewer than 150 words, you should have no difficulty seeing the entirety of the passage on the screen while you work through the question.

13. Give every question your best effort.

With fewer questions on the digital PSAT, each question has a larger impact on your score. Given the adaptive nature of the digital PSAT, the questions you will be given on the later modules are designed to be of a difficulty appropriate for you. Be sure to give every question your very best effort—do not allow yourself to become frustrated and quickly guess.

14. When in doubt about your strategy, give the PSAT the benefit of the doubt.

On poorly written tests, tricks and gimmicks can help you succeed—such shortcuts *will not* help you perform well on the exam. The digital PSAT is an extraordinarily well-constructed assessment, given the amount of time and resources the College Board has devoted to its overhaul. As a result, do not waste your time and energy while taking the PSAT looking for flaws in the test. Instead, give the PSAT Reading section the benefit of the doubt and focus on how *you* can improve your reading comprehension and critical thinking skills.

15. Understand the order of difficulty in the Reading and Writing questions.

Each set of questions of the same type, like the word-in-context or the inference questions, progresses from easy to hard in difficulty. When you get to a new type of question, the order of difficulty will begin again. Use this knowledge to your advantage: don't overthink the first question in a new category of questions, and don't underthink the later questions in the same category.

Central Ideas and Details

These questions will ask you to interpret the overall meaning of the text. For example, they may ask you something like this:

Which choice best states the main idea of the text?

How should you handle these specific types of questions?

- **Carefully read and thoroughly paraphrase the text before examining the answer choices.** While this is good advice on almost all PSAT Reading questions, it is particularly important on central ideas questions. The meaning will likely be based on the text as a whole rather than one small part of it, so understand the entirety of what is given.
- **Be careful of latching on to answers just because they mention specific parts from the text.** If you don't fully grasp the general meaning of the text, it will be easy to become trapped by answers that are partially right in citing specific language in the selection.

Practice Exercises

1. *The following text is from Anatole France's 1912 French novel* The Gods Will Have Blood.

   "As an appetizer for your capon, I've made some vegetable soup with a slice of bacon and a big beef bone. There's nothing gives soup a flavor better than a marrow bone."

   "A praiseworthy maxim, (Gamelin)," replied old Brotteaux. "And you will do wisely, if tomorrow, and the next day, and all the rest of the week, you put this precious bone back into the pot, so that it will continue to flavor it. The wise woman of Panzoust used to do that: she made a soup of green cabbages with a rind of bacon and an old *savorados*. That is what they call the tasty and succulent medullary bone in her country, which is also my country."

   "This lady you speak of, monsieur," . . . Gamelin put in, "wasn't she a little on the careful side, making the same bone last so long?"

   Based on the text, Citizen Brotteaux and Citizeness Gamelin have what respective attitudes toward the reuse of food?

   (A) Both agree that no effort should be spared to make food as delicious as possible to give refuge from the political difficulties of the time.
   (B) There is no need for conservation, given the abundant supply of poultry; use every part of the poultry—let nothing go to waste.

   (C) Both agree that given the scarcity of food, every effort should be made to conserve and reuse food.
   (D) Be wise by craftily reusing food as much as possible; don't take conservation of food to an extreme.

2. *The text is from Booker T. Washington's 1901 autobiography.*

   My mother, I suppose, attracted the attention of a purchaser who was afterward my owner and hers. Her addition to the slave family attracted about as much attention as the purchase of a new horse or cow. Of my father I know even less than of my mother. I do not even know his name. I have heard reports to the effect that he was a white man who lived on one of the near-by plantations. Whoever he was, I never heard of his taking the least interest in me or providing in any way for my rearing. But I do not find especial fault with him.

   The source of information Washington primarily draws upon for the information in the text is most likely

   (A) a publication.
   (B) hearsay.
   (C) statistical analysis.
   (D) a scholarly article.

3. Finding a job directly out of college is, for many, a catch-22. Employers want experience, and graduates are hard pressed to gain the experience needed to, well, gain experience. As a remedy, universities are encouraging internships, opportunities to enter the workforce temporarily and train in a position of interest. The idea is that both sides will come out the better—the intern strengthening his or her resume and building a strong social network, the employer expanding its workforce and investing in a prospective employee. But now, more students are questioning exactly who is getting their money's worth when many internships are unpaid. Rather than doubting the value of experience, they wonder at its fairness and practicality. Internships, when paid, are not only more valuable, but also more meaningful.

Which choice best states the main argument of the text?

(A) Ambitious college students should embrace any work opportunity that becomes available.

(B) Employers should do away with the obsolete practice of college internships.

(C) In order to create a mutually beneficial opportunity, internships should be compensated.

(D) So that employers do not have to waste time training inexperienced new hires, they should focus on only hiring applicants with experience.

4. *The following is Carl Sandburg's 1916 poem "Fog."*

The fog comes
on little cat feet.

It sits looking
over harbor and city
on silent haunches
and then moves on.

What is the most suitable description of fog as presented in the poem?

(A) Gentle and fleeting

(B) Invasive and dominating

(C) Quiet and subversive

(D) Animalistic and destructive

5. *This selection is adapted from Lincoln's 1863 Gettysburg Address.*

Now we are engaged in a great civil war, testing whether that nation, or any nation so conceived and so dedicated, can long endure. We are met on a great battle-field of that war. We have come to dedicate a portion of that field, as a final resting place for those who here gave their lives that that nation might live. It is altogether fitting and proper that we should do this.

Which choice best states the main idea of the text?

(A) Defeating the enemy is essential to creating the type of nation the United States should become.

(B) While the civil war rages on, we must have hope that there will be a peaceful resolution.

(C) It is important for policy makers to understand the importance of constructing a burial ground.

(D) Dedicating a cemetery for those who died in a vital national battle is the right thing to do.

6. *The following text is from Ralph Waldo Emerson's 1862 lecture "American Civilization."*

The power of Emancipation is this, that it alters the atomic social constitution of the Southern people. Now their interest is in keeping out white labor; then, when they must pay wages, their interest will be to let it in, to get the best labor, and, if they fear their blacks, to invite Irish, German, and American laborers. Thus, whilst Slavery makes and keeps disunion, Emancipation removes the whole objection to union. Emancipation at one stroke elevates the poor white of the South, and identifies his interest with that of the Northern laborer. [...]

What is the main idea of the text?

(A) Emancipation will lead to the political dominance of European immigrants.

(B) Emancipation will ensure an equitable redistribution of income across the races.

(C) An end to slavery will cause the Southern constitution to be amended.

(D) An end to slavery will realign Southern economic interests in favor of union.

Answer Explanations

1. **(D)** Brotteaux's attitude is seen when he advocates reusing a cooking bone; Gamelin's attitude is seen in the final paragraph of the text in which she questions the sensibility of reusing a bone so much. Neither would support choice (A) or (B), and only Brotteaux would support (C).

2. **(B)** Washington has acquired the little knowledge he has of his family through informal conversations and speculation. This is most evident when Washington states that he has "heard reports" about his family. This type of conjecture and secondary-witness testimonial is best represented as *hearsay*. There were no *publications* of his family; he mentions nothing written at all. Similarly, there were no *statistics*. Washington did not learn of his family through *scholarship* or academia; there was nothing to be studied.

3. **(C)** The passage initially presents the dilemma that both employers and potential employees face—workers will be better prepared with experience, but they can only get experience if they become workers. The author argues that a way to solve this dilemma is for internships to be paid so that they are both valuable and meaningful. This argument aligns with choice (C). Neither (A) nor (B) is presented in the passage, whereas (D) inaccurately summarizes the general argument given.

4. **(A)** The fog comes in very gently "on little cat feet." Then it sticks around for a bit before it "moves on," showing that it is impermanent or *fleeting*. It does not have the negative and violent elements suggested in (B) with *invasive and dominating*, in (C) with *subversive*, or in (D) with *destructive*. While the fog could be described as *quiet* and also having some animal qualities, the entirety of the answer must be correct to work.

5. **(D)** Lincoln sets the stage by stating that there is a great civil war going on. He then states that he is dedicating a portion of the battlefield as a "final resting place" for deceased soldiers, and that this is a "fitting and proper" thing to do. This aligns with choice (D). It is not (A) or (B), because there is not a primary focus on defeating an enemy and on ending the war, but on taking a pause to dedicate this cemetery. It is not (C), because the burial ground has already been made—it is just being ceremonially dedicated at this point.

6. **(D)** To paraphrase the main idea of the text, emancipation will change Southern culture in ways that will unify the nation. Thus, (D) best captures this idea. Emerson only mentions immigrants to argue that emancipation opens up labor options. Choice (B) is a distorted exaggeration. A Southern constitution, as in (C), was never mentioned. Choice (A) is incorrect because the text suggests that European immigrants will have their interests represented, not that they will be politically dominant.

Command of Evidence

These questions will ask you to analyze textual and quantitative evidence to determine what is justified based on the given information. For example, they may ask you things like this:

Which quotation from Hamlet *most effectively illustrates this idea?*

Which choice most effectively uses information from the graph to complete the example?

Which finding from the experiments, if true, would most strongly support the scientist's theory?

How should you handle these specific types of questions?

- **Realize that you do not need to understand everything, just enough to answer the question.** It will likely be easiest to read the question first to focus on what context clues you should pay close attention to.
- **Recognize that you do not need any background knowledge.** Do not let yourself be intimidated by unfamiliar graphs or concepts—everything you need to figure out evidence-based problems will be right there in the material.
- **Give yourself plenty of time to understand the graphs, poems, text, or other information.** On graph questions be sure to carefully examine the labels and axes so you can evaluate the data. With challenging texts, like poems, allow yourself time to read through the text a couple of times if need be.

Practice Exercises

1. Intentional cultivation of non-native invasive plants is generally far more beneficial than accidental introduction.

   Which of the following, if true, would most undermine the statement made above?

   (A) A historical investigation into the origins of invasive plants that demonstrates that the majority were introduced by accident

   (B) A global statistical analysis that demonstrates the net harmful effect from purposefully introduced invasive plant species

   (C) A genetic analysis that establishes that invasive plant species share several fundamental characteristics in their DNA

   (D) Discovery of three instances of invasive plant introduction that had a beneficial impact on the surrounding environments

2. "A Jelly-Fish" is an early 1900s poem by Marianne Moore. In the poem, the speaker metaphorically alludes to giving up on trying to find meaning:

   _____

   Which quotation from "A Jelly-Fish" most effectively illustrates the claim?

   (A) "Visible, invisible, / A fluctuating charm, / An amber-colored amethyst / Inhabits it;"

   (B) "your arm / Approaches, and / It opens and / It closes"

   (C) "You have meant / To catch it, / And it shrivels; / You abandon / Your intent—"

   (D) "It opens, and it / Closes and you / Reach for it— / The blue / Surrounding it / Grows cloudy,"

3. "Grimms' Fairy Tales" is a German collection of over 200 tales that has influenced much of modern stories. They published seven editions of this book, constantly adding and deleting stories they acquired. In a paper for history class, a student claims the Grimm brothers—Jacob and Wilhelm—should be considered as collectors and literary historians rather than authors.

   Which finding, if true, would most directly support the student's hypothesis?

   (A) The Grimm Brothers recorded oral history and poetry of German-speaking countries, documenting oral and written accounts from informants.

   (B) The Grimm Brothers were talented writers, creating stories that have stood the test of time; some have even become major motion pictures.

   (C) While the Grimm Brothers' works can be considered in the genre of fairy tales, other parts of their collection could be categorized as short stories.

(D) The Grimm Brothers' tales have received more recognition in countries outside of Germany than in Germany itself.

4. A historical passage presents an overview of the history of the War of 1812. Which quotation from the passage best illustrates the claim that the War of 1812 gradually shifted from being fought in the wilderness to being fought in urban areas?

(A) "By concentrating their defenses in Ontario, the Canadians left Quebec vulnerable to invasion along the St. Lawrence River."

(B) "In April of 1814 Napoleon was defeated in Europe, and a greater brunt of the British military fell upon the United States."

(C) "The primary theatres of war, in turn, shifted from the Canadian frontier to coastal American cities such as Baltimore, Washington, D.C., and New Orleans."

(D) "Canada's role in the conflict was by that time essentially at an end, though fighting continued intermittently in the North until the signing of the Treaty of Ghent in December of that year."

5.

Principal USDA Food Guides, 1940s–1980s

U.S. Food Guide Time Period	Number of Food Groups	Protein-Rich Foods	Breads	Fruits and Vegetables	Other
1940s Basic Seven Foundation Diet	7	Milk and milk products: 2 or more cups Meat, poultry, fish, eggs, dried beans, peas, nuts: 1–2	Bread, flour, and cereals: Every day	Leafy green/yellow: 1 or more Potatoes, other fruit/veg: 2 or more Citrus, tomato, cabbage, salad greens: 1 or more	Butter, fortified margarine: some daily
1956–70s Basic Four Foundation Diet	4	Milk group: 2 or more cups Meat group: 2 or more (2–3 oz. serving)	Bread, cereal: 4 or more (1 oz. dry, 1 slice, ½–¾ cup cooked)	Vegetable-fruit group: 4 or more (including dark green/yellow vegetables frequently and citrus daily, ½ cup or average-size piece)	None
1979 Hassle-Free Foundation Diet	5	Milk-cheese group: 2 (1 cup, 1 ½ oz. cheese) Meat, poultry, fish, and beans group: 2 (2–3 oz. serving)	Bread-cereal group: 4 (1 oz. dry, 1 slice, ½–¾ cup cooked)	Vegetable-fruit group: 4 (including vitamin C source daily and dark green/yellow vegetable frequently, ½ cup or typical portion)	Fats, sweets, alcohol: Use dependent on calorie needs
1984 Food Guide Pyramid Total Diet	6	Milk, yogurt, cheese: 2–3 (1 cup, 1 ½ oz. cheese) Meat, poultry, fish, eggs, dry beans, nuts: 2–3 (5–7 oz. total/day)	Breads, cereals, rice, pasta: 6–11 servings –Whole grain –Enriched (1 slice, ½ cup cooked)	Vegetable: 3–5 –Dark green/deep yellow –Starchy/legumes –Other (1 cup raw, ½ cup cooked) Fruit: 2–4 –Citrus –Other (½ cup or average)	Fats, oils, sweets: Total fat not to exceed 30% of calories Sweets vary according to calorie needs

Source: USDA.Gov

The U.S. Government has made dietary recommendations to citizens over the past several decades. The recommendations regarding sweets have historically been ambiguous: _____ .

Which choice most effectively uses data from the table to complete the statement?

(A) with 6 different food groups in 1984.

(B) with vague statements in 1979 and 1984 to use sweets "according to calorie needs."

(C) with a recommendation to consume "6–11 servings" of pasta, breads, cereals, and rice in 1984.

(D) with guidance to consume 2 servings of the milk-cheese group in 1979.

6.

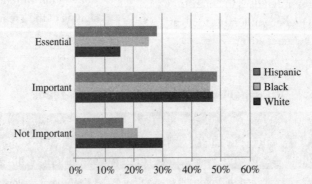

Forbes: How Important Is It That Americans Learn a Second Language?

Most Americans agree on the importance of language education—in fact, the approximate percent of white, Black, and Hispanic Americans who believe that learning another language is important or essential is _____ .

Which choice most effectively uses data from the chart to complete the example?

(A) 20 percent

(B) 50 percent

(C) 70 percent

(D) 100 percent

7.

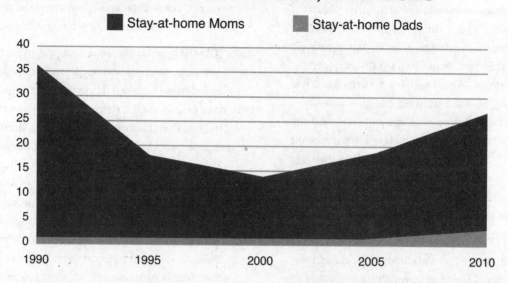

STAY-AT-HOME PARENTS, IN MILLIONS

■ Stay-at-home Moms   ■ Stay-at-home Dads

An often-overlooked change in a workforce evermore reliant on technology is the increasing number of employees who find themselves staying at home during the workday. _____

Which choice most effectively uses data from the chart to complete the example?

(A) From 1990 to 2000, the number of stay-at-home moms declined, whereas the number of stay-at-home dads remained steady.

(B) From 1995 to 2005, the number of stay-at-home moms increased slightly, whereas the number of stay-at-home dads remained steady.

(C) From 1990 to 2010, the number of stay-at-home moms somewhat declined, whereas the number of stay-at-home dads slightly increased.

(D) From 2000 to 2010, the number of stay-at-home moms and stay-at-home dads both increased.

Answer Explanations

1. **(B)** The author argues in these lines that intentional cultivation of non-native plants is usually a good thing. A global analysis demonstrating that non-native plants are typically harmful when introduced would therefore undermine—i.e., weaken—this argument. It is not (A), because knowing that most invasive plants were introduced by accident would not give information about their relative benefit. It is not (C), because this too would not give any facts about how harmful the plants were to their surroundings. And it is not (D), because this would be too small a sample size to make such a sweeping claim.

2. **(C)** In the last part of choice (C) it states *You abandon / Your intent*, which metaphorically illustrates that the speaker is giving up on trying to find meaning. The other options focus on the physical description of and the narrator's interaction with the jelly-fish.

3. **(A)** The student's hypothesis is that the Grimm Brothers should be thought of as collectors and literary historians rather than authors. Choice (A) would provide direct support for this hypothesis, because it would show that they compiled the stories based on the input of others instead of writing the stories themselves. It is not choice (B) because this does not focus on the authorship, instead focusing on the long-term impact of the stories. It is not choice (C) because this looks at how the stories should be categorized. It is not choice (D) because it focuses on which countries most appreciate the stories.

4. **(C)** This option illustrates a shift from fighting in the wilderness, "the Canadian frontier," to fighting in urban areas— "cities such as Baltimore, Washington, D.C., and New Orleans." The other options do not illustrate this sort of shift in setting.

5. **(B)** Analyze the table for this question. Never is there a definite, clear recommendation for how many servings of sweets one should or should not eat. This is an example of something *ambiguous*, which is another word for *unclear*. Choice (B) correctly provides evidence for this ambiguity by stating that the government provided vague guidance to eat sweets "according to calorie needs." The other answers do not relate to ambiguity.

6. **(C)** Analyze the accompanying graph for this question. The best way to determine the percentage of those who feel it is essential or important is to determine the percentage of people who do *not* feel that it is important, and then subtract this percentage from 100. Analyzing the graph, 30 percent of white people do not feel that it is important, whereas the percentages of Blacks and Hispanics who do not feel it is important are roughly 20 percent and 15 percent, respectively. Theoretically, the mathematics could become a little complicated because there are more whites than Blacks or Hispanics, but the percentage of people who do feel that is important must be somewhere between 70 percent and 85 percent; only choice (C) falls in this range.

7. **(D)** The correct answer is (D) because in 2000, both the number of stay-at-home moms and the number of stay-at-home dads were lower than they were in 2010; this data supports the claim in the previous sentence that there is an "increasing number of employees who find themselves staying at home during the workday." Choices (A), (B), and (C) make accurate statements based on the data in the graph, but they would not support the claim made in the previous sentence.

Inferences

These questions will ask you to read between the lines as you demonstrate deeper understanding of a text—what the author is implying or what the reader can infer. For example, they may ask you something like this:

Which choice most logically completes the text?

How should you handle these specific types of questions?

- **Do not be overly literal.** Look for what the author may be saying indirectly—what is being suggested or implied? Especially watch out for overly literal interpretations when you read genres like fiction, poetry, and drama.
- **Create a possible insertion of your own before evaluating the options.** Inference questions often involve asking you to consider what would most logically complete the text. Although it is tempting to immediately plug each of the choices into the text, you will likely perform better on these types of questions if you create a possible insertion in your own words first. Doing so will make you less susceptible to persuasive yet incorrect answer choices.

Practice Exercises

1. Socioeconomic status has such a strong influence on diet and activity level. Fast food is often cheap food. Most fast-food restaurants have $1 menus. People with a low socioeconomic status might be drawn to this fast and cheap food. It takes time and money to prepare a meal using fresh ingredients. Additionally, those ingredients could spoil before cooking, and that would be financially impactful. Researchers have discussed the link between low socioeconomic status and sedentary lifestyle. Interestingly, they found that socioeconomic stress even in childhood was associated with sedentary lifestyle as an adult. Further, communities in economically challenged areas may lack the necessary green spaces and recreational opportunities _____

   Which choice most logically completes the text?

   (A) to network with potential employers.
   (B) to meet one's neighbors and socialize.
   (C) to improve oneself through literary education.
   (D) to easily take part in an active lifestyle.

2. It might be easy to chalk up the younger generation as careless and unconcerned and altogether misdirected, but that's the easy way out, and it is flawed. Students are largely civic-minded; they volunteer, worry about public policies, and even congregate to debate solutions to everything from environmental issues to human rights to health care. Significant events like the war in Iraq in 2003 or Barack Obama's running for president in 2008 or gay marriage rights may generate an influx in youth participation, but overall, young voters are disengaged from American democracy and looking at other ways of tackling society's problems. It is not that they are merely apathetic, but instead that they have lost faith in electoral politics and are highly suspicious of party labels. Therefore, it is most likely that younger Americans will take the following approach to solving societal problems: _____.

   Which choice most logically completes the text?

   (A) Active participation in the political process
   (B) General apathy and lack of activity
   (C) Attacking problems outside of a governmental paradigm
   (D) Focusing on their own individual interests above all

3. Many accounts from people immersed in a language that is not their own have, throughout several centuries, pointed to profanity as by far the most difficult aspect of a novel language to master. There is, in our profanity, a high cultural learning curve that demands intimate knowledge and sensitivity to the subtleties of social interactions. Therefore, certain professionals will find the idea of the difficulty of fully understanding another language's profanity helpful in accomplishing their particular goals, like _____

Which choice most logically completes the text?

(A) a film censor who wishes to eliminate controversial vocabulary from an upcoming movie.

(B) a world language teacher who wants to pacify students eager to immediately learn translated swear words.

(C) a businessperson who wants to communicate the benefits of her products to potential clients in other countries.

(D) a translator of cookbooks who wants to convert customary measurements to metric ones.

4. As a compassionate and passionate educator, I know the competition your child faces. I am interested in breaking down the barriers that intimidate students and providing the path that will get them better college offers, better careers, and, most significantly, a better quality of life. To do this, I adopt a perspective of peak preparation at all costs and wholeheartedly embrace a focus on _____ .

Which choice most logically completes the text?

(A) physical exertion.

(B) intellectual contemplation.

(C) rigorous expectations.

(D) logical reasoning.

5. Employees say working from home means fewer dollars spent on gas and daycare. Employers brag that they can reduce real estate, diminish employee turnover, and end the practice of employees' disregarding their attendance obligations. _____

Which choice most logically completes the text?

(A) Employees find working from home to be an unneeded chore.

(B) All in all, working from home may be a win-win.

(C) Gas prices may impact the willingness of employers to pay for employee commutes.

(D) To summarize, the culture of an office is difficult to replicate at home.

Answer Explanations

1. **(D)** The text focuses on how socioeconomic status can have an impact on diet and activity level. The final sentence of the text refers to a lack of things that would be detrimental to health, making it logical to complete this idea with a statement like "to easily take part in an active lifestyle." The other options do not relate directly to personal health.

2. **(C)** Given the overall argument in the text, it is safe to assume that the author believes the younger generation is concerned with solving social issues but prefers to do so outside of political spheres. They are looking at "other ways of tackling society's problems." The text argues against (A). Choices (B) and (D) are refuted in the first sentence of the text.

3. **(B)** The text states that profanity is the most difficult aspect of a new language to learn, so if a world language teacher wanted to discourage students from learning translated swear words, the teacher could explain the inherent difficulty in doing so. It is not (A), because this has nothing to do with different languages. It is not (C) or (D), because the passage focuses on profanity, not on descriptive business prose or the language of measurement.

4. **(C)** The text conveys the author's priority to prepare students for the challenges ahead "at all costs." So, we can assume that the author places an emphasis on (C), rigorous expectations. There is no evidence that the author values physical exertion as in (A). Choice (B) more closely resembles what the author of Text 1 might stress. Finally, (D) usually refers to a process by which one supports and gives logical evidence for an argument or position.

5. **(B)** The first sentence states the benefits that employees receive from at-home work, and the second sentence states the benefits that employers receive. Choice (B) summarizes this by stating that both employers and employees can win from this arrangement. Choices (A) and (C) only focus on one group instead of both, and (D) is overly negative based on the context.

Words in Context

These questions will ask you determine which words are the best fit for a given context and what the definitions of words are based on context clues. For example, they may ask you things like this:

Which choice completes the text with the most logical and precise word or phrase?

As used in the text, what does the word compromise *most nearly mean?*

How should you handle these specific types of questions?

- **Create a synonym of your own when asked to complete the text with a word or phrase.** Having a synonym before reviewing the answer choices is like having a shopping list before going to the store—you will be more decisive and accurate in picking what you actually need.
- **Just because you do not know a word's meaning does not mean it is wrong.** One of the most frequent mistakes students make on word-in-context questions is going with a word that *sort of works* simply because they know the meaning of the word. If you narrow the question down to two words, one of which you know and doesn't quite fit, and the other of which you do not know, *go with the word you do not know since it has the <u>potential</u> to be 100-percent correct.*
- **Work on picking up on context clues with word definitions.** While memorizing vocab will still help you prepare for these types of questions, you should especially sharpen your skills in picking up on the meanings of words based on context. Even if you know the definitions of words, you will need to determine which definition is most applicable in the particular situation. Build on this skill by making a habit of trying to pick up on definitions as you read.

Practice Exercises

1. The author's rebuttal to such concerns is _____. First, he uses tongue-in-cheek humor to brush off such concerns, by assuring his parents that he will not end up homeless. Second, and more effectively, he uses facts to the contrary.

   Which choice completes the text with the most logical and precise word?

   (A) complex
   (B) understated
   (C) lacking
   (D) twofold

2. The skills developed through studying philosophy train us to clear up confusions. Sometimes, when two people are discussing a significant life issue, they <u>talk past</u> one another and use the same terms in different ways. Learning to analyze concepts helps us to step back and clarify what we mean by the terms we use, to realize the assumptions we are making in holding certain views, and to make important distinctions.

   As used in the text, what does the phrase "talk past" most nearly mean?

   (A) Speak about the same topic but with different understandings of the topic
   (B) Enter into verbal altercations with one another
   (C) Clearly define the topics about what one another is speaking
   (D) Carefully analyze the shortcomings of the other person's argument

3. Outward expansion of cities was necessary as we continued to deplete the resources near our urban centers. Modern transportation _____ that need, as the necessities for life could be brought in over long distances.

   Which choice completes the text with the most logical and precise word?

   (A) encouraged
   (B) designated
   (C) created
   (D) nullified

4. Why does one listen to music? Or dance? Or look to the stars? Amusement, surely. Communication and complex stimulation, absolutely. But mostly, I write in the name of indomitable creativity. I am of the distinct opinion that creativity is the most _____ ingredient of erudition, expression, and future success, and being so, must be encouraged inside the classroom.

Which choice completes the text with the most logical and precise word?

(A) effusive
(B) essential
(C) attainable
(D) discouraging

5. President Franklin Delano Roosevelt signed into effect the first minimum wage law in 1933. The Supreme Court overturned this first minimum wage law as unconstitutional, arguing that Congress lacked the legislative _____ for such a far-reaching mandate.

Which choice completes the text with the most logical and precise word or phrase?

(A) authority
(B) ideology
(C) consensus
(D) disparity

6. The bad rap of traditional dietary fats is unjustified. While fats may be high in calories, the human body is excellent at transforming fats into long-lasting energy. This isn't to say that all fats are good; the highly processed fats that in the last fifty years have become ubiquitous are bad for the body because the body cannot easily process them. However, modern studies have demonstrated that unrefined fat—e.g., that in milk, butter, eggs, and meat—<u>poses</u> no danger to a healthy person. Instead, in contrast to the 1950s AMA recommendations, people should monitor their intake of sugars and highly processed foods to maintain healthy lifestyles.

As used in the text, what does the word "poses" most nearly mean?

(A) Postures
(B) Positions
(C) Presents
(D) Displays

7. An Enigma operator was given a message to encrypt. As he typed in each letter, a lamp randomly selected a letter different from the first. The letter substituted by the lamp was recorded as the encrypted message. Each key press moved a rotor so that the subsequent key would use a different electrical pathway, which led to the substitution of a whole new letter. The entire <u>initial</u>, unencrypted message would be typed in, and Enigma would produce the encrypted message.

As used in the text, what does the word "initial" most nearly mean?

(A) Original
(B) Personalized
(C) Literary
(D) Decoded

8. The governmental structure of the League was rather uncomplicated. The women of each tribe would select men to represent the tribe at the council. Each village and tribe operated independently outside of the council and the council came together to discuss issues important to the entire league. The Iroquois did not vote individually but as tribes. Debates would <u>rage</u> for long periods of time because the Iroquois never had majority rule; they would come to a consensus. All decisions made were made unanimously. The league had no power to enforce decisions; if a tribe did not agree, it could simply ignore the decision. Thus, consensus was crucial.

As used in the text, what does the word "rage" most nearly mean?

(A) Embitter
(B) Go on
(C) Cause ire
(D) Dispute

9. The electoral college served its purpose in years past when smaller states were concerned that larger states would _____ their authority.

Which choice completes the text with the most logical and precise word or phrase?

(A) usurp
(B) invade
(C) touch
(D) decline

Answer Explanations

1. **(D)** The sentence goes on to state two things about what describes the rebuttal, making *twofold* the most logical word. The response has just two aspects, making *complex* too extreme. It is not *understated*, because the author is very direct and vocal with his arguments. It is not *lacking*, because the text speaks of the author's rebuttal in positive terms.

2. **(A)** The sentence clears this up with the later context that states that the people "use the same terms in different ways." So, this would go with (A) because the people would speak about the same topic but have different understandings of it. It is not (B), because while there is confusion, there is no mention of hostility. It is not (C), because the people are not clearly defining the topics. It is not (D), because the people are entrenched in their own points of view, unable to carefully analyze the other person's argument.

3. **(D)** The second sentence states that necessities could be brought into cities over long distances, making the outward expansion of cities no longer necessary, thereby *nullifying* this need. It is not (A) or (C), because these would suggest that modern transportation made this need for outward expansion rather than getting rid of it. It is not (B), because to *designate* is to "name" something, which would not make sense in this context.

4. **(B)** The narrator speaks of creativity in extremely positive terms, making it most logical to call it the *essential* ingredient for success. It is not (A), because the narrator does not suggest that creativity is essentially expressive. It is not (C), because the narrator does not suggest that it is easy to be creative. It is not (D), because this is overly negative.

5. **(A)** Since the Supreme Court overturned this law, the Court would have argued that Congress lacked the *authority* to do so—in other words, Congress would not have had the legitimate power to pass this law. While Congress may have had an *ideology* or *consensus*, these would not necessarily give Congress the rightful power to pass the law.

Disparity means "difference," which is illogical in this context.

6. **(C)** Substitute the choices into the sentence to determine which option is most appropriate in context. The sentence "Modern studies have demonstrated that unrefined fat . . . *presents* no danger to a healthy person" is the most sensible substitution, because the fats do not cause a danger in the author's estimation.

7. **(A)** The sentence in which we find "initial" states that "The entire initial, unencrypted message would be typed in, and Enigma would produce the encrypted message." It is most reasonable to conclude that an unencrypted message would be the original message that would need to be put into coded form. Thus, choice (A) makes the most sense. It is not choice (B), because the message would not necessarily be personalized. It is not choice (C), because it is unlikely that military communication would take on literary qualities. It is not choice (D), because the message would not likely have been decoded since it had not yet been put into coded form.

8. **(B)** The paragraph states that debates would rage for "long periods of time" until consensus was reached—this is a process that has the potential to be quite inefficient, making choice (B) the best option. It is not choice (A) or choice (D), because with all the debates there would surely be communication and transparency (openness). It is not choice (C), because there is no tyrannical dictatorial structure in this governmental arrangement.

9. **(A)** *Usurp* means to "seize power," usually inappropriately. This would be the best word to convey the fears that the smaller states had. The larger states are not going to literally *invade*, *touch*, or *decline* authority over smaller states.

Text Structure and Purpose

These questions will ask you determine the primary purpose and function of both entire texts and smaller selections within texts. For example, they may ask you things like this:

Which choice best states the main purpose of the text?

Which choice best states the function of the underlined sentence in the text as a whole?

How should you handle these specific types of questions?

- **Distinguish between *purpose* and *summary*.** Students often answer structure/purpose questions by summarizing the text instead of finding the purpose of the text. A summary tells you what the text is about, whereas the purpose tells you why the text was written—these are two very different tasks.
- **Use the surrounding context to pick up on the function of underlined selections.** To understand the purpose of an underlined sentence, you will likely need to fully grasp the entirety of the text. Do not limit yourself to just the underlined sentence when you need to determine the sentence's function and purpose.
- **If the question asks about the purpose of the entire text, be sure you keep the big picture in mind.** It might be tempting to pick an answer that gives you the purpose of some small part of the text instead of the entirety of the text. Be aware of this temptation when doing these types of questions.

Practice Exercises

1. Think traditions. Think stories, dances, jokes, and old fairy tales. But don't stop there. Think about ways of living and expressing oneself—maybe through language, or cooking, or laughing, or rituals. The Center for Folklore Studies at Ohio State University defines it this way: <u>"Folklore may be seen as the products of human work and thought that have developed within a limited community and that are communicated directly from generation to generation, usually orally, with the author or creator unknown."</u>

   Which choice best states the function of the underlined sentence in the text as a whole?

   (A) To explain a method whereby a topic will be researched
   (B) To analyze a specific work of folklore artistry
   (C) To cite an authoritative source in order to clarify an idea
   (D) To highlight the shortcomings of folklore as a communication approach

2. *The following text is from Kate Chopin's 1899 novel* The Awakening.

   The very first chords which Mademoiselle Reisz struck upon the piano sent a keen tremor down [Edna's] spinal column. It was not the first time she had heard an artist at the piano. Perhaps it was the first time she was ready, perhaps the first time her being was tempered to take an impress of the abiding truth.

   [Edna] waited for the material pictures which she thought would gather and blaze before her imagination. She waited in vain. She saw no pictures of solitude, of hope, of longing, or of despair. But the very passions themselves were aroused within her soul, swaying it, lashing it, as the waves daily beat upon her splendid body. She trembled, she was choking, and the tears blinded her.

   Which choice best states the main purpose of the text?

   (A) To show that Edna was relatively unaffected by the songs
   (B) To illustrate that Edna was surprised at her newfound reaction to the music
   (C) To demonstrate that Edna was weary at the lengthy delay in her entertainment
   (D) To point out that Edna was distraught at her inability to visualize as she listened

3. It is important to acknowledge that research has identified several serious health risks associated with the chronic overconsumption of sugar, and perhaps of fructose in particular. These risks, however, are by no means limited to foodstuffs containing high fructose corn syrup. Depending on the formula, corn syrup contains between 42 percent and 55 percent fructose by volume. For comparison, cane sugar, honey, and agave nectar—three popular sweeteners touted as *natural*, and therefore, more healthful—contain 50 percent, 52 percent, and 85 percent fructose, respectively. Thus, whereas it is true that fructose should be consumed only in moderation, the singling out of products that contain high fructose corn syrup is not merely insufficient action to curb the fructose-associated obesity epidemic in our country, it's also patently misleading to consumers.

Which choice best states the function of the underlined sentence in the text as a whole?

(A) Demonstrate that corn syrup is especially harmful to consumers

(B) Show that corn syrup is undeservingly singled-out for criticism

(C) Argue that fructose is but one reason that corn syrup is maligned

(D) Illustrate that many foodstuffs contain great quantities of sugar

4. Research shows that animal companionship supports mental and physical health, increasing life expectancy despite the lack of tyrannous flora or fauna. Pets are associated with lower blood pressure, lower triglyceride and cholesterol levels, and a reduced risk of heart disease. Pet owners are known to be more active, less anxious, and more socially adept. Similarly, pets can improve relationship bonds and unite families around a shared responsibility.

Which choice best states the main purpose of the text?

(A) Discuss the latest advances in medical science

(B) Present a method to improve heart health

(C) Critique those who dislike animal owners

(D) Describe the benefits of pet ownership

5. Consider the work that you most enjoy doing. How do you figure out what to do when complications arise? Relationships with family members, friends, and others enrich our lives. What makes those relationships go well? Many forms of recreation contribute to living a good life. But is there any ultimate meaning or purpose to these temporary activities, or even to life itself? Studying philosophy equips us with the skills needed to understand these and many other important questions.

Which choice best states the main purpose of the text?

(A) Ask questions critical to picking an ideal career

(B) Persuade the reader of the need to study a particular subject

(C) Encourage readers to seek out more recreational activities

(D) Suggest the ultimate answer to life's major questions

6. *The following text is from* Meditations on First Philosophy, *by René Descartes, 1641, in which he muses about the nature of knowledge.*

Several years have now elapsed since . . . I was convinced of the necessity of undertaking once in my life to rid myself of all the opinions I had adopted, and of commencing anew the work of building from the foundation, if I desired to establish a firm and abiding superstructure in the sciences. But as this enterprise appeared to me to be one of great magnitude, I waited until I had attained an age so mature as to leave me no hope that at any stage of life more advanced I should be better able to execute my design. On this account, I have delayed so long that I should henceforth consider I was doing wrong were I still to consume in deliberation any of the time that now remains for action.

Which choice best states the function of the underlined selection in the text as a whole?

(A) Argue why he believes that the foundations for knowledge are error ridden

(B) Show why the intellectual project he is tackling is so important

(C) Demonstrate that his mental and physical health have begun to decline

(D) Explain why he has chosen this point in time to write this work

Answer Explanations

1. **(C)** Prior to the underlined sentence, the narrator states that the idea of folklore can be defined in this way, and the narrator defines folklore by citing the Center for Folklore Studies—an authoritative source. So, (C) is the most logical option. It is not (A), because there is no mention of the methodology that will be used to study folklore. It is not (B), because the description of folklore is very general, not of a specific work. It is not (D), because the selection is a definition, not a mentioning of shortcomings.

2. **(B)** The text demonstrates that Edna expected to have mental images of various emotions in response to the emotion. Instead, though, it states that she could *feel* those emotions instead of simply picturing them, which is a far stronger response than Edna anticipated. She was, thus, *surprised at her newfound reaction to the music.* Choice (A) is flawed because Edna does indeed experience an emotional reaction to the songs. Choice (C) is flawed because there is nothing to express fatigue. Choice (D) is flawed because she *can* in fact visualize as she listens, so she certainly would not be distraught.

3. **(B)** The text states that the health risks are misdirected at corn syrup; realistically, they are associated with fructose, which is prevalent in "cane sugar, honey, and agave nectar" as well. So, (B) is correct. Corn syrup has comparable or even lesser amounts of fructose than the author's other examples, so (A) is not supported. (C) misunderstands the argument—fructose, not corn syrup, is problematic. (D), although true, does not address the fact that the high amounts of fructose in other foodstuffs contradict the case against corn syrup.

4. **(D)** The text presents numerous reasons that pet ownership can be beneficial: it can increase life expectancy, help heart health, and improve social skills. So, choice (D) best captures this overall presentation. It is not (A), because while the text does make references to research, it does not focus on the latest research developments throughout. It is not (B), because the reference to heart health is only in the second sentence. It is not (C), because the text has a positive tone, suggesting the benefits for those who choose to own pets instead of criticizing those who do not do so.

5. **(B)** The last sentence of the text is key in summarizing the main purpose—the author encourages the reader to study philosophy in order to develop the skills needed to understand the important questions of life. This most logically aligns with (B), because the text serves to persuade the reader to study the subject of philosophy. It is not (A), because the focus is not on career choices. It is not (C), because the narrator is encouraging the reader to develop philosophical thinking skills instead of embark on a particular course of recreation. It is not (D), because the narrator emphasizes the importance of asking questions without giving an idea as to what the ultimate answer to those questions will be.

6. **(D)** The underlined portion refers to the fact that Descartes has waited until an optimal age to try to break down his false principles, making (D) accurate. (A) and (B) are alluded to earlier in the text, and (C) is not supported by the text.

Cross-Text Connections

These questions will ask you determine the primary purpose and function of both entire texts and smaller selections within texts. For example, they may ask you something like this:

Based on the texts, how would the author of Text 2 most likely describe the view of the historians presented in Text 1?

How should you handle these specific types of questions?

- **Paraphrase the thesis of each text.** With non-fiction texts in particular, each text will most likely have some sort of argument it is making. Determine each author's position on the topic, and you will be in excellent shape with the question.
- **Recognize the complexity of the text relationship.** It is unlikely that the relationship between the two texts will be completely in opposition to each other. Instead, the texts will likely have some overlapping thoughts and some opposing thoughts. Try not to oversimplify the relationship between the texts.

Practice Exercises

1. **Text 1**

   If both Chicago and Indianapolis expanded their radii by fewer than 100 miles, they would spill into one another. All the farmland between the two would be gone. It's a rather scary enigma: we expand our cities because our population is growing, yet we decrease our ability to sustain ourselves by doing so.

   Text 2

   If done correctly, vertical expansion would greatly decrease our need for cars. A *large city* would actually be made up of many *mini-communities*. Each community would be a self-serving network of high rises. Food would likely still need to be imported, but the people in each community would be able to walk to the grocery store. Residents would walk to work. Each community would have workers specialized in the various essential professions.

   Which of the following best describes the relationship between the texts?

   (A) Text 1 demonstrates how the approach advocated in Text 2 is impractical.
   (B) Text 2 provides a possible solution to the problem described in Text 1.
   (C) Text 1 argues that existing technology can overcome the obstacles in Text 2.
   (D) Text 2 is focused on urban developments while Text 1 is not.

2. **Text 1**

   Students should be permitted to leave school during lunch periods. Having the opportunity to get off school grounds and recharge will build student morale and empower students to be more focused when they return from their meal. Additionally, giving students the chance to leave school for lunch will likely encourage more physical activity, as many students will walk home or to a nearby restaurant.

   Text 2

   Many people are rightly concerned that some students cannot be trusted to act appropriately with the freedom to leave school during lunch. Rather than letting a few bad apples spoil the barrel, schools should prohibit troublemakers from leaving the school grounds, while allowing responsible students the freedom to make their own choices.

   The two texts differ in arguments in that

   (A) Text 2 uses metaphorical language, whereas Text 1 does not.
   (B) Text 1 argues for students to be free to leave during lunch periods, whereas Text 2 disagrees.
   (C) Text 2 does not consider the likely objections of others, whereas Text 1 does.
   (D) Text 1 cites evidence from scholarly publications, whereas Text 2 does not.

3. **Text 1**

Some non-native plants are introduced to new territories accidentally via interregional soil and food trade. Accidental introduction of non-native organisms can often have negative and unforeseen consequences. For example, the Asian chestnut blight fungus was unexpectedly brought to the United States through the trade of plants; this fungus nearly wiped out the entire American chestnut population, harming many animals that depended on chestnuts for food.

Text 2

For the past fifty years, it has been the conventional credence of ecologists and biologists alike that invasive, non-native plant species are, without exception, detrimental to the host ecosystem. However, recent studies at Penn State University indicate that the eradication of invasive plants—specifically fruit-bearing shrubs—can do more harm than good for the native animal populations.

Based on the texts, how would the author of Text 2 describe the overall view presented in Text 1?

(A) Unusual

(B) Typical

(C) Unfounded

(D) Correct

4. **Text 1**

If the eruption of smartphones has been the vanguard of anything, it is the near societal takeover of social media. Within the workplace, most supervisors quickly block sites like Facebook, Twitter, and Instagram from company computers, and for good reason. Productivity is likely to decrease if three hours of an eight-hour workday are spent *liking* and *tweeting* and *pinning*. Then there is company bad-mouthing to consider. In the digital age, nothing one says or does or records online is private—nothing.

Text 2

The unique ability of social media to market company services and extend company reputation is indispensable. Many startup businesses find that they simply cannot compete without a social media page to deliver their mission and broaden their contacts. It can simply be the best tool available for advertising, marketing, expansion, and customer feedback. Likewise, it provides an unrivaled medium for market research.

It can be reasonably concluded that the authors of both Text 1 and Text 2 would most likely agree with which of the following statements?

(A) Social media has definitely had a significant impact on the modern workplace.

(B) Social media provides an unnecessary distraction to both businesses and to their employees and should be removed from the workplace.

(C) Employers often overstep their bounds by interfering with the social media use of their employees.

(D) Privacy is the foremost concern for internet users, and strict measures should be taken to safeguard personal information.

5. **Text 1**

According to the American Academy of Sleep Medicine, teenagers (13–18 years old) should aim for 8–10 hours of sleep during each 24-hour period. According to a national survey, however, 73 percent of students reported not getting enough sleep during school nights.

Text 2

The early start time for high school is a major problem for students. When I was of high school age, I found it exceedingly difficult to fall asleep before midnight, despite my best efforts to go to bed around 10 PM. When the alarm clock woke me up at 6 AM, I was exhausted and certainly not in the best frame of mind to learn.

What would the authors of the texts most likely consider to be a reasonable solution to teenage sleep deprivation?

(A) Mandate that high school students get at least 12 hours of sleep every evening

(B) Find an alternative waking notification method to the relatively shrill noise of an alarm clock

(C) Shift the start time of high school to later in the day so students can get more sleep

(D) Educate teens on the importance of being alert during the school day so that they can maximize learning

6. *Text 1 is from Sojourner Truth's 1815 speech at the Women's Convention in Akron, Ohio. Text 2 is from Carrie Chapman Catt's 1917 Address to the Congress on Women's Suffrage.*

Text 1

That man over there says that women need to be helped into carriages and lifted over ditches, and to have the best place everywhere. Nobody ever helps me into carriages, or over mud-puddles, or gives me any best place! And ain't I a woman? Look at me! Look at my arm! I could have ploughed and planted, and gathered into barns, and no man could head me! And ain't I a woman?

Text 2

Your party platforms have pledged women suffrage. Then why not be honest, frank friends of our cause, adopt it in reality as your own, make it a party program, and *fight with us*? . . . We shall all be better friends, we shall have a happier nation, we women will be free to support loyally the party of our choice, and we shall be far prouder of our history.

Both texts use which of the following argumentative techniques?

(A) Rhetorical questions

(B) Individual attacks

(C) Personal anecdotes

(D) Historical references

Answer Explanations

1. **(B)** The problem outlined in Text 1 is that as cities grow, the land available for the cities decreases. Text 2 proposes a solution of vertical expansion to overcome this, making (B) the most logical option. It is not (A) or (C), because Text 1 does not address the specifics of the solution discussed in Text 2. It is not (D), because both texts consider urban developments—i.e., cities.

2. **(A)** Text 2 uses the phrase "letting a few bad apples spoil the barrel," which is metaphorical, not literal, language. Text 1 does not use any metaphorical language and is very matter-of-fact. It is not (B), because Text 2 also believes that students should have the freedom to leave school during lunch periods. It is not (C), because Text 2 begins by considering the objections of others. It is not (D), because neither text cites scholarly evidence.

3. **(B)** Text 1 describes invasive plants as generally negative in their influence on the environment, which would align with the "conventional credence" that non-native species are detrimental. *Conventional* is close to *typical* in meaning, making choice (B) correct. It is not (A), because Text 2 would consider this text *usual* rather than *unusual*. To call it *unfounded* would be overly negative—Text 2 would most likely acknowledge that there are justifications to this viewpoint, although recent research has shown exceptions. It is not (D), because Text 2 argues that the general view in Text 1 is not completely correct.

4. **(A)** Text 1 argues that due to time wasting and privacy considerations, employers are correct in blocking social media use by employees at work. Text 2 argues that there are tremendous benefits to businesses that can use social media. So, choice (A) would be the best fit since it states that both texts would find social media to be influential. It is not (B), because Text 2 argues that businesses should be able to use social media. It is not (C), because neither text argues that a social media ban in the workplace is an invasion of boundaries. It is not (D), because whereas Text 1 acknowledges concerns about privacy, Text 2 does not give evidence in support of this position.

5. **(C)** Text 1 states that 73 percent of students are not getting enough sleep during school nights, and Text 2 gives a personal anecdote about the difficulty of getting to sleep as a high school student. Putting these arguments together, both authors would likely consider shifting the start time of high school to later in the day to be a good solution. It is not (A), because this would be too extreme a solution. It is not (B), because the issue is not about the annoyance from an alarm clock but about the lack of sleep. It is not (D), because a lack of education does not seem to be at the heart of the issue.

6. **(A)** Both passages use rhetorical questions—i.e., questions given for dramatic effect in which the answer is already known. Text 1 asks, "ain't I a woman?" and Text 2 asks, "why not be honest, frank friends of our cause?" Neither uses individual attacks. Text 1 uses personal anecdotes, whereas Text 2 does not. Text 2 puts the situation in a historical context, whereas Text 1 focuses on the present.

Troubleshooting

Here are some further pointers for common issues.

"I can't stay focused when I read."

- Be certain you get a good night's sleep before the PSAT. You will start the PSAT with the Reading and Writing section. So if you are tired and groggy, it will go poorly. Staying focused is extremely difficult when you are exhausted. Don't stay up late the night before the test doing last-minute cramming; it is not worth it.

- Don't try to remember too much when you read. You only need to remember the general meaning of the text—you should go back when you need to find details. This is not a school-based test for which you need to memorize many details.

- Try doing the questions in an order you choose. The simple act of choosing what texts to try first empowers you to take more ownership of what you read, instead of feeling that you're stuck reading a boring text out of necessity. You could even begin with the grammar questions that come later in the module so you feel less rushed on the reading questions. Build momentum by starting with the texts that come easiest to you.

"I finish too early."

- Consider what would be the best use of your extra time—surely it is not to just sit there and stare off into space for several minutes at the end of the test. Perhaps you can spend more time reading the texts, formulating your own answers to questions, or carefully dissecting the answer choices. Experiment with some practice texts to see where the extra time will be most helpful for you.

- Have a watch when you take the test so you can be mindful of how quickly you are working. Try to maintain about a 70 second per question pace. You can also use the timer that is embedded into the testing program if you would rather not wear a watch.

"I go too slowly."

- Diagnose what is taking you the most time. Typically, students spend too much time either reading the texts or evaluating each answer choice. If you are spending too much time reading the text, remind yourself that this is an open-book test and that you only need to paraphrase an answer to the question. If you are spending too much time breaking down the choices, shift your energy to reading the questions more carefully and formulating your own answer; that way, you will be much more decisive when you go to the answer choices.

- Let go of perfectionist tendencies. You may not have time to double-check every answer, and you may not have time to do every question. The PSAT is heavily curved, and you can likely still achieve National Merit recognition even if you miss some questions.

"I get it down to two choices, and I can't decide."

- Even though this isn't the Math section, know that there will be one answer that is definitely correct. If you are not seeing it, make sure you understand the context and make sure you have a firm grasp of what the question is asking. Do not allow yourself to become frantic and panicked because you feel you have come across a "trick" question.

- Look for "contamination" in the choices. Even one incorrect word can ruin an entire answer choice. Instead of looking for the "best" answer, look for the "flawless" answer—this mindset will help you more rigorously analyze the answer choices without being seduced by the incorrect options.

Further Preparation

What else can I do beyond this book to prepare for the PSAT Reading Test?

- Practice with Barron's books for the SAT: *Barron's Digital SAT* has plenty of practice tests you can try.
- Use the online vocabulary resource that accompanies this book if you have trouble with the words-in-context questions. See the card at the front of this book for online access.
- Try the online PSAT Reading exercises that accompany this book for more targeted practice.
- Use the free reading practice tests and resources provided by the College Board on *KhanAcademy.org*.
- Focus on your most difficult passage types—and turn them into strengths. To challenge yourself even further, you may want to try reading passages for the GRE, GMAT, and MCAT; the passages you find on graduate school admissions tests will surely be more challenging than what you will face on test day.
- Read, read, read. At a minimum, read high-quality books for pleasure, such as ones that have won the Pulitzer Prize or Booker Prize. At a maximum, seek out articles and books that you find most challenging, and read those in your spare time. The more widely you read, the greater the likelihood that you will have some baseline familiarity with the topics you encounter on the PSAT.

TIP

Don't forget to try the next chapter, "Advanced Reading Drills," for more challenging practice.

2

Advanced Reading Drills

The following drills are designed to represent the most difficult types of texts and questions you could encounter on the Digital PSAT Reading section.

Advanced Reading Drill 1

1. Throughout our evolution, the neurons that make up our brain and spinal cord have adapted to detect the presence of adenosine, and to react to it by increasing the secretion of melatonin from the pineal gland, which in turn mediates _____ of "drowsiness" or somnolence. The purpose, one might reason, is simply to promote sleep: a state that is minimally taxing to the metabolism of the central nervous system and will allow its cells an opportunity to replenish their energy stores.

   Which choice completes the text with the most logical and precise word or phrase?

   (A) emissions
   (B) opinions
   (C) replacements
   (D) feelings

2. The following text is from the 1845 autobiography of Frederick Douglass.

   I was born in Tuckahoe, near Hillsborough, and about twelve miles from Easton, in Talbot County, Maryland. I have no accurate knowledge of my age, never having seen any authentic record containing it. By far the larger part of the slaves know as little of their ages as horses know of theirs, and it is the wish of most masters within my knowledge to keep their slaves thus ignorant. I do not remember to have ever met a slave who could tell of his birthday. They seldom come nearer to it than planting-time, harvest-time, cherry-time, spring-time, or fall-time. A <u>want</u> of information concerning my own was a source of unhappiness to me even during childhood. The white children could tell their ages. I could not tell why I ought to be deprived of the same privilege.

   As used in the text, what does the word "want" most nearly mean?

   (A) Desire
   (B) Obstacle
   (C) Lack
   (D) Command

3. The following text is from the 1895 novel Almayer's Folly by Joseph Conrad.

   One of those drifting trees grounded on the shelving shore, just by the house, and Almayer, neglecting his dream, watched it with languid interest. The tree swung slowly round, amid the hiss and foam of the water, and soon getting free of the obstruction began to move down stream again, rolling slowly over, raising upwards a long, denuded branch, like a hand lifted in mute appeal to heaven against the river's brutal and unnecessary violence. Almayer's interest in the fate of that tree increased rapidly. He leaned over to see if it would clear the low point below. It did; then he drew back, thinking that now its course was <u>free</u> down to the sea, and he envied the lot of that inanimate thing now growing small and indistinct in the deepening darkness.

   As used in the text, what does the word "free" most nearly mean?

   (A) Willful
   (B) Unhindered
   (C) Empowered
   (D) Inexpensive

4. The following text is adapted from a 1777 letter from Thomas Jefferson to Benjamin Franklin, writing about the situation in the American colonies.

I think nothing can bring the security of our continent and its cause into danger, if we can support the credit of our paper. To do that, I apprehend one of two steps must be taken. Either to procure free trade by alliance with some naval power able to protect it; or, if we find there is no prospect of that, to shut our ports totally to all the world, and turn our colonies into manufactories. The former would be most eligible, because most conformable to the habits and wishes of our people.

Which choice best describes the function of the underlined sentence in the text as a whole?

(A) It suggests that Americans would prefer to continue to be able to purchase manufactured goods from abroad.

(B) It shows that Americans are eager to achieve economic independence by creating domestic factories.

(C) It argues that Americans are unwilling to engage in an entangling alliance with another country that would require the United States to enter foreign conflicts.

(D) It states that Americans are weary of the revolutionary conflict and would like to see its swift end.

5. The following text is from the 1912-13 poem "The Walk" by Thomas Hardy. Hardy wrote this poem in the aftermath of his first wife's death.

You did not Walk with me
Of late to the hil-tio tree
    By the gated ways,
    As in earlier days;
    You were weak and lame,
    So you never came,
And I went alone, and I did not mind,
Not thinking of you as left behind.

I walked up there to-day
Just in the former way:
    Surveyed around
    The familiar ground

By myself again:
What difference, then?
Only that underlying sense
Of the look of a room on returning thence.

Which choice best describes the overall structure of the text?

(A) The speaker starts by bemoaning the lack of a walking companion and eventually reaches satisfaction through the restoration of such a partner.

(B) The speaker initially expresses dismay at the illness of his companion but goes on to express gratitude that his companion's illness had been cured.

(C) The speaker begins by noting the gradual loss of companionship and ends by observing how he has become used to no longer having the companionship.

(D) The speaker begins his journey by traveling to a nearby tree and ends his journey by going to a familiar room.

6. It would not be overstating the matter to say that statins have transformed the treatment of both acquired and congenital cholesterol-related diseases. But what's more, the first generation of statins was discovered, oddly enough, by Japanese scientist Akira Endo during his research into the antimicrobial properties of the mold *Penicillium citrinum*. Not unlike Alexander Fleming's accidental discovery of penicillin one-half century earlier, Endo serendipitously discovered yet another compound from this curious genus of fungi destined to do no less than revolutionize the medical maintenance of human health. One must wonder, therefore, what more we stand to learn from fungi, and what still-greater mysteries they may yet be concealing in the soil.

According to the text, what is true about some of the most important fungi-related medical innovations?

(A) They came about because of luck.

(B) They are a product of evolution.

(C) They resulted from significant economic investment.

(D) They were designed by genetic engineering.

7.

Average Salaries for Legal Occupations, 2014

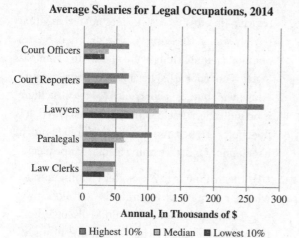

Annual, In Thousands of $

■ Highest 10% ☐ Median ■ Lowest 10%

Source: Onetonline.org

The occupational skills valued in a court reporter encompass clerical, listening, and writing skills; selective hearing; attention to detail; and knowledge of legal codes, jargon, and court procedures. It might surprise you to learn that most entry-level positions require only an associate degree or certificate program, and completion of licensing exams. You could be on your way to a front-row seat at local, state, or federal court proceedings in as little as two years. In addition, this job can likely provide a predictable amount of compensation since_____

Which choice most effectively uses data from the graph to illustrate the claim?

(A) a given court reporter's salary is more likely to be within a consistent range than the salaries of lawyers or paralegals.

(B) court reporters earn an average salary that exceeds the median legal professional salary.

(C) court reporters are more likely to be hired for entry-level positions.

(D) a given court reporter's compensation is likely to be as much as the salaries of the attorneys who appear before them.

8. "Adventure" is a 1919 short story by Sherwood Anderson. The primary character, Alice Hindman, faithfully loved a man who moved away from her hometown. As an adult and many years after the man moved away, Alice exhibits an unsettled attitude toward her past: _____

Which quotation from "Adventure" most effectively illustrates the claim?

(A) "At twenty-seven Alice was tall and somewhat slight. Her head was large and overshadowed her body."

(B) "[Alice's] shoulders were a little stooped and her hair and eyes brown. She was very quiet but beneath a placid exterior a continual ferment went on."

(C) "The young newspaper man did not succeed in getting a place on a Cleveland paper and went west to Chicago."

(D) "Alice worked in the dry goods store from eight in the morning until six at night and on three evenings a week went back to the store to stay from seven until nine."

Answer Explanations

1. **(D)** *Drowsiness* is best described as a human *feeling*, not as an *emission* or a *replacement*. Also, drowsiness is not a spoken or reasoned *opinion*— it is more a general mood or state of mind, making *feelings* most appropriate.

2. **(C)** Douglass expresses his distress at not having access to his own basic personal information. If you replace *want* with *absence*, you can see that choice (C) is appropriate. Although choice (A) might be tempting, read the sentence with obstacle substituted for *want*. You'll quickly see that the desire for information is not what produced unhappiness but that the need was denied. It isn't appropriate to say the *obstacle* or *command* of information produced unhappiness.

3. **(B)** Here, the powerless and formerly stuck tree is now *free* to drift into the sea. So, you could substitute "unimpeded" or "no longer restrained," which makes choice (B) correct. Choice (A) conveys the idea that the tree has a feeling or an attitude of its own. Choice (C) is tempting but evokes the idea that the tree has gained power rather than merely escaped to freedom. Choice (D) refers to *free* as a financial concept, as in without cost, which does not fit here.

4. **(A)** Check the sentence before this one. Jefferson says free trade with an alliance is preferable because it aligns with the American people's "habits and wishes." Here, he implies that Americans would like to have access to imports from abroad rather than making everything themselves. This coincides with choice (A) but contradicts choices (B) and (C). Choice (D) brings up the American Revolution. Although it seems plausible that Americans do not desire further conflict, that is not the subject of these lines.

5. **(C)** The first half of the poem talks about how the narrator left his wife behind on his walks late in her life because she was too sick to accompany him. The second half of the poem refers to a later point after his wife's death in which he has emotionally moved on to the point of feeling somewhat normal when he comes back from his walk. Instead of missing his wife, as would be expected, he now feels a sense of "the look of a room" when he

returns—in other words, he does not feel anything terribly strong. He seems to have returned to an emotional equilibrium in the aftermath of her passing. It is not choice (A) because the partner is no longer with him. It is not choice (B) because there is no indication that an illness has been cured. It is not choice (D) because the "room" is not literal, but a metaphor for his returning feeling of normalcy.

6. **(A)** The text refers to Alexander Fleming somewhat accidentally discovering the antibiotic properties of penicillin and Akiro Endo discovering the benefits of statins while attempting to study *Penicillium citrinum's* antimicrobial properties. What these major discoveries have in common is that they were somewhat accidental. Thus, the answer is choice (A). These discoveries weren't a product of evolution or genetic engineering as in choice (B) or choice (D). Although they may have required economic investment, as in choice (C), the author doesn't mention this.

7. **(A)** Given that the claim is that the job as a court reporter can provide a predictable paycheck, the correct answer will connect information from the graph to show how court reporters can have a standard idea of what their compensation will be. The range of court reporter salaries is far narrower than the ranges for the salaries of lawyers and paralegals, making choice (A) correct. It is not choice (C) because there is no information in the graph about how likely it is that court reporters will be hired for entry-level positions. It is not choice (B) or (D) because, according to the graph, attorney (i.e., lawyer) salaries are generally much higher than the salaries for court reporters.

8. **(B)** This selection says that Alice is "stooped" and "quiet," despite the "ferment" brewing under her surface. Synonyms of *ferment* include *tumult, turmoil,* and *disquiet,* so *unsettled* is the correct answer. It is not choice (A) because this option describes her physical appearance, not her emotional state. Choice (C) refers to a different character, describing his moving plans. It is not choice (D) because this describes her long hours of work but does not describe her emotions about her circumstances.

Advanced Reading Drill 2

1. Although some invasive species do cause tremendous and irreparable damage to their ecosystems, environments are not static; they change, develop, and adapt to transitions, whether they be natural or manmade. We must learn to be more <u>discriminating</u> in our eradication of invasive plants from those areas where they have become an integral part of the greater ecosystem.

   As used in the text, what does the word "discriminating" most nearly mean?

   (A) Biased
   (B) Intolerant
   (C) Tasteful
   (D) Selective

2. While the light and sound pollution may trigger veterans and frighten pets, the environmental pollution caused by fireworks can harm us all. Those who set off fireworks are at most risk for experiencing the negative respiratory effects but add up all the firework displays in the weeks surrounding the Fourth of July and the _____ for air quality are profound. Many fireworks are also set off above bodies of water. Runoff of pollutants from firework displays into lakes and streams can harm the waterways, affecting wildlife and water quality.

   Which choice completes the text with the most logical and precise word or phrase?

   (A) consequences
   (B) enhancements
   (C) admiration
   (D) benefits

3. The following text is from Matthew Arnold's 1885 work Discourses in America.

   It is impossible to deny that Plato's ideas do often seem unpractical and impracticable, and especially when one views them in connection with . . . a great work-a-day world like the United States. The necessary staple of the life of such a world Plato regards with disdain; handicraft and trade and the working professions he regards with disdain; but what becomes of the life of an industrial modern community if you take handicraft and trade and the working professions out of it? The base mechanic arts and handicrafts, says Plato, bring about a natural weakness in the principle of excellence in a man, so that he cannot govern the ignoble growths in him, but nurses them, and cannot understand fostering any other. Those who exercise such arts and trades, as they have their bodies, he says, marred by their vulgar businesses, so they have their souls, too, bowed and broken by them.

   According to the text, what would best summarize Arnold's description of Plato's philosophy toward work?

   (A) Genuine strength is evident only in those who put the needs of others before themselves.
   (B) Those who cannot make themselves useful to society are little more than parasites.
   (C) The demands of one's profession will limit the loftiness of one's being.
   (D) True nobility of soul is more likely to be found among those who work by hand than in those who use machines.

4. Even when a laceration as small as a paper cut happens to a person, complex reactions begin within the body almost instantaneously. Were these processes to be disrupted for any number of reasons, even the most insignificant of scrapes could prove fatal for the victim. Immediately after the initial laceration transpires, the body responds and initiates action. Known as the "inflammatory phase" of wound healing, this is when the body first begins to repair the damage it encountered. To prevent excessive blood loss, the first step is vasoconstriction in which the blood vessels near the affected area are constricted. Nearly concurrently, phagocytosis begins as white blood cells are sent to the wound. <u>Phagocytes are cells that consume the debris in the wound, which aids in the cleansing of damaged tissue as well as foreign matter.</u>

   Which choice best describes the function of the underlined sentence in the text as a whole?

   (A) It clarifies a specialized term.
   (B) It explains the derivation of a word.
   (C) It highlights an irony.
   (D) It offers a solution to a health care predicament.

5. The following text is adapted from F. Scott Fitzgerald's 1920 novel This Side of Paradise. The book opens with the character introduction of Fitzgerald's semi-autobiographical protagonist, Amory Blaine.

All in all Beatrice O'Hara absorbed the sort of education that will be quite impossible ever again; a tutelage measured by the number of things and people one could be contemptuous of and charming about; a culture rich in all arts and traditions, barren of all ideas, in the last of those days when the great gardener clipped the inferior roses to produce one perfect bud.

In her less important moments, she returned to America, met Stephen Blaine and married him— this almost entirely because she was a little bit weary, a little bit sad. Her only child was carried through a tiresome season and brought into the world on a spring day in ninety-six.

Based on the text, Beatrice married Stephen for what reason?

(A) True love
(B) Because she settled
(C) Because she was forced
(D) Because of vengeance

6. **Text 1**

Melaleuca trees were brought to the Florida Everglades from Australia; developers thought these trees would help dry up vast swampy areas, enabling residential and commercial construction. Unfortunately, the trees spread widely, and covered up large swaths of the Everglades, displacing native plants. Florida has had to spend a great deal of money to remove these invasive trees.

Text 2

Though common protocol would dictate that an invasive species like honeysuckle be removed from areas where it becomes dominant, these new findings demonstrate that such action would likely strike a significant blow to native bird populations. What's more, areas that today are abundant in honeysuckle typically host 30 to 40 percent more birds than these same regions did 30 years ago, indicating a long-term change for the better.

The author of Text 2 would most likely agree with which statement about Text 1?

(A) While invasive species may cause damage, not all invasive species should be considered harmful.
(B) Melaleuca trees demonstrate the importance of uniformly removing invasive species from the environment.
(C) Honeysuckle plants and melaleuca plants show the need for a consistent approach to invasive species management.
(D) So long as invasive plants are not transported across oceans, they are unlikely to be harmful.

7.

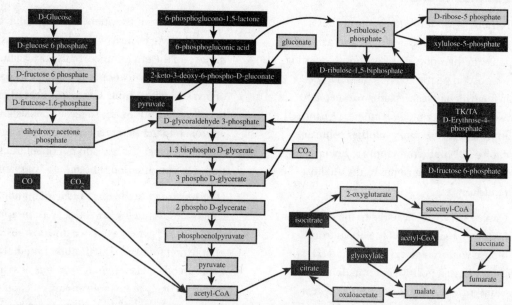

Figure 1. The intermediates in the black boxes are ones that *M. stadtmanae* cannot use or does not have. The intermediates in the gray boxes are ones that *M. stadtmanae* does use or have.

Methanosphaera stadtmanae, the first single-celled (archaeal) commensal (i.e., two organisms have a relationship wherein one benefits, and the other has no harm nor benefit) organism to have its genome sequenced, is an anaerobic, non-moving, sphere-shaped organism that inhabits the human gastrointestinal tract. Of all methanogenic (methane-producing) archaea, *Methanosphaera stadtmanae* is known to have the most restrictive energy metabolism (having relatively few intermediates available to it) because it can generate methane only by a reduction of methanol with hydrogen. This unique energy conservation of *Methanosphaera stadtmanae* is what makes it beneficial to its human host and not an opportunistic pathogen. It is therefore reasonable to conclude that another intestinal methanogenic archea, *Methanobrevibacter smithii*, is likely to be _____

Which choice most effectively uses information from the chart to complete the statement?

(A) more energy efficient than *Methanosphaera stadtmanae* with relatively more of the boxes in a similar accompanying figure shaded gray.

(B) less energy efficient than *Methanosphaera stadtmanae* with relatively fewer of the boxes in the accompanying figure shaded gray.

(C) more energy efficient than *Methanosphaera stadtmanae* with relatively more of the boxes in the accompanying figure shaded black.

(D) less energy efficient than *Methanosphaera stadtmanae* with relatively fewer of the boxes in the accompanying figure shaded black.

8. It's a common fixture in household kitchens across the United States, but remarkably few of us who use them have any real idea of how our microwave ovens work. Contrary to most other food-heating appliances—the toaster, the convection oven, and the stove, for instance—the microwave itself has no internal heating element: flame, coil, or otherwise. Instead, the microwave oven uses the principle of dipole rotation to_____

Which choice most logically completes the text?

(A) create a healthy alternative to highly processed foods.

(B) give consumers an affordable alternative to restaurant meals.

(C) generate heat from the molecules within the food itself.

(D) provide structural support to the walls of the appliance.

Answer Explanations

1. **(D)** Although *discriminating* typically has a negative connotation that people associate with prejudice, in this context, the author is asserting that we need to be more careful and *selective* in picking which invasive plants we keep and which ones we exterminate. Choices (A) and (B) can apply to *discriminating* in other contexts, and choice (C) would only apply to being *discriminating* when it comes to the quality of art, food, music, etc.

2. **(A)** Choice (A) correctly refers to the results, or *consequences*, that would come about from setting off fireworks. Choices (B), (C), and (D) all incorrectly have a positive connotation, which is not supported by the surrounding context that refers to "negative respiratory effects" and "pollutants."

3. **(C)** According to the text, Plato is generally scornful of all working professions, thinking they will cause people to focus too much of their minds on work. So, look for an answer that says something to the effect of labor detracting from one's self-worth. That is choice (C). Choices (A) and (D) favor those who work or service others and so contradict Plato's belief. Choice (B) doesn't work because the text states that Plato disdains the "necessary staple" of working in society.

4. **(A)** Consider the context here. The previous sentence introduces the term *phagocytosis*. Because this is a scientific term that not all readers will know, the author then clarifies what phagocytes do in the process of phagocytosis. Therefore, the author is clarifying a specialized term, making choice (A) correct. Choice (B) is incorrect because the author doesn't tell where the word comes from. Choices (C) and (D) are incorrect because the sentence does neither of these things.

5. **(B)** The text states that Beatrice married Stephen because she was "weary" and "sad," making (B) the correct answer. There is no evidence that she fell in love with or was forced to marry him. Likewise, vengeance implies retaliation or a punishment for a wrongdoing, which is not mentioned.

6. **(A)** Text 2 presents evidence showing that an invasive plant, honeysuckle, can have a positive impact on the environment; this goes against the general suggestion about the negative impact of invasive plants from Text 1. It is not (B) or (C) because Text 2 does not suggest a consistent approach to the treatment of invasive plants. It is not (D) because the texts do not detail transportation recommendations about invasive plants.

7. **(A)** According to the text, "of all methanogenic (methane-producing) archaea, *Methanosphaera stadtmanae* is known to have the most restrictive energy metabolism." Thus, another methanogenic archaea, like *Methanobrevibacter smithii*, would be likely to be *more* energy efficient than *Methanosphaera stadtmanae* because it would have more pathways to metabolizing energy. If *Methanobrevibacter smithii* has more pathways available for energy metabolism, it is likely that it would have more of the intermediates boxes shaded gray. Thus, choice (A) is correct. It is not choice (B) or (D) because these incorrectly state that *Methanobrevibacter smithii* would be less energy efficient. It is not choice (C) because the boxes would be shaded gray, not black.

8. **(C)** The text indicates that microwaves are different from other food-heating appliances because they do not have an internal heating element. Stating that the microwave generates heat from the molecules in the food would logically complete this text, showing how microwaves can successfully heat food without having an internal heating element. The other options do not focus on the heating of food.

Advanced Reading Drill 3

1. The following text is from Nathaniel Hawthorne's 1852 novel, The Blithedale Romance.

   "Nothing," answered I; "nothing, that I know of, unless to make pretty verses, and play a part, with Zenobia and the rest of the amateurs, in our pastoral. It seems but an unsubstantial sort of business, as viewed through a mist of fever. But, dear Hollingsworth, your own vocation is evidently to be a priest, and to spend your days and nights in helping your fellow-creatures to <u>draw</u> peaceful dying breaths."

   As used in the text what does the word "draw" most nearly mean?

   (A) Inhale
   (B) Provoke
   (C) Infer
   (D) Sketch

2. The following text is from the 1919 poem "Anne Rutledge" by Edgar Lee Master. Anne Rutledge was thought by some to be the first true love of Abraham Lincoln, who went on to become President of the United States during the Civil War.

   Out of me unworthy and unknown
   The vibrations of deathless music;
   "With malice toward none, with charity for all."
   Out of me the forgiveness of millions toward millions,
   And the beneficent face of a nation
   Shining with justice and truth
   I am Anne Rutledge who sleep beneath these weeds,
   Beloved in life of Abraham Lincoln,
   Wedded to him, not through union,
   But through separation,
   Bloom forever, O Republic,
   From the dust of my bosom!

   Which choice best states the main purpose of the text?

   (A) To show that death cannot prevent the ideals of a country from continuing
   (B) To express despair that the narrator's true love was not reciprocated

   (C) To demonstrate the regret at the outcome of a national conflict
   (D) To condemn those who would doubt the love she felt toward Lincoln

3. The following text is from the 1839 short story "The Fall of the House of Usher" by Edgar Allan Poe.

   Although, as boys, we had been even intimate associates, yet I really knew little of my friend. His reserve had been always excessive and habitual. I was aware, however, that his very ancient family had been noted, time out of mind, for a peculiar sensibility of temperament, displaying itself, through long ages, in many works of exalted art, and manifested, of late, in repeated deeds of munificent yet unobtrusive charity, as well as in a passionate devotion to the intricacies, perhaps even more than to the orthodox and easily recognizable beauties, of musical science. I had learned, too, the very remarkable fact, that the stem of the Usher race, all time-honored as it was, had put forth, at no period, any enduring branch; in other words, that the entire family lay in the direct line of descent, and had always, with very trifling and very temporary variation, so lain.

   The text suggests that at any point in its history, the Usher family would most likely have had how many heirs at a given time?

   (A) None
   (B) One
   (C) Two or more
   (D) The family had no heirs.

4. The following text is from Ralph Waldo Emerson's 1836 essay "Nature." The essay is considered a foundational text of transcendentalism.

   Our age is retrospective. It builds the sepulchres of the fathers. It writes biographies, histories, and criticism. The foregoing generations beheld God and nature face to face; we, through their eyes. Why should not we also enjoy an original relation to the universe? Why should not we have a poetry and philosophy of insight and not of tradition, and a religion by revelation to us, and not the history of theirs? Embosomed for a season in nature, whose floods of life stream around and through us, and invite us by the powers they supply, to action proportioned to nature, why should we grope among the dry bones of the past, or put the living generation into masquerade out of its faded wardrobe? The sun shines to-day also. There are new lands, new men, new thoughts. Let us demand our own works and laws and worship.

Which choice best describes the main question posed by the text?

(A) Why is it that scientific inquiry is dismissed in favor of political dogma?
(B) Why are philosophers considered superior to more practical professionals?
(C) Why shouldn't archaeology take precedence over historical research?
(D) Why can't modern society directly have transcendental experiences?

5. Russia, the geographically largest country in the world, is facing the biggest long-term problem any country can: depopulation. This problem is difficult to solve, however, as no one factor caused it. The beginning of the demographic problem is in Russia's low life expectancy. The life expectancy at birth for Russian males is only 64.7 years, and while the life expectancy for women is much longer, having the male half of the population die so early, before many of them can reach retirement age, causes great concern. Low birth rates are another critical factor in the Russian population crisis. The average fertility rate for Russian women is at 1.61 children per woman; this results in a population growth rate of −0.04 each year. A social scientist claims that without an increase in Russian life expectancy and the fertility rate of Russian women, the population of Russia is destined to grow ever smaller.

Which finding, if true, would most directly support the social scientist's claim?

(A) A newfound openness to immigrant resettlement has the potential to bolster the Russian population, despite low birthrates and life expectancy.
(B) In a demographically similar country to Russia, in a five-year period when there was a life expectancy in the high sixties for men and a fertility rate for women of 1.7, the country's population declined.
(C) In a decade fifty years before the authorship of this text, the Russian population steadily increased when men had a life expectancy of 62 and women had a fertility rate of 2.8.
(D) An annual population growth rate of −0.05 percent resulted from a country that is geographically similar to Russia when it was subject to widespread epidemic disease that reduced the life expectancy of men from 72 to 68.

6.

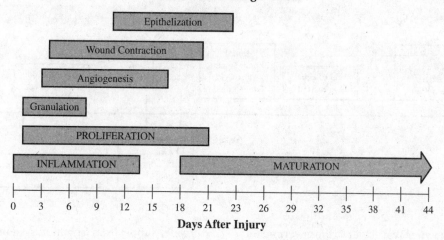

It is critical to be protective of a newly healed wound at the beginning of the third stage of wound healing (following inflammation and proliferation): maturation. The new skin is quite fragile and can easily reopen if too much stress is placed on it. The maturation stage can last up to two years as the scar forms and hardens. In some cases, the scar will disappear with time, but in others it's a permanent addendum to a person's body. Even once the scar has fully matured, scar tissue is only 80% as strong as skin, meaning it is prone to re-injury. The nurse who created the above chart wishes to extend the *x*-axis of the figure to portray the point at which a wound would nearly certainly be healed without extending the graph unnecessarily. Given these criteria, the nurse would most logically end the revised *x*-axis at _____

Which choice most effectively uses data from the table to complete the statement?

(A) 10 days.

(B) 100 days.

(C) 1,000 days.

(D) 10,000 days.

7. A historian argues that the primary advantage of the Fraktur variety of blackletter font was that it balanced elegance with functionalism. Which quotation from the historian's essay most effectively illustrates this claim?

(A) Though far less calligraphic than textualis, Fraktur is nonetheless more intricate than Schwabacher, and combines the soft readability of the latter with the bold regality of the former.

(B) Antiqua's subversion of blackletter began gradually, appearing primarily in scientific texts (which valued readability over appearance).

(C) By far the most familiar blackletter style, Fraktur originated at the end of the 15th century through a commission of the Holy Roman Emperor Maximilian I.

(D) The revolutionary scale of his innovation firmly established blackletter—particularly the Schwabacher and Fraktur varieties—as the preferred script for printed texts throughout Europe.

8.

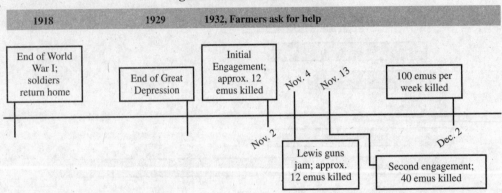

Significant Events in Emu War

| 1918 | 1929 | 1932, Farmers ask for help |

End of World War I; soldiers return home

End of Great Depression

Initial Engagement; approx. 12 emus killed

Nov. 4   Nov. 13

100 emus per week killed

Nov. 2

Lewis guns jam; approx. 12 emus killed

Second engagement; 40 emus killed

Dec. 2

In Australia after World War 1, the government encouraged British veterans to take up farming. Subsidies were guaranteed but either failed to be provided or weren't enough. As a result, by October 1932, wheat prices fell dangerously low. Justifiably outraged, the farmers and government entered a time of rising tensions. Matters were made appreciably worse when over 20,000 emus entered the scene. Emus follow predictable migration patterns and when the farmers settled the land, the emus were undeterred from moving into the newly settled farms. In fact, due to the extensive farming that had taken place, the land had been cleared—allowing easier migration—and there was a plentiful water supply from irrigation systems, giving the emus an ideal habitat. After the emus destroyed much of their crops, the farmers demanded the government provide them military aid. The military's effectiveness in fighting the emus can best be described as _____

Which choice most effectively uses information from the graphic to complete an accurate generalization?

(A) gradually increasing over time.
(B) steadily decreasing over time.
(C) relatively constant over time.
(D) generally inconsistent.

Answer Explanations

1. **(A)** The sentence refers to drawing breaths, so *inhale* is the best choice. Breathing is not directly associated with *provoking, inferring,* or *sketching*.

2. **(A)** Despite the death of Anne Rutledge, who sleeps "beneath the weeds" indicating she has been buried, the ideals like justice and truth of the "Republic"—i.e., the United States—continue to "bloom forever." It is not choice (B) because the poem states that she was "beloved in life" of Abraham Lincoln, indicating the love was reciprocal. It is not choice (C) because there is nothing to indicate that Rutledge regretted the outcome of the U.S. Civil War. It is not choice (D) because there is nothing indicating a feeling of condemnation toward others.

3. **(B)** This is tough reading, but don't be intimidated; break it down. The family is peculiar, or odd; has a great interest in art, charity, and musical science; but is not enduring. In fact, the line of descent is direct and has always been so. Thus, there is most likely only one descendant. The word "direct" implies that the inheritance has always been passed down from one to the next without any extra heirs, eliminating choice (C). It is not choice (A) or (D) because the family line continues to the time of the story, referring to "his very ancient family."

4. **(D)** According to the text, Emerson is concerned with why the current age is retrospective, or always looking back into the past. He advocates, instead, for "a poetry and philosophy of insight" rather than relying on traditional discourses. Similarly, he says we should "demand our own works" and interrogate what is natural. Hence, he raises the question of why we rely on what others have said instead of having our own transcendental (i.e., spiritual) experiences and creating our own theories, making choice (D) correct. He is not concerned with feuds or inconsistencies between separate fields as in choice (A), (B), or (C).

5. **(B)** The stated claim is that "without an increase in Russian life expectancy and the fertility rate of Russian women, the population of Russia is destined to grow ever smaller." The circumstances in choice (B) are similar to those of Russia, with a life expectancy for men in the high 60s and a fertility rate at 1.7. In fact, the circumstances in this other country are more positive with respect to population increase than would be expected in Russia, since in the other country, the men live relatively longer lives and the women have relatively more children. Thus, if there is a population decline in the alternative country, it is likely that there would be a relative decline of at least this severity in Russia, if not of greater severity. It is not choice (A) because this would cause an increase in Russian population, undermining the social scientist's claim. It is not choice (C) because the birthrate was far higher fifty years ago than when the social scientist makes the claim. It is not choice (D) because there is no indication that Russia has an epidemic of disease, making this information irrelevant to the social scientist's claim.

6. **(C)** The text states that the last step of healing, the maturation stage, may last up to two years. The inflammatory phase lasts between 2 and 14 days, and the proliferative phase lasts between 3 and 21 days. Therefore, the whole healing phase may last $14 + 21 + 365 + 365 = 765$ days. Thus, the closest answer is 1,000. In 1,000 days, the wound will almost certainly be healed, choice (C).

7. **(A)** This option shows "elegance" by stating that Fraktur is "intricate" and has "regality"; it also shows functionalism by mentioning "readability." It is not (B), (C), or (D) because these choices focus on the timeline of the font's development.

8. **(A)** From the figure, you can see that the forces were generally ineffective at first, improved with time, and then became particularly efficient by December 2 with 100 emus per week killed. Choice (A) accurately accounts for this gradual increase in efficiency. Choices (B) and (C) do not reflect this improvement, and choice (D) inaccurately implies that you cannot find a general pattern.

Writing

3

Writing

Frequently Asked Questions

How Is the Writing Component Structured?

- Part of the Reading and Writing section (2 modules of 27 questions each, 32 minutes each)
- The first Reading and Writing module will be of standard difficulty, and the second module will be more or less difficult depending on your performance on the first module.
- Approximately 25 of the 54 total Reading and Writing questions are Writing ones.
- Out of these 25 questions, about 14 relate to Standard English conventions and about 11 relate to the expression of ideas.

What Are the Most Important Things I Can Do to Be Successful?

1. **CAREFULLY REVIEW THIS CHAPTER.** It comprehensively covers the major grammar and editing concepts you will need to know for the PSAT.
2. **WORK THROUGH THE READING AND WRITING TESTS IN THIS BOOK.** They are carefully designed to align with what you will face on test day and are based on careful analysis of the released materials from the College Board.
3. **READ WIDELY.** The more familiar you are with what good writing should look like, the easier it will be for you to spot the best options in this section.
4. **PRACTICE WITH OTHER MATERIALS IF NEEDED.** The PSAT Reading and Writing section is virtually identical to the SAT Reading and Writing section. So, if you run out of practice materials in this book, check out *Barron's Digital SAT* or any of the other Barron's books for the SAT. You can find further practice at *KhanAcademy.org*, the official College Board practice website. Also, since the PSAT Writing questions closely mirror the content covered by the ACT English section, you can improve your PSAT Writing performance by practicing ACT English passages.

Writing Strategies

1. Use the full amount of time.

The PSAT Writing questions are typically easy to finish for most students. You can take approximately 70 seconds to complete each Writing question. You are much more likely to make careless errors if you rush through the questions. Instead, do the questions one time well so that you do not miss the subtle issues that many questions test. Even though with many tests it makes sense to finish early so that you have time to check your work, it is advisable with the PSAT Writing questions to pace yourself to finish right on time. You are more likely to avoid careless errors if you catch them the first time, rather than if you go through the test quickly and then quickly scan over your answers to check.

2. Mouth it out as you read.

"Hear" the text in your head and test out the sound of the different options. You don't have to know the exact rules for misplaced modifiers and proper sentence construction to recognize that this sounds wrong: "Excited was I the brand new science fiction movie to see." When you are doing the PSAT Reading and Writing modules, you must answer the questions correctly—you do not need to write out a justification for each answer. This chapter comprehensively covers the grammar rules you will need to know—study them, and you will be much more confident and decisive. Coupled with this knowledge, you will put yourself in the best position to succeed if you filter the questions not just through your eyes but through your ears as well.

3. Make sure that everything makes sense given the context.

To determine if a sentence provides an effective transition, you must understand the text as a whole. To see if a verb has the correct tense, you must see how the verbs in nearby sentences are used. Some questions will require that you look only at the sentence that the underlined portion is in, whereas other questions will require the entire text. When you have any doubt about how much of the surrounding context to consider, err on the side of reading *too much* rather than *too little*. Since the Reading and Writing section is relatively easy to finish, you should take the necessary time to be certain everything is consistent and logical.

4. Understand that there will not be grammar gimmicks—just grammar rules.

The PSAT will only test you on topics where there are clearly defined grammar rules. Topics on which there is disagreement on proper English usage (using the Oxford comma, using "but" or "because" to start a sentence, and whether it is OK to use the first person "I" or second person "you" in formal papers) will not be tested. In addition, you do not need to worry about if there will be two right answers—the PSAT is an extremely well-crafted test, and it is a virtual certainty that it will be free of errors. So, instead of wasting your time trying to determine the "tricks" of the test, boost your grammar knowledge and go in with confidence.

5. Guess intelligently, not just randomly.

Remember—there is no penalty for guessing on the PSAT. Thus, be certain that you answer every single test question. If two or three of the answers are extremely similar, it is highly unlikely that one of those will be the correct choice. For example, if a question has these choices—(A) but, (B) however, (C) nevertheless, and (D) consequently—the answer is most likely choice (D) because the other choices are all synonymous. Flag and then come back to questions if you do not feel confident. Doing this will allow you to reexamine the question with fresh eyes after you've given your mind a chance to subconsciously process what the question was asking.

Transitions Questions

Questions about the best connections between different parts of the text *are among the most frequent question types on the PSAT.* These questions require you to consider what wording would make the flow of the text most logical and meaningful. Be sure you know the "big three" transitional words—"but," "also," and "because"—and some of their common synonyms.

BUT: however, on the other hand, in contrast to, yet, still, nevertheless, conversely, in spite of, despite, unlike, besides, although, instead, rather, otherwise, regardless, notwithstanding

ALSO: additionally, moreover, further, as well, besides, likewise, what is more, furthermore, in addition, similarly

BECAUSE: consequently, so, therefore, as a result, thus, hence, in order to, if . . . then, since, so that, due to, whenever

Tactic: Treat the Transitional Wording as a Blank, and Then Consider What Type of Transition Is Needed Given What Comes Around It.

What comes around the transitional wording could be in contrast to one another, be in support of one another, or have some other relationship. Look at as much of the text as needed—sometimes just a couple of sentences, sometimes the entire paragraph—to determine what wording is needed.

> Example

Those not accustomed to the effects of caffeine may experience jitteriness upon initial consumption. Despite this, many students try caffeine for the first time the morning of the PSAT in an effort to be alert. _____ they should rely on a good night's sleep and natural adrenaline to maximize performance.

23. Which choice completes the text with the most logical transition?

   (A) As a result,
   (B) Instead,
   (C) Consequently,
   (D) Moreover,

The sentence that precedes the question states that students try caffeine in order to improve their test performance. The sentence that follows states that students should rely on more natural solutions to improve performance. Choice (B) is the only option that shows the needed contrast between these two ideas. "As a result" and "consequently" both show cause and effect, and "moreover" is synonymous with "also."

Transitional Wording Drill

Write appropriate transitional words in the underlined portions. Use the "word bank" of transitions—each word will be used only once.

Word Bank

while	and	in fact
but	since	perhaps

_____ it is unusual that I enjoy waiting in line for hours on the opening night of a big movie, _____ I am not alone. _____, dozens of other moviegoers wait along with me, _____ we enjoy passing the time speculating on the movie's potential plot twists. _____ it could be expected that tempers would be short as people stood patiently in line, the truth is that people are extremely polite. _____ we are all full of hopeful anticipation, everyone is in a fairly good mood.

Answer

Perhaps it is unusual that I enjoy waiting in line for hours on the opening night of a big movie, but I am not alone. In fact, dozens of other moviegoers wait along with me, and we enjoy passing the time speculating on the movie's potential plot twists. While it could be expected that tempers would be short as people stood patiently in line, the truth is that people are extremely polite. Since we are all full of hopeful anticipation, everyone is in a fairly good mood.

Transitions Practice Drill 1

1. The students had been without their regular teacher for several weeks, and the substitute teacher was only mildly proficient in the subject matter. _____ the students consistently performed well on the semester exam, much to the surprise of both the teacher and the students themselves.

   Which choice completes the text with the most logical transition?

   (A) Indeed,
   (B) Nevertheless,
   (C) Consequently,
   (D) Similarly,

2. Scientific generalizations are, like many rules, susceptible to the occasional exception. Water, _____ unlike many other liquids, has a greater density than its corresponding solid form. Without this exception to the general scientific rule, icebergs and ice cubes would sink to the bottom of water instead of floating on top.

   Which choice completes the text with the most logical transition?

   (A) for example,
   (B) furthermore,
   (C) eventually,
   (D) meanwhile,

3. Typically, an inverted yield curve—i.e., the condition when long-term interest rates fall below short-term interest rates—precedes an economic recession. _____ there have been occasional exceptions to this macroeconomic tendency.

   Which choice completes the text with the most logical transition?

   (A) As a result,
   (B) Likewise,
   (C) However,
   (D) Additionally,

4. Melanie Matchett Wood is a recipient of the MacArthur Fellowship, giving her a no-strings-attached grant to pursue her research in number theory. _____ Tomeka Reid earned a MacArthur Fellowship; in her case, it was to give her the opportunity to further her innovation in cello improvisation.

   Which choice completes the text with the most logical transition?

   (A) Nonetheless,
   (B) Soon,
   (C) Meanwhile,
   (D) Similarly,

5. Lyme disease, which is transmitted by ticks, has become an increasing threat to people in the Northeastern United States. _____ researchers are working on developing an effective vaccine so that hikers can make their way through the forest with minimal concern.

   Which choice completes the text with the most logical transition?

   (A) Consequently,
   (B) Eventually,
   (C) Besides,
   (D) Later,

6. Public libraries have become increasingly adept at integrating technology, like computers and 3D printing, into their buildings. _____ the libraries have ensured that patrons from a wide variety of backgrounds have access to these innovative resources.

   Which choice completes the text with the most logical transition?

   (A) Conversely,
   (B) Additionally,
   (C) However,
   (D) Eventually,

7. The high school principal has empowered the student body to have more autonomy over fund-raising and social event planning. _____ she has listened to students when they have made specific suggestions for an anti-bullying initiative.

   Which choice completes the text with the most logical transition?

   (A) Furthermore,
   (B) Therefore,
   (C) Nonetheless,
   (D) By contrast,

8. Many students prefer doing their homework on a computer or tablet. A researcher recommends that students _____ try using paper for assignments that require a great deal of concentration; after all, it is easier to avoid becoming distracted by social media when technology is kept to a minimum.

   Which choice completes the text with the most logical transition?

   (A) eventually
   (B) later
   (C) then
   (D) instead

9. The head of the political science department was an excellent manager, able to skillfully delegate coursework among the different professors. _____ she was a well-regarded researcher in her own right, which earned her the respect of her department colleagues.

   Which choice completes the text with the most logical transition?

   (A) Nevertheless,
   (B) Instead,
   (C) Moreover,
   (D) Still,

10. To be comfortable with quantum mechanics, one must embrace paradox. _____ to understand many of the concepts underpinning quantum mechanics, one must wrap one's mind around the possibility of two seemingly incompatible ideas being true at the same time.

    Which choice completes the text with the most logical transition?

    (A) Additionally,
    (B) In other words,
    (C) Conversely,
    (D) Rather,

Answer Explanations

1. **(B)** *Nevertheless* shows a contrast between the lack of quality instruction the students receive and the strong performance the students had on their exam. *Indeed* would designate a clarification, *consequently* would show cause and effect, and *similarly* would build off an idea.

2. **(A)** *For example* shows how water is an example of how scientific rules may have exceptions. *Furthermore* would be like "also," *eventually* would pertain to the passage of time, and *meanwhile* would refer to a different sort of event.

3. **(C)** *However* gives a contrast between the typical circumstances surrounding an inverted yield curve and the occasional exceptions that have occurred. *As a result* shows cause and effect, and *likewise* and *additionally* show a continuation of an idea.

4. **(D)** *Similarly* gives a logical transition to show how Tomeka Reid also received a MacArthur Fellowship. *Nonetheless* and *meanwhile* would show a contrast, and *soon* would refer to the passage of time.

5. **(A)** *Consequently* gives a cause-and-effect relationship between the threat of Lyme disease and the fact that researchers are working on a vaccine for this illness. *Eventually* and *later* deal with the passage of time, and *besides* would designate an additional idea.

6. **(B)** *Additionally* logically transitions from the first sentence about how public libraries have integrated technology into their buildings and the notion that the libraries are ensuring access to these resources. *Conversely* and *however* would both illustrate a contrast, and *eventually* would designate that an event will occur in the future.

7. **(A)** *Furthermore* is synonymous with "additionally" or "also," making it a logical transition between the fact that the principal is empowering the students in certain areas and that she is listening to student policy suggestions in another area. The other options would all express a contrast.

8. **(D)** *Instead* expresses a contrast between the students' preferred way of doing homework and the researcher's recommended way of doing the homework. The other options would all designate points in time, which would be illogical in this case.

9. **(C)** *Moreover* is similar to "also," which makes the most sense here to provide a transition between the two sentences, because they are both expressing positive characteristics of the head of the political science department. All the other answers would show a contrast, which would not make sense here.

10. **(B)** The text begins with a broad statement about the need to embrace paradox and follows with a specific explanation of what it means to embrace paradox. Thus, *in other words* would provide a logical transition to this clarification. *Additionally* would show a continuation of an idea, and *conversely* and *rather* would both show a contrast.

Transitions Practice Drill 2

1. The friends' relationship dissolved after a break-down in trust. _____ when one friend lied about their whereabouts the previous week, the other friend began to question where he had been on previous occasions.

   Which choice completes the text with the most logical transition?

   (A) Alternatively,
   (B) Besides,
   (C) Therefore,
   (D) Specifically,

2. The theoretical physicists continued to fine-tune their predictive models about the subatomic particle's properties. _____ electrical engineers continued to work on the equipment that could be used to assess the accuracy of these models.

   Which choice completes the text with the most logical transition?

   (A) In particular,
   (B) Meanwhile,
   (C) Thus,
   (D) In fact,

3. Attendance at the amusement park has steadily declined over the years; over the past decade, annual attendance has decreased by approximately 30%. _____ many families consider it a must-go destination for their annual family reunions, providing a steady base of attendees.

   Which choice completes the text with the most logical transition?

   (A) Still,
   (B) Likewise,
   (C) For example,
   (D) Similarly,

4. There was an unfortunate shortage in one of the raw materials needed to manufacture the medicine. _____ many patients who regularly took the medication had to ration their doses. As the shortage continued, these patients had to go completely without the medicine, resulting in severe withdrawal symptoms.

   Which choice completes the text with the most logical transition?

   (A) Instead,
   (B) First,
   (C) Similarly,
   (D) Nevertheless,

5. The coastal region was recently recategorized from a Category 1 risk, able to withstand winds between 156–165 MPH, to a Category 3 risk, able to withstand winds between 180–185 MPH. _____ new builds in the region need to be constructed with more structural reinforcement than had been required for builds in previous years.

   Which choice completes the text with the most logical transition?

   (A) Thus,
   (B) Moreover,
   (C) However,
   (D) In addition,

6. Test performance generally improves when students have gotten sufficient rest, usually nine hours on a given night. _____ when students get little rest, five to six hours or even less, their performance on assessments usually deteriorates. Therefore, students should avoid cramming the night before a test as it may undermine their performance on problem-solving exercises.

   Which choice completes the text with the most logical transition?

   (A) Similarly,
   (B) Therefore,
   (C) Likewise,
   (D) Conversely,

7. Although earthquakes are often called natural disasters, in and of themselves, they are part of the forces of nature that actually help to sustain life on Earth. _____ the carbon cycle is made possible by moving continental plates which, together with the water cycle, keep nutrients, water, and land available for life.

Which choice completes the text with the most logical transition?

(A) On the other hand,
(B) For example,
(C) As a result,
(D) Nevertheless,

8. After the baseball team's dramatic loss to their archrival, the coach was deeply frustrated with his players. _____ he was disappointed with the two players who made errors late in the game that enabled the other team to score a game-winning run. Going forward, he was determined to keep the mistakes his players made to an absolute minimum.

Which choice completes the text with the most logical transition?

(A) In particular,
(B) Meanwhile,
(C) Nonetheless,
(D) Nevertheless,

9. August 1 was a momentous anniversary for the political science institute _____ . Not only did the date commemorate the founding of the institute, but it was the date on which it secured its most prestigious accolades. Understandably, the institute members were excited to celebrate, using the anniversary as inspiration for further advances.

Which choice completes the text with the most logical transition?

(A) first
(B) alternately
(C) furthermore
(D) indeed

10. The gardener was initially determined to eradicate invasive plants from all parts of his yard; if the plant was not indigenous to his area, he thought it should be removed and replaced with a native species. _____ however, the gardener has learned to live with the non-native honeysuckle plant, because it provides thick foliage that acts as a visual barrier between his yard and his neighbor's.

Which choice completes the text with the most logical transition?

(A) Increasingly,
(B) In particular,
(C) Meanwhile,
(D) Additionally,

Answer Explanations

1. **(D)** *Specifically* provides a transition between the broad statement about the friendship in the first sentence and the specific details about what caused the friendship to deteriorate. *Alternatively* would show a contrast, *besides* would show a continuation of an idea, and *therefore* would show cause and effect.

2. **(B)** *Meanwhile* means "at the same time," making it the most logical transition to join these two sentences. The first sentence talks about the work the physicists were doing, and the second sentence talks about the simultaneous work of the engineers. It is not choice (A) or (D) because the second sentence does not provide specific details to elaborate on the first sentence. It is not choice (C) because what happens in the first sentence does not directly cause what happens in the next sentence.

3. **(A)** *Still* expresses a contrast between the decline in attendance and the desire that many families feel to attend the park. It is not choice (B) or (D) because the second sentence does not show a similarity. It is not choice (C) because the second sentence provides a new idea, not an example of the idea expressed in the first sentence.

4. **(B)** *First* logically introduces the first step that patients had to take to cope with the lack of their needed medication. Choices (A) and (B) do not work because there is no contrast expressed. Choice (C) doesn't work because the second sentence of the text provides new information, not a similar example.

5. **(A)** *Thus* logically transitions between the fact that the increased risk assessment for the area caused it to require more stringent building codes. It is not choice (B) or (D) because what follows is not a continuation of the idea expressed in the first sentence. It is not choice (C) because the two sentences do not present a contrast.

6. **(D)** *Conversely* transitions between the statement about increased sleep leading to better test performance and the statement about how, when students get little sleep, their performance declines. The other options all incorrectly would show a continuation of the previous idea.

7. **(B)** *For example* connects the previous statement that earthquakes are life sustaining and the example of the carbon cycle that follows. Choices (A) and (D) incorrectly show a contrast, and choice (C) incorrectly shows a cause-and-effect relationship.

8. **(A)** *In particular* provides a transition between the broad claim about the coach's frustration and the specific reasons why he felt the disappointment. Choice (B) doesn't work since the second sentence is an elaboration on the first, not a statement about a simultaneous event. Choices (C) and (D) do not work because there is not a logical contrast between the first two sentences.

9. **(D)** *Indeed* serves to emphasize that the date was quite momentous, a statement supported by the details in the following sentence. The other options do not provide any sort of emphasis on the significance of August 1.

10. **(A)** *Increasingly* expresses that with the passage of time, the gardener went from a more extreme view about the need to kill all invasive plants to a more moderate view that he could tolerate some presence of invasive plants. It is not choice (B) because there is no elaboration on specific details. It is not choice (C) because there is no expression of simultaneous events. It is not choice (D) because the final sentence does not continue the idea of the first sentence.

Rhetorical Synthesis Questions

A new type of question on the Digital PSAT is the rhetorical synthesis question. You will be asked to consider the notes that a student has taken on a topic and determine the best way to use the information in the notes to present or emphasize a particular idea. On questions like these, be sure to really focus on what the question asks so that you can zero in on the most relevant evidence.

❯ Example

While researching a topic, a student has taken the following notes:

- A solar eclipse occurs when the moon passes between the Earth and the sun, thereby blocking the sun's light.
- Some solar eclipses are partial, in which some of the sunlight is obscured by the moon.
- On rare occasions, there can be a total solar eclipse in which the moon fully blocks the sun's circular disk.
- Astronomy enthusiasts sometimes travel to the site of a solar eclipse to observe it, since at any given spot on the Earth, it may take about four centuries for an eclipse to occur.
- Ancient societies understandably were unsettled by solar eclipses, since they often feared some unusual supernatural force was at work.

The student wants to draw a contrast between partial and total solar eclipses. Which choice most effectively uses relevant information from the notes to accomplish this goal?

(A)   Even though it might take nearly 400 years for a total solar eclipse, it is exciting to see one if possible.

(B)   Since ancient societies felt that eclipses were the result of supernatural forces, they did not see any difference between total and partial eclipses.

(C)   A total eclipse occurs when the moon is between the Earth and the sun, whereas a partial eclipse occurs when the Earth is between the moon and the sun.

(D)   While a partial eclipse shows some of the sun's light, a total eclipse will fully block the sun's circular disk.

❯ Explanation

The question asks you to draw a contrast between a partial and total solar eclipse. Choice **(D)** effectively accomplishes this task by incorporating the information about the partial eclipse only blocking out some of the sun's light, while a total eclipse blocks out the sun's circular disk. It is not choice (A) because it does not highlight a difference between the two types of eclipse. It is not choice (B) because it ignores the possibility of a difference between the eclipse types. It is not choice (C) because both eclipse types occur when the moon is between the Earth and the sun.

Rhetorical Synthesis Practice

1. While researching a topic, a student has taken the following notes:

    - People hold their writing utensil in many ways.
    - A functional grasp is one that produces legible writing and does not cause pain or inefficiency for the writer.

    - An inefficient grasp can cause illegible writing, pain, very slow writing, and excessive fatigue when writing.
    - Three common functional writing utensil grasps are dynamic tripod, quadrupod, and modified tripod.
    - Many people write using a grasp that falls outside of the common functional grasps. As long as the unique grasp is functional for the individual and not inefficient, there is no cause for concern.

The student wants to emphasize the potential negative consequences if someone does not hold a pen properly. Which choice most effectively uses relevant information from the notes to accomplish this goal?

(A) An inefficient grasp is less preferable than a functional one.

(B) Individuals can decide as to what type of grasp best suits them.

(C) Without a proper grasp of the writing utensil, pain, fatigue, and slow writing may result.

(D) Increased legibility might be an undesirable outcome of not holding a pen properly.

2. While researching a topic, a student has taken the following notes:

- The French Legion of Honor is an award for great personal and professional merit.
- This award is given to both military and non-military recipients.
- Following similar categories to ranks of chivalry, the Legion of Honor was established by Napoleon Bonaparte in 1802.
- The American Congressional Medal of Honor is the highest military decoration in the United States.
- The Medal of Honor was established during the U.S. Civil War to recognize those who distinguished themselves with acts of bravery.

The student wants to describe a difference between the general types of recipients of the Medal of Honor and Legion of Honor. Which choice most effectively uses relevant information from the notes to accomplish this goal?

(A) Though the Medal of Honor is given to members of the military, the Legion of Honor is given only to citizens who are not in the armed forces.

(B) While both military and non-military persons can receive the Legion of Honor, the Medal of Honor is given to military recipients.

(C) The French Legion of Honor was established at an earlier historical date than the U.S. Medal of Honor.

(D) The U.S. Medal of Honor deemphasizes recognition of accomplishment, while the French Legion of Honor seeks to reestablish a medieval feudal order.

3. While researching a topic, a student has taken the following notes:

- The creator of *Star Wars* is George Lucas.
- George Lucas made episodes 4–6 and waited to make episodes 1–3 until further technological advancement.
- Lucas Films produced the movies, which were later bought by Disney in 2012.
- Upon Disney taking over the *Star Wars* franchise, Dave Filoni and Jon Favreau became the new creative directors.
- As of 2022, there have been nine core films, multiple spinoffs, and TV shows.

The student wants to highlight the change in the management of the *Star Wars* franchise at a particular point in time. Which choice most effectively uses relevant information from the notes to accomplish this goal?

(A) The number of *Star Wars* films created—at least nine as of 2022—is quite impressive.

(B) Dave Filoni, Jon Favreau, and George Lucas are among the persons who have managed the famous *Star Wars* franchise.

(C) While initially created by George Lucas, Disney took over the *Star Wars* franchise in 2012.

(D) George Lucas, famously known as the creator of *Star Wars*, held off on making new *Star Wars* films until technology could advance.

4. While researching a topic, a student has taken the following notes:

- Many people experience eye floaters.
- Eye floaters often appear as clear squiggles or small spots that float across the field of vision.
- Eye floaters appear as they do because they are shadows cast on the retina from small stuck-together pieces of vitreous in the eye.
- Most of the time, eye floaters are not a cause for concern, but they can have serious causes, such as retinal detachment.
- If there is a sudden change in eye floaters, an eye care professional should be alerted.

The student wants to emphasize floater symptoms that should not prompt concern. Which choice most effectively uses relevant information from the notes to accomplish this goal?

(A) If the retina becomes detached, be sure to seek out a doctor.

(B) When the spots from floaters rapidly increase, try to remain calm.

(C) Stuck-together pieces of vitreous in the eye can cause one's vision to be impeded.

(D) Consistently small squiggles in the field of vision are likely nothing to worry about.

5. While researching a topic, a student has taken the following notes:

- Digestion means the breakdown of food.
- There are two kinds of digestion: chemical and mechanical.
- Chemical digestion is the breakdown of food through enzymes and hormones.
- Mechanical digestion is simply breaking down the food into smaller pieces.
- In the mouth, chewing (a mechanical digestive process) is the main type of digestion that occurs, but small amounts of salivary amylase are released to chemically degrade starches.

The student wants to point out a similarity between chemical and mechanical digestion. Which choice most effectively uses relevant information from the notes to accomplish this goal?

(A) Chemical and mechanical digestion equally contribute to the digestion that takes place in the mouth.

(B) While mechanical digestion is more prevalent in the mouth, chemical digestion is more prevalent in the intestines.

(C) Both mechanical and chemical digestion involve breaking down food.

(D) Saliva is used as a key component of both mechanical and chemical digestion.

Answer Explanations

1. **(C)** This option is the only choice that accomplishes the goal of showing what negative consequences will result from not holding a pen correctly. Choices (A) and (B) do not focus on negative consequences, and Choice (D) is a positive outcome.

2. **(B)** This option accurately points out that there is a general difference between the possible recipients of the two honors since civilians are only eligible for the Legion of Honor. The other options do not accurately reflect the information in the notes.

3. **(C)** This question asks the student to highlight a small portion of the information presented, namely about how the management of the franchise changed at a point in time. Choice (C) is the only option that connects to the change in management.

4. **(D)** This choice is the only option that emphasizes specific symptoms of floaters—like small squiggles—that should not make patients worry. Choices (A) and (B) focus on more severe symptoms, and Choice (C) focuses on the causes of floaters.

5. **(C)** This option points out a similarity between chemical and mechanical digestion—they both break down food. Choice (A) is not supported by the given information. Choice (B) points out a difference. Choice (D) is inaccurate since saliva is involved in chemical, not mechanical, digestion.

Sentence Structure

Sentence Fragments and Run-On Questions

*A **sentence** expresses a complete thought with both a subject and predicate (i.e., a subject and a verb).* A subject will be a noun—a person, place, or thing. The predicate will have a verb—a word that expresses an *action*, such as "is," "were," "ate," "choose," or "eat." Here are some examples of complete sentences:

> What is this?
> He won the match.
> There is great trouble brewing in the town.

*A **sentence fragment** expresses an incomplete thought. It typically has just a subject or a predicate.* Here are some examples of sentence fragments:

> From my place.
> Homework for tomorrow's big test.
> Your neighbor's house, which is next to the spooky mansion on the hill.

*A **run-on sentence** consists of two or more complete sentences that are not joined together with appropriate punctuation or transitions.* Here are some examples of run-on sentences.

> Finish your meal it is really good for you to do so.
> I was excited to see the new show I stayed up really late to see it.
> The moon will be full tonight, let's stay up and enjoy its beauty.

Tactic: Evaluate Whether a Sentence Is Complete by Determining If It Has a Subject and a Verb—Don't Make Assumptions Based Simply on the Length of the Sentence.

A sentence can be complete while being quite short. For example, "I am" is a complete sentence. A selection can be a fragment even though it is rather long. For example, "For the benefit of the United States of America, today, tomorrow, and in the years to come" is a fragment. Consider each sentence on a case-by-case basis to make a determination.

> **Example**

We will need to get to the bottom of this news _____ he is a winner in the hotly contested election.

19. Which choice completes the text so that it conforms to the conventions of Standard English?

   (A) story. Whether
   (B) story. If
   (C) story. Whether or not
   (D) story as to whether

Choices (A), (B), and (C) all have a sentence fragment after the period. Choice (D) is the only option that joins the wording together in a way that provides one complete sentence.

Complete and Incomplete Sentences Drill

Determine if the sentence is complete, a run-on, or a fragment.

1. To whom this letter may concern.
2. She wept.
3. I am looking forward to the movie I plan on standing in line for a couple of hours.
4. Whenever they leave the doors unlocked of their brand new automobile.
5. My best friend, whom I have known since childhood, will be visiting from out of town this upcoming weekend.

Answers

1. Fragment
2. Complete
3. Run-on
4. Fragment
5. Complete

Modifier Placement Questions

Consider these two improper sentences:

The fish loved its new aquarium, swimming quickly.

While reading the brand new book, many people were annoying.

These two sentences have confusing meaning. The first sentence literally expressed that the aquarium is swimming quickly. In the second sentence, it is unclear who is reading the new book. These sentences can be fixed by making sure the modifying words, like adjectives, and the words they modify, like nouns, are clearly stated and in a proper sequence. Here are proper versions of the two sentences:

The fish, swimming quickly, loved its new aquarium.

While I was reading the brand new book, many people annoyed me.

When it comes to modifier clarity and placement, remember this tip:

Tactic: Make Sure That the *Literal* Meaning and the *Intended* Meaning Are the Same.

> **Example**

My teacher asked me a question, but _____ a prompt response.

22. Which choice completes the text so that it conforms to the conventions of Standard English?

   (A) too tired was I for giving
   (B) giving was too tired for me
   (C) I was giving too tired
   (D) I was too tired to give

To clearly express what is doing the action, "I" should follow the "but." Choices (A) and (B) have convoluted word order. Choice (C) has the correct placement of "I," but jumbles the wording later in the selection. Choice (D) has clarity of wording and a logical sequence throughout.

Modifier Placement Drill

Make corrections, if needed, to give the sentences proper modifier placement and word order. There are multiple ways to fix these sentences.

1. While reading the book, forgot to leave a bookmark I did.
2. My car was unavailable for the road trip, which was in the repair shop.
3. The player's last game was rather abysmal, not practice very well leading up to it.
4. Route 1 was a beautiful stretch of freeway on our way to vacation, a six-lane superhighway.
5. Read all the way to the end of the book, and confusion will be replaced with clarity.

Answers with Possible Corrections

1. While reading the book, **I forgot to leave a bookmark.**
2. My car**, which was in the repair shop,** was unavailable for the road trip.
3. The player's last game was rather abysmal **since he did** not practice very well leading up to it.
4. Route 1, **a six-lane superhighway,** was a beautiful stretch of freeway on our way to vacation.
5. Fine as is. The sentence implies that the reader is being directly addressed.

Verb Use Questions

The PSAT requires you to be comfortable with the essentials of verb conjugation. Most students become familiar with the terminology for proper verb conjugation when they take a foreign language in high school—here is an overview of the key verb conjugation information that you may already know intuitively.

Table 3.1 contains a summary of some of the basic conjugation patterns of verbs.

Table 3.1 Basic Verb Conjugations

Past	Present	Future
He ate They were She ran We walked	He eats They are She runs We walk	He will eat They will She will run We will walk
Past Perfect	**Present Perfect**	**Future Perfect**
I had eaten They had been She had run We had walked	I have eaten They have been She has run We have walked	I will have eaten They will have been She will have run They will have walked

Although many verbs follow a simple pattern, quite a few verbs have irregular conjugations, particularly for the past and past perfect forms. These irregular verbs are often called "strong" verbs since they form a past tense without the aid of the "ed" ending as with "weak" verbs. Table 3.2 shows a sampling of some irregular verbs you might encounter.

Table 3.2 Irregular Verb Conjugations

Present Tense (*I am.*)	Past Tense (*I was.*)	Past Participle (What comes after "have" in the Present Perfect— "*I have been.*")
Become	Became	Become
Begin	Began	Begun
Bring	Brought	Brought
Choose	Chose	Chosen
Do	Did	Done
Draw	Drew	Drawn
Drink	Drank	Drunk
Drive	Drove	Driven
Fly	Flew	Flown
Get	Got	Gotten
Go	Went	Gone
Grow	Grew	Grown

Present Tense (*I am.*)	Past Tense (*I was.*)	Past Participle (What comes after "have" in the Present Perfect— "*I have been.*")
Have	Had	Had
Hear	Heard	Heard
Know	Knew	Known
Lay (i.e., place)	Laid	Laid
Lead	Led	Led
Lie (i.e., recline)	Lay	Lain
Light	Lit	Lit
Ride	Rode	Ridden
Ring	Rang	Rung
Rise	Rose	Risen
Run	Ran	Run
See	Saw	Seen
Shine	Shone	Shone
Show	Showed	Shown
Sing	Sang	Sung
Sink	Sank	Sunk
Swim	Swam	Swum
Swing	Swung	Swung
Take	Took	Taken
Wake	Woke	Woken
Wear	Wore	Worn

Tactic: Look at the Context Surrounding the Verb to See What Verb Tense, Mood, or Voice Is Appropriate.

> **Example**

Three years ago on our trip to India, we visited Humayan's Tomb and _____ the Siddhivinayak Temple.

20. Which choice completes the text so that it conforms to the conventions of Standard English?

 (A) see
 (B) saw
 (C) seeing
 (D) shall see

The sentence refers to events that took place three years ago, making the entire sentence in the past tense. Choice (B) is the only option in the past tense. Choice (A) is in the present tense, choice (C) uses the gerund form of the verb, and choice (D) uses the future tense.

Verb Use Drill

Make corrections, if needed, to give the sentences proper verb use. There are multiple ways to fix these sentences.

1. A decade ago, I decide to focus more intently on my studies.
2. The customer service message needs to be answered by you.
3. If you was able to find a job, you would not have the financial worries you currently did.
4. In 1992, Caitlin won the prize, but only after she practice for many months.
5. My teacher demands that I am quiet during the test.

Answers with Possible Corrections

1. A decade ago I **decided** to focus more intently on my studies. *Put it in the past tense since it was a decade ago.*
2. **You need to answer** the customer service message. *Avoid the passive voice—use the active voice instead.*
3. If you **were** able to find a job, you would not have the financial worries you currently **do**. *Use the subjunctive mood to express something contrary to fact, and use the present tense since the sentence says "currently."*
4. In 1992, Caitlin won the prize, but only after she **had practiced** for many months. *Use the past perfect tense to indicate that the practice was ongoing for a period in the past.*
5. My teacher demands that I **be** quiet during the test. *Since this is a demand, use "be" rather than "is."*

Subject-Verb Agreement Questions

Subject-verb agreement would be easy to determine if all sentences had the subject and verb close to one another. For example,

Birds fly in the air.

When the subject and verb are separated from each other, creating agreement can be more challenging. For example,

The movie about the terrifying monsters and evil ghosts were most frightening.

The subject "movie" and the verb "were" do not match numerically. Here is the corrected version:

The movie about the terrifying monsters and evil ghosts was most frightening.

When you encounter subject-verb agreement questions remember this next tactic.

Tactic: Cut Out the Words Between the Subject and Verb to See If the Subject and Verb Are Both Singular or Both Plural.

> **Example**

The general who led legions of soldiers _____ triumphant in the battle.

20. Which choice completes the text so that it conforms to the conventions of Standard English?

(A) were
(B) are
(C) was
(D) have been

The subject in the sentence is "general," which is singular. Choice (C) is the only option that has a singular verb. Choices (A), (B), and (D) are all plural, and thus incorrect. It would be easy to be confused about the subject and think that it was the plural "legions" or "soldiers."

Number Agreement Drill

Make corrections, if needed, to a lack of number agreement. There are multiple ways to fix these sentences.
1. The company of actors do a wonderful production.
2. My teacher or his teaching assistant is in charge of grading the assignment.
3. Gender roles over the past century has evolved significantly.
4. My favorite summer diversion, reading and swimming, are quite enjoyable.
5. Each person on the train were glad to arrive at the destination.

Answers with Possible Corrections
1. The company of actors **does** a wonderful production.
2. Fine as is.
3. Gender roles over the past century **have** evolved significantly.
4. My favorite summer **diversions**, reading and swimming, are quite enjoyable.
5. Each person on the train **was** glad to arrive at the destination.

Pronoun Number Questions

Matching pronouns with the nouns they represent is easy when the words are close to each other. For example,

Jennifer ate her entire lunch.

It becomes more challenging to match pronouns when the pronouns and the nouns are more separated. For example,

The man who left the calculator on top of the board games cabinet needs to pick up his property.

Tactic: Match Singular Pronouns with Singular Nouns and Plural Pronouns with Plural Nouns.

Even though the pronouns and nouns may be separated from one another, be sure they are numerically consistent. These types of questions take a bit more focus because simply "mouthing them out" won't necessarily alert you to a grammatical problem; the separation between the pronouns and nouns makes the sentences sound pretty good as they are.

> Example

When two scientists work together, _____ become smarter than would be possible if working independently.

17. Which choice completes the text so that it conforms to the conventions of Standard English?

    (A) he
    (B) you
    (C) they
    (D) it

In the first part of the sentence, "two scientists" are mentioned as working together—this is a plural subject. So, it would be logical to have the plural pronoun "they" match up with this. The other pronouns are singular, and so would not work.

Pronoun Number Drill

Make corrections, if needed, to give the sentences proper pronoun number. There are multiple ways to fix these sentences.

1. No matter your feelings on the vote, be sure that you are true to oneself.
2. Whenever I see someone struggling with math, I can't help but wonder if they missed some of the fundamentals earlier in school.
3. A sperm whale will probably have scars from deep-sea battles with giant squids all over their skin.
4. Members of the orchestra have to submit practice records before you are allowed to attend rehearsal.
5. Skilled surgeons are likely quite proud of their training.

Answers with Possible Corrections

1. No matter your feelings on the vote, be sure that you are true to **yourself**. *Keep it consistent with "your" throughout.*
2. Whenever I see someone struggling with math, I can't help but wonder if **he or she** missed some of the fundamentals earlier in school. *This is referring to a singular person given the use of "someone."*
3. A sperm whale will probably have scars from deep-sea battles with giant squids all over **its** skin. *This refers to "a" sperm whale, so use the singular.*
4. Members of the orchestra have to submit practice records before **they** are allowed to attend rehearsal. *"They" will be consistent with "members of the orchestra."*
5. No change is needed to this sentence because "surgeons" is plural and "their" is also plural.

Sentence Structure Drill 1

1. Pet owners may notice that their cats and dogs tend to shed quite a bit of hair as summer approaches. This is a way that the animals have evolved _____ for the warmer summertime temperatures.

   Which choice completes the text so that it conforms to the conventions of Standard English?

   (A) prepare
   (B) preparing
   (C) to prepare
   (D) will prepare

2. Walt Disney, an American entertainment innovator, was the creator of the eponymous Disneyland and Disney World. Disney World is the larger development, _____ several major theme parks within its boundaries.

   Which choice completes the text so that it conforms to the conventions of Standard English?

   (A) including
   (B) include
   (C) have included
   (D) has included

3. An eclipse that _____ when the moon passes directly between the sun and the Earth, completely blocking out the sun, is known as a total solar eclipse.

   Which choice completes the text so that it conforms to the conventions of Standard English?

   (A) had occurred
   (B) occurring
   (C) occurs
   (D) has occur

4. After visiting the Great Barrier Reef when he was a college student, John _____ that he would one day take his entire family there to explore its wonders.

   Which choice completes the text so that it conforms to the conventions of Standard English?

   (A) promised
   (B) promise
   (C) promises
   (D) will promise

5. Larry King, a radio and television personality known for his trademark suspenders, made _____ a wide range of politicians an important part of his programs.

   Which choice completes the text so that it conforms to the conventions of Standard English?

   (A) interview
   (B) interviewing
   (C) to interview
   (D) will interview

6. After a major disaster, like a tornado or hurricane, the U.S. Federal Emergency Management Agency has staff members who _____ those affected by the disaster with emergency aid.

   Which choice completes the text so that it conforms to the conventions of Standard English?

   (A) supply
   (B) has supplied
   (C) had supplied
   (D) supplying

7. From the Santa Monica Mountains to the Malibu lagoons, from the gorgeous Cascades and Mount Rainier to Puget Sound, the entirety of the coast from California to Washington is breathtaking. Tucked beneath that striking veneer, sinister and lurking, however, _____ geological secrets of a magnitude of which we are suspicious but uncertain.

   Which choice completes the text so that it conforms to the conventions of Standard English?

   (A) is
   (B) was
   (C) are
   (D) has

8. In a recent recording of Mozart's "*The Magic Flute*," a male soloist exhibits true virtuosity. In a notable excerpt, he _____ an impossibly high note and sings an extraordinary vibrato.

Which choice completes the text so that it conforms to the conventions of Standard English?

(A) struck
(B) strikes
(C) striking
(D) had stricken

9. Teachers have found that students are more likely to finish their homework when their parent or guardian asks whether _____ had completed the assignment.

Which choice completes the text so that it conforms to the conventions of Standard English?

(A) it
(B) one
(C) they
(D) us

10. Science fiction writer Isaac Asimov wrote stories that often foretold the future; _____ prediction of a mobile computerized object is very much like the smartphone of today.

Which choice completes the text so that it conforms to the conventions of Standard English?

(A) his
(B) its
(C) it's
(D) there

Answer Explanations

1. **(C)** This option correctly uses the infinitive "to prepare" to explain what the animals have evolved to do over time. The other options use incorrect verb tenses given the context.

2. **(A)** "Including" correctly uses the present participle to give a dependent clause that clarifies the statement made in the independent clause that precedes it. The other options would be used in an independent clause, which this final clause of the sentence is not.

3. **(C)** This option correctly uses the present tense of the verb, making it consistent with the present tense "is" used later in the sentence. The other options use incorrect conjugations of "occur" given the context.

4. **(A)** "Promised" is the only option that maintains the past tense as used throughout the sentence, like with the verb "was." Choices (B) and (C) are in the present tense and choice (D) is in the future.

5. **(B)** "Interviewing" uses the correct gerund form of the verb to make the word a noun—since "interviewing" would follow "made," "interviewing" acts as an object in the sentence. The other verb conjugation options would not act as a noun and would therefore be incorrect.

6. **(A)** "Supply" is both consistent with the plural subject of "staff members" and with the present tense as with the earlier verb "has." Choice (B) would be for a singular subject. Choice (C) would designate past actions instead of present ones. Choice (D) would need an "are" to precede it to be in the present tense.

7. **(C)** The subject comes after the verb, which can be confusing. Nonetheless, the subject is "secrets," a plural noun that requires a plural verb for agreement. Choices (A), (B), and (D) are all singular verbs and therefore must be eliminated. "Are" is the only acceptable option.

8. **(B)** This is the only option that correctly conjugates the verb to match the singular subject "he" and the present tense to be consistent with the other verbs "exhibits" and "sings." The other options are not in the present tense.

9. **(C)** "They" stands for the plural "students" earlier in the sentence. Choices (A) and (B) would stand for singular nouns, and (D) could be used if the sentence were in the second person (you, we, us) instead of the third person.

10. **(A)** The word "his" refers to the singular writer Isaac Asimov. Choices (B) and (C) would not work because these would refer to things, not people. Choice (D) incorrectly uses "there," which designates a place, not a person.

Sentence Structure Drill 2

1. In the Canadian Yukon Territory in 2022, miners _____ a 30,000-year-old mummified baby mammoth, the first discovery of this type in North America. Many paleontologists were excited to come face-to-face with this extraordinary specimen.

   Which choice completes the text so that it conforms to the conventions of Standard English?

   (A) have unearthed
   (B) are unearthing
   (C) to unearth
   (D) unearthed

2. The lamprey, an eel-like cartilaginous fish, is a parasite of larger fish species, causing them to have their immune systems gradually weakened. The lamprey attaches _____ to another fish by using its suction disk mouth.

   Which choice completes the text so that it conforms to the conventions of Standard English?

   (A) themselves
   (B) it
   (C) itself
   (D) oneself

3. The U.S. National Wireless Emergency Alert System _____ the U.S. President and the head of the Federal Emergency Management Agency to communicate with the American people during a large-scale emergency.

   Which choice completes the text so that it conforms to the conventions of Standard English?

   (A) are enabling
   (B) enabling
   (C) enables
   (D) enable

4. After the evacuation of Fort Lee, General George Washington and his revolutionary troops suffered a significant loss of equipment. Despite this setback, _____ and had an impressive victory at the Battle of Trenton.

   Which choice completes the text so that it conforms to the conventions of Standard English?

   (A) Washington's army regrouped
   (B) the regrouping of Washington's Army
   (C) regrouping of Washington
   (D) it was the Army of Washington that regrouped

5. While the new roller coaster at the amusement park is the first of its kind, similar rides to it _____ imagined before. Just last year, many independent bloggers drew sketches of such a ride.

   Which choice completes the text so that it conforms to the conventions of Standard English?

   (A) has been
   (B) is
   (C) are
   (D) have been

6. Overconsumption of ground water in the community, through both direct human consumption and indirect consumption via agriculture, may _____ the local government to institute conservation measures.

   Which choice completes the text so that it conforms to the conventions of Standard English?

   (A) force
   (B) forcing
   (C) forces
   (D) forced

7. When Wikipedia was first introduced, many were concerned about the potential for poorly cited articles. Nowadays, Wikipedia _____ often used as an excellent place to find links to primary sources on various topics.

   Which choice completes the text so that it conforms to the conventions of Standard English?

   (A) is
   (B) was
   (C) are
   (D) had been

8. A community that has experienced violent flooding in recent years is considering creating a large dam for its river. While a large upfront investment, this new infrastructure would ensure that the community is no longer devastated by storms and _____ bountiful hydroelectric energy to the residents.

   Which choice completes the text so that it conforms to the conventions of Standard English?

   (A) provided
   (B) providing
   (C) provides
   (D) provide

9. In an effort to put aside the divisions of the Cold War, the European Union was founded in 1993 with 12 participating countries. Since then, the European Union _____ to well over double that number.

   Which choice completes the text so that it conforms to the conventions of Standard English?

   (A) have expanded
   (B) expand
   (C) expanding
   (D) has expanded

10. Someone who is an empath is quite attuned to the emotions of others, at times even _____ the same emotions that others are, making them exceptional listeners.

    Which choice completes the text so that it conforms to the conventions of Standard English?

    (A) will feeling
    (B) will have felt
    (C) feeling
    (D) had felt

Answer Explanations

1. **(D)** "Unearthed" is the only option that is in the past tense, making it consistent with the past tense "were" used later in the text. The other options are not in the past tense.

2. **(C)** "Itself" makes sense as a reflexive pronoun when referring to an animal that is attaching "itself" to another fish. It is not (A) because the lamprey is singular. It is not (B) because "it" is not reflexive. It is not (D) because "one" is not used elsewhere in the text.

3. **(C)** "Enables" is the only option that correctly uses the singular verb form to align with the singular subject "System." Choices (A) and (D) use plural forms of the verb, and (B) uses a gerund.

4. **(A)** This is the only option that puts the words in a logical sequence, making it clear that "Washington's army" was the thing that "regrouped" after a setback. Choices (B) and (C) would mean that "regrouping" had a setback, and choice (D) would mean that "it" had a setback without clarifying what "it" stood for.

5. **(D)** The plural present perfect "have been" makes sense here to state that rides like this roller coaster have been imagined over a period up to the present. It is not choice (A) or (B) because these are singular verbs. It is not choice (C) because this would not support that people have contemplated such rides beginning in the past, as stated in the final sentence of the text.

6. **(A)** "Force" would be the correct conjugation of the verb to accompany the present tense verb "may," as in "may force." "Forces" and "forced" could be used on their own, but not in conjunction with "may." "Forcing" is a gerund.

7. **(A)** Since the sentence starts with the word "Nowadays," it is correct to use the present tense in this sentence. "Is" correctly matches with the singular subject of "Wikipedia." Choices (B) and (D) would refer to past events, and choice (C) needs a plural subject.

8. **(D)** "Provide" would work in conjunction with the earlier "would," making this parallel to the verb "ensure" used earlier in the sentence. The other options all lack a parallel construction to "ensure."

9. **(D)** The singular present perfect "has expanded" is appropriate, because the subject "European Union" is singular, and the events of the sentence begin in the past and continue to the present day. It is not choices (A) or (B) because these would need a plural subject. It is not (C) because this would not make the sentence complete.

10. **(C)** This option correctly uses the present participle "feeling" to express a continuous action aligned with the present tense "is." It is not choice (A) or (B) because these would designate future actions; choice (D) refers to past action.

Punctuation

Proper use of punctuation is a major area that is tested on the PSAT. Tables 3.3 through 3.7 show the rules for proper usage of commas, semicolons, colons, dashes, and apostrophes. These tables also include examples showing the correct usage of punctuation marks.

Commas

Table 3.3 Comma Rules and Examples

General Rule	Proper Use
Separate a phrase (dependent clause) from a complete sentence (independent clause).	When you open your birthday present, remember to whom you should send thank you notes.
Join two complete sentences when there is a transitional word, like the "FANBOYS": *for, and, nor, but, or, yet,* and *so.*	I am eager to receive my PSAT test scores online, but they will not come out for a few weeks.
Separate extra information from the rest of the sentence.	The Hubble Telescope, which orbits our planet, has provided fantastic pictures of deep space.
Separate items in a list with commas.[1]	I will order a pizza topped with cheese, pepperoni, mushrooms, and green peppers.
Don't use commas to separate parts of a sentence if everything in the sentence is needed to make it clear and logical (in this case, clarifying that the boat is sinking).	The boat that is sinking needs Coast Guard personnel to come rescue its passengers.
Just because a sentence is long doesn't mean that it needs a comma. Look more at the structure of the sentence than at its length.	The Great Barrier Reef off the coast of Australia offers some of the best snorkeling and scuba diving anywhere in the world.
A clarifying parenthetical phrase needs to be separated with commas. If the name is sufficient to know who the person is, commas are needed to separate the description. If the description is too vague to precisely narrow down the item, then no commas should separate descriptive phrases.	Eddie George, winner of the 1995 Heisman Trophy, had a successful professional football career after college.

[1]The PSAT has traditionally preferred the serial or "Oxford" comma (i.e., having a comma between the second-to-last and last items in a list), but since there is not a universally accepted rule about whether the serial comma should be used, it is extremely unlikely that the PSAT would include a test question about it.

Comma Drill

Make changes, if needed, to the comma usage.

1. Joe Montana winner of multiple Super Bowls, is undoubtedly one of the best to ever play football.
2. You are doing pretty well but you could be doing even better.
3. No I did not call the doctor.
4. *Gone With the Wind,* a nearly four-hour-long movie is so long that it has an intermission.
5. The horse currently winning the race will probably finish first.

Answers

1. Joe Montana, winner of multiple Super Bowls, is undoubtedly one of the best to ever play football.
2. You are doing pretty well, but you could be doing even better.
3. No, I did not call the doctor.
4. *Gone With the Wind,* a nearly four-hour-long movie, is so long that it has an intermission.
5. Fine as is.

Semicolons

Table 3.4 Semicolon Rules and Examples

General Rule	Proper Use
You can use a semicolon to separate two complete, related sentences.	My friend did most of the driving on our trip; she has much better stamina than I do.
Use a semicolon to separate items in a list when an item has punctuation within it.	On my European trip during college, I went to Paris, France; London, England; and Rome, Italy.
Put a semicolon before a conjunctive adverb (e.g., *however*, *consequently*, and *nevertheless*) when it joins two independent clauses.	Be sure to wear a raincoat today; otherwise, you will be soaked.

Semicolon Drill

Make changes, if needed, to the semicolon usage.

1. Please clean up after yourself I don't want to find any messes.
2. My dad was convinced she was lying, however, I was not so sure.
3. Although my husband's snoring is quite annoying, I try my best to ignore it.
4. Cyberbullying is a major problem, consequently, we need to do something to stop it.
5. On our "foundation of the nation" vacation we traveled to Boston, Massachusetts, Philadelphia, Pennsylvania, and Washington, D.C.

Answers

1. Please clean up after yourself; I don't want to find any messes.
2. My dad was convinced she was lying; however, I was not so sure.
3. Fine as is.
4. Cyberbullying is a major problem; consequently, we need to do something to stop it.
5. On our "foundation of the nation" vacation we traveled to Boston, Massachusetts; Philadelphia, Pennsylvania; and Washington, D.C.

Colons

Table 3.5 Colon Rules and Examples

General Rule	Proper Use
Use a colon after a complete sentence to set off a list.	Whenever I go on a trip, I am certain to take the following items: my passport, a cell phone, and my wallet.
Use a colon after a complete sentence to set off a clarification. (A colon can work if it can be replaced by the word *namely*.)	I was surprised at how my boyfriend proposed to me: he did so at the spot of our very first date.

Colon Drill

Make changes, if needed, to the colon usage.

1. Be sure to do the following in the interview, make eye contact, listen carefully, and answer from the heart.
2. I whiffed something burning from downstairs it was the stove.
3. Lead paint should be avoided it can cause lower intelligence and delayed growth.
4. The player had a major announcement: he was retiring for good.
5. Both of the job candidates have major flaws, one candidate is inexperienced and the other is unprofessional.

Answers

1. Be sure to do the following in the interview: make eye contact, listen carefully, and answer from the heart.
2. I whiffed something burning from downstairs: it was the stove.
3. Lead paint should be avoided: it can cause lower intelligence and delayed growth.
4. Fine as is.
5. Both of the job candidates have major flaws: one candidate is inexperienced and the other is unprofessional.

Dashes

Table 3.6 Dash Rules and Examples

General Rule	Proper Use
While other punctuation can often work (in this case, a colon or semicolon could work instead of the dash), the dash can provide variety in your writing when you need to indicate an interruption or change of thought.	Shut the door behind you—it is freezing outside.
A dash can be used to interrupt a sentence and provide a change of voice.	She won the prize—this came as no surprise to me—and shared her prize money with all her friends.
Dashes can set off a parenthetical phrase. If you start with a dash on one end of the phrase, you need to use a dash on the other end of it for consistency.	Summer vacation—considered by many educators to be outdated—is probably my favorite time of year.

Dash Drill

Make changes, if needed, to the dash usage.

1. Hold on a second please wait for me to finish.
2. Sam took just three things with him to class a laptop, reading glasses, and a ballpoint pen.
3. New York City—home of the Statue of Liberty and the Empire State Building, is a major tourist attraction.
4. My brand new phone charger does not work nearly as well as my old one did.
5. My stomach was full I couldn't eat another bite.

Answers

1. Hold on a second—please wait for me to finish.
2. Sam took just three things with him to class—a laptop, reading glasses, and a ballpoint pen.
3. New York City—home of the Statue of Liberty and the Empire State Building—is a major tourist attraction.
4. Fine as is.
5. My stomach was full—I couldn't eat another bite.

Apostrophes

Table 3.7 Apostrophe Rules and Examples

General Rule	Proper Use
Use an apostrophe before the "s" to indicate that a singular entity possesses something.	The cat's claws needed to be trimmed.
Use an apostrophe after the "s" to indicate that a plural entity possesses something.	The class officers' retreat was extremely productive.
Use an apostrophe before the "s" to indicate possession after an already-plural noun.	Children's theater is often far more interesting than adults'.

Apostrophe Drill

Make changes, if needed, to the apostrophe usage.

1. One dog's leash is sometimes just as expensive as two dog's leashes.
2. Womens restrooms frequently have longer lines than mens.
3. Your car's windows are so dirty I can write my name on them with my finger.
4. My one friends house is quite a bit more spacious than his.
5. Whale's skin is extremely thick in order to protect the animals from cold water.

Answers

1. One dog's leash is sometimes just as expensive as two **dogs'** leashes.
2. **Women's** restrooms frequently have longer lines than **men's**.
3. Fine as is.
4. My one **friend's** house is quite a bit more spacious than his.
5. **Whales'** skin is extremely thick in order to protect the animals from cold water.

Possession Questions

The PSAT will assess your understanding of possessive pronouns. Table 3.8 summarizes what you need to know.

Table 3.8 Possessive Pronouns

Pronoun	Meaning	Example
There vs. Their vs. They're	there: place their: possession they're: "they are"	They're excited to implement their new ideas when they travel over there.
Its vs. It's	its: possession it's: "it is" (its' is always incorrect)	It's a great day to take the car to be washed and vacuum all of its carpeting.
Your vs. You're	your: possession you're: "you are"	Your best friend tells you when you're not acting like yourself.
Whose vs. Who's	whose: possession who's: "who is"	Who's about to decide whose project wins the grand prize?

Tactic: Pronouns That Show Possession Do Not Have Apostrophes, Unlike Most Nouns.

Pronouns that use apostrophes are the contraction forms, like "they're" and "you're." Pronouns are different from most other words in that they show possession without apostrophes.

> **Example**

When you try to turn on your computer, be sure that _____ plugged into the wall outlet.

18. Which choice completes the text so that it conforms to the conventions of Standard English?

(A) it's
(B) its
(C) its'
(D) it is going to be

In the above sentence, the required meaning of the underlined portion is "it is," making choice (A) correct. Choice (B) is used to show possession, choice (C) is never correct, and choice (D) is too wordy.

Possession Drill

Make corrections, if needed, to clarify possession. There are multiple ways to fix these sentences.

1. The chair was nonfunctional—its' legs no longer worked.
2. You're patience is appreciated as you wait for the next customer service representative.
3. I am confident that they're going to be on time.
4. Whose calculator needs new batteries?
5. While it's a nice day, please be sure to wash your car—it's windows are filthy.

Answers with Possible Corrections

1. The chair was nonfunctional—**its** legs no longer worked.
2. **Your** patience is appreciated as you wait for the next customer service representative.
3. Fine as is.
4. Fine as is.
5. While it's a nice day, please be sure to wash your car—**its** windows are filthy.

Frequent Types of Punctuation Questions

End-of-Sentence Questions

It is unlikely that you will find an end-of-sentence punctuation question that asks you to identify the basic usage of a period or a question mark, since these concepts are typically mastered in elementary school.

Tactic: End-of-Sentence Punctuation Questions Will Probably Be About Unusual Situations.

❯ Example

My friend was wondering if it would be OK for me _____

16. Which choice completes the text so that it conforms to the conventions of Standard English?

    (A) to take him home?
    (B) taking him home?
    (C) to take him home.
    (D) take him home!

Although the friend is asking a question, it is given indirectly. As a result, no question mark is needed, making choice (C) the correct choice. Choices (A) and (B) both improperly make this into a direct question, and choice (D) incorrectly makes this into an exclamation.

Items-in-a-Series Questions

As with end-of-sentence punctuation questions, items-in-a-series questions are unlikely to test basic concepts, such as knowing that a list of three or more items requires each item to be separated by punctuation of some kind. Be on the lookout for unusual situations with items-in-a-series of questions, paying close attention to this next tactic.

Tactic: Make Sure the Punctuation Separates One Complete Item from Another.

> **Example**

When traveling in the Western United States, be sure to visit _____

19. Which choice completes the text so that it conforms to the conventions of Standard English?

     (A) Yosemite National Park, Yellowstone National Park, and San Francisco.
     (B) Yosemite National Park Yellowstone National Park, and San Francisco.
     (C) Yosemite, National Park, Yellowstone National Park, and San Francisco.
     (D) Yosemite National Park Yellowstone National Park and San Francisco.

Choice (A) is the only option that correctly separates each destination from one another. Choices (B) and (D) jumble the destination names together, and choice (C) breaks up "Yosemite National Park" unnecessarily.

Parenthetical-Phrase Questions

A parenthetical phrase provides extra, clarifying information that can be removed and the sentence will still be complete. For example,

> My good friend Jen—a champion horseback rider—is one of the most talented people I have ever met.

Commas, dashes, and parentheses can all set off parenthetical phrases. Be sure of one thing:

Tactic: Start a Parenthetical Phrase in the Same Way That You End It.

If the parenthetical phrase begins with a comma, end it with a comma; if it starts with a dash, end it with a dash. Do not mix and match punctuation types in these cases.

> **Example**

The widely respected _____ able to develop a solution to the seemingly intractable problem.

18. Which choice completes the text so that it conforms to the conventions of Standard English?

     (A) engineer, winner of numerous industry awards—was
     (B) engineer—winner of numerous industry awards—was
     (C) engineer, winner of numerous industry awards was
     (D) engineer winner of numerous industry awards was

The phrase "winner of numerous industry awards" is not essential to making this sentence complete, although it does provide helpful clarifying information. The only option that sets this phrase out of the way using consistent punctuation is choice (B). Choice (A) mixes a comma with a dash, and choices (C) and (D) do not set the parenthetical phrase aside.

Unnecessary-Punctuation Questions

Some students tend to over-punctuate, feeling that PSAT answer choices with more elaborate punctuation are more sophisticated. Other students tend to under-punctuate, picking options that read like a stream of consciousness.

Tactic: Find a Balance Between Too Much and Too Little Punctuation. Use Exactly What Is Needed, No More and No Less.

> **Example**

In the _____ sure to enjoy time with your family and high school friends.

22. Which choice completes the text so that it conforms to the conventions of Standard English?

    (A) summer months before, you start college, be

    (B) summer months, before you start college be

    (C) summer months before you start college, be

    (D) summer months before you start college be

The introductory phrase of the sentence, "In the summer months before you start college," needs to be kept unified because it gives a precise description of the time period under discussion. Choices (A) and (B) interrupt this phrase. Choice (D) has no punctuation to separate the introductory clause from the complete sentence that follows. Choice (C) is the only option that correctly places a comma just after the introductory phrase.

Punctuation Drill 1

1. In the new medical study, scientists will test _____ to the new medication, assessing the significance of the antibody response relative to the control group of patients who did not take the medication.

   Which choice completes the text so that it conforms to the conventions of Standard English?

   (A) patient's antibody response's
   (B) patient's antibody responses'
   (C) patients antibody responses
   (D) patients' antibody responses

2. *The Nutcracker* ballet is a work _____ consistently comprises the bulk of a ballet company's revenue for the fiscal year. A long run of this production allows a company to put on more specialized pieces that do not appeal to as wide an audience.

   Which choice completes the text so that it conforms to the conventions of Standard English?

   (A) that,
   (B) that
   (C) that;
   (D) —that

3. Zora Neale Hurston was a famous Harlem Renaissance intellectual whose interests included anthropology and filmmaking. While she first authored the novel *Mules and* _____is most renowned for her novel *Their Eyes Were Watching God*.

   Which choice completes the text so that it conforms to the conventions of Standard English?

   (A) *Men* (1935), and she
   (B) *Men* 1935 she
   (C) *Men* (1935) she
   (D) *Men* (1935), she

4. The Empire State building became the world's tallest building at the time thanks to a dirigible, or blimp, docking tower built on its top. Did _____ Although a photograph of a navy dirigible landing at the Empire State building's tower is widely circulated, it was a fake that was made to promote the new building.

   Which choice completes the text so that it conforms to the conventions of Standard English?

   (A) any dirigibles ever use the docking station?
   (B) any dirigibles ever use the docking station.
   (C) any dirigibles ever use the docking station!
   (D) docking station of the dirigibles ever use.

5. Prior to the opening of the Panama Canal in 1914, ships traveling from the East Coast of the United States to the West Coast of the United States typically took over two months to make the journey. Through connecting the Atlantic and Pacific oceans over the narrow Isthmus of _____ saved weeks of transportation time for shipping companies.

   Which choice completes the text so that it conforms to the conventions of Standard English?

   (A) Panama the canal,
   (B) Panama the canal
   (C) Panama, the canal
   (D) Panama; the canal

6. Local assemblies of board game and video game _____have been meeting to determine the next location of their worldwide convention.

   Which choice completes the text so that it conforms to the conventions of Standard English?

   (A) enthusiasts,
   (B) enthusiasts—
   (C) enthusiasts
   (D) enthusiasts:

7. Some animals exhibit the unique capacity of autotomy, enabling them to purposefully discard a limb as a way of escaping an external threat and regrowing the limb later. The axolotl, a Mexican salamander, takes autotomy to an extreme level with its ability to regenerate _____ heart tissue, and even brain matter.

Which choice completes the text so that it conforms to the conventions of Standard English?

(A) its limbs

(B) its limbs,

(C) it's limbs

(D) its' limbs,

8. Living "off the grid" from electricity lines provided by a large corporation comes with the risk of more frequent _____ solar powers or a gas-powered generator can help minimize disruptions to homes that are disconnected from a larger electricity network.

Which choice completes the text so that it conforms to the conventions of Standard English?

(A) blackouts installing

(B) blackouts, the installation of

(C) blackouts, installing

(D) blackouts. Installing

9. The city of Dubai in the United Arab Emirates is world-renowned for its incredible _____ them the Burj Khalifa, rising over half of a mile into the sky.

Which choice completes the text so that it conforms to the conventions of Standard English?

(A) skyscrapers among,

(B) skyscrapers; among

(C) skyscrapers, among

(D) skyscrapers among

10. Virginian Patrick Henry, one of the foremost advocates of individual liberty, was purported to have said "Give me liberty, or give me _____ that a revolution was increasingly necessary.

Which choice completes the text so that it conforms to the conventions of Standard English?

(A) death," arguing

(B) death" arguing

(C) death." Arguing

(D) death;" arguing

Answer Explanations

1. **(D)** The plural "patients" possess their antibody responses, making "patients'" work. Choices (A) and (B) incorrectly use apostrophes to show singular possession, as well as incorrectly adding apostrophes to "response." Choice (C) incorrectly has no apostrophe to show possession.

2. **(B)** "That" is used to introduce essential phrases—ones that are vital to identifying something in the sentence—and therefore do not require punctuation. The other options all unnecessarily introduce punctuation to designate an essential descriptive phrase.

3. **(D)** This option correctly places a comma after the introductory dependent clause that starts with "While." Choices (B) and (C) do not have a comma to separate the dependent clause that introduces the sentence from the independent clause that follows. Choice (A) incorrectly inserts the word "and," which is unneeded because "While" is already providing the logical connection between the two clauses in the sentence.

4. **(A)** This is the only option that correctly uses a question mark to clearly mark this sentence as a question. Choices (B) and (C) would make this into a statement instead of a question, and choice (D) puts the words in an illogical sequence.

5. **(C)** The comma correctly separates the dependent introductory clause in this sentence from the independent clause that follows. Choice (A) incorrectly places a comma amid the independent clause, separating the subject "canal" from the verb "saved." Choice (B) provides no pause whatsoever. Choice (D) incorrectly uses a semicolon, because what comes before the semicolon in this case is not a complete sentence.

6. **(C)** No punctuation is needed to separate the long subject, "Local assemblies of board game and video game enthusiasts," from the corresponding verb, "have been meeting." All the other options use some sort of punctuation to separate the subject from the verb.

7. **(B)** This option correctly uses no punctuation with "its" to show possession, and it also has a comma after "limbs" to set up the first item in the list of three things at the end of this sentence. Choice (A) has no comma to separate the first item in this list. Choice (C) incorrectly uses the contraction for "it is," and choice (D) uses the word "its'" that is always incorrect.

8. **(D)** This is the only option that prevents the formation of a run-on sentence, giving a period to end the first complete sentence. The other options would all result in run-ons.

9. **(C)** The sentence begins with an independent clause and a comma then separates the dependent clause that follows. Choice (A) places the comma amid the dependent clause instead of before it begins. Choice (B) incorrectly uses a semicolon to separate the independent and dependent clauses—the semicolon should be used to separate two independent clauses. Choice (D) provides no break at all.

10. **(A)** The comma correctly separates the independent clause making up the sentence through the end of the quotation from the dependent clause that begins with "arguing." Choice (B) provides no break whatsoever, and choices (C) and (D) could only be used if what followed the period/semicolon were also an independent clause.

Punctuation Drill 2

1. The new restaurant on Main Street, featuring a fusion between cuisines of the Iberian Peninsula and North Africa, was an incredible addition to the town, such _____ he had "nothing less than the best meal of my life there."

   Which choice completes the text so that it conforms to the conventions of Standard English?

   (A) that columnist, Joseph Ducasse, declared
   (B) that columnist Joseph Ducasse declared
   (C) that columnist Joseph Ducasse, declared
   (D) that columnist—Joseph Ducasse—declared

2. Tourists in search of incredible shifts in the skies above find that Iceland is a great _____ the summer, there can be more than 21 hours of sunlight on days in June, and in the winter, the Northern lights paint a beautiful symphony of colors in the nighttime sky.

   Which choice completes the text so that it conforms to the conventions of Standard English?

   (A) destination whereas in
   (B) destination, in
   (C) destination in
   (D) destination: in

3. Tennis player Billie Jean King is famous for advocating gender equality. Her victory in the "battle of the sexes" tennis match against male tennis player Bobby _____ watched by approximately 90 million people around the world.

   Which choice completes the text so that it conforms to the conventions of Standard English?

   (A) Riggs' was,
   (B) Riggs was
   (C) Riggs, was
   (D) Rigg's, was

4. Jesse Owens was an elite track star at Ohio State University, where he won 8 individual championships in 1935–36, a record for the time. His climb to fame was only _____ the 1936 Berlin Olympics, he won an incredible four gold medals in a variety of events.

   Which choice completes the text so that it conforms to the conventions of Standard English?

   (A) beginning, however; in
   (B) beginning; however, in
   (C) beginning, however, in
   (D) beginning however, in

5. The Hubble Space Telescope, orbiting around the Earth, has been a ground-breaking tool for astronomers since it can gather light from distant galaxies without the interference of Earth's atmosphere. If a newer telescope could be developed that did not rely only on visual imagery for its data, could more distant galactic phenomena _____ what the James Webb Space Telescope is designed to do, with its capacity to observe infrared phenomena.

   Which choice completes the text so that it conforms to the conventions of Standard English?

   (A) observed be? That is
   (B) be observed. That is
   (C) be observed? That is
   (D) be observed. That, is

6. The ancient Native American Earthworks of Ohio were recently added to the prestigious UNESCO World Heritage list. The application to have them on this list was ultimately _____ full public access to the earthworks was assured.

   Which choice completes the text so that it conforms to the conventions of Standard English?

   (A) successful. Once
   (B) successful and once
   (C) successful; once
   (D) successful once

7. While many artworks are designed to stand the test of time, some art is purposefully designed to be fleeting. In the fall of 2021, the Arc de Triomphe in Paris was draped in fabric for 16 days under a design created by the _____ Jeanne-Claude.

Which choice completes the text so that it conforms to the conventions of Standard English?

(A) late artists Christo and
(B) late, artists Christo and
(C) late artists, Christo and
(D) late, artists Christo, and

8. During the Great Depression, many unemployed workers in the United States found a constructive outlet through the Works Progress Administration (WPA). Many parks needed trails, bridges, and other _____ workers used their talents to create such improvements; many of these useful constructions are still around today.

Which choice completes the text so that it conforms to the conventions of Standard English?

(A) infrastructure for WPA
(B) infrastructure, WPA
(C) infrastructure. WPA
(D) infrastructure WPA

9. An important invention that has improved car safety is the antilock braking system. When a _____ indicate that its brakes are locking up, the system quickly applies and releases the brakes so that the car will not skid on the pavement.

Which choice completes the text so that it conforms to the conventions of Standard English?

(A) car's sensor's
(B) cars sensors'
(C) car's sensors
(D) cars' sensors

10. Noting that "everything has its beauty, but not everyone _____ Andy Warhol captured his personal artistic philosophy; rather than having traditional subjects for his portraits, Warhol created "pop art" by using motifs like a can of soup.

Which choice completes the text so that it conforms to the conventions of Standard English?

(A) sees it;" American artist
(B) sees it" American, artist
(C) sees it." American artist
(D) sees it," American artist

Answer Explanations

1. **(B)** The description of "columnist" is not sufficiently specific to narrow the designation to a single person, making it necessary to have the name stated to have a clear and logical sentence. Choices (A) and (D) would set the name off to the side, which does not work since this is not specific enough to be an appositive. It is not (C) because no comma is needed to separate the subject from the verb.

2. **(D)** The colon correctly separates the complete sentence that comes before and the extensive clarification that follows. Choice (A) incorrectly would show a contrast with "whereas." Choice (B) uses a comma that would not designate a strong enough pause to come before the clarification. Choice (C) gives no punctuation whatsoever, providing no needed break.

3. **(B)** Although the subject is quite long, "Her victory in the 'battle of the sexes' tennis match against male tennis player Bobby Riggs," no comma would be needed to separate this subject from the verb "watched" that follows. All the other options incorrectly insert commas, with choices (A) and (D) also incorrectly showing possession.

4. **(A)** Typically, when you see "however" to separate two independent clauses, it is found after the semicolon. In this case, it is logical to place it before the semicolon because it is showing a contrast with the sentence that comes before the sentence "however" is in, not showing a contrast with the independent clause that comes after "however." Because the Digital PSAT doesn't test as wide a range of grammar concepts as other assessments, be prepared for exceptions to general "rules of thumb" to come up. It is not choice (B) because this would show a contrast with the last independent clause in the text. It is not choice (C) or (D) because a comma is insufficient to break up two independent clauses when a conjunctive adverb like "however" is used.

5. **(C)** This option correctly uses a question mark to designate this sentence as a question. Choice (A) also uses a question mark, but it inverts the order of the words to make the sentence illogical. It is not choice (B) or (D) because neither uses a question mark.

6. **(D)** No punctuation is needed to interrupt this continuous phrase. Choices (A) and (C) incorrectly use punctuation needed to have both what comes before and after be a complete sentence—the last part of the text is not a complete sentence. It is not choice (B) because a comma would be needed before "and."

7. **(A)** "Late" in this case means that the artists are no longer alive. No comma is needed to separate the adjective from the noun "artists." Choices (B) and (D) incorrectly separate the adjective "late" from the noun "artists." Choice (C) would not work because "late artists" is not sufficiently descriptive to make naming the artists unnecessary, as would be required if a comma is going to precede an appositive.

8. **(C)** Choice (C) keeps this from being a run-on sentence by breaking up two independent clauses with a period. Choices (B) and (D) do not provide the needed punctuation to separate two independent clauses. Choice (A) unnecessarily inserts "for" which would provide an illogical transition.

9. **(C)** "Car's" correctly shows a singular car possessing its sensors. This is needed since "a" comes before the word "car's," making it clearly singular. Choice (D) would be used with plural cars. Choices (A) and (B) unnecessarily show that the sensor or sensors possess something.

10. **(D)** The comma in this choice correctly separates the introductory dependent clause from the independent clause that follows. Choices (A) and (C) do not work because there is not a complete sentence before the semicolon/period. Choice (B) does not work because it incorrectly places a comma after "American" instead of between the two clauses.

Expression of Ideas Practice Questions

1. While researching a topic, a student has taken the following notes:

   - Inflation involves an increase in the money supply.
   - Inflation is associated with increasing prices for goods and services.
   - Those who have fixed prices for their long-term debt payments may find inflation beneficial.
   - Fixed debt payments will become relatively less expensive over time with inflation.
   - Those who are on fixed incomes may find inflation detrimental.
   - Fixed income recipients may find their purchasing power decrease in an inflationary environment.

   The student is doing a presentation in which she wants to create an example of a person who would most likely be harmed by inflation. Which choice most effectively uses relevant information from the notes to accomplish this goal?

   (A) A homeowner with fixed monthly mortgage payments

   (B) A retiree on a pension with a set income every month

   (C) A car owner who has $500 monthly payments until the car is fully paid off in five years

   (D) A gardener who grows most of his food at home, thereby avoiding purchasing food at stores

2. Still, modernism isn't let off easy in Fitzgerald's well-liked short story. _____ Marjorie is preferred socially, she is flagrantly rude and always needing to be entertained.

   Which choice completes the text with the most logical transition?

   (A) When
   (B) While
   (C) Because
   (D) Since

3. Reading is an enriching activity that is well worth making part of one's regular habits. Starting from an early age, children who read for pleasure encounter many new words and concepts that expand their minds. _____ images are frequently used in society today, words, unlike images, require using one's mind to understand them, ponder their meaning, and consider whether they are communicating something true or false.

   Which choice completes the text with the most logical transition?

   (A) Although
   (B) Since
   (C) Because
   (D) In addition,

4. Athenians collected their most lavish possessions inside the Parthenon among a host of statues, sculptures, precious metals, and treasures taken in the conquest of the Persians. _____ the project and all it stood for were short-lived: just seven years after the Parthenon was constructed, war broke out with Sparta.

   Which choice completes the text with the most logical transition?

   (A) Yet,
   (B) Additionally,
   (C) In conclusion,
   (D) As a result,

5. Sociologically, sports unite us far more than they divide us. Take, _____ Americans and football. Regardless of where you're from, what you believe, what team you like, or what ideologies you believe, when it's football season you can connect with other people, strangers even, through this unifying agent.

   Which choice completes the text with the most logical transition?

   (A) though,
   (B) on the other hand,
   (C) still,
   (D) for example,

6. Perhaps nowhere are timeless marital troubles better illustrated than in the second narrative of the suite, "The Clerk's Tale." _____ we find the greatest power imbalance of any of Chaucer's unhappy couples.

Which choice completes the text with the most logical transition?

(A) However,
(B) Additionally,
(C) Here
(D) Therefore

7. When researching a topic, a student has made the following notes:

- The Heliocentric model has the Earth and other planets revolving around the sun.
- Ancient Greek philosopher Aristotle was a proponent of the Heliocentric model.
- The Geocentric model has the sun and other planetary bodies revolving around the Earth.
- Ancient Greek philosopher Ptolemy was a proponent of the Geocentric model.
- The Heliocentric model eventually became dominant after Copernicus demonstrated that it better explained astronomical observations mathematically.

The student wants to emphasize a similarity between the Heliocentric and Geocentric theories. Which choice most effectively uses relevant information to accomplish this goal?

(A) The Heliocentric and Geocentric models are both widely accepted by scientists today.
(B) Both the Heliocentric and Geocentric models incorporate rotational movement.
(C) The Geocentric and Heliocentric models both were widely known by the citizens of Ancient Greece.
(D) Aristotle and Copernicus were both eminent scientists who lived in Ancient Greece.

Answer Explanations

1. **(B)** The student wants to create an example of someone who is likely to be harmed by inflation. Based on the notes, someone who has fixed income payments would likely find inflation detrimental because their purchasing power would decrease over time. A retiree with a set income each month would fall under this description. It is not (A) or (C), because these represent fixed debt payments that would become relatively less expensive over time. It is not (D), because this person would not be significantly impacted by changes in the money supply since they do not need as much money to grow their own food as they would if they purchased the food at a store.

2. **(B)** *While* is the only option that provides a contrast within the sentence between how Marjorie is preferred socially and her rudeness.

3. **(A)** A contrasting transition is required here. Essentially, the idea of the text is that "while images are used often in society, words require more cognitive processing." "Although" is the only option to achieve that contrast. Choices (B) and (C) express cause and effect, while choice (D) is acceptable when the passage is listing multiple things along the same thought process.

4. **(A)** This is the only option that expresses the needed contrast between the previous sentence and the current one since there is a contrast between the glorious construction of the Parthenon and the fact that the glory was very short-lived. The other options do not express the needed contrast.

5. **(D)** "Take, for example, . . . " or "take, for instance, . . . " are common English phrases. Moreover, Americans and football function as an example of how sports can "unite us far more than they divide us." Either of these two thought processes would have led you to the correct answer, choice (D).

6. **(C)** Choice (C) logically connects the previous sentence that makes a general claim about the story, and the following sentence that provides specific support for the claim. It is not choice (A) because there is not a contrast. It is not choice (B) because the following sentence provides an elaboration, not additional information. Choice (D) is incorrect because the current sentence is simply expanding on the previous one, not showing cause and effect.

7. **(B)** Both the Geocentric and Heliocentric models involve "revolving" of astronomical bodies, meaning they both incorporate rotational movement. It is not (A) because the notes indicate that the Heliocentric theory became dominant. It is not (C) because there is no evidence in the notes to suggest that citizens in Ancient Greece widely knew these theories. It is not (D) because the nationality of Copernicus is not mentioned in the notes.

Standard English Conventions Practice Questions Set 1

1. The United States is the only country in the world to use an electoral college system to elect its chief executive. Each state has a certain number of electors based on _____ of senators and congresspersons.

   Which choice completes the text so that it conforms to the conventions of Standard English?

   (A) there number
   (B) their numbers
   (C) its number
   (D) our number

2. The areas of _____ of ways people use their time—that an occupational therapist considers when working with clients include activities of daily living, instrumental activities of daily living, rest and sleep, education, work, play, leisure, and social participation.

   Which choice completes the text so that it conforms to the conventions of Standard English?

   (A) occupations—or categories
   (B) occupations: categories
   (C) occupations; or categories
   (D) occupations, or categories

3. Among many discoveries, the Voyager 2 spacecraft _____volcanic activity—the first time another astronomical body was found to have this earth-like characteristic.

   Which choice completes the text so that it conforms to the conventions of Standard English?

   (A) found that Io a moon of Jupiter has
   (B) found that Io, a moon of Jupiter has
   (C) found that Io, a moon of Jupiter, has
   (D) found that Io a moon, of Jupiter has

4. Following physicist Carl D. Anderson's 1932 gamma ray _____ anticipated the discovery of negatively baryon-charged antimatter throughout the universe in quantities that would precisely counterbalance the positive baryon charge of matter.

   Which choice completes the text so that it conforms to the conventions of Standard English?

   (A) experiment which demonstrated the existence of antimatter, scientists
   (B) experiment, which demonstrated the existence of antimatter, scientists
   (C) experiment; which demonstrated the existence of antimatter, scientists
   (D) experiment which demonstrated the existence of antimatter scientists

5. The innate immune system _____ of two major barriers: the skin and the natural flora (i.e., naturally occurring bacteria).

   Which choice completes the text so that it conforms to the conventions of Standard English?

   (A) consist
   (B) consists
   (C) consisting
   (D) to consist

6. When struck by a wave of electromagnetic radiation, every element _____ an *excited state*, in which the electrons surrounding the nucleus *jump* to higher energy levels.

   Which choice completes the text so that it conforms to the conventions of Standard English?

   (A) enter
   (B) entering
   (C) enters
   (D) entries

7. Now, more than ever, science is beginning to understand the deleterious effects of prolonged stress, _____

   Which choice completes the text so that it conforms to the conventions of Standard English?

   (A) including—but far from limited to, hypertension, obesity, and heart disease.
   (B) including—but far from limited to hypertension, obesity, and heart disease.
   (C) including—but far from limited to; hypertension, obesity, and heart disease.
   (D) including—but far from limited to—hypertension, obesity, and heart disease.

Answer Explanations

1. **(C)** "Its" refers to each singular state taken on its own, not as part of a group, while the other options do not have the number agreement established in the context.

2. **(A)** A dash is needed to set off the parenthetical phrase in the same way the parenthetical phrase is ended, namely with another dash. (B) and (C) are incorrect because a complete sentence must come before a semicolon or a colon. (D) would start the parenthetical phrase with a comma, while it ends with a dash—this would be fine if it also ended with a dash.

3. **(C)** The commas correctly surround the clarification of what Io is. This is known as an "appositive," which is when an interchangeable name for what comes before is surrounded with commas. For example: "My oldest daughter, the Prime Minster, is well respected." The other options do not provide sufficient pauses.

4. **(B)** The sentence can still function as a complete sentence without the phrase "which demonstrated the existence of antimatter," so it is appropriate to use commas to set it aside. Choice (A) does not have a necessary pause before the phrase, choice (C) does not have the necessary completed sentence before the semicolon, and choice (D) has no pauses whatsoever.

5. **(B)** The subject is "system," a singular subject requiring a corresponding singular verb: "consists" is a singular verb. Eliminate choice (A) for using a plural verb. Eliminate choice (C), which uses a gerund, ultimately leading to a sentence fragment. Choice (D) uses an infinitive verb, and conjugation is required for a full sentence.

6. **(C)** The subject of this sentence, "element," is singular. Even though the author is referring to many different elements, she is doing so one element at a time. So the singular verb *enters* is needed. Choice (A) is plural, choice (B) is progressive, and choice (D) is a noun.

7. **(D)** "But far from limited to" is a parenthetical phrase; remove it and the sentence still functions effectively. Parenthetical phrases can be surrounded with two commas or two dashes. Choice (A) is close, but it breaks parallelism by using a dash and then a comma instead of the same punctuation mark twice, as required.

Standard English Conventions Practice Questions Set 2

1. She instructs Bernice in social protocol in a
_____ sentences, causing the reader to question the frivolous hedonism that dominates the early twentieth century.

   Which choice completes the text so that it conforms to the conventions of Standard English?

   (A) few short
   (B) short few
   (C) few, short
   (D) short, few

2. Although the digital age has understandably discouraged popularity in some traditional forms of _____
_____ is the digital platform more than making up for the moderate declines in traditional news sources, but also research shows that Americans are spending more time consuming news than they have since the early 1990s.

   Which choice completes the text so that it conforms to the conventions of Standard English?

   (A) news media the field itself is optimistic, not only
   (B) news media, the field itself is optimistic, not only
   (C) news media, the field itself is optimistic: not only
   (D) news media the field itself; is optimistic not only

3. The building's miraculous design comes not from its magnitude, but from the curvatures between its platform and columns that offer an illusion of symmetry that exceeds its true dimensions, and in the elaborate engravings within its marble surfaces _____ centuries of calamity.

   Which choice completes the text so that it conforms to the conventions of Standard English?

   (A) that having to outlast
   (B) which has to outlast
   (C) that have outlasted
   (D) which had outlasted

4. While Neanderthals appear to have maintained a stable population during the Ice Age,
_____ leaving only the strongest and most intelligent to survive and carry on the species.

   Which choice completes the text so that it conforms to the conventions of Standard English?

   (A) a drastic genetic bottleneck was experienced by our African ancestors,
   (B) a drastic genetic bottleneck by our African ancestors was experienced,
   (C) our African ancestors drastically experienced a bottleneck that was genetic,
   (D) our African ancestors experienced a drastic genetic bottleneck,

5. Griselda consents to each demand precisely as she promised on their wedding day, and one begins to imagine that the Marquis is not so much testing his wife's devotion _____ exploring the extent to which his power reaches.

   Which choice completes the text so that it conforms to the conventions of Standard English?

   (A) so they are
   (B) when they were
   (C) so he was
   (D) as he is

6. Occupational therapists work with many clients on any given day. If activities occupy _____ schedules, occupational therapists can provide treatments.

   Which choice completes the text so that it conforms to the conventions of Standard English?

   (A) their clients'
   (B) they're clients
   (C) there client's
   (D) their clients

7. Although in life the two considered themselves plenary _____ begin to realize that the worlds envisioned by Strindberg and Ibsen were perhaps not so different as they believed.

   Which choice completes the text so that it conforms to the conventions of Standard English?

   (A) opposites as drama continues to evolve into the postmodern era, we may
   (B) opposites as drama continues, to evolve into the postmodern era we may
   (C) opposites, as drama continues to evolve into the postmodern era, we may
   (D) opposites as drama continues to evolve into the postmodern era we may

Answer Explanations

1. **(A)** When adjectives have to be ordered a certain way to provide a logical meaning, there should be no commas separating them. In this case, it only makes sense to use *few short sentences*, not *short few sentences*, making choice (A) the only viable option. Choices (B) and (D) change the meaning, and choice (C) has an unnecessary comma.

2. **(C)** This choice places a comma after the introductory dependent clause ending in *media* and puts a colon before a clarification of how the field is optimistic. Choice (A) lacks a necessary comma after *media* and leads to a run-on sentence. Choice (B) leads to a run-on. Choice (D) puts a semicolon between a subject and a verb, which should not be separated.

3. **(C)** The fact that these engravings have lasted for a long time is an essential part of their description, so *that* is needed instead of *which*. Choice (C) also uses the proper tense. Choice (A) uses the incorrect verb tense. Choices (B) and (D) use *which*, which works for nonessential characteristics of described objects.

4. **(D)** This choice concisely expresses the idea using logical word order. Choices (A) and (B) use passive voice. Choice (C) jumbles the word order such that the meaning is confused.

5. **(D)** This phrase completes the idiomatic expression *is not so much . . . as he is*. The other options do not connect appropriately to this earlier phrasing.

6. **(A)** "Their" shows possession by the occupational therapists, and "clients'" shows that the time belongs to the plural "clients." It is not (B) because "they're" is the conjunction for "they are," and it is not (C) because "there" refers to a place. Choice (D) is missing the apostrophe that shows possession.

7. **(C)** The commas set aside the phrase *as drama continues to evolve into the postmodern era* that leads into the rest of the sentence. Choice (A) lacks a needed comma. Choice (B) breaks up the phrase *continues to evolve*. Choice (D) gives no break whatsoever.

Troubleshooting

Here are some further pointers for common issues.

"I never learned grammar rules."
- Review the concepts presented throughout this chapter—the rules are presented in an extremely concise, easy-to-grasp way.
- Realize that you don't need to know the precise grammatical terminology for a concept being tested. As long as you have a good sense of what is correct, you do not need to give an elaborate justification for your answer—simply get it right.
- Actually read the editing marks and comments teachers make on your papers. Instead of just looking at your grade, look at what grammar mistakes you made and be sure you understand *why* they were mistakes. That way, you will gradually remedy gaps in your grammar knowledge.

"I finish too quickly."
- Try reading the text before you look at the question and choices. Having a sense of the broad flow of the text can be useful to you in answering many of the writing questions, especially the ones about transitions. Throughly reviewing the text will be a more effective use of your time than doing nothing for several minutes at the end of the Reading and Writing section.
- Pace yourself to take the full amount of time per question. If you do not check your time as you go, you will likely rush to the end. Try to take the full 70 seconds per question.

"I finish too slowly."
- Do not spend time overanalyzing your choice after you have made it. If you have read enough context and fully understand the requirements of the question, you have done all you can do; it is time to pick an answer choice and move on.
- Practice with timing so that on test day you do not fall prey to "paralysis by analysis." Any tendencies you have to go too slowly will only be exacerbated by the stresses of the actual PSAT.
- Try to spend no more than 90 seconds on a difficult question. If you have spent this much time and are not getting anywhere, you should cut your losses and take a guess. After all, there is no guessing penalty on the PSAT. You will not need to answer every question correctly to achieve National Merit recognition.

Further Preparation

What else can I do beyond the drills and practice tests in this book to prepare for the PSAT Writing?

TIP

Don't forget to try the drills in chapter 4, "Advanced Writing Drills," for more challenging practice.

- Try the online PSAT Writing exercises that accompany this book for more targeted practice.
- Practice with the other Barron's books for the SAT: *Barron's Digital SAT* has plenty of practice tests you can try.
- Use the free practice tests and resources provided by the College Board on *KhanAcademy.org*.
- Practice with ACT English tests—the grammar concepts and editing skills tested on the ACT are virtually identical to those tested on the PSAT Writing questions.
- Edit your friends' papers, and have them edit yours. The more practice you have with editing, the better you will do.
- Read a variety of high-quality texts so that you develop a great feel for excellent writing.

4

Advanced Writing Drills

The following drills are designed to represent the most difficult types of questions you could encounter on the Digital PSAT Writing section.

Advanced Writing Drill 1

1. Cliff's novel is within the tradition of Jamaica Kincaid's *Annie John* _____ Kempadoo's *Buxton Spice* (1999), and Edwidge Danticat's *Clare of the Sea Light* (2013), in which young Caribbean girls' gender awakenings coincide with their political awakenings while they struggle to construct a Black female self without coherent mother-daughter relationships and without a clear sense of history.

   Which choice completes the text so that it conforms to the conventions of Standard English?

   (A) (1985) Merle Hodge's *Crick Crack Monkey* (1981), Oonya
   (B) (1985), Merle Hodge's *Crick Crack Monkey* (1981) Oonya
   (C) (1985) Merle Hodge's, *Crick Crack Monkey* (1981) Oonya
   (D) (1985), Merle Hodge's *Crick Crack Monkey* (1981), Oonya

2. In a court of law, a judge is the public official who presides over the hearing and is ultimately responsible for the administration of justice. An attorney or a lawyer advises and represents individuals, businesses, or agencies in legal disputes. Defense attorneys and prosecutors are the specific names given to lawyers who represent the accused or who represent local, state, or federal agencies as they accuse others of crimes, respectively. The jury consists of a body of people appointed to listen, consider evidence, and give a verdict on a _____ of the defendant's peers. Responsible for maintaining order in the court is an officer, much like a police officer.

   Which choice completes the text so that it conforms to the conventions of Standard English?

   (A) specific trial—essentially, jurors represent a panel
   (B) specific trial, essentially jurors represent a panel
   (C) specific trial: essentially jurors represent, a panel
   (D) specific trial; essentially jurors, represent a panel

3. The increased use of smartphones and Internet technology has profoundly affected how we interact with our friends and family. Class reunions and opening holiday greeting cards _____ highly anticipated events that would offer updates on the goings-on of distant acquaintances. Now, a quick scan of a social media feed gives a real-time update.

   Which choice completes the text so that it conforms to the conventions of Standard English?

   (A) was once
   (B) has been the
   (C) were once
   (D) is now

4. In contemporary critical work examining female subjectivities in _____ fiction, there is a tendency to privilege the overt insurgent over more subtle representations of resistance. For most, it seems that the better story lies with psychically fragmented protagonists deviating from the world in which they live.

Which choice completes the text so that it conforms to the conventions of Standard English?

(A) womens'
(B) women's
(C) womans'
(D) womens

5. He understood firsthand how being ashamed of your dental health can _____ your whole demeanor. He was so conscientious about his smile that he would never show his teeth in photographs.

Which choice completes the text so that it conforms to the conventions of Standard English?

(A) effect
(B) effects
(C) affects
(D) affect

6. The scientist's findings from her research showed great promise. Unfortunately, the scientist's grant for her biomedical research project was drastically cut. _____ she persisted with the project by making her processes more efficient and finding a new, albeit less generous, source of funding.

Which choice completes the text with the most logical transition?

(A) In other words,
(B) Regardless,
(C) Thus,
(D) In fact,

7. While researching a topic, a student has taken the following notes:

- Most *Microbial* products for crops consist of four specific microbes: *Rhizobia*, *Arbuscular mycorrhizal fungi*, *Trichoderma*, and *Bacillus*.
- These bacteria are naturally occurring in most soils, but there may not be enough to make an impact.
- Research has shown varying results for the success of these microbial products in improving crop production.
- The bacteria can help with disease suppression and increase nutrient uptake.
- They are also highly dependent on the pre-existing microbial communities in the soil, climate, and the soil pH.

The student wants to make a qualified statement about the possible impact of microbial products on improving crop yields. Which choice most effectively uses relevant information from the notes to accomplish this goal?

(A) Microbial products, like *Bacillus* and *Arbuscular mycorrhizal fungi*, are unfortunately able to have a positive impact on improving crop production due to their dependence on pre-existing microbial communities.
(B) While microbial products, like *Rhizobia* and *Trichoderma*, may help to suppress disease, their impact may be limited since much depends on other factors like the climate and soil pH.
(C) Bacterial species, which come in several different subtypes like *Bacillus* and *Rhizobia*, have been instrumental in helping farmers fight disease by increasing the nutrients in their soil.
(D) Even though microbial products are used by some farmers to combat disease and low nutrient consumption, their use among agricultural operators has been generally limited.

8. While researching a topic, a student has taken the following notes:

- Impressionism was a revolutionary art movement that started in France around the 19th century.
- A famous American painter of that time was Frederick Childe Hassam, producing over 3,000 painting oils, watercolors, etchings, and lithographs.
- He played a pivotal role in promoting impressionism to American collectors.
- Inspired by a "Preparedness Parade" in New York, Hassam created "The Flag" series comprised of 30 paintings.
- The patriotic parade showed local support for U.S. entry into WWI.

The student wants to highlight the artistic mediums utilized by an important artist. Which choice most effectively uses relevant information from the notes to accomplish this goal?

(A) The inspiration for Hassam's work "The Flag" was a newspaper report advocating U.S. entry into the first World War.

(B) American collectors became interested in purchasing non-traditional impressionist artworks in large part thanks to the influence of Frederick Childe Hassam.

(C) Both French and American artists made use of the revolutionary impressionist approach as they created works that increasingly became popular in the 20th century.

(D) The important American impressionist Frederick Childe Hassam used oils, watercolors, etchings, and lithographs to create his works.

Answer Explanations

1. **(D)** Notice the pattern here: there is an author, a title, a year, and then a comma. Eliminate choices (A) and (C) for neglecting the comma after "(1985)." Eliminate choice (B) since it does not include a comma after "(1981)."

2. **(A)** The clause up to the word "trial" is independent, as is the clause after "trial." Accordingly, sufficient punctuation is needed to separate the two. Eliminate choice (B) because it is a comma splice. In the second clause, "jurors represent a panel of the defendant's peers," there should be no punctuation separating the subject and predicate. Choices (C) and (D) both add unnecessary commas.

3. **(C)** Choice (C) uses a plural and past tense verb, "were," which is consistent with the fact that this refers to a past situation and that there is a compound subject of "reunions" and "cards." All the other choices use singular verb forms.

4. **(B)** A choice is needed that encompasses fiction of women. A possessive is required, and possession is demonstrated using "s." "Women" is unusual in that because the word is already plural without an "s," the apostrophe comes before the "s" even though the word is plural. Choice (D) can be eliminated, as it has no apostrophe. Choice (C) can be eliminated, as it reads as fiction of womans. Choice (A) can be eliminated as it reads as fiction of womens. Choice (B) is the only logical option.

5. **(D)** After the verb "can," an infinitive verb is required. Eliminate choices (B) and (C) because they are conjugated verbs. "Effect" is rarely used as a verb, but when it is, it means "to bring about." "Affect" means "to influence." The sentence is much more logical with "influence," so "affect" is the correct answer.

6. **(B)** "Regardless" is synonymous with "despite," which makes sense as the transition here because it would show that even though the scientist didn't have as much funding, she still managed to figure out a way to make her project work. This transition does not introduce a clarification, making "in other words" and "in fact" illogical. It also is not showing a cause-and-effect relationship, making "thus" incorrect.

7. **(B)** A "qualified" statement indicates that there will be an exception to a broader statement. Choice (B) effectively accomplishes this goal by stating that "while" certain products can help suppress disease, their impact may be limited. Choices (A) and (C) make broader statements without any qualification. Choice (D) makes a qualifying statement but does not incorporate sufficient information from the notes to do so.

8. **(D)** An artistic medium refers to what an artwork is made of. Choice (D) refers to "oils, watercolors, etchings, and lithographs," making this the only option that refers to the artistic mediums. Choice (A) focuses on the inspiration for an artwork, choice (B) focuses on how Hassam influenced American collectors, and choice (C) talks about an artistic philosophy.

Advanced Writing Drill 2

1. The extent of one's extracurricular participation is a vital factor in college admissions decisions. There are innumerable ways to become involved in your school and _____ a new club, and volunteering as a tutor or mentor.

    Which choice completes the text so that it conforms to the conventions of Standard English?

    (A) community, running for class office, starting
    (B) community running, for class office starting
    (C) community running for class office; starting
    (D) community: running for class office, starting

2. Carbon dioxide—a carbon atom joined to two oxygen atoms—can be detrimental in excess quantities. Furthermore, when joined with only one oxygen atom, carbon forms a toxic gas known as carbon monoxide and _____ sometimes the cause of fatal poisonings.

    Which choice completes the text so that it conforms to the conventions of Standard English?

    (A) are
    (B) is
    (C) were
    (D) am

3. Like many of history's most legendary battles, the lawless family feud between the Hatfields and McCoys boiled down to the differences between two men. William Anderson Hatfield, known widely as "Devil Anse," was a mountain dweller and successful timber merchant. Randolph McCoy, or "Ole Ran'l," _____. The clash between the two families brands the American memory—in the Midwest, the vendetta rivals that of the Capulets and Montagues.

    Which choice completes the text so that it conforms to the conventions of Standard English?

    (A) owned some land, and livestock in the same region; the borderlands dividing Kentucky and West Virginia.
    (B) owned some land, and livestock in the same region, the borderlands dividing Kentucky and West Virginia.

    (C) owned some land and livestock in the same region, the borderlands dividing Kentucky and West Virginia.
    (D) owned some land and livestock in the same region the borderlands dividing Kentucky and West Virginia.

4. For centuries, North America's continental shelf has ground against the Juan de Fuca plate, and the shelf has been compressed upward all the while—every moment, every day, every century, a little bit more all the time. Predictions are that this sort of unrelenting stress _____ breaking point of both literal and figurative nature.

    Which choice completes the text so that it conforms to the conventions of Standard English?

    (A) is approaching its
    (B) is approaching their
    (C) are approaching its
    (D) are approaching their

5. Enjoyment of fiction novels stimulates the _____ consider what it would have been like to be at some historical event, or to form a picture of what one could accomplish in life.

    Which choice completes the text so that it conforms to the conventions of Standard English?

    (A) imagination to identify with a hero in a story, to
    (B) imagination: to identify with a hero in a story, to
    (C) imagination; to identify with a hero in a story, to
    (D) imagination, to identify with a hero in a story to

6. When I was young, I could not put down books. I read all the Harry Potter books several times over and was a big fan of other fantasy and science fiction texts. Once I entered middle school, I lost much of the joy of reading. _____ reading for fun, I had to read certain books for summer reading. Not only did I have to read them, but I also had to take careful notes on the texts because when school started again, there would inevitably be a major reading test.

Which choice completes the text with the most logical transition?

(A) Since I loved

(B) As a result of

(C) In addition to

(D) Instead of

7. While researching a topic, a student took the following notes:

- There are many theories in psychology that work to explain the personalities of humans and how they come about.
- The Trait theory takes the stance that people are born with established personality characteristics.
- The traits are inherited at birth and are consistent in all situations.
- The Social Learning Behavior theory states that all behavior is learned through interaction with the environment.
- People who follow this line of thinking tend to look at the family of origin to find behavioral patterns.

The student wants to emphasize a similarity between two psychological theories. Which choice most effectively uses relevant information from the notes to accomplish this goal?

(A) Social Learning Behavior theory and Trait theory are both widely used by behavioral scientists and psychologists across a variety of medical settings.

(B) While Trait theory suggests that personality characteristics are inherited, the Social Learning Behavior theory suggests that personalities are molded through nurturing.

(C) Both the Social Learning Behavior theory and the Trait theory are used by psychologists to explain the origins of human personalities.

(D) Both the Trait theory and Social Learning Behavior theory emphasize the importance of observational analysis of the interpersonal interactions of a research subject's family.

8. While researching a topic, a student has taken the following notes:

- Comparative mythology is the comparison of myths from different cultures.
- This study has helped with tracing the origins of culture and religions.
- An example of this can be seen in a sky god's name in Greek, Roman, and Indian traditions.
- Zeus Pater, Jupiter, and Dyaus Pitr are all linguistically similar names of a Greek, Roman, and Indian sky god.
- Some suggest that this similarity points to a common ancestral culture.

The student wants to give an example of comparative mythological analysis so that a reader may be able to better recognize this sort of analysis in other cases. Which choice most effectively uses relevant information from the notes to accomplish this goal?

(A) By evaluating the linguistic similarities among names of the same spiritual entity, comparative mythologists can explain why many cultures today have the same fundamental religious beliefs.

(B) Zeus Pater, Jupiter, and Dyaus Pitr are names used to identify the same god of the sky, illustrating the common religious beliefs of Greeks, Romans, and Indians in the modern era.

(C) Comparative mythologists trace the origins of culture and religions by looking for underlying connections, such as by noting that the names of the Greek, Roman, and Indian sky god have linguistically similar names.

(D) The linguistic analysis of the names of Zeus Pater, Jupiter, and Dyaus Pitr is the most influential example of the comparative mythological academic discipline.

Answer Explanations

1. **(D)** A colon is appropriate here as it sets off a list of three different ways that one can become involved. Choices (A) and (B) do not provide a sufficient pause, and choice (C) does not work because a semicolon must have a complete sentence both before and after.

2. **(B)** The subject is difficult to isolate, but it is "carbon." This is a singular noun that requires a singular verb, making "is" the correct option. "Are" and "were" are used with plural nouns. "Am" would be used with the first-person "I," not the third person "carbon" as in this sentence.

3. **(C)** The first issue is not to include an unnecessary comma between "land and livestock." No comma is required in a list of just two items. Eliminate choices (A) and (B) for that reason. Choice (D) neglects necessary punctuation after "region," rendering it a run-on sentence. Choice (C) correctly places a comma before the dependent clause that clarifies "region."

4. **(A)** The subject is the singular word "stress," making a singular verb like "is" necessary. Eliminate choices (C) and (D) for using plural verbs. Next, the possessive pronoun form of one thing is "its." "Their" is used for multiple items, as in choice (B). Choice (A) is therefore the correct answer.

5. **(B)** The independent clause is "Enjoyment of fiction novels stimulates the imagination." The sentence best functions by using a colon, and then listing the various ways it stimulates the imagination. Choice (B) does this perfectly. Choice (A) is a run-on sentence. Choice (C) incorrectly uses a semicolon; there must be a full sentence on both sides of the semicolon, but there isn't a full sentence after the semicolon here. Choice (D) incorrectly attaches a list to the independent clause.

6. **(D)** The previous sentence establishes that the narrator has lost joy in reading. The current sentence explains how this shift in attitude came about—namely, rather than reading recreationally, the narrator was required to read certain texts. Choice (D) is the only option that shows this contrast. Choices (A) and (B) both show cause and effect, and choice (C) indicates a list of ideas.

7. **(C)** Since the Trait theory argues that human personality traits are inherited and the Social Learning Behavior theory argues that human personality traits are learned, they would both be used to explain the origins of human personalities, making choice (C) correct. It is not choice (A) because the notes do not talk about the use of these theories in medical settings. It is not choice (B) because this would state a difference between the theories. It is not choice (D) because only the Social Learning Behavior theory focuses on the family of origin.

8. **(C)** Choice (C) is the only option that gives an example of a comparative mythological analysis by mentioning how the names of the different gods have similar names. Choice (A) does not give a specific example of the analysis. Choice (B) incorrectly confuses the beliefs of ancient cultures and modern ones. Choice (D) mentions the linguistic analysis but fails to explain its conclusion, making it difficult for a reader to recognize similar analysis in the future.

Advanced Writing Drill 3

1. U.S. presidents tend to be married with children and hold advanced degrees in law or business from elite universities. Most candidates possess resumes boasting of years in public service and political positions; the fast track to presidential candidacy comprises elected posts like mayor, governor, and senator. _____ years in diplomatic service are a dime a dozen in presidential races. One needs money, and plenty of it, to run for the presidency.

    Which choice completes the text so that it conforms to the conventions of Standard English?

    (A) Still allure, a spotless background, and
    (B) Still, allure, a spotless background, and
    (C) Still, allure a spotless background and
    (D) Still, allure a spotless background, and

2. Taking a risk involves the understanding that various outcomes can arise when you make a choice. _____ But hiding behind every one of these possible futures is the uncertainty of which one or some hybrid of several will actually occur. An effective manager has the confidence to face these outcomes and the inherent unknowns.

    Which choice completes the text so that it conforms to the conventions of Standard English?

    (A) Some outcomes may spell disaster for your company, others may create exceptional financial returns for the shareholders.
    (B) Some outcomes, may spell disaster for your company: others may create exceptional financial returns for the shareholders.
    (C) Some outcomes—may spell disaster for your company—others may create exceptional financial returns for the shareholders.
    (D) Some outcomes may spell disaster for your company; others may create exceptional financial returns for the shareholders.

3. If you are on vacation, take advantage of "away" messages and _____ informing people that you will be available to respond upon your return. If you can take control of technology rather than letting it control you, you will be empowered to

have the benefits of new technology while minimizing its pitfalls.

Which choice completes the text so that it conforms to the conventions of Standard English?

(A) as your gatekeeper let the computer serve,
(B) the computer you should let as your gatekeeper serve,
(C) let the computer serve as your gatekeeper,
(D) the computer should be served by you as the gatekeeper,

4. The title of Erna Brodber's third novel, *Louisiana*, has a triple meaning: it refers to a state in the United States, a place of the same name in Jamaica, and the name taken by Ella _____ Ultimately, the word's fluidity emphasizes the connection between African Americans and African Caribbeans, as well as between the living and dead.

    Which choice completes the text so that it conforms to the conventions of Standard English?

    (A) Townsend the novel's protagonist.
    (B) Townsend; the novel's protagonist.
    (C) Townsend, the novel's protagonist.
    (D) Townsend: the novels protagonist.

5. The career office is called by different names on different campuses, but its job remains the same—_____ Be sure to take full advantage of this resource when you are on your college campus.

    Which choice completes the text so that it conforms to the conventions of Standard English?

    (A) a job upon graduation to help students secure.
    (B) helping upon graduation to secure a student job.
    (C) to help students secure jobs upon graduation.
    (D) helping secure upon graduation for students jobs.

6. Court reporting, an often-overlooked occupation of legal services, is essential to trials, depositions, committee meetings, and basically any legal proceeding you can think of. A court reporter provides a verbatim record of court proceedings using recording equipment, stenographs, and steno-masks. _____ a court reporter transcribes any spoken dialogue, recorded speech, gestures, actions, etc. that occur in a legal environment where exact record of occurrences is mandatory. Hence, the oversight does not reflect the significance of the occupation itself. Court reporters are very important to the judicial system.

Which choice completes the text with the most logical transition?

(A) For this reason,
(B) In other words,
(C) In contrast,
(D) Because of this

7. While researching a topic, a student has taken the following notes:

- In 1728, Benjamin Franklin came up with the idea to make a magazine for the North American colonies.
- The magazine was named *The Pennsylvania Gazette*.
- Publication ended in the 1800s, but the old print shop remained in business.
- In 1821, *The Saturday Evening Post* began publishing in that same printing shop at 53 Market Street.
- Ben Franklin's old printing press was used to publish these new issues.
- The publisher of *The Saturday Evening Post* also used the same style as Franklin.

The student wants to point out the connections between *The Pennsylvania Gazette* and *The Saturday Evening Post* to an audience unfamiliar with these publications. Which choice most effectively uses relevant information from the notes to accomplish this goal?

(A) While *The Pennsylvania Gazette* focused on colonial affairs, *The Saturday Evening Post* brought a more cosmopolitan focus to the news when the United States expanded West.

(B) Utilizing the same printing press and location as Ben Franklin used for *The Pennsylvania Gazette*, *The Saturday Evening Post* continued a North American publication tradition.

(C) Using more modern printing techniques, *The Saturday Evening Post* built on the example of *The Pennsylvania Gazette* as it grew its base of subscribers.

(D) Under the direction of Ben Franklin, *The Saturday Evening Post* and *The Pennsylvania Gazette* were influential news publications in the state of Pennsylvania.

8. While researching a topic, a student has taken the following notes:

- Temporomandibular disorder (TMD) is a secondary headache disorder that affects more than a quarter of the general population.
- Issues in the muscles and joints of the jaw cause clicking, jaw locking, and disability.
- Dr. Jordan Keys, DO, investigated the use of osteopathic manipulative treatment (OMT) to improve patients' symptoms.
- They try unilateral TMJ dysfunction muscle energy to target the muscles involved in chewing, i.e., the ones in pain.
- This approach involves the direct movement of the joint and joint musculature.
- Current literature shows these techniques to be an effective, conservative, first-line treatment.

The student wants to emphasize the extent to which OMT could be used to treat TMD. Which choice most effectively uses relevant information from the notes to accomplish this goal?

(A) For patients in need of a non-invasive, low-risk initial treatment option for TMD, OMT could make sense.

(B) OMT provides a comprehensive cure for those patients suffering from the painful effects of TMD, including jaw locking and clicking.

(C) Unfortunately, the treatment options for TMD are limited to the rather conservative OMT technique; research is needed to uncover a more effective treatment option.

(D) While OMT is a good option for first-line treatment of TMD, surgical options may be necessary for those with a more severe prognosis.

Answer Explanations

1. **(B)** "*Still*" is separate from the main clause. (In effect if you remove "still," the clause is still logical.) So, you must place a comma after "*still*" to denote that required separation. Eliminate choice (A) accordingly. From that point in the sentence is a list of three things: "allure, a spotless background, and years in diplomatic service." Eliminate choices (C) and (D) for neglecting the comma after "allure."

2. **(D)** There are two independent clauses, with the first ending at "company" and the second beginning at "others." Choice (A) is a comma splice. Choice (B) includes an unnecessary comma after "outcomes." Choice (C) incorrectly attempts to employ a parenthetical phrase. Choice (D), however, correctly links the two independent clauses with a semicolon.

3. **(C)** Choice (C) maintains the parallel structure established earlier in the sentence in which the narrator directly addresses the reader, stating that he or she should "take advantage." The other options all lack this parallel structure.

4. **(C)** This choice properly places a comma before the clarifying description; it also correctly uses the apostrophe and an "s" after "novel" to indicate singular possession. Choice (A) is incorrect because there is no break before the clarifying phrase. The answer is not choice (B) because a semicolon must have a complete sentence both before and after it. Choice (D) is incorrect because this option does not properly show possession.

5. **(C)** Choice (C) puts the wording in a logical sequence. The other options do not have word sequences that flow logically, making it difficult for the reader to fully grasp what is happening.

6. **(B)** Notice that choices (A) and (D) convey the exact same meaning. As there can be only one correct answer, eliminate those two (the relationship is not causal). Choice (C) declares a contrast, but this sentence does not contrast with the previous one. What does happen is that the second sentence restates the first sentence in a more explanatory fashion. "In other words" is the correct answer.

7. **(B)** As stated in the question, the goal is to point out the connections between *The Pennsylvania Gazette* and *The Saturday Evening Post* to an audience unfamiliar with these publications. Choice (B) effectively does this by noting that both publications used the same location and the same printing press. Choice (A) focuses on a difference between the publications. Choice (C) is incorrect because there is no indication that the printing techniques in *The Saturday Evening Post* were more modern than those in the other publication. It is not choice (D) because this is overly vague.

8. **(A)** The goal is to state how much OMT could be used to treat TMD. According to the notes, OMT techniques are an "effective, conservative, first-line treatment." This corresponds to the statement in choice (A) about a "*non-invasive, low-risk initial treatment*" option. It is not choice (B) because the text does not indicate that this treatment is comprehensive. It is not choice (C) because the notes do not clarify the extent of treatment options available. It is not choice (D) because there is no discussion of surgical possibilities.

Math

5

Math Review

What Is Tested on the Math Section?

The following is the typical breakdown of all the Math Test questions from both modules combined:

- Algebra (primarily linear equations and systems): approximately 14 questions
- Problem-Solving and Data Analysis (primarily demonstrating literacy with data and real-world applications): approximately 8 questions
- Advanced Math (primarily more complicated equations): approximately 13 questions
- Geometry and Trigonometry: approximately 5 questions

If you have studied Algebra 1, Geometry, and Algebra 2, then you most likely will have covered the concepts tested on the PSAT Math sections.

How Should I Use This Chapter?

Examine the following list. If there is anything you need to review or practice, check it out. After you complete the review, try the "Math Essentials Review Quiz" to be sure that you don't have any gaps in your knowledge.

Algebra

- Order of Operations (page 181)
- Substitution and Elimination to Solve a System of Equations (page 183)
- Fractions (page 187)
- Inequalities (page 189)
- Absolute Value (page 191)
- Linear Relationships (page 192)

Problem-Solving and Data Analysis

- Interpreting Functions (page 195)
- Percentages (page 200)
- Ratios, Proportions, and Direct and Inverse Variation (page 202)
- Mean, Median, and Mode (page 205)
- Probability and Statistics (page 207)

Advanced Math

Geometry and Trigonometry

Algebra

Order of Operations

Remember the proper sequence of mathematical operations by using the acronym **PEMDAS:** *Please Excuse My Dear Aunt Sally.*

<u>P</u>arentheses ( ) or other grouping symbols, like $\sqrt{}$ or { }
<u>E</u>xponents x^y
<u>M</u>ultiplication $x \times y$
<u>D</u>ivision $x \div y$
<u>A</u>ddition $x + y$
<u>S</u>ubtraction $x - y$

❯ Example

$$(-2)(4 + 3)^2 = ?$$

✓ Solution

Simplify what is in the parentheses first, square it, and then multiply it by -2.

$$(-2)(4 + 3)^2 =$$
$$(-2)(7)^2 =$$
$$(-2)49 = -98$$

FOIL

Remember how to multiply simple polynomials by "FOILing" the expression. This corresponds to the order in which you multiply parts of the factored expression:

<u>F</u>irst, <u>O</u>uter, <u>I</u>nner, <u>L</u>ast

In the expression $(a + b)(x + y)$, you can simplify by multiplying parts in the FOIL sequence and then simplifying like terms by combining them together:

First $= ax$ Outer $= ay$ Inner $= bx$ Last $= by$

Add them all together: $ax + ay + bx + by$

Here are examples of FOIL in action:

$$(4 + x)(2 - x) = 4 \cdot 2 - 4x + 2x - x^2 = 8 - 2x - x^2$$
$$(x + 2y)(x - 3y) = x \cdot x - 3xy + 2xy - 6y^2 = x^2 - xy - 6y^2$$

Order of Operations Drill

1. $(x + 4) + (x - 2) = ?$

2. $3(m + n) - n = ?$

3. $x^2 + 2x^2 = ?$

4. $\dfrac{2x + 3x}{x} = ?$

5. $\dfrac{3 \times (5n)^2}{n} = ?$

6. $(2 + x)(5 + x) = ?$

7. $(3x - 4)(2x + 5) = ?$

8. $5n(2n + 1)^2 = ?$

9. Solve for x: $2x + 5 = 7$

10. Solve for x: $\dfrac{-5}{x} = 10$

Solutions

1. The parentheses can be ignored since there is nothing on the outside of the parentheses:

$$(x + 4) + (x - 2) =$$
$$x + 4 + x - 2 = 2x + 2$$

2. Distribute the 3 and multiply it by each term within the parentheses. Then combine like terms to simplify:

$$3(m + n) - n =$$
$$3m + 3n - n = 3m + 2n$$

3. Add the like terms together:

$$x^2 + 2x^2 =$$
$$1x^2 + 2x^2 = 3x^2$$

4. Combine the parts on the top, and then divide both the top and bottom by x:

$$\frac{2x + 3x}{x} =$$
$$\frac{5x}{x} =$$
$$\frac{5\cancel{x}}{\cancel{x}} = 5$$

5. First simplify what is in the parentheses by squaring it, and then multiply and divide:

$$\frac{3 \times (5n)^2}{n} =$$
$$\frac{3 \times (25n^2)}{n} =$$
$$\frac{75n^2}{n} = 75n$$

6. FOIL the expression:

$$(2 + x)(5 + x) =$$
$$10 + 2x + 5x + x^2 =$$
$$10 + 7x + x^2 \rightarrow x^2 + 7x + 10$$

7. FOIL the expression:

$$(3x - 4)(2x + 5) =$$
$$6x^2 + 15x - 8x - 20 = 6x^2 + 7x - 20$$

8. First FOIL what is in the parentheses, and then distribute the $5n$ through the expression:

$$5n(2n + 1)^2 =$$
$$5n((2n + 1)(2n + 1)) =$$
$$5n(4n^2 + 4n + 1) = 20n^3 + 20n^2 + 5n$$

(handwritten margin notes)
$$an^2 + bn + c = 0$$
$$an^2 + bn = c \qquad a\left(n^2 + \frac{bn}{a} + \frac{c}{a}\right) = 0$$
$$\frac{a^2bn^2}{ab} + \frac{abn}{ab} = c \qquad a\left(\left(n + \frac{bn}{2a}\right)^2 - \left(\frac{b}{2a}\right)^2 + \frac{c}{a}\right)$$
$$n(an + b) = c \qquad a\left(n + \frac{b}{2a}\right)^2 - \frac{b^2}{4a} + c$$
$$n \cancel{a}$$

9. $2x + 5 = 7$

$\qquad 2x = 7 - 5$

$\qquad 2x = 2$

$\qquad x = 1$

10. $\dfrac{-5}{x} = 10$

$\qquad -5 = 10x$

$\qquad -\dfrac{5}{10} = x$

$\qquad -\dfrac{1}{2} = x$

Substitution and Elimination to Solve a System of Equations

Substitution

A common way to solve a system of equations with two variables is through *substitution* of one variable in terms of the other.

> **Example**

Solve for x and y in the equations below.

$$2x = y$$
$$y - 3x = -5$$

✓ **Solution**

Substitute $2x$ for y in the second equation:

$$(2x) - 3x = -5$$
$$-x = -5$$
$$x = 5$$

Plug 5 in for x into the first equation to solve for y:

$$2x = y$$
$$2(5) = 10$$
$$y = 10$$

Elimination

When two equations are similar to one another, *elimination* of terms and variables may be the easiest way to solve for the variables. Multiply both sides of one of the equations by a number that allows you to add or subtract one equation easily from another, making it easy to eliminate one of the variables.

Two equations have infinitely many solutions if the equations are identical. For example, $x + y = 2$ and $2x + 2y = 4$ together have infinitely many solutions since the equations are simply multiples of one another. Some equations, like $x + y = 2$ and $2x + 2y = 10$, have no solutions. They do not intersect at all because their graphs are parallel to each other.

❯ Example

Solve for both x and y in the system of equations below:

$$3x + 2y = 7$$
$$2x - y = 0$$

✓ Solution

Multiply the second equation by 2:

$$3x + 2y = 7$$
$$4x - 2y = 0$$

Then add the second equation to the first equation to eliminate the y-variables:

$$3x + 2y = 7$$
$$\underline{+4x - 2y = 0}$$
$$7x + 0 = 7$$

Divide both sides by 7 to get the answer: $x = 1$.

Then solve for y by plugging 1 in for x in the first equation:

$$3x + 2y = 7$$
$$3 \times 1 + 2y = 7$$
$$2y = 4$$
$$y = 2$$

The PSAT will generally have systems of equations with one or two variables. Be mindful that there should typically be as many *equations* as there are *variables* in order to solve a given system. For example, in order to solve for two variables, you should have two equations; to solve for three variables, you should have three equations.

Distance, Rate, and Time

When considering the relationship among distance, speed/rate, and time, use the following formula:

$$\text{Distance} = \text{Rate} \times \text{Time}$$

For example, if you were biking 80 miles at 10 miles per hour, it would take you 8 hours to do so. See how that situation fits into the equation:

$$80 \text{ miles} = 10 \, \frac{\text{miles}}{\text{hour}} \times 8 \text{ hours}$$

Variations on the distance, speed/rate, and time formula can also be used to solve for whichever variable is needed:

$$\text{Rate} = \frac{\text{Distance}}{\text{Time}} \text{ and Time} = \frac{\text{Distance}}{\text{Rate}}$$

❯ Example

If Fred has to drive 200 miles in 5 hours, at what average speed should he drive?

✓ **Solution**

Insert the given information into the formula and solve for rate (speed):

$$\text{Distance} = \text{Rate} \times \text{Time}$$

$$200 \text{ miles} = \text{Rate} \times 5 \text{ hours}$$

$$\frac{200}{5} = 40 \text{ miles per hour}$$

With distance, rate, and time questions, be sure to check that the units in the solution (mph, miles, hours, etc.) match the units required by the question.

Substitution and Elimination to Solve a System of Equations Drill

In questions 1 to 5, solve for x and y in these systems of equations:

1. $3x = 2y$
    $x = y + 1$

2. $y = x - 1$
    $7x = -3y + 2$

3. $x + 4y = 2$
    $-x + y = 8$

4. $x - \frac{1}{2}y = 3$
    $2x + y = 10$

5. $4x + 2y = 1$
    $8x + 4y = 2$

6. If Nischal is traveling at 40 miles per hour for 3 hours, how far will he have traveled?

7. What is the rate in feet per second a hockey puck travels if it goes 30 feet in 10 seconds?

Solutions

1. Use substitution to solve this system of equations:

$$3x = 2y$$
$$x = y + 1$$

Plug in $y + 1$ for x into the first equation:

$$3(y + 1) = 2y$$
$$3y + 3 = 2y$$
$$y + 3 = 0$$
$$y = -3$$

Then substitute -3 in for y into the second equation:

$$x = y + 1$$
$$x = -3 + 1$$
$$x = -2$$

So the solution is $x = -2$ and $y = -3$.

2. Use substitution to solve this system of equations:

$$y = x - 1$$
$$7x = -3y + 2$$

Plug in $x - 1$ for y into the second equation:

$$7x = -3(x - 1) + 2$$
$$7x = -3x + 3 + 2$$
$$7x = -3x + 5$$
$$10x = 5$$
$$x = \frac{1}{2}$$

Now, plug this value of x into the first equation:

$$y = x - 1$$
$$y = \frac{1}{2} - 1$$
$$y = -\frac{1}{2}$$

So the solution is $x = \frac{1}{2}$ and $y = -\frac{1}{2}$.

3. Use elimination to solve this system of equations:

$$x + 4y = 2$$
$$\underline{-x + y = 8}$$
$$0 + 5y = 10$$

Then, solve for y:

$$5y = 10$$
$$y = \frac{10}{5}$$
$$y = 2$$

Then, plug 2 back in for y and solve for x:

$$x + 4y = 2$$
$$x + 4(2) = 2$$
$$x + 8 = 2$$
$$x = -6$$

So the solution set is $x = -6$ and $y = 2$.

4. Solve using elimination by doubling the first equation and adding it to the second:

$$2\left(x - \frac{1}{2}y = 3\right) \rightarrow 2x - y = 6$$
$$2x - y = 6$$
$$\underline{2x + y = 10}$$
$$4x + 0 = 16$$

Then solve for x and plug it into either original equation to solve for y:

$$4x = 16$$
$$x = 4$$

$$2x + y = 10$$
$$2(4) + y = 10$$
$$8 + y = 10$$
$$y = 2$$

So the solution is $x = 4$ and $y = 2$.

5. Multiply the first equation by 2 to notice a pattern:

$$4x + 2y = 1$$
$$8x + 4y = 2$$

As you may recognize, this is identical to the second equation: $8x + 4y = 2$.

Since the two equations are identical and would therefore overlap if graphed in the *xy*-plane, there would be *infinitely* many solutions.

6. Multiply the rate by the time to find the total distance:

$$40 \times 3 = 120$$

So Nischal has traveled a total of 120 miles.

7. Divide the distance by the time to find the rate:

$$30 \div 10 = 3$$

So the puck is traveling 3 feet/second.

Fractions

The *numerator* is the number on top of a fraction, while the *denominator* is the number on the bottom of the fraction. For example, in the fraction $\frac{1}{2}$, "1" is the numerator and "2" is the denominator. To simplify fractions, put them in their *lowest terms*. Do so by canceling out the same number as a factor of both the numerator and the denominator. For example:

$$\frac{6}{10} = \frac{3 \cdot 2}{5 \cdot 2} = \frac{3 \cdot 2}{5 \cdot 2} = \frac{3}{5}$$

The number 2 can be taken out of both the numerator and denominator, leaving just $\frac{3}{5}$. We know that the fraction is now in lowest terms because no factors are shared by 3 and 5 besides 1.

Adding and Subtracting Fractions

To add two fractions, follow these two simple steps.

STEP 1 Find the least common denominator of each fraction (i.e., the lowest common multiple of the denominators) so that the fractions have the same number on the bottom.

Consider the problem $\frac{3}{7} + \frac{5}{14}$. The least common multiple of the denominators is 14, so $\frac{3}{7}$ can be rewritten like this:

$$\frac{3}{7} \times \frac{2}{2} = \frac{6}{14}$$

Now both fractions have 14 as the denominator. The addition problem looks like this:

$$\frac{6}{14} + \frac{5}{14} =$$

Let's do our second step to solve the problem.

STEP 2 Once you have the same denominator for the fractions, add their numerators.

With $\frac{6}{14} + \frac{5}{14}$, just add the 6 and 5 together:

$$\frac{6}{14} + \frac{5}{14} = \frac{6 + 5}{14} = \frac{11}{14}$$

To subtract a fraction from another, find the least common denominator and subtract the numerators. For example:

$$\frac{8}{9} - \frac{1}{6} =$$

$$\frac{2}{2}\left(\frac{8}{9}\right) - \frac{3}{3}\left(\frac{1}{6}\right) = \frac{16}{18} - \frac{3}{18}$$

The least common denominator is 18. Now subtract one numerator from the other:

$$\frac{16 - 3}{18} = \frac{13}{18}$$

Multiplying and Dividing Fractions

Multiply fractions using this rule:

$$\frac{a}{b} \cdot \frac{c}{d} = \frac{ac}{bd} \quad \text{(Neither } b \text{ nor } d \text{ can equal zero, or it will be undefined.)}$$

Visualize fraction multiplication with actual numbers:

$$\frac{3}{4} \cdot \frac{2}{5} = \frac{3 \cdot 2}{4 \cdot 5} = \frac{6}{20} \rightarrow \text{reduce the fraction} \rightarrow \frac{3}{10}$$

Divide fractions using the following rule:

$$\frac{a}{b} \div \frac{c}{d} = \frac{a}{b} \cdot \frac{d}{c} \text{ (} b, c, \text{ and } d \text{ cannot equal zero, or it will be undefined.)}$$

Visualize fraction division with actual numbers:

$$\frac{2}{5} \div \frac{3}{4} = \frac{2}{5} \cdot \frac{4}{3} = \frac{8}{15}$$

Fractions Drill

1. Reduce $\frac{12}{18}$ to its lowest terms.

2. Reduce $\frac{2}{7}$ to its lowest terms.

3. $\frac{1}{4} + \frac{3}{4} = ?$

4. $\frac{2}{3} + \frac{1}{9} = ?$

5. $\frac{7}{8} - \frac{1}{2} = ?$

6. $\frac{15}{16} - \frac{3}{4} = ?$

7. $\frac{2}{9} \times \frac{4}{5} = ?$

8. $\frac{2}{3} \times \frac{3}{8} = ?$

9. $\frac{4}{3} \div \frac{1}{3} = ?$

10. $\frac{5}{8} \div \frac{2}{3} = ?$

Solutions

1. $\frac{12}{18} =$

   $\frac{2 \cdot 6}{3 \cdot 6} =$

   $\frac{2 \cdot 6}{3 \cdot 6} = \frac{2}{3}$

2. $\frac{2}{7}$ cannot be reduced further.

3. $\frac{1}{4} + \frac{3}{4} =$

   $\frac{1 + 3}{4} =$

   $\frac{4}{4} = 1$

4. $\frac{2}{3} + \frac{1}{9} =$

   $\frac{6}{9} + \frac{1}{9} = \frac{7}{9}$

5. $\frac{7}{8} - \frac{1}{2} =$

   $\frac{7}{8} - \frac{4}{8} = \frac{3}{8}$

6. $\frac{15}{16} - \frac{3}{4} =$

   $\frac{15}{16} - \frac{12}{16} =$

   $\frac{15 - 12}{16} = \frac{3}{16}$

7. $\frac{2}{9} \times \frac{4}{5} =$

   $\frac{2 \times 4}{9 \times 5} = \frac{8}{45}$

8. $\frac{2}{3} \times \frac{3}{8} =$

   $\frac{2}{3} \times \frac{3}{8} =$

   $\frac{2}{8} = \frac{1}{4}$

9. $\frac{4}{3} \div \frac{1}{3} =$

   $\frac{4}{3} \times \frac{3}{1} =$

   $\frac{4}{3} \times \frac{3}{1} =$

   $\frac{4}{1} = 4$

10. $\frac{5}{8} \div \frac{2}{3} =$

    $\frac{5}{8} \times \frac{3}{2} =$

    $\frac{5 \times 3}{8 \times 2} = \frac{15}{16}$

Inequalities

An inequality is an expression that indicates that something is less than or greater than something else. The open end of the ">" goes toward the larger number. For example:

$$4 < 8 \text{ and } 7 > 2$$

When an inequality has a line underneath the "greater than" sign or the "less than" sign, it indicates that the terms on either side can also equal one another. For example:

$$x \leq 5 \text{ means that } x \text{ is less than or equal to } 5$$

When working with inequalities, solve them just as you would typical equations EXCEPT in two situations:

1. When you multiply or divide both sides of the inequality by a *negative* number, change the direction of the inequality sign.

❯ Example

Solve for x: $-5x > 2$

✓ Solution

Divide both sides by -5 and turn the $>$ around to $<$.

$$-5x > 2$$
$$\frac{-5x}{-5} < \frac{2}{-5}$$
$$\frac{-5x}{-5} < \frac{2}{-5}$$
$$x < -\frac{2}{5}$$

2. If you take the reciprocal with an inequality, and the variables have the same sign (positive or negative), you must change the direction of the inequality sign. If the variables have opposite signs, do not change the direction of the inequality sign.

⟩ Example

Simplify this expression, in which x and y are both positive: $\frac{1}{x} > \frac{1}{y}$

✓ Solution

Cross multiply, and then flip the sign to put the variables in the numerator:

$$\frac{1}{x} > \frac{1}{y}$$
$$x < y$$

When graphing inequalities on a number line, a hollow circle indicates < or > and a solid circle indicates ≤ or ≥. Figure 1 shows the graph of two different inequalities.

$n > 2$ is graphed as:

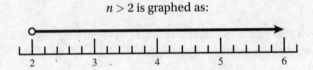

$n \leq 5$ is graphed as:

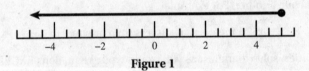

Figure 1

Inequalities Drill

1. Solve for x: $4x + 2 \leq 6$

2. How would you graph the inequality $x > 2$ on a number line?

3. Solve for x: $-3x \geq 9$

Solutions

1. $4x + 2 \leq 6$

    $4x \leq 4$

    $x \leq 1$

2. Since the inequality includes a > sign with no "equal" underneath, make the circle where it intersects 2 *hollow*:

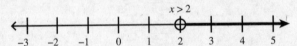

3. When you multiply or divide an inequality by a negative number, the direction of the inequality sign changes:

$$-3x \geq 9 \rightarrow x \leq -3$$

Absolute Value

Absolute value is the distance that a number is from zero along the number line. It doesn't matter if you are considering -3 or $+3$. Since both are the same distance from zero on the number line, both have an absolute value of 3.

If you want the absolute value of 9, express it like this: $|9|$.

When computing the value of an absolute value expression, simply determine the value of what is inside the two bars and then make that number positive, no matter if it was originally positive or negative. Here are some examples:

$$|25| = 25$$
$$|-12| = 12$$
$$|-3 + 8| = 5$$
$$|-2 \times 9| = 18$$

When solving absolute value equations, set them up as equal to both a positive and a negative value. If, for example, you are going to solve $|x + 2| = 4$, you should write it as two different equations since what occurs inside the absolute value signs can have either a positive or a negative value and can make the expression true.

$$|x + 2| = 4$$

$$x + 2 = 4 \qquad \text{and} \qquad x + 2 = -4$$
$$x = 2 \qquad\qquad\qquad\qquad x = -6$$

So x could be either 2 or -6.

Absolute Value Drill

1. What is the value of $|8|$?

2. What is the value of $|-25 + 4|$?

3. What are the possible solutions for x: $|x + 5| = 7$?

4. How many solutions are there for x in this equation? $|x - 5| = -2$

Solutions

1. 8

2. $|-25 + 4| \rightarrow |-21| \rightarrow 21$

3. Turn $|x + 5| = 7$ into two equations and solve:

$$x + 5 = 7 \qquad \text{and} \qquad x + 5 = -7$$
$$x = 2 \qquad\qquad\qquad\qquad x = -12$$

So the solutions for x are 2 and -12.

4. Since an absolute value must give a value that is greater than or equal to zero, there are *no* solutions to this equation.

Linear Relationships

Slope-Intercept Form

Determine the graph of a line by putting it in *slope-intercept form*:

$$y = mx + b$$

m = slope of the line, the "rise" over the "run," calculated with $\dfrac{(y_2 - y_1)}{(x_2 - x_1)}$

b = y-intercept of the line, i.e., where the line intersects the y-axis

> **Example**

Graph the following equation:

$$y = 3x + 2$$

> **Solution**

Based on the slope-intercept formula, the line has a slope of 3 and a y-intercept of 2.

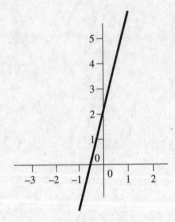

Parallel and Perpendicular Lines

Lines that are *parallel* to one another have *identical slopes*—they will never cross one another. (Parallel lines should have different y-intercepts, or they will simply be overlapping lines.) Figure 2 is a graph of two parallel lines in the xy-plane, $y = 3x$ and $y = 3x + 2$:

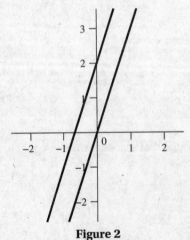

Figure 2

Perpendicular lines intersect at a 90° angle and have slopes that are *negative reciprocals* of one another. For example, if one line has a slope of 4, a line perpendicular to it has a slope of $-\frac{1}{4}$. Figure 3 is an example of two perpendicular lines and their graph, $y = -\frac{1}{5}x - 1$ and $y = 5x - 3$:

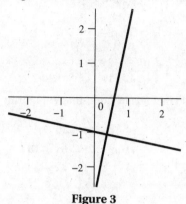

Figure 3

Slope Formula, Positive and Negative Correlations

To find the slope between two points, (x_1, y_1) and (x_2, y_2), plug the coordinates of the points into this formula:

$$\text{Slope} = \frac{\text{Change in } y}{\text{Change in } x} = \frac{(y_2 - y_1)}{(x_2 - x_1)}$$

(It is not important which point you consider the first or second set of coordinates, so long as your calculation is consistent.)

> Example

If a line includes the points (6, 4) and (2, 9), what is the slope of the line?

✓ Solution

You can determine the slope as follows:

$$\frac{(y_2 - y_1)}{(x_2 - x_1)} = \frac{(9 - 4)}{(2 - 6)} = -\frac{5}{4}$$

You can examine the slope of a line to see whether the variables have a positive or a negative correlation. If the *x*-values and *y*-values increase together or decrease together, the variables have a *positive correlation*. The line has a *positive slope*. If the *x*-values increase while the *y*-values decrease, or vice versa, the variables have a *negative correlation*. The line has a *negative slope*.

Linear Relationships Drill

1. What is the *y*-intercept of the line given by $y = -4x + 13$?

2. What is the slope of a line with points $(1, -2)$ and $(-4, 6)$?

3. What is the slope of the line given by $-8x + 2y = 10$?

4. If $(3, 5)$ is a point on a line that goes through the origin, what is the slope of this line?

5. If a line has a slope of $-\frac{2}{3}$, what is the slope of a line perpendicular to it?

6. If two lines have the same slope but different *y*-intercepts, how often will the lines intersect?

7. In the equation $y = 5x$, are *x* and *y* positively or negatively correlated?

Solutions

1. The line is in slope-intercept form, $y = mx + b$, so the y-intercept corresponds to the b: 13.

2. Use the slope formula, $\dfrac{(y_2 - y_1)}{(x_2 - x_1)}$, to solve for the slope of the line with these points:

$$\frac{(y_2 - y_1)}{(x_2 - x_1)}$$

$$\frac{(6 - -2)}{(-4 - 1)} = \frac{8}{-5} = -\frac{8}{5}$$

3. Rearrange the parts of the equation so that it is in slope-intercept form:

$$-8x + 2y = 10$$
$$2y = 8x + 10$$
$$y = 4x + 5$$

    The slope is 4.

4. The origin has the coordinates $(0, 0)$. So take the slope of the two points using the slope formula:

$$\frac{(y_2 - y_1)}{(x_2 - x_1)}$$

$$\frac{(5 - 0)}{(3 - 0)} = \frac{5}{3}$$

5. Take the negative reciprocal of $-\frac{2}{3}$ to find the slope of a perpendicular line. Multiply $-\frac{2}{3}$ by -1 and flip the fraction.

$$-\frac{2}{3} \times -1 = \frac{2}{3}$$
$$\frac{3}{2}$$

6. Lines with the same slope but different y-intercepts are parallel to each other. Therefore, they never intersect. For example, the lines $y = 2x$ and $y = 2x + 2$ have identical slopes but different y-intercepts, making them parallel:

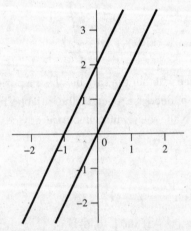

7. The variables are *positively* correlated with one another because the line of this equation has a positive slope. As x increases, y also increases.

Problem-Solving and Data Analysis

Interpreting Functions

Linear, Quadratic, and Exponential Models

A *linear relationship* between two variables is represented by a graph with a *constant slope*. For example, the equation $y = x$ represents a linear relationship between x and y, as you can see in the graph in Figure 4.

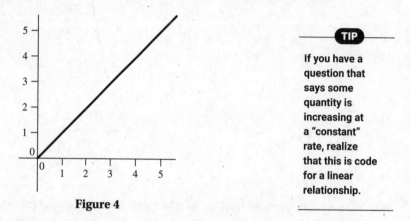

Figure 4

A *quadratic relationship* between two variables, x and y, is generally represented by an equation of the form $y = kx^2$ or $y = ax^2 + bx + c$, in which k, a, b, and c are constants. It is called a quadratic relationship because *quad* means "square." Figure 5 shows a portion of the graph of $y = x^2$, in which x and y have a quadratic relationship.

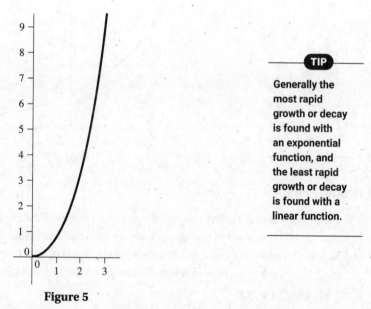

Figure 5

An *exponential relationship* between two variables, x and y, is generally expressed in the form $y = cbx$ or $y = abx + c$, in which a, b, and c are constants. Figure 6 shows a portion of the graph of $y = 3x - 1$, which is an exponential function. (Notice that the exponential relationship puts the x in the exponent part of the equation.)

Figure 6

Keep in mind that functions can have negative linear, quadratic, and exponential relationships. In other words, these functions can express decay rather than growth. For example, the function $y = 20 \times 0.5^x$ shows decay because as x increases to infinity, the y-value decreases. The graph of the function is shown in Figure 7.

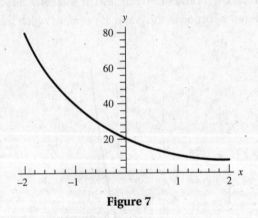

Figure 7

Scatter Plots

The PSAT will test your understanding of scatter plot graphs. Scatter plots provide a graph of different points that together show a relationship among data. To see the relationship among the data, draw a "line of best fit" that shows a line that best approximates the data points. A line of best fit typically has roughly the same number of points above it and beneath it, unless there are significantly outlying points. Figure 8 is an example of a scatter plot with a line of best fit.

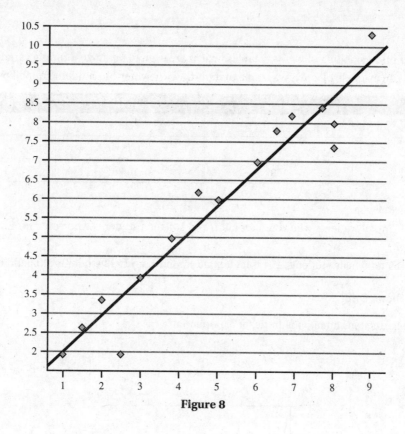

Figure 8

Histograms

Another type of graph on the PSAT is the histogram—it shows the frequency of different values in a data set. For example, consider the histogram in Figure 9.

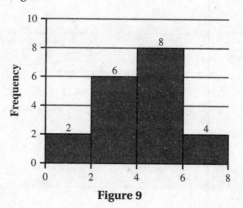

Figure 9

What does this histogram portray?

- 2 values in the set between 0 and 2
- 6 values between 2 and 4
- 8 values between 4 and 6
- 4 values between 6 and 8

Two-Way Tables

The PSAT tests your understanding of two-way tables, which are used to organize multiple variables and their frequencies. Here is an example of a two-way table that portrays the votes in a student council president election:

	Male	Female	Total
Voted for Liam	48	59	107
Voted for Emma	61	45	106
Total	109	104	213

What does this table tell you?

- There are 107 total students who voted for Liam and 106 total students who voted for Emma. So Liam won the election.
- There are 109 total male students, 104 total female students, and 213 students altogether.

Interpreting Functions Drill

1. Are the following functions linear, quadratic, or exponential?

   a. $y = 2x^2 - 5$
   b. $y = 4x + 2$
   c. $y = 6^x + 5$

2.

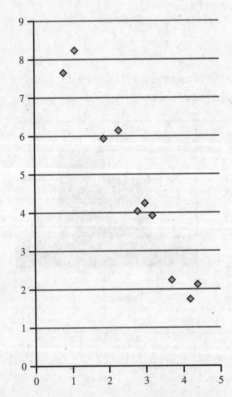

Consider the scatter plot above. When rounded to the nearest whole number, what is the slope of the line of best fit for this scatter plot?

3.

	Seniors Graduating with Honors	Seniors Graduating without Honors	Total
Lincoln High School	50	240	290
Jefferson High School	80	170	250
Total	130	410	540

Consider the table above.

   a. How many seniors are graduating from Jefferson High School without honors?

   b. How many seniors are at both schools?

   c. How many seniors are at just Lincoln High School?

Solutions

1. a. $y = 2x^2 - 5$ is a quadratic function since the x is raised to the second power.

   b. $y = 4x + 2$ is a linear function since it has a constant slope of 4.

   c. $y = 6^x + 5$ is an exponential function since the 6 is raised to the x power.

2. To estimate the slope, sketch a best-fit line:

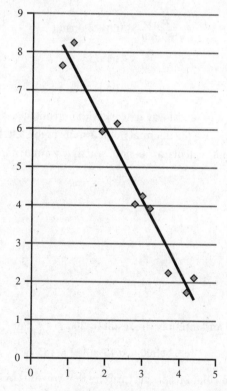

The line roughly has points at (1, 8) and (3, 4). So the slope would approximately be:

$$\frac{(y_2 - y_1)}{(x_2 - x_1)}$$

$$\frac{8 - 4}{1 - 3} =$$

$$\frac{4}{-2} = -2$$

3. a. 170
    b. 540. Include seniors from both schools, both those who are graduating with honors and those who are graduating without honors.
    c. 290. Include only seniors from Lincoln, both those who are graduating with honors and those who are graduating without honors.

Percentages

The general formula for percentages is:

$$\frac{\text{Part}}{\text{Whole}} \times 100 = \text{Percent}$$

> Example

You took a test with 80 questions, and you answered 60 of them correctly. What percentage of the questions did you answer correctly?

✓ Solution

$$\frac{\text{Part}}{\text{Whole}} \times 100 = \text{Percent}$$

$$\frac{60}{80} \times 100 =$$

$$0.75 \times 100 = 75\%$$

On the calculator-permitted section, a practical way to work with percentages is to convert them to decimals. First, remove the percent sign. Then, move the decimal point 2 spots to the left. Finally, multiply the last decimal expression by 100. Note that on the non-calculator section, you may want to convert the percentages to a fraction, like $\frac{1}{2} = 50\%$.

> Example

What is 45 percent of 300?

✓ Solution

Convert the percentage to a decimal and multiply the result by 300:

$$45\% \text{ of } 300 = 0.45 \times 300 = 135$$

When doing multistep percentage calculations, be very careful that you are considering the increases or decreases from previous steps in your later calculations.

> Example

A book regularly costs $20, but it is on sale for 10% off. A customer also has a coupon for 30% off the price of the book in addition to any sale discounts. What will be the price of the book the customer pays using only the sale? What will then be the price also using the coupon? Ignore any sales tax.

✓ Solution

First determine the sale price of the book by subtracting the 10% discount from the original price:

$$\$20 - (0.1 \times \$20) = \$20 - \$2 = \$18$$

Then subtract 30% of the new price from the new price to find the fully discounted price:

$$\$18 - (0.3 \times \$18) = \$18 - \$5.40 = \$12.60$$

Alternatively, you could calculate 90% of the original amount and then calculate 70% of that new amount. This method takes away the need to do subtraction:

$$\$20 \times 0.9 = \$18 \rightarrow \$18 \times 0.7 = \$12.60$$

Another useful approach to percentage calculations is to use 100 as a sample starting value.

⟩ Example

If Michal's blood pressure increased by 20% from 6 P.M. to 7 P.M. and then decreased by 10% from 7 P.M. to 8 P.M., what was the overall percentage change in her blood pressure from 6 P.M. to 8 P.M.?

✓ Solution

Although you can calculate this percentage change using variables, it is far easier if you use 100 as the original number. If you assume Michal's initial blood pressure at 6 P.M. is 100, then a 20% increase will result in a new blood pressure of 120 at 7 P.M. Why? Because 20% of 100 is 20, and you add it to 100, giving 120. Then to calculate the change from 7 P.M. to 8 P.M., simply take 10% of 120, which is $120 \times 0.10 = 12$, and subtract it from 120: $120 - 12 = 108$. So 108 represents an 8% increase over 100. The overall percentage change in her blood pressure is 8%.

Sometimes you can save time on percentage problems by substituting fractions for the percentage. Certain percentages are easily converted to fractions, like $25\% \rightarrow \frac{1}{4}$ or $50\% \rightarrow \frac{1}{2}$.

⟩ Example

If a shirt that costs $60 is on sale for 50% off, what is the discounted price of the shirt?

✓ Solution

To solve this without the use of a calculator, use the fraction $\frac{1}{2}$ instead of 50% to easily find the discounted price:

$$\$60 \times \frac{1}{2} = \$30$$

$30 taken away from $60 gives you a discounted price of $30.

Percentages Drill

1. What is 25% of 200?

2. What is 110% of 50?

3. If there are 50 questions on a test and you answered 36 questions correctly, what is your percent score on the test?

4. If a book regularly costs $20 but you have a coupon for 15% off the book, what would you pay altogether for the book after 7% sales tax is added?

5. Lydia has $1,000 in her savings account on January 1 of this year. If she earns 2% interest, compounded annually, how much money will she have on January 1 two years from now (assuming she makes no additional deposits or withdrawals)?

Solutions

1. $0.25 \times 200 = 50$

2. $1.10 \times 50 = 55$

3. $\dfrac{36}{50} \times 100 = 72\%$

4. First determine the discounted price for the book:

$$\$20 - (0.15 \times \$20) = \$17$$

Then, add the 7% sales tax to the price to get the total price paid:

$$\$17 + (0.07 \times \$17) = \$18.19$$

Alternatively, combine the addition and subtraction steps to save time in your calculations:

$$\$20 \times (0.85) = \$17$$
$$\$17 \times (1.07) = \$18.19$$

5. A 2% increase on an original amount of x is calculated like this:

$$x + 0.02x = 1.02x$$

To compound the 2% interest on the original sum of $1,000 over two years, multiply the original amount by 1.02 *twice* to get the total amount of money:

$$1.02 \times 1.02 \times \$1,000 = \$1,040.40$$

Ratios, Proportions, and Direct and Inverse Variation

Ratios and Proportions

Recognize when numbers and expressions involve the application of ratios and proportions. This will most frequently occur with word problems.

> **Example**

A cookie recipe calls for 6 cups of sugar and 4 cups of milk. Brendan has 18 cups of sugar. If Brendan wants to use all of that sugar, how many cups of milk will he need?

✓ **Solution**

Set up a ratio that has the same units in the numerator and the same units in the denominator:

$$\frac{4 \text{ cups milk}}{6 \text{ cups sugar}} = \frac{x \text{ cups milk}}{18 \text{ cups sugar}}$$

$$\frac{2}{3} = \frac{x}{18}$$

Cross multiply:

$$2 \times 18 = 3x$$

Divide both sides by 3:

$$\frac{2 \times 18}{3} = x$$

$$\frac{36}{3} = 12 = x$$

Brendan will need 12 cups of milk.

Direct and Inverse Variation

The variables a and b vary *directly* with one another (also called "directly proportional") if as a increases, then b increases, and if as a decreases, then b also decreases. The general form for an equation in which a and b are directly proportional is:

$$b = ka \ \ (k = \text{constant})$$

As a real-world example, the greater the quantity of a certain food, the more calories there are in that food. You could say the food quantity and caloric quantity are directly proportional.

The variables a and b vary *indirectly* with one another (also called "inversely proportional") if as a increases, then b decreases, and if as a decreases, then b increases. The general form for an equation in which a and b are inversely related is:

$$b = \frac{k}{a} \ \ (k = \text{constant})$$

As a real-world example, the more people who split a pizza, the smaller the size is of each person's piece of pizza. The number of people and the size of each piece are inversely related.

❯ Example

Consider the variable n in this equation:

$$n = \frac{x}{y}$$

To which variable is n directly proportional, and to which variable is n inversely proportional?

✓ Solution

Since n and x are both on top in the equation, if x becomes greater, so does n. (You can consider n to be a fraction with n as the numerator and 1 as the denominator.) The variable y is in the denominator, so as y increases, n decreases. As a result, n is directly proportional to x and is inversely proportional to y.

Ratios, Proportions, and Direct and Inverse Variation Drill

1. If 3 teaspoons are in 1 tablespoon, how many teaspoons are in 4 tablespoons?

2. If the U.S. dollar exchanges for 71 Indian rupees, how many dollars will be needed to purchase a toy that costs 426 rupees?

3. A town requires that in every new development, there are 2 acres of park for every 3 acres that are zoned for residential and/or commercial purposes. How many acres of park would be required in a new development that is 50 acres total?

4. When a car is traveling 40 kilometers per hour, how fast will it be going in meters per second (to the nearest tenth)? Note: There are 1,000 meters in a kilometer.

5. The physics equation that describes the relationship among pressure (p), force (F), and surface area (A) is $p = \dfrac{F}{A}$. Based on this equation, pressure is directly proportional and is inversely related to which variables?

6. Variables a and b are related by the equation $b = ka$, in which k is the constant of proportionality. If b is 5 when a is 10, what is the value of k?

Solutions

1. Set up a proportion to solve the problem:

$$\frac{3 \text{ teaspoons}}{1 \text{ tablespoon}} = \frac{x \text{ teaspoons}}{4 \text{ tablespoons}}$$

   Cross multiply:

$$3 \times 4 = 12 \text{ teaspoons}$$

2. Solve using a proportion:

$$\frac{1 \text{ dollar}}{71 \text{ rupees}} = \frac{x \text{ dollars}}{426 \text{ rupees}}$$

   Cross multiply:

$$426 = 71x$$

$$\frac{426}{71} = 6 \text{ dollars}$$

3. For a given development, there will be 2 park acres for every 5 total acres since 2 park acres + 3 non-park acres = 5 total acres. Solve this question using a proportion:

$$\frac{2 \text{ park acres}}{5 \text{ total acres}} = \frac{x \text{ park acres}}{50 \text{ total acres}}$$

   Cross multiply:

$$50 \times 2 = 5x$$

$$\frac{100}{5} = 20 \text{ park acres}$$

4. There are 1,000 meters in 1 kilometer and 3,600 seconds in an hour (60 minutes $\times$ 60 seconds = 3,600). Solve by converting the units:

$$40\,\frac{\text{kilometers}}{\text{hour}} \times 1,000\,\frac{\text{meters}}{\text{kilometer}} \times \frac{\text{hour}}{3,600 \text{ seconds}} \rightarrow$$

$$40\,\frac{\cancel{\text{kilometers}}}{\cancel{\text{hour}}} \times 1,000\,\frac{\text{meters}}{\cancel{\text{kilometer}}} \times \frac{\cancel{\text{hour}}}{3,600 \text{ seconds}} = \frac{40 \times 1,000}{3,600} = 11.1\,\frac{\text{meters}}{\text{second}}$$

5. In this equation, $p = \dfrac{F}{A}$, p and F are both in the numerator. So pressure (p) and force (F) are directly proportional to one another—as p increases, F also increases. Surface area (A) is in the denominator while p is in the numerator. So A and p are inversely related to one another—as A increases, p decreases.

6. Plug the values for a and b into the equation to solve for k:

$$b = ka$$

$$5 = k(10)$$

$$\frac{5}{10} = k$$

$$\frac{1}{2} = k$$

Mean, Median, and Mode

Table 5.1 gives the definitions of mean, median, and mode.

Table 5.1 Mean, Median, and Mode

	Definition
Mean	$$\frac{\text{Sum of Items}}{\text{Number of Items}} = \text{Mean}$$ What you usually think of when you calculate the average.
Median	The middle term of a set of numbers when those numbers are lined up from smallest to largest. When the number of terms is even and the two terms in the middle are not the same, take the mean of the two middle terms to find the median.
Mode	The most frequent term in a set of numbers. In a set of numbers, if each number appears only once, there is no mode. However, if two or more numbers are tied for appearing the most times, that set has multiple modes.

> **Example**

Compute the mean, median, and mode for the following set of numbers:

$$\{1, 4, 4, 5, 8, 13, 22\}$$

✓ **Solution**

The mean:

$$\frac{1 + 4 + 4 + 5 + 8 + 13 + 22}{7} = \frac{57}{7} \approx 8.14$$

The mean is 8.14.

The median:

The numbers are already in order from smallest to largest. There are 7 numbers in the set. The median is 5 since it is in the middle of the set.

The mode:

The most frequent term is 4, so it is the mode.

A common application of the mean is when you calculate the missing term in a set when you already know the mean. Here is an example.

> **Example**

Sam has taken three exams, each worth a maximum of 50 points, over the course of her semester. She scored 40, 35, and 27 on her three exams. What must she score on a fourth exam, also out of 50 points, in order to average 35 points on her four exams?

✓ **Solution**

Set up the problem using the formula for finding the mean:

$$\frac{\text{Sum of Items}}{\text{Number of Items}} = \text{Mean}$$

Plug in the terms that you know:

$$\frac{40 + 35 + 27 + x}{4} = 35$$

Cross multiply by 4:

$$(4)\frac{40 + 35 + 27 + x}{4} = 35(4)$$

$$40 + 35 + 27 + x = 140$$

Solve for x:

$$40 + 35 + 27 + x = 140$$

$$102 + x = 140$$

$$x = 38$$

Sam would need to score a 38 on her fourth exam.

Mean, Median, and Mode Drill

1. Consider this set of numbers: {1, 3, 4, 5, 5, 7, 10}.
   a. What is the mean of this set?
   b. What is the median of this set?
   c. What is the mode of this set?

2. If the set of numbers {4, 6, 7, 7, 9} had the number 10 added to it, what would change?
   I. The set's mean
   II. The set's mode
   III. The set's median

3. A restaurant wants the average calories for each item in a meal to be 300. If a meal is to consist of a serving of pasta (500 calories), a salad (200 calories), and a side dish, what must the calories in the side dish be to meet the restaurant's requirement?

Solutions

1. a. The formula for the mean is $\frac{\text{Sum of Items}}{\text{Number of Items}} = \text{Mean}$. Add the numbers in the set together, and divide by how many numbers there are in the set:

   $$\frac{1 + 3 + 4 + 5 + 5 + 7 + 10}{7} = \frac{35}{7} = 5$$

   b. The numbers are already organized in order from least to greatest, so find the fourth value of the set since it is in the middle:

   $$(1, 3, 4, \mathbf{5}, 5, 7, 10)$$

   The median is therefore 5.

   c. The mode is the most frequent member of the set. Since 5 appears twice while the other numbers appear only once, 5 is the mode of the set.

2. The current set is {4, 6, 7, 7, 9}, and the new set is {4, 6, 7, 7, 9, 10}.

The mean of the set would change. The original mean is $\frac{4+6+7+7+9}{5} = \frac{33}{5} = 6.6$, while the new mean would be $\frac{4+6+7+7+9+10}{6} = \frac{43}{6} \approx 7.2$. You could also estimate that the mean would change because if you add only a number that is greater than the mean to a set, it will make the mean larger as a result.

The mode of the set would NOT change because 7 is still the most frequent number in each set.

The median of the set would NOT change. In the original set, 7 is the middle number. In the new set, 7 is the value we get when we take the average of the two middle values of the new set (since there is an even number of members of the set): $\frac{7+7}{2} = 7$. If the two middle values in a set that has an even number of elements are the same, then the median will simply be one of these middle values.

3. Set up an equation for the mean, where x represents the calories in the side dish:

$$\frac{500 + 200 + x}{3} = 300$$

$$\frac{700 + x}{3} = 300$$

Cross multiply:

$$700 + x = 3 \times 300$$
$$700 + x = 900$$
$$x = 200$$

There must be 200 calories in the side dish.

Probability and Statistics
Probability Basics

Probability is the *likelihood that a given event will happen*, expressed as a fraction, decimal, or percentage. If there is no chance an event will occur, it has a probability of 0. If there is a 100 percent chance something will happen, it has a probability of 1.

To calculate probability, take the number of cases of a success and divide it by the total number of possible outcomes:

$$\text{Probability} = \frac{\text{Number of Successes}}{\text{Number of Possible Outcomes}}$$

> Example

If Janice has 3 red marbles out of the 200 total marbles in her collection, what is the probability that she will randomly pick a red marble?

✓ Solution

The number of successes is 3, and the number of possible outcomes is 200:

$$\frac{\text{Number of red marbles}}{\text{Number of total marbles}} = \frac{3}{200} = 0.015 = 1.5\%$$

Independent/Dependent Counting Problems

Counting problems are either independent or dependent.

Independent Counting Problems (Drawing With Replacement)

Independent counting problems involve drawing an object and then replacing it before drawing again. In these types of problems, each choice is computed *independently*. In other words, what you pick the first time has *no impact* on what you pick the second time, which has no impact on what you pick the third time, and so on. Such problems include flipping a coin several times because the flip of one coin has no impact on the later coin flips.

> **Example**

Hazel is choosing a 3-letter combination for her safe. Whether or not the letters are repeated does not matter. How many unique combinations can Hazel make?

✓ **Solution**

What Hazel picks for one letter does not impact what she picks for another letter. Since there are 26 letters in the alphabet, calculate the total number of possible combinations as follows:

$$26 \times 26 \times 26 = 17{,}576 \text{ possible combinations}$$

Dependent Counting Problems (Drawing Without Replacement)

Dependent counting problems involve drawing an object and not replacing it before drawing again. In these types of problems, each choice *depends* on what was previously chosen. In other words, what you pick the first time *has an impact* on what you pick the second time, which has an impact on what you pick the third time, and so on. Such problems include drawing names out of a hat because you do not want to pick the same name more than once.

✓ **Example**

John is choosing a 3-letter combination for his locker. The letters *cannot* be repeated. How many unique combinations can John make?

✓ **Solution**

What John picks for the first letter does impact what he picks for the second, which impacts what he picks for the third. So he will have one fewer possible letters for each subsequent choice. He can compute the total number of unique 3-letter combinations with no repeating letters as follows:

$$26 \times 25 \times 24 = 15{,}600 \text{ possible combinations}$$

Range and Standard Deviation

The PSAT will emphasize analyzing data sets. So be comfortable with the important concepts of range and standard deviation.

Range

Range is defined as the difference between the smallest and the largest values in a set of data.

Standard Deviation

Standard deviation measures how spread out or how varied the data points are in a set. It can be calculated using the following equation:

$$\text{Standard deviation} = \sqrt{\text{Average of the squared distances of the data points from their mean}}$$

Rather than having you conduct elaborate calculations to find the standard deviation of a set of data, you will need to have a feel for what the standard deviation represents. If the standard deviation is small, the data points have little variation. If the standard deviation is large, the data points have great variation.

❯ Example

Compare the ranges and standard deviations of Set A and Set B.

Set A: {1, 3, 4, 6, 8}

Set B: {1, 8, 50, 200, 380}

✓ Solution

The range and standard deviation of Set B are greater than the range and standard deviation of Set A. Why? The values in Set A range from only 1 to 8 and do not vary much from the average of Set A (4.4). The values in Set B range from 1 to 380 and vary quite a bit from the average of Set B (127.8). The sets are simple enough that you can likely determine the general trends with standard deviation and range without doing detailed calculations.

The most common graph involving standard deviation is the *normal distribution*—the typical distribution of a large sampling of values in a bell curve shape. Figure 10 shows a normal distribution. About 68% of the values are within 1 standard deviation of the mean. About 95% of the values are within 2 standard deviations of the mean. About 99.7% of the values are within 3 standard deviations of the mean.

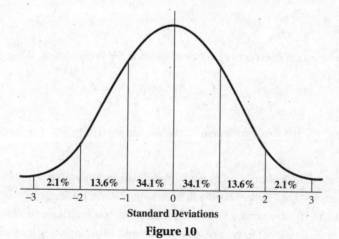

Figure 10

Confidence Interval and Margin of Error

When collecting a sample of data from a population, you need to be sure that the results give a true snapshot of the population as a whole. Two important terms are associated with the quality of data sampling: confidence interval and margin of error.

> Use common sense when thinking about data. To get an accurate snapshot of public opinion, you want to ask as MANY RANDOM people your questions as you can!

Confidence Interval

The confidence interval is a range of values defined so that there is a predetermined probability that the value of an unknown parameter under investigation will fall within the range. The higher the confidence level is, the more likely the parameter will fall within that interval.

⟩ Example

Suppose a stockbroker has research indicating a 95% confidence interval that a company's stock will have a return between −7.8% and +9.5% during the next year. What does this mean?

✓ Solution

In this case, the unknown parameter is the average stock return for the year. This means that if all economic conditions remain the same, there is a 95% chance that the stock will have an average return in this interval of −7.8% to +9.5%.

Margin of Error

The margin of error is the maximum expected difference between the actual (unknown) parameter and the estimate for that parameter obtained through a sample. The smaller the margin of error is, the more accurate the survey results are.

⟩ Example

Suppose that a survey has a margin of error of plus or minus 5% at 96% confidence. What does this mean?

✓ Solution

This means that 96% of the time the survey is repeated, the results are within 5% of the amount reported in the original survey.

You do not need to know the details of calculating confidence level and margin of error for the PSAT. Instead, you need to have a feel for what will make survey results more reliable. The confidence level and margin of error for survey results are interrelated. If you want a smaller margin of error, you may have to have less confidence in the results. If you want to be more confident in your results, you should allow for a larger margin of error. In order to maximize confidence in the results and minimize the margin of error, make sure that the sample is *as large and as random* as possible.

Probability and Statistics Drill

1. If a particular pet store has five dogs, four cats, and 12 guinea pigs available for purchase (and no other pets for sale), what is the probability that a randomly purchased pet will be a cat?

2.

	Write Using Cursive	Write Using Print	Total
Teachers	12	4	16
Students	40	280	320
Total	52	284	336

Consider the table above that portrays the teachers and students at a particular high school and their preferred writing styles.

a. What is the probability that a randomly selected teacher prefers to write using print?

b. What is the probability that a randomly selected person at the school prefers to write using cursive?

3. At the school cafeteria, there are three main courses and four desserts from which to choose. What is the total number of possible meals that a student can choose, assuming he or she wants both a main course and a dessert?

4. In Kim's closet, she has eight different dresses. She is packing for a three-day trip; she wants to wear a different dress on each day of the trip. What is the total number of combinations of dresses Kim could pack?

5. Consider the set of numbers {3, 4, 7, 11}. What positive number could be added to the set to double the set's range?

6. If someone added the number 20 to the set of numbers {1, 2, 4, 5, 12}, would that increase or decrease the standard deviation of the set?

7. Which of these approaches would give the best indication of how a particular town is planning on voting on an issue in an election?

a. Interviewing 100 political activists in the town as to their predictions

b. Taking a phone survey of 500 randomly selected likely voters

c. Having 500 pedestrians in the main city park complete a survey

Solutions

1. Total the number of pets:

$$5 + 4 + 12 = 21$$

Then divide the number of cats (4) by the number of total pets (21) to get the probability that a randomly purchased pet will be a cat:

$$\frac{4}{21}$$

2. a. There are 16 total teachers, and 4 of them prefer to write using print. So divide 4 by 16 to get the probability:

$$\frac{4}{16} = \frac{1}{4}$$

This is the same as 0.25 if you want to express the answer as a decimal.

b. There are 336 total people in the school, and 52 of them prefer to write using cursive. So divide 52 by 336. Your answer can be expressed as a reduced fraction or as a decimal:

$$\frac{52}{336} = \frac{13}{84} \text{ or } 0.155$$

3. Multiply the number of main courses by the number of desserts to find the total number of possible meals:

$$3 \times 4 = 12$$

4. After Kim wears one dress, she does not want to wear it again. Therefore, the number of dress options each day decreases by 1. Calculate the total number of combinations as follows:

$$8 \times 7 \times 6 = 336 \text{ total possible combinations}$$

5. The range of the set $\{3, 4, 7, 11\}$ is currently $11 - 3 = 8$.

   Double the current range to find the new range:

$$8 \times 2 = 16$$

   Since the smallest number in the set is 3, add 16 to 3 to find the number that would need to be added to make the range of the set 16:

$$3 + 16 = 19$$

   So the new set would be $\{3, 4, 7, 11, 19\}$ with 19 as the added number. It would have a range of 16, twice the original range of 8.

6. If 20 was added to this set, the new set would be $\{1, 2, 4, 5, 12, 20\}$. The average deviation from the mean would increase since the spread of the numbers would increase. Therefore, the standard deviation would increase.

7. Interviewing the political activists and the park pedestrians would not be ideal since the sample set would not be randomized. Performing a phone survey of the randomly selected voters would ensure that the sample was randomized, giving much better results.

Advanced Math

Factoring

When simplifying an equation, take out any common factors.

> **Example**

Factor $nx + ny$.

✓ **Solution**

$nx + ny$ can be expressed as $n(x + y)$ by factoring out the n.

> **Example**

Factor $\dfrac{2x^3 + 6x}{3x}$.

✓ **Solution**

$\dfrac{2x^3 + 6x}{3x}$ can be expressed as $\dfrac{2x(x^2 + 3)}{3x}$ since you can factor $2x$ out of the numerator. Then you can cancel out an x from the numerator and denominator:

$$\frac{2x(x^2 + 3)}{3x} = \frac{2x(x^2 + 3)}{3x} = \frac{2}{3}(x^2 + 3)$$

You also should know how to factor equations like $x^2 - x - 12 = 0$. Try to express it as two binomials that are multiplied by each other. The factored form looks like:

$$(x + \text{something})(x - \text{something}) = 0$$

In the case of $x^2 - x - 12 = 0$, you can rewrite it as $(x + 3)(x - 4) = 0$. -12 is equal to 3×-4, and $-x$ is equal to $-4x + 3x$, making it possible to visualize how the expression can be factored. If you use FOIL to multiply the left-hand side (i.e., multiply the **F**irst terms together, then the **O**uter terms, then the **I**nner terms, and finally the **L**ast terms), you will get the original equation:

$$(x + 3)(x - 4) = 0$$
$$x^2 - 4x + 3x - 12 = 0$$
$$x^2 - x - 12 = 0$$

Common Factoring Patterns

Memorize these patterns so you can recognize them on the PSAT Math Test and save time.

- Multiplying Binomials

$$(a + b)(a + b) = a^2 + 2ab + b^2$$

Example:

$$(x + 3)(x + 3) = x^2 + 6x + 9$$

$$(a + b)(a - b) = a^2 - b^2$$

Example:

$$(m + 2)(m - 2) = m^2 - 4$$

$$(a - b)(a - b) = a^2 - 2ab + b^2$$

Example:

$$(3 - y)(3 - y) = 9 - 6y + y^2$$

- Sum of Cubes

$$(a + b)(a^2 - ab + b^2) = a^3 + b^3$$

Example:

$$(2 + x)(4 - 2x + x^2) = 2^3 + x^3 = 8 + x^3$$

- Difference of Cubes

$$(a - b)(a^2 + ab + b^2) = a^3 - b^3$$

Example:

$$(y - 4)(y^2 + 4y + 16) = y^3 - 4^3 = y^3 - 64$$

Factoring Drill

1. Factor this expression: $4x + 8y$
2. Simplify this expression: $\dfrac{3x - 6y}{3}$
3. Simplify this expression: $\dfrac{12x^4}{3x^2}$
4. Factor this expression: $25x^2 - 9y^2$
5. Factor this expression: $27 - 8x^3$

Solutions

1. $4x + 8y \rightarrow 4(x + 2y)$
2. $\dfrac{3x - 6y}{3} =$

   $\dfrac{3(x - 2y)}{3} =$

   $\dfrac{3(x - 2y)}{3} = x - 2y$

3. $$\frac{12x^4}{3x^2} =$$

   $$\frac{3 \cdot 4 \cdot x^2 \cdot x^2}{3x^2} =$$

   $$\frac{3 \cdot 4 \cdot x^2 \cdot x^2}{3x^2} = 4x^2$$

4. $25x^2 - 9y^2 = (5x - 3y)(5x + 3y)$

5. This is a difference of cubes, where $a^3 - b^3 = (a - b)(a^2 + ab + b^2)$. In this case, a is equal to 3, and b is equal to $2x$. So the solution is:

$$27 - 8x^3 =$$

$$3^3 - ((2x)^3) =$$

$$(3 - 2x)(3^2 + 3(2x) + (2x)^2) = (3 - 2x)(9 + 6x + 4x^2)$$

Advanced Equation Concepts

Quadratic Formula

A second-degree equation containing the variable x and the constants a, b, and c, and written in the form $ax^2 + bx + c = 0$, can be solved using the quadratic formula:

$$x = \frac{-b \pm \sqrt{b^2 - 4ac}}{2a}$$

> **Example**

What are the values of x in the equation $2x^2 - 2x - 12 = 0$?

✓ **Solution**

The values of the constants are $a = 2$, $b = -2$, and $c = -12$. Solve for x by plugging a, b, and c into the quadratic formula:

$$x = \frac{-b \pm \sqrt{b^2 - 4ac}}{2a}$$

$$x = \frac{-(-2) \pm \sqrt{(-2)^2 - 4(2)(-12)}}{2(2)}$$

$$x = \frac{2 \pm \sqrt{4 + 96}}{4}$$

$$x = \frac{2 \pm \sqrt{100}}{4}$$

$$x = \frac{2 \pm 10}{4}$$

$$x = \frac{1}{2} \pm \frac{5}{2}$$

$$x = 3 \text{ or } -2$$

Completing the Square

Another way to solve quadratic equations is by completing the square—turning each side of the equation into parts that can be squared. Here is how you can solve for x using this method. Consider the following equation:

$$x^2 - 6x - 16 = 0$$

Start by adding 16 to both sides so the x-terms are all on the left.

$$x^2 - 6x = 16$$

Then take half of -6, which is -3, square it, and add it to both sides of the equation.

$$x^2 - 6x + 9 = 16 + 9$$

You can now rewrite the left-hand side in simplified, squared form:

$$(x - 3)^2 = 25$$

Take the square root of both sides:

$$x - 3 = \pm 5$$

Solve for x:

$$x - 3 = -5 \quad \text{and} \quad x - 3 = 5$$
$$x = -2 \quad\quad\quad\quad x = 8$$

Therefore, $x = 8$ and $x = -2$

Undefined Functions

A function can be undefined when *it is divided by zero*. The value at which a function is undefined indicates that the function has *no solution* for that value. This makes sense because it would be impossible to divide something into *zero* parts.

> Example

When is this function undefined?

$$f(x) = \frac{x^2 + 5}{x - 7}$$

✓ Solution

Find the value of x that would make this function have zero in the denominator. The denominator is $x - 7$, so set this equal to zero and solve for x:

$$x - 7 = 0$$
$$x = 7$$

So the function is undefined when $x = 7$.

Extraneous Solutions

Sometimes you should test solutions to see if they work in the original expression.

> **Example**

What is (are) the solution(s) for x in this equation?

$$x = \sqrt{24 - 2x}$$

✓ **Solution**

The logical first step to solve this equation is to square both sides:

$$x^2 = 24 - 2x$$

This can then be arranged and factored:

$$x^2 + 2x - 24 = 0$$
$$(x - 4)(x + 6) = 0$$

$$x - 4 = 0 \quad x + 6 = 0$$
$$x = 4 \qquad x = -6$$

So 4 and −6 both appear to be solutions. However, only 4 works in the original expression since the square root of a real number cannot be negative. Therefore, just 4 is the answer. Check for extraneous solutions when you start multiplying and dividing expressions containing square root symbols.

Advanced Equation Concepts Drill

1. Solve for x: $2x^2 - 5x + 1 = 0$

2. For what value of x is the following function undefined?

$$y = \frac{14x - 5}{2x + 3}$$

3. What is the solution (or solutions) to this equation?

$$x = \sqrt{12 - x}$$

4. Solve for x by completing the square: $x^2 - 8x - 20 = 0$

Solutions

1. Use the quadratic equation to solve:

$$x = \frac{-b \pm \sqrt{b^2 - 4ac}}{2a}$$
$$x = \frac{-(-5) \pm \sqrt{(-5)^2 - 4(2)(1)}}{2 \cdot 2}$$
$$x = \frac{5 \pm \sqrt{25 - 8}}{4}$$
$$x = \frac{5 \pm \sqrt{17}}{4}$$

2. In order for the function $y = \frac{14x - 5}{2x + 3}$ to be undefined, the denominator, $2x + 3$, should equal zero. Set up an equation to solve:

$$2x + 3 = 0 \rightarrow 2x = -3 \rightarrow x = -\frac{3}{2}$$

3. Start by squaring both sides of the equation:

$$x = \sqrt{12 - x}$$
$$x^2 = 12 - x$$
$$x^2 + x - 12 = 0$$

Then factor the equation:

$$x^2 + x - 12 = 0$$
$$(x + 4)(x - 3) = 0$$

It looks like -4 and 3 will work as solutions. However, you need to check for extraneous solutions by plugging these possible solutions back into the original equation.

Plug in 3 for x:

$$x = \sqrt{12 - x}$$
$$3 = \sqrt{12 - 3}$$
$$3 = \sqrt{9}$$
$$3 = 3$$

So 3 works.

Now plug in -4 for x:

$$-4 = \sqrt{12 - (-4)}$$
$$-4 = \sqrt{12 - (-4)}$$
$$-4 = \sqrt{16}$$
$$-4 \neq 4$$

So -4 is extraneous, and the only solution is 3.

4. Start by adding 20 to each side of the equation:

$$x^2 - 8x - 20 = 0$$
$$x^2 - 8x = 20$$

Now take half of -8, which is -4, square it, and add it to both sides:

$$x^2 - 8x + 16 = 20 + 16$$
$$x^2 - 8x + 16 = 36$$
$$(x - 4)^2 = 6^2$$
$$\sqrt{(x - 4)^2} = \sqrt{6^2}$$
$$x - 4 = \pm 6$$

The two solutions for x can be found as follows:

$$x - 4 = 6 \qquad \text{and} \qquad x - 4 = -6$$
$$x = 10 \qquad\qquad\qquad x = -2$$

So x can be either 10 or -2.

Synthetic Division

Synthetic division is the way students typically learn how to divide polynomials. Here is a brief review of how $2x^2 - 5x + 7$ would be divided by $x + 1$ using synthetic division.

Set up the synthetic division by taking the coefficients of the terms of the polynomial $(2, -5, 7)$ and placing the numerical term of the divisor $x + 1$ (multiplied by -1) to the left of them as follows:

$$-1 \,\vert\, 2 \quad -5 \quad 7$$

Then, bring down each of the coefficients, multiplying the columns one by one by the -1. Create sums to determine the divided polynomial and remainder:

$$
\begin{array}{r|rrr}
-1 & 2 & -5 & 7 \\
   &   & -2 & 7 \\
\hline
   & 2 & -7 & 14
\end{array}
$$

So the answer is $2x - 7$ with a remainder of $\dfrac{14}{x+1}$.

Important fact: $x + 1$ is NOT a factor of $2x^2 - 5x + 7$ since the remainder is not zero.

Synthetic Division Drill

1. Is $(x - 2)$ a factor of $x^2 + 3x - 10$?

2. What is the remainder when $5x^2 - 3x + 2$ is divided by $x - 2$?

Solutions

1. To determine if $(x - 2)$ is a factor of $x^2 + 3x - 10$, divide $x^2 + 3x - 10$ by $(x - 2)$ to see if there is a remainder. If the remainder is zero, then $(x - 2)$ is a factor. Use synthetic division to divide:

$$
\begin{array}{r|rrr}
2 & 1 & 3 & -10 \\
  &   & 2 & 10 \\
\hline
  & 1 & 5 & 0
\end{array}
$$

The remainder is zero, so $(x - 2)$ is a factor.

2. Use synthetic division to divide:

$$
\begin{array}{r|rrr}
2 & 5 & -3 & 2 \\
  &   & 10 & 14 \\
\hline
  & 5 & 7 & 16
\end{array}
$$

The remainder is 16 divided by $x - 2$:

$$\frac{16}{x - 2}$$

Function Notation and Manipulation

In school, you are probably comfortable with equations written in one of the following two ways:

A function written like this:

$$y = 4x - 2$$

is the same as a function written like this:

$$f(x) = 4x - 2$$

If you are told that $x = 3$, you can just plug 3 in for x into each equation:

$$y = 4(3) - 2$$
$$f(3) = 4 \cdot 3 - 2$$

The PSAT will also assess your understanding of *composite functions*, which involve functions that depend on one another. For example, consider these two functions:

$$f(x) = x + 5$$
$$g(x) = 3x - 1$$

If you are asked to solve $f(g(2))$, you need to work from the *inside out*. Start with the $g(x)$ function, plugging in 2 for x:

$$g(x) = 3x - 1$$
$$g(2) = 3 \cdot 2 - 1$$
$$g(2) = 5$$

Then, plug 5 into $f(x)$:

$$f(x) = x + 5$$
$$f(5) = 5 + 5$$
$$f(5) = 10$$

So $f(g(2)) = 10$.

Function Notation and Manipulation Drill

1. If $f(x) = -3x + 5$, what is the value of $f(4)$?

2. If $f(x) = 3x$ and $g(x) = x - 4$, what is the value of $f(g(5))$?

3. What is the value of $f(x + 2) = 5x - 6$ when $x = 4$?

Solutions

1. Plug in 4 for x:

$$f(x) = -3x + 5$$
$$f(4) = -3(4) + 5$$
$$f(4) = -12 + 5$$
$$f(4) = -7$$

2. Start by calculating the value of $g(5)$:

$$g(x) = x - 4$$
$$g(5) = 5 - 4$$
$$g(5) = 1$$

Now, plug 1 into $f(x)$:

$$f(x) = 3x$$
$$f(1) = 3(1)$$
$$f(1) = 3$$

3. Plug in 4 for x on the left-hand side to determine what value should be plugged in for x on the right-hand side:

$$f(x + 2) = 5x - 6$$
$$f(4 + 2) = 5(4 + 2) - 6$$
$$f(6) = 5(6) - 6$$
$$f(6) = 24$$

Exponents

Table 5.2 shows the most important exponent rules along with some concrete examples. It also includes ways to remember these rules.

Table 5.2 Exponent Rules

Exponent Rule	Concrete Example	Way to Remember
$x^a x^b = x^{(a + b)}$	$x^3 x^4 = x^{(3 + 4)} = x^7$	Remember the acronym **MADSPM**. Multiply exponents, Add them. Divide exponents, Subtract them. Parentheses with exponents, Multiply them.
$\dfrac{x^a}{x^b} = x^{a-b}$	$\dfrac{x^7}{x^2} = x^{7-2} = x^5$	
$(x^a)^b = x^{ab}$	$(x^3)^5 = x^{15}$	
$x^{-a} = \dfrac{1}{x^a}$	$x^{-5} = \dfrac{1}{x^5}$	If you are "bad" (negative), you are sent down below!
$x^{\frac{a}{b}} = \sqrt[b]{x^a}$	$x^{\frac{2}{7}} = \sqrt[7]{x^2}$	The root of a tree is on the bottom. Similarly, the root is on the bottom and on the left-hand side!

Exponential Growth and Decay

One of the most common ways that the PSAT will assess your understanding of exponents is by asking you to calculate the future value of a quantity after interest is applied to it. Here is a formula you can use to determine *exponential growth*:

$$(\text{Future Value}) = (\text{Present Value})(1 + (\text{Interest Rate as a Decimal}))^{\text{Number of Periods}}$$

The number of periods indicates the number of times the interest is compounded.

> ### Example

If Sara starts a savings account with $500 and the money in the account earns 3% interest compounded once a year, how much money will she have in the account after two years?

✓ Solution

The present value of the money is $500. The interest rate, expressed as a decimal, is 0.03. The number of periods for which the money is compounded is 2 since there are two years. By plugging this all into the formula, you get the following:

$$(\text{Future Value}) = (500)(1 + (0.03))^2$$

$$500 \times 1.03^2 = \$530.45$$

If a function decreases exponentially over time, slightly modify the formula by subtracting the interest rate to determine *exponential decay*:

$$(\text{Future Value}) = (\text{Present Value})(1 - (\text{Interest Rate as a Decimal}))^{\text{Number of Periods}}$$

> ### Example

Suppose the cost of a television is currently $600, but the price of the television will decrease by 5% each year. What will be price of the television exactly three years from now?

✓ Solution

The present value of the price is $600. The interest rate, expressed as a decimal, is 0.05. The number of periods for which the price is compounded is 3 since there are three years. By plugging this all into the formula, you get the following:

$$(\text{Future Value}) = (600)(1 - (0.05))^3$$

$$600 \times 0.95^3 \approx \$514.43$$

Exponents Drill

1. Simplify: $3x^2 + 7x^2$

2. Simplify: $4(x^3)^2$

3. Simplify: $\dfrac{5x^3 + 10x}{5x}$

4. Simplify without the negative exponent: $2x^{-4}$

5. Simplify without the exponent form: $x^{\left(-\frac{2}{5}\right)}$

6. Simplify this expression: $\dfrac{x^{\left(\frac{3}{4}\right)}}{x^{-\left(\frac{1}{4}\right)}}$

7. Simplify this expression: $\left(\sqrt[3]{x^2}\right)\left(\sqrt[6]{x^8}\right)$

8. If Neha is 50 inches tall and she grows 5% in height each year, what is her height after two years have passed?

Solutions

1. $3x^2 + 7x^2 = 10x^2$

2. $4(x^3)^2 = 4x^{(3\times 2)} = 4x^6$

3. $\dfrac{5x^3 + 10x}{5x} =$

   $\dfrac{5x(x^2 + 2)}{5x} =$

   $\dfrac{5\cancel{x}(x^2 + 2)}{5\cancel{x}} = x^2 + 2$

4. $2x^{-4} = \dfrac{2}{x^4}$

5. $x^{\left(-\frac{2}{5}\right)} = \dfrac{1}{x^{\left(\frac{2}{5}\right)}} = \dfrac{1}{\sqrt[5]{x^2}}$

6. $\dfrac{x^{\left(\frac{3}{4}\right)}}{x^{-\left(\frac{1}{4}\right)}} =$

   $x^{\left(\frac{3}{4}\right)}x^{\left(\frac{1}{4}\right)} =$

   $x^{\left(\frac{3}{4}+\frac{1}{4}\right)} = x^1 = x$

7. $\left(\sqrt[3]{x^2}\right)\left(\sqrt[6]{x^8}\right) =$

   $\left(x^{\frac{2}{3}}\right)\left(x^{\frac{8}{6}}\right) =$

   $\left(x^{\frac{2}{3}}\right)\left(x^{\frac{4}{3}}\right) =$

   $x^{\left(\frac{2}{3}+\frac{4}{3}\right)} = x^{\left(\frac{6}{3}\right)} = x^2$

8. You can use this equation to solve:

$$(\text{Future Value}) = (\text{Present Value})(1 + (\text{Interest Rate as a Decimal}))^{\text{Number of Periods}}$$

The present value is 50 inches, the interest rate expressed as a decimal is 0.05, and the number of periods is 2 since you need the height after two years. By plugging this all into the formula, you get the following:

$$(\text{Future Value}) = (50)(1 + 0.05)^2 = 55.125 \text{ inches}$$

Zeros and Parabolas

Roots or Zeros

The root or zero of a function is the value for which the function has a value of zero. A function can have more than one root/zero. To find the root(s) of a function, either examine the equation of the function or look at the function's graph.

> **Example**

What are the zeros of $y = x^2 - 10x + 21$?

☑ **Solution**

The equation is graphed below:

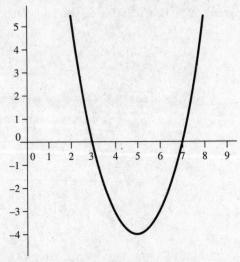

The function has roots/zeros at 3 and 7 since that is where the function intersects the *x*-axis. Since the function intersects the *x*-axis twice, the function has 2 solutions.

You can also determine the roots/zeros of the function by factoring it and setting the function equal to zero. Then solve for *x*. Let's do that with the above function:

$$y = x^2 - 10x + 21$$
$$0 = (x - 3)(x - 7)$$
$$(x - 3) = 0 \text{ and } (x - 7) = 0$$
$$x = 3 \text{ and } 7$$

The values of *x* that give a *y*-value of 0 are 3 and 7. Depending on the situation, use the graph or a simplified equation to determine roots/zeros.

Alternatively, you can use the quadratic formula to determine the roots:

$$y = x^2 - 10x + 21$$
$$x = \frac{-b \pm \sqrt{b^2 - 4ac}}{2a}$$
$$x = \frac{-(-10) \pm \sqrt{(-10)^2 - 4(1)(21)}}{2(1)}$$
$$x = \frac{10 \pm \sqrt{100 - 84}}{2}$$
$$x = \frac{10 \pm \sqrt{16}}{2}$$
$$x = \frac{10 \pm 4}{2}$$
$$x = 5 \pm 2$$
$$x = 3 \text{ or } 7$$

Parabolas

Sometimes you will need to look at the equation of a U-shaped curve, known as a parabola, and determine certain properties of it.

- The vertex form of a parabola is $y = a(x - h)^2 + k$.
- The vertex has the coordinates (h, k). If the parabola is facing up, the vertex is the bottom point of the U-shape. If the parabola is facing down, the vertex is the top point of the U-shape.
- The x-coordinate of the vertex provides the *axis of symmetry* for the parabola.

A parabola with the equation $y = (x - 1)^2 + 2$ has a vertex of $(1, 2)$. The equation for the axis of symmetry for the parabola is $x = 1$. The parabola is graphed in Figure 11:

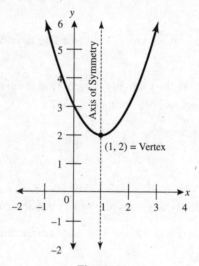

Figure 11

When a parabola is written in the form $y = ax^2 + bx + c$, you can determine the x-coordinate of the parabola's vertex using this formula:

$$x = -\frac{b}{2a}$$

> **Example**

Given a parabola with the equation $y = 5x^2 - 4x + 7$, what is the x-coordinate of the parabola's vertex?

✓ **Solution**

Use the formula $x = -\frac{b}{2a}$, and plug in the correct values: $a = 5$ and $b = -4$. Therefore:

$$x = -\frac{b}{2a}$$
$$x = -\frac{(-4)}{2 \cdot 5}$$
$$x = \frac{4}{10}$$
$$x = 0.4$$

Zeros and Parabolas Drill

1. What are the zeros of the function $y = (x - 9)(x + 1)$?

2. Where does the function $y = (x + 4)(x - 7)$ intersect the x-axis?

3. What are the zeros of the parabola $y = x^2 + x - 12$?

4. What is the x-coordinate of the vertex of a parabola with the equation $y = (x + 2)(x - 4)$?

5. A parabola with the equation $y + 4 = 3(x - 5)^2$ has what coordinates for its vertex?

6. What are the x- and y-coordinates for the vertex of a parabola with the equation $y = 3x^2 - 6x + 5$?

Solutions

1. Consider where y will equal zero. If $x - 9 = 0$ or $x + 1 = 0$, the function will equal zero. Therefore, x can equal 9 or -1.

2. The function intersects the x-axis where the value of y is zero. Find the zeros of $y = (x + 4)(x - 7)$ to solve. If $(x + 4) = 0$ or $(x - 7) = 0$, y will be zero. So x could be -4 or 7.

3. Factor the equation to determine the zeros:

$$y = x^2 + x - 12$$
$$y = (x + 4)(x - 3)$$

So the zeros are at -4 and 3 since those two values of x make y equal zero.

4. The parabola $y = (x + 2)(x - 4)$ has zeros at -2 and 4. To easily determine the x-coordinate of the vertex, find the midpoint between -2 and 4:

$$\frac{-2 + 4}{2} = \frac{2}{2} = 1$$

So the x-coordinate of the vertex is simply 1.

Alternatively, you could FOIL the equation and find $-\frac{b}{2a}$ in the new expression:

$$y = (x + 2)(x - 4)$$
$$y = x^2 - 4x + 2x - 8$$
$$y = x^2 - 2x - 8$$

For this equation, $a = 1$ and $b = -2$. So:

$$-\frac{b}{2a} \rightarrow -\frac{-2}{2(1)} = \frac{2}{2} = 1$$

Therefore, this approach also results in 1 as the x-coordinate of the vertex.

5. Put the parabola with the equation $y + 4 = 3(x - 5)^2$ into vertex form, $y = a(x - h)^2 + k$. Easily do so by subtracting 4 from both sides:

$$y + 4 = 3(x - 5)^2$$
$$y = 3(x - 5)^2 - 4$$

In parabolas of the form $y = a(x - h)^2 + k$, (h, k) is the vertex. Therefore, in the equation $y = 3(x - 5)^2 - 4$, the vertex is $(5, -4)$.

6. For parabolas in the form $y = ax^2 + bx + c$, the x-coordinate of the vertex is found using this formula: $x = -\dfrac{b}{2a}$. For the equation $y = 3x^2 - 6x + 5$, find the x-coordinate of the vertex:

$$x = -\frac{(-6)}{2(3)} = \frac{6}{6} = 1$$

Then, solve for the y-coordinate of the vertex by plugging 1 into the equation for the parabola:

$$y = 3x^2 - 6x + 5$$
$$y = 3(1)^2 - 6(1) + 5$$
$$y = 3 - 6 + 5$$
$$y = 2$$

The coordinates of the vertex are (1, 2).

Geometry and Trigonometry

Trigonometry

The three sides in a right triangle (a triangle with a 90° angle) each have special names that are based on the angles.

- **Hypotenuse:** This side is always the longest and is across from the 90° angle.
- **Opposite:** This side depends on the location of the angle you are using. It is always *directly opposite* the angle.
- **Adjacent:** This side also changes depending on the location of the angle you are using. It is always *adjacent* (next) to the angle you are using.

People often confuse the adjacent with the hypotenuse. Just remember that the hypotenuse is always the longest side in a right triangle. All three sides in a right triangle are shown in Figure 12.

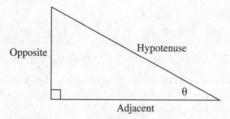

Figure 12

Use the acronym **SOH-CAH-TOA** to remember the key trigonometric ratios, as shown in Table 5.3.

Table 5.3 A Mnemonic to Remember Trigonometric Ratios

SOH	CAH	TOA
$\sin \theta = \dfrac{\text{Opposite}}{\text{Hypotenuse}}$	$\cos \theta = \dfrac{\text{Adjacent}}{\text{Hypotenuse}}$	$\tan \theta = \dfrac{\text{Opposite}}{\text{Adjacent}}$

Let's take a look at an example to see what the different trigonometric values are in the same right triangle.

> Example

A right triangle has side lengths of 3, 4, and 5. The angle θ is opposite from the side with length 3. What are the different trigonometric values for angle θ?

✓ Solution

Draw the triangle to determine the different trigonometric values.

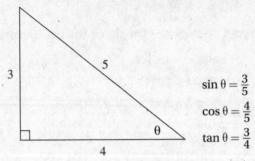

$$\sin \theta = \frac{3}{5}$$
$$\cos \theta = \frac{4}{5}$$
$$\tan \theta = \frac{3}{4}$$

To solve for an unknown angle in a right triangle, use an *inverse* of one of the trigonometry functions. In the triangle above, use an inverse function to solve for θ:

$$\sin \theta = \frac{3}{5}$$
$$\sin^{-1}(\sin \theta) = \sin^{-1}\left(\frac{3}{5}\right)$$
$$\theta \approx 36.87°$$

This could have been calculated using an inverse of the tangent or the cosine functions as well.

You can save time in your calculations if you recognize common special right triangles and Pythagorean triples:

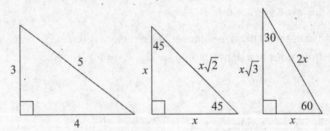

Some other common triples are **5-12-13** and **7-24-25**—you can plug these in to the Pythagorean theorem, and they will work as sides in a right triangle:

$$5^2 + 12^2 = 13^2 \text{ and } 7^2 + 24^2 = 25^2$$

Trigonometry Drill

1.

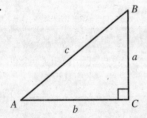

In this right triangle, what are the values of the following?

a. $\sin A$

b. $\cos B$

c. $\tan A$

2. What is the length of the hypotenuse of a right triangle with two legs that each have a length of 4?

3. If $\sin X = \frac{1}{2}$ and angle X is between $0°$ and $90°$, what is the degree measure of angle X?

4. If a right triangle has a hypotenuse of 13 and one of its legs is 5, what is the measure of the smallest angle in the triangle to the nearest whole degree?

Solutions

1.

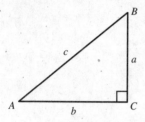

   a. $\sin A = \dfrac{\text{side opposite of angle A}}{\text{hypotenuse of the triangle}} = \dfrac{a}{c}$

   b. $\cos B = \dfrac{\text{side adjacent to angle B}}{\text{hypotenuse of the triangle}} = \dfrac{a}{c}$

   c. $\tan A = \dfrac{\text{side opposite of angle A}}{\text{side adjacent to angle A}} = \dfrac{a}{b}$

2. Use the Pythagorean theorem to solve, plugging in 4 for both a and b since the length of each leg is 4:

$$a^2 + b^2 = c^2$$
$$4^2 + 4^2 = c^2$$
$$16 + 16 = 32$$
$$c^2 = 32$$
$$c = \sqrt{32}$$
$$c = \sqrt{2 \times 16}$$
$$c = 4\sqrt{2}$$

Alternatively, you could recognize this is a multiple of a special right triangle: $x, x, \sqrt{2}\,x$. You could then just multiply 4 by $\sqrt{2}$ and get the same result.

3.

$$\sin X = \frac{1}{2}$$
$$\sin^{-1}(\sin X) = \sin^{-1}\left(\frac{1}{2}\right)$$
$$X = \sin^{-1}\left(\frac{1}{2}\right)$$

With the calculator set in degree mode (not radian mode), find that $\sin^{-1}\left(\frac{1}{2}\right) = 30°$.

4. If a right triangle has a hypotenuse of 13 and one of its legs as 5, the length of the other leg will be 12. You can find this by either realizing this is a 5-12-13 special right triangle or by calculating the unknown side by using the Pythagorean theorem:

$$a^2 + b^2 = c^2$$

$$5^2 + x^2 = 13^2$$
$$25 + x^2 = 169$$
$$x^2 = 169 - 25$$
$$x^2 = 144$$
$$\sqrt{x^2} = \sqrt{144}$$
$$x = 12$$

The triangle will look like this:

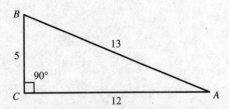

The smallest angle will be the one across from the side of length 5, angle A. So find the measure of angle A using trigonometry:

$$\sin A = \frac{5}{13}$$
$$\sin^{-1}(\sin A) = \sin^{-1}\left(\frac{5}{13}\right)$$
$$A \approx 22.62°$$

The answer is 23° since the question asks for the nearest whole degree. You could have calculated the value of this angle using tangent or cosine as well.

Circles

Circumference and Area

You should know some important circle definitions.

■ The *radius* goes from the center of the circle to the circle itself, as shown in Figure 13.

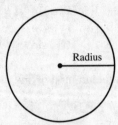

Figure 13

- The *diameter* goes from one point on a circle, through the center, to another point on the circle, as shown in Figure 14.

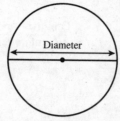

Figure 14

- A circle has 360°, as shown in Figure 15.

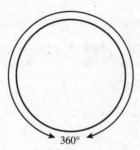

Figure 15

The *area* of a circle is computed with the following formula, where r is the radius:

$$\text{Area} = \pi r^2$$

For example, the area of a circle that has a radius of 6 is $\pi 6^2 = 36\pi$.

The *circumference* of a circle is computed with the following formula, where r is the radius:

$$\text{Circumference} = 2\pi r$$

For example, the circumference of a circle that has a radius of 6 is $2\pi 6 = 12\pi$.

A common application of circle concepts on the PSAT is calculating the length of an arc or the area of a sector. The formula for *arc length* is the following:

$$\frac{\text{Part}}{\text{Whole}} = \frac{\text{Angle}}{360°} = \frac{\text{Length of Arc}}{\text{Circumference}}$$

> **Example**

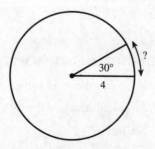

If a circle has a radius of 4 with an arc of 30° as shown above, what is the length of the arc?

✓ **Solution**

Use the part-whole ratio to solve this problem:

$$\frac{\text{Part}}{\text{Whole}} = \frac{30°}{360°} = \frac{1}{12} = \frac{\text{Length of Arc}}{\text{Circumference}} = \frac{x}{2\pi4} = \frac{x}{8\pi}$$

Set up a proportion to solve for the arc length:

$$\frac{1}{12} = \frac{x}{8\pi}$$
$$8\pi = 12x$$
$$\frac{8\pi}{12} = x$$
$$\frac{2}{3}\pi = x$$

The formula for *sector area* is the following:

$$\frac{\text{Part}}{\text{Whole}} = \frac{\text{Angle}}{360°} = \frac{\text{Area of Sector}}{\text{Area of Circle}}$$

> **Example**

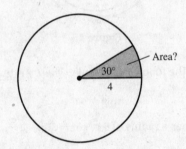

If a circle has a radius of 4 with a sector of 30° as shown above, what is the area of the sector?

✓ **Solution**

Use the part-whole ratio to solve this problem:

$$\frac{\text{Part}}{\text{Whole}} = \frac{30°}{360°} = \frac{1}{12} = \frac{\text{Area of Sector}}{\text{Area of Circle}} = \frac{x}{\pi4^2} = \frac{x}{16\pi}$$

Set up a proportion to solve for the sector area:

$$\frac{1}{12} = \frac{x}{16\pi} \rightarrow \frac{16\pi}{12} = x \rightarrow \frac{4}{3}\pi = x$$

Circle Formula

The following formula provides the graph of a circle in the xy-plane:

$$(x - h)^2 + (y - k)^2 = r^2$$

$h = x$-coordinate of center

$k = y$-coordinate of center

$r = $ radius

> **Example**

What are the center and radius of the following equation? What is its graph?

$$(x - 3)^2 + (y - 2)^2 = 9$$

✓ **Solution**

$(x - 3)^2 + (y - 2)^2 = 9$ has a center at (3, 2) and a radius of 3. Its graph is shown:

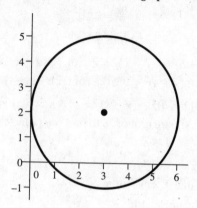

Circles Drill

1. What is the circumference of a circle with radius 5?

2. What is the area of a circle with a diameter of 6?

3. Consider a circle with the equation $(x - 1)^2 + (y + 4)^2 = 36$.

   a. What are the coordinates of the center of the circle?

   b. What is the radius of the circle?

4.

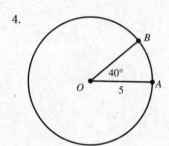

Consider a circle with a radius of 5 as shown above. Arc $\widehat{AB}$ in this circle has a measure of 40°.

   a. What is the length of arc $\widehat{AB}$?

   b. What is the area of the sector formed by arc $\widehat{AB}$?

Solutions

1. Use the formula for circumference, $2\pi r$, and plug in 5 for the radius:

$$C = 2\pi r$$
$$C = 2\pi 5$$
$$C = 10\pi$$

2. Use the area formula for a circle, πr^2, and plug in half the diameter, 3, for the radius:

$$A = \pi r^2$$
$$A = \pi(3)^2$$
$$A = 9\pi$$

3. a. From the formula for a circle, $(x - h)^2 + (y - k)^2 = r^2$, the center of the circle is point (h, k). So in the circle with the equation $(x - 1)^2 + (y + 4)^2 = 36$, the center is $(1, -4)$.

   b. The radius of a circle of the form $(x - h)^2 + (y - k)^2 = r^2$ is r. So in the circle with the equation $(x - 1)^2 + (y + 4)^2 = 36$, take the square root of 36 to find the radius:

$$\sqrt{36} = 6$$

4. a. $\dfrac{\text{Part}}{\text{Whole}} = \dfrac{40°}{360°} = \dfrac{1}{9} = \dfrac{\text{Length of Arc}}{\text{Circumference}} = \dfrac{x}{2\pi 5} = \dfrac{x}{10\pi}$

   Set up a proportion to solve for the arc length:

$$\frac{1}{9} = \frac{x}{10\pi}$$
$$10\pi = 9x$$
$$\frac{10\pi}{9} = x$$

   If you simplify without the π, the solution is approximately 3.49.

   b. $\dfrac{\text{Part}}{\text{Whole}} = \dfrac{40°}{360°} = \dfrac{1}{9} = \dfrac{\text{Area of Sector}}{\text{Area of Circle}} = \dfrac{x}{\pi 5^2} = \dfrac{x}{25\pi}$

   Set up a proportion to solve for the sector area:

$$\frac{1}{9} = \frac{x}{25\pi}$$
$$25\pi = 9x$$
$$\frac{25\pi}{9} = x$$

   If you simplify without the π, the solution is approximately 8.73.

PSAT Reference Formulas

The PSAT will provide you with the following facts and formulas. Memorizing these facts will save you time and help you think about what formula may be needed for a particular problem. However, if you do forget a formula, you can always click open the option to see it.

Radius of a circle $= r$
Area of a circle $= \pi r^2$
Circumference of a circle $= 2\pi r$

Area of a rectangle $=$ length $\times$ width $= lw$

Area of a triangle $= \frac{1}{2} \times$ base $\times$ height $= \frac{1}{2} bh$

Pythagorean theorem: $a^2 + b^2 = c^2$

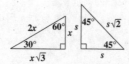

Special right triangles: 30-60-90 and 45-45-90

Volume of a box $=$ length $\times$ width $\times$ height $= lwh$

Volume of a cylinder $= \pi r^2 h$

Volume of a sphere $= \frac{4}{3}\pi r^3$

Volume of a cone $= \frac{1}{3}\pi r^2 h$

Volume of a pyramid $=$
$\frac{1}{3}$ length $\times$ width $\times$ height $= \frac{1}{3}lwh$

Key Facts:

- A circle has 360 degrees.
- There are 2π radians in a circle.
- There are 180 degrees in a triangle.

Math Essentials Review Quiz

Even though the PSAT provides you with some formulas, it doesn't provide all the ones you will need. Complete this quiz to determine which concepts you may still need to memorize.

1. To find the perimeter P of a rectangle with length L and width W, what is the correct formula?

    (A) $P = L \times W$ OR   (B) $P = 2L + 2W$

2. Which of these statements is true?

    (A) An isosceles triangle is always equilateral.   OR   (B) An equilateral triangle is always isosceles.

3.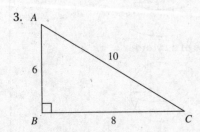

    What is the value of the sine of angle C in the triangle above?

    (A) $\frac{3}{5}$ OR   (B) $\frac{4}{5}$

4. What is the y-intercept and slope of the line with the equation $y = 4x + 3$?

    (A) y-intercept: 4 and slope: 3   OR   (B) y-intercept: 3 and slope: 4

5. What is an expression to calculate the slope between the points (A, B) and (C, D)?

    (A) $\frac{B - D}{A - C}$ OR   (B) $\frac{A - C}{B - D}$

6. A line that is parallel to the line $y = 5x - 3$ would have what slope?

    (A) 5   OR   (B) -3

7. What is the slope of a line perpendicular to the line with the equation $y = -\frac{1}{5}x - 7$?

    (A) -5 OR   (B) 5

8. What is another way of writing $(a + b)(a - b)$?

    (A) $a^2 - b^2$ OR   (B) $a^2 + b^2$

9. What does $(4x - 3)^2$ equal?

    (A) $16x^2 - 24x + 9$ OR   (B) $16x^2 + 9$

10. Which of these expresses an equivalent relationship?

    (A) $|-3| = -|3|$ OR   (B) $|3| = |-3|$

11. Which of these expresses that x is 40% of y?

    (A) $x = 0.4y$ OR   (B) $y = 0.4x$

12.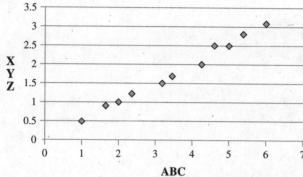

    What is the best approximation of the slope of a best-fit line for the graph above?

    (A) $\frac{1}{2}$ OR   (B) 2

13. How should you calculate the arithmetic mean of this set of numbers?

    $$\{2, 3, 5, 7, 11\}$$

    (A) Simply choose the middle value, 5   OR   (B) $\dfrac{2 + 3 + 5 + 7 + 11}{5}$

14. Which is larger for this set of numbers, the mode or the range?

    $$\{1, 1, 4, 5, 12, 71\}$$

    (A) Mode   OR   (B) Range

15. What is the probability that a two-sided coin will turn up heads when flipped?

    (A) 0.5   OR   (B) 2

16. Which of these expressions states that x is less than or equal to 3?

    (A) $x < 3$ OR   (B) $x \leq 3$

17. If $f(x) = 2x$ and $g(x) = x + 3$, what is the value of $f(g(2))$?

    (A) 10   OR   (B) 13

18. Which of these is the correct quadratic formula for equations in the form $ax^2 + bx + c = 0$?

    (A) $x = \dfrac{-b \pm \sqrt{b^2 - 4ac}}{2a}$ OR   (B) $x = \dfrac{b \pm \sqrt{b^2 + 4ac}}{a}$

19. Which of these systems of equations has infinitely many solutions?

    (A) $y = 2x$ OR   (B) $y = 2x + 1$
         $y = x + 5$ $3y = 6x + 3$

20. The function $f(x) = \frac{x^2 + 5}{x - 3}$ is undefined when x equals what number?

    (A) $x = 3$ OR   (B) $x = \sqrt{5}$

21. $\frac{2}{3} + \frac{1}{4} = ?$

    (A) $\frac{11}{12}$ OR   (B) $\frac{3}{7}$

22. $\frac{x + 3}{3} = ?$

    (A) x OR   (B) $\frac{x}{3} + 1$

23. $x^3 x^4 = ?$

    (A) x^7 OR   (B) x^{12}

24. $(x^2)^5 = ?$

    (A) x^7 OR   (B) x^{10}

25. If $x > 0$, $\frac{\sqrt[3]{x^2}}{\sqrt[6]{x}} = ?$

    (A) $\sqrt[3]{x}$ OR   (B) $\sqrt{x}$

26. What is 40% of 80?

    (A) 32   OR   (B) 48

27. If someone travels 200 miles in 4 hours, what is the person's speed in miles per hour?

    (A) 40 mph   OR   (B) 50 mph

28. What are the zeros of the function $y = (x + 2)(x - 4)$?

    (A) -2 and 4   OR   (B) 2 and -4

29. What is the vertex of a parabola with the equation $y = 2(x - 4)^2 - 5$?

    (A) $(4, -5)$ OR   (B) $(2, 4)$

30. What is the x-coordinate of the vertex of a parabola with the equation $y = 2x^2 + 3x - 6$?

    (A) $\frac{1}{3}$ OR   (B) $-\frac{3}{4}$

Answer Explanations

Solutions	Concept Review
1. **(B)** $P = 2L + 2W$ Perimeter is the sum of the lengths of the sides in the figure. As you can see in the figure below, the rectangle has two sides of width W and two sides of length L. The sum of all these sides is $L + L + W + W = 2L + 2W$. 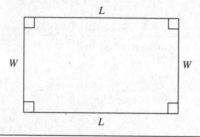	**Rectangle Area = Length × Width** and **Rectangle Perimeter = (2 × Length) + (2 × Width)**
2. **(B)** An equilateral triangle is always isosceles. An isosceles triangle needs to have only *two* sides and angles equivalent. In contrast, an equilateral triangle must have *all three sides and angles equivalent.* (An isosceles triangle can also have three angles and sides equivalent, but it is not a necessary condition to be isosceles.) So if a triangle is equilateral, it will definitely be isosceles as well. (This is similar to stating that a square is always a rectangle.)	**Isosceles Triangle:** At least 2 equal sides; at least 2 equal angles. **Equilateral Triangle:** 3 equal sides; 3 equal angles (all 60°).
3. **(A)** $\frac{3}{5}$ Here is a drawing of the sides of the triangle relative to angle C: 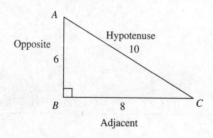	$\sin \theta = \dfrac{\text{Opposite}}{\text{Hypotenuse}}$ $\cos \theta = \dfrac{\text{Adjacent}}{\text{Hypotenuse}}$ $\tan \theta = \dfrac{\text{Opposite}}{\text{Adjacent}}$ **Pythagorean Theorem:** $$a^2 + b^2 = c^2$$

Calculate the sine of angle *C* by taking the length of the opposite side (length 6) and dividing it by the length of the hypotenuse (length 10):

$$\frac{6}{10} = \frac{3}{5}$$

Special Right Triangles and Pythagorean Triples:

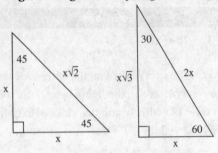

3-4-5   5-12-13   7-24-25

---

4. **(B)** *y*-intercept: 3 and slope: 4

The equation is in slope-intercept form. So the slope of the line is 4 and its *y*-intercept is 3. Here is a drawing of the line:

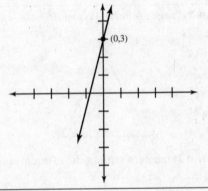

Slope-Intercept Form of a Line:

$y = mx + b$

$m = $ slope $b = $ *y*-intercept

---

5. **(A)** $\dfrac{B - D}{A - C}$

Slope is the rise over the run. For the given two points, take the difference between the *y*-coordinates and divide it by the difference between the *x*-coordinates. Be careful to maintain the same order. If you subtract the *y*-coordinate of point 1 from the *y*-coordinate of point 2, you must subtract the *x*-coordinate of point 1 from the *x*-coordinate of point 2.

For a line with the points (x_1, y_1) and (x_2, y_2):

Slope $= \dfrac{y_2 - y_1}{x_2 - x_1}$

---

6. **(A)** 5

Parallel lines never intersect since they run parallel to one another. They therefore have identical slopes. Since this line is in slope-intercept form, we can tell that the slope is 5. So any line parallel to it will also have a slope of 5.

Parallel Lines: Slopes are the same.

7. **(B)** 5

Perpendicular lines intersect at a 90-degree angle and have slopes that are negative reciprocals of each other. The slope of the line in the equation is $-\frac{1}{5}$. To find the negative reciprocal, first find the reciprocal and then multiply that result by -1. To find the reciprocal of $-\frac{1}{5}$, determine what number you would multiply $-\frac{1}{5}$ by to get 1.

$$-\frac{1}{5} \times (-5) = 1$$

So the reciprocal is -5. To get the negative reciprocal, multiply this by -1, giving $(-1)(-5) = 5$. Thus, the slope of the line perpendicular to the given line is 5.

A shortcut to finding the slope of a line perpendicular to another is simply to invert the fraction and flip the sign.

Perpendicular Lines: Slopes are *negative reciprocals of each other* $\left(\text{e.g., } 3 \text{ and } -\frac{1}{3}\right)$.

8. **(A)** $a^2 - b^2$

If you don't remember this pattern, you can use FOIL (first, outer, inner, last) with this expression:

$$(a + b)(a - b) \rightarrow$$
$$a^2 - ab + ab - b^2 \rightarrow$$
$$a^2 - b^2$$

9. **(A)** $16x^2 - 24x + 9$

FOIL the expression:

$$(4x - 3)^2 \rightarrow$$
$$(4x - 3)(4x - 3) \rightarrow$$
$$16x^2 - 12x - 12x + 9 \rightarrow$$
$$16x^2 - 24x + 9$$

Common Factoring Patterns:

$$(a + b)(a + b) = a^2 + 2ab + b^2$$

Example:

$$(x + 4)(x + 4) = x^2 + 8x + 16$$

$$(a + b)(a - b) = a^2 - b^2$$

Example:

$$(m + 2)(m - 2) = m^2 - 4$$

$$(a - b)(a - b) = a^2 - 2ab + b^2$$

Example:

$$(5 - y)(5 - y) = 25 - 10y + y^2$$

Sum of Cubes

$$(a + b)(a^2 - ab + b^2) = a^3 + b^3$$

Example:

$$(2 + x)(4 - 2x + x^2) = 8 + x^3$$

Difference of Cubes

$$(a - b)(a^2 + ab + b^2) = a^3 - b^3$$

Example:

$$(y - 4)(y^2 + 4y + 16) = y^3 - 4^3 = y^3 - 64$$

10. **(B)** $\left|3\right| = \left|-3\right|$

Treat the absolute value sign like parentheses with the order of operations. Just like parentheses come first in the order of operations, you should calculate the absolute value expressions first before dealing with the negatives outside the absolute values. In choice (A), the left-hand side equals 3 since -3 is 3 units away from 0. However, on the right-hand side, the negative sign on the outside of the absolute value makes the expression negative:

$$-\left|3\right| = -3$$

Absolute Value: Distance along the number line from zero.

Examples:

$$\left|8\right| = 8 \text{ and } \left|-8\right| = 8$$

Remark: Taking the absolute value of something should always give a nonnegative result since absolute value represents a distance.

11. **(A)** $x = 0.4y$

To find the percent, turn 40% into a fraction by dividing 40 by 100:

$$\frac{40}{100} = 0.4$$

Write an equation to show that x equals 40% of y:

$$x = 0.4y$$

General Percent Formula:

$$\frac{\text{Part}}{\text{Whole}} \times 100 = \text{Percent}$$

12. **(A)** $\frac{1}{2}$

Estimate the coordinates of a couple of points in the graph. Then calculate the slope. We can use $(0, 0)$ and $(6, 3)$. Plug these into the slope formula to solve:

$$\frac{y_2 - y_1}{x_2 - x_1} = \frac{3 - 0}{6 - 0} = \frac{3}{6} = \frac{1}{2}$$

Best-Fit Lines: Look for a general trend in the data (if it exists), and draw a line to model the trend.

13. **(B)** $\frac{2 + 3 + 5 + 7 + 11}{5}$

The mean is the simple average. Add the individual values $(2 + 3 + 5 + 7 + 11)$, and divide by the total number of values (5).

$$\text{Mean} = \frac{\text{Sum of Items}}{\text{Number of Items}}$$

Median: The middle term of a set of numbers when lined up small to large. Note that when the number of terms is even and the two terms in the middle are not equal, take the mean of the two middle terms to find the median.

Mode: The most frequent term in a set of numbers. Note that if in a set of numbers each number appears only once, there is no mode. If a set of numbers has 2 or more numbers tied for appearing the most times, the set has multiple modes.

14. **(B)** Range The mode is 1 for this set of numbers since 1 appears more frequently than any other number. The range is $71 - 1 = 70$ since that is the difference between the smallest and largest terms in the set. Therefore, the range is greater than the mode.	**Range:** The difference between the smallest and largest values in a set of data.
15. **(A)** 0.5 When the coin is flipped, it can land on either heads or tails. So there is a 1 out of 2 chance it will land on heads. In other words, 1 outcome results in success (heads) out of 2 possible outcomes (heads or tails). So the probability is $\frac{1}{2} = 0.5$.	**Probability:** The likelihood that a given event will happen, expressed as a fraction or decimal between 0 and 1 inclusive. Note that a probability of 0 means an event has no chance of occurring. A probability of 0.5 means there is a 50% chance it will occur. A probability of 1 means the event is certain to occur. In general, we can find the probability by taking the number of successes divided by the number of possible outcomes.
16. **(B)** $x \leq 3$ The line underneath the $>$ or $<$ sign signifies equivalence.	$<$ means less than. $>$ means greater than. $\leq$ means less than or equal to. $\geq$ means greater than or equal to.
17. **(A)** 10 First, calculate the value of $g(2)$: $$g(x) = x + 3$$ $$g(2) = 2 + 3 = 5$$ Then plug 5 into $f(x)$: $$f(x) = 2x$$ $$f(5) = 2 \times 5 = 10$$	**Composite Functions:** Calculate the value of the *inside* function first. Then calculate the value of the *outside* function, just as in the example problem.
18. **(A)** $x = \dfrac{-b \pm \sqrt{b^2 - 4ac}}{2a}$ This is a formula you absolutely must memorize.	**Quadratic Formula:** $x = \dfrac{-b \pm \sqrt{b^2 - 4ac}}{2a}$ An equation with the variable x and constants a, b, and c written in the form $ax^2 + bx + c = 0$ can be solved with the quadratic formula.

19. **(B)** $y = 2x + 1$

$$3y = 6x + 3$$

These two equations have infinitely many solutions because the second equation is 3 times the first equation, making them different expressions of the same equation. Thus, any solution to one equation is a solution to the other as well. Since there are infinitely many solutions to the equations (both equations are linear and a line has infinitely many points), the system itself must have infinitely many solutions.

A system of equations will have **infinite solutions** if the equations are simple multiples of each other. The graphs of the equations are exactly the same.

A system of equations will have **no solutions** if no points are solutions to all equations in the system. Graphically, the graphs of the equations never intersect. In other words, the graphs are parallel.

20. **(A)** $x = 3$

If $x = 3$, the denominator (bottom) of the equation equals zero since $3 - 3 = 0$. If you divide a number by zero, the result is undefined. You cannot divide a number into zero parts.

A function is **undefined** at a point if inputting that value into the function produces an undefined number, such as $\frac{5}{0}$.

21. **(A)** $\frac{11}{12}$

$$\frac{2}{3} + \frac{1}{4} \rightarrow \frac{8}{12} + \frac{3}{12} \rightarrow \frac{11}{12}$$

Add fractions by (1) finding the least common denominator, (2) changing each fraction to have the same denominator, and (3) adding the numerators together.

22. **(B)** $\frac{x}{3} + 1$

$$\frac{x + 3}{3} = \frac{x}{3} + \frac{3}{3} = \frac{x}{3} + 1$$

In general,

$$\frac{xy}{x} = \frac{\cancel{x}y}{\cancel{x}} = y \text{ and}$$

$$\frac{x + y}{y} = \frac{x}{y} + \frac{y}{y} = \frac{x}{y} + 1$$

23. **(A)** x^7

$$x^3 x^4 = x^{3 + 4} = x^7$$

Exponent Rules:

$$a^x a^y = a^{x + y}$$

$$\frac{a^x}{a^y} = a^{x - y}$$

$$(a^x)y = a^{xy}$$

$$a^{-x} = \frac{1}{a^x}$$

$$a^{\frac{x}{y}} = \sqrt[y]{a^x}$$

24. **(B)** x^{10}

$$(x^2)^5 = x^{2 \times 5} = x^{10}$$

25. **(B)** $\sqrt{x}$

For $x > 0$,

$$\frac{\sqrt[3]{x^2}}{\sqrt[6]{x}} = \frac{x^{\frac{2}{3}}}{x^{\frac{1}{6}}} = x^{\frac{2}{3} - \frac{1}{6}} = x^{\frac{4}{6} - \frac{1}{6}} = x^{\frac{3}{6}} = x^{\frac{1}{2}} = \sqrt{x}$$

26. **(A)** 32

$$0.40 \times 80 = 32$$

$$\frac{\text{Part}}{\text{Whole}} \times 100 = \text{Percent}$$

Move the decimal point over two spots to calculate a percentage.

$$40\% = 0.40$$

27. **(B)** 50 mph

$$\frac{200 \text{ miles}}{4 \text{ hours}} = 50 \text{ mph}$$

$$\text{Distance} = \text{Rate} \times \text{Time}$$

28. **(A)** -2 and 4 For $y = (x+2)(x-4)$, y will be zero when x equals -2 and 4.	**Zeros:** The root or zero of a function is the value for which the function has a value of zero. In other words, it is where the function intersects the x-axis.
29. **(A)** $(4, -5)$ In the function $y = 2(x-4)^2 - 5$, 4 is the h and -5 is the k.	The vertex form of a parabola is $y = a(x-h)^2 + k$ and the vertex (the bottom point of the U-shape) has the coordinates (h, k).
30. **(B)** $-\frac{3}{4}$ For $y = 2x^2 + 3x - 6$, the a is 2 and the b is 3: $$-\frac{b}{2a} = -\frac{3}{2 \cdot 2} = -\frac{3}{4}$$	When a parabola is written in the form $y = ax^2 + bx + c$, the x-coordinate of the parabola's vertex is $x = -\frac{b}{2a}$.

Further Preparation

- Try the online PSAT Math exercises that accompany this book for more targeted practice.
- Practice with other materials if needed. The PSAT Math sections are very similar to the SAT Math sections. You can use *Barron's Digital SAT* for additional practice. Also, you can find further practice at *Khanacademy.org*, the official College Board practice website.
- Take the most rigorous math courses offered by your school.
- Practice all of the word problems and algebra problems you can find—these are the most prevalent types of problems you will find on the test.

6

Math Strategies, Tactics, and Problem-Solving

How Is the PSAT Math Test Designed?

- Math Test structure:
  - 2 modules, 22 questions each, 35 minutes each
  - First module is of a standard difficulty, second module of an adaptive difficulty (will be easier or more difficult depending on student performance on the first module)
  - 4 of the questions (2 per module) are experimental and will not count toward the score.
  - The questions generally become more difficult as you go.
- Breakdown of Math Test questions:
  - Algebra (primarily linear equations and systems): approximately 14 questions
  - Problem-Solving and Data Analysis (primarily demonstrating literacy with data and real-world applications): approximately 8 questions
  - Advanced Math (primarily more complicated equations): approximately 13 questions
  - Geometry and Trigonometry: approximately 5 questions

How Can I Prepare for and Be Successful on the PSAT Math Test?

- Brush up on your content knowledge with the "Math Review" chapter.
- Review the timing strategies, question strategies, and math tactics in this chapter.
- Practice PSAT-style math questions in this chapter, targeting the question types that are most challenging to you. They are organized as follows:
  - Algebra
  - Problem-Solving and Data Analysis
  - Advanced Math
  - Geometry and Trigonometry
- Use the "Troubleshooting" guide at the end of this chapter to help you work through strategic issues you have encountered in the past or are finding as you work through problems.

PSAT Math Timing Strategies

1. Take about 1.5 minutes per question, adjusting based on where you are in the test.

Since the math questions will get gradually more difficult as you progress through each module, spend a little less than 1.5 minutes per question on the earlier questions and a little more than 1.5 minutes per question on the later questions.

If you are having trouble finishing the Math Test, on which questions would it make sense to guess? In general, if you are having difficulty finishing the Math Test, guess on the later questions within a module—these are usually the toughest ones. Every question is worth the same point value, and there is no penalty for guessing; so be sure to try the easy and medium questions. If you end up doing the more difficult second math module, be mindful that your pacing may be more challenging for that module than on the first math module.

2. Don't rush through the PSAT math.

Compared to other major standardized tests, like the ACT, the PSAT will be easier to finish in the given time. Practice your pacing on the practice Math Tests in this book, and go into the test ready to be thorough rather than hasty. On school math tests if you finish early, you can typically take the remainder of the class period to do something else. On the PSAT, however, you won't be able to do anything but the test if you finish early—you might as well use all the time available. Rushing to the end may feel good and make you look smart to your fellow test takers, who may glance at you resting on your desk and assume you are a math genius. However, there is no prize for finishing early. There is a prize—thousands of dollars in scholarship money—if you answer the questions correctly. Also, even if you are a fast reader, realize that the dense, technical prose of PSAT Math questions will require more time and focus than other sorts of reading material.

3. Don't overthink early questions, and don't underthink later questions.

Solutions to earlier questions in the PSAT Math Test will be more straightforward, while solutions to later multiple-choice and student-produced response questions will involve more critical thinking.

4. Do the questions one time well, instead of double-checking.

The PSAT Math generally has far more challenging word problems than you may be accustomed to seeing on typical school math tests, making it more difficult to correct careless reading errors. Instead of rushing through the questions and spending time second-guessing and double-checking your work, focus on doing the questions *one time well.* If you misread a PSAT Math question because you are going too quickly and then come back and read it over again quickly to double-check, it is far less likely that you will answer the question correctly than if you had simply taken the time to get it right the first time. If you are very thorough and *still* finish with some time remaining, go ahead and double-check. Go back to problems that are particularly susceptible to careless errors, like ones with negative numbers, fractions, and long word problems. Also, as you go through the test the first time, you can flag any questions you would like to come back to and double-check if time permits.

5. Come back to questions you don't understand.

Don't underestimate the power of your subconscious mind to work through something while your conscious mind is focused on a different problem. If you have given a problem a decent attempt to no avail, flag the question and come back. While you are working on other problems, your subconscious mind will be unlocking possible approaches to the problem you left behind. By coming back to the problem later and with fresh eyes, it may seem much easier than it did before. Since the math problems are of gradually increasing difficulty, you will likely want to return to the earlier problems rather than the later ones in the test if you want to attempt them again. Whatever you do, don't allow yourself to become bogged down on a single problem—you can still earn a top score while missing questions.

6. Check your pace at reasonable intervals.

Every five questions or so on the PSAT Math is typically a good time to see if you are on track with your pacing. If you are going significantly faster than the 1.5 minutes per question, you may want to slow down. If you are going slower than 1.5 minutes per question, speed things up or consider guessing on the harder questions. If you never check your pacing, you may finish way ahead or way behind. If you check the pace too frequently, you will spend too much time looking at your watch instead of solving problems. Use the included timer to monitor your pacing and hide it if you find it distracting.

7. Since the PSAT is curved, do your best to stay levelheaded.

If the PSAT seems more challenging or less challenging than you anticipated, do your best to keep a level head and not to get too confident or too worried. The curve will reflect the relative difficulty of the test that particular day. As a point of reference, in 2018, a math score of 650 out of 760 would still be in the 95th percentile for a nationally representative sample; a math score of 480 out of 760 was approximately average for all test takers nationwide.*

PSAT Math Question Strategies

1. Focus on what the question is asking.

Make notations on your scrap paper to paraphrase the question. Rather than going on autopilot and quickly jumping into solving the question, really pay attention to what the question is asking you to do. Unless you are mindful about focusing on what the questions are asking, you will get tunnel vision and tune out vital information in the questions.

2. Stay in the moment—don't skip ahead to the next step.

When solving a problem, a desire to finish quickly will make you jump ahead to the next step instead of working through the step you are on. Fortunately, the PSAT Math problems generally *do not require many steps to solve them*. Many of the wrong answers, however, will be what many students would calculate if they skipped or rushed through a step. Channel all of your intellectual energy into rigorously solving the problem, one step at a time.

3. Don't overthink the questions.

Don't allow yourself to over-complicate the questions at the beginning of the test, as they will be more straightforward and simple to solve than the later questions. The PSAT questions may all be solved in fairly straightforward ways once you get past the surface.

- Drawings and figures are always drawn to scale, unless otherwise noted in the question.
- If a question involves factoring, it will typically use a common factoring pattern, e.g., $(x + 1)(x - 1) = x^2 - 1$.

---

* *https://collegereadiness.collegeboard.org/pdf/psat-nmsqt-understanding-scores.pdf*

- If a question involves right triangles, it will often use a special right triangle, e.g., 45°–45°–90° or 3-4-5.
- If a question asks you to calculate the value of an expression, like x^3 or $x - 9$, look for ways that the expression can be simplified. For example, if you are asked to solve for x^4 in the equation $x^8 = 49$, simply take the square root of both sides to reach your answer: $x^8 = 49 \rightarrow \sqrt{x^8} = \sqrt{49} \rightarrow x^4 = 7$. This is much easier than solving for just the variable x and having to plug that value back in to x^4.
- Since the PSAT mainly tests algebra, many advanced students who are taking calculus or precalculus may overthink relatively easy questions. You will not need higher-order math to solve the questions on the PSAT—you will just need a firm grounding in the basics. If you have not studied algebra and geometry for a while, be sure to read the "Math Review" chapter in this book thoroughly—it should not take you very long to get back up to speed.

4. Take advantage of the desmos calculator, but don't rely on calculators for everything.

PSAT Math problems will not require elaborate calculations, and having a bunch of sophisticated programs on your calculator won't make a difference. In fact, many of the answers to the problems keep radicals and fractions in their non-decimal form, so calculating too far ahead could set you behind. Use the calculator when necessary, but rely on your critical thinking first and your calculator second. You may find it helpful to use the Desmos calculator on problems that involve graphing functions like lines, parabolas, and circles. You could also use the Desmos calculator to double-check your answers on certain problems, like solving systems of equations. Try working through a PSAT math practice test using only the Desmos calculator and not your regular calculator to become more familiar with when you would like to use it.

5. Mistakes can lead to success.

If the PSAT problems involved 20–30 steps of calculations, a simple mistake would jeopardize your entire problem-solving process and would waste valuable time. In actuality, the PSAT Math problems generally do not require great numbers of steps, so a small mistake will not be catastrophic. As long as you find your mistakes quickly and are able to restart your thought process on a problem quickly, you will be fine.

6. Give the questions the benefit of the doubt.

The College Board has spent a couple of years developing the materials you will see on the PSAT, and it has extensively field-tested possible questions on students to ensure the fairness and accuracy of those questions. As a result, when you encounter a tough problem on the PSAT Math, do not immediately assume that it is an unfair or a stupid question. Instead, know that quite a bit of work and care went into crafting the questions, and try to reexamine your understanding of the question.

7. It's fine if you cannot precisely justify your answers.

You simply need to answer the question correctly—you do not need to explain yourself. There are many ways to solve the PSAT Math problems; as long as you have a method that arrives at the correct answer, you are doing things perfectly. Let go of the little voice in your head that tells you that if you can't explain yourself, you must not truly understand it. Trust your intuition.

Math Tactics with Examples

Tactic 1: Translate Word Problems into Algebraic Expressions.

A major difference between the PSAT and school tests is the widespread use of word problems on the PSAT. Many PSAT problems will require you to translate several sentences into an algebraic expression. Table 6.1 lists some of the key phrases that may be used in place of mathematical notations.

Table 6.1 Key Phrases and Mathematical Operators

Wording Examples	Translation
Is, are, was, were, will be, results in, gives, yields, equals	$=$
Sum, increased by, more than, together, combined, total(s), added to, older than, farther than	$+$
Difference, decreased by, less than, fewer than, minus, younger than, shorter than	$-$
Multiplied by, times, of, product of, twice	$\times$
Divided by, per, out of, ratio of, half of, one third of, split	$\div$ or $\frac{x}{y}$

Here is an example of a typical PSAT word problem that is much easier to solve by translating the wording into algebra.

> **Example**

Katie rents an apartment in the spring and will rent it for the rest of the calendar year. To rent it, she must pay a $500 security deposit and a monthly rent of $750. In addition, she must pay monthly utilities of $40 for water and $50 for electricity. What expression gives the total amount of money Katie will spend if she rents the apartment for x months that year?

(A) $840 + 500x$
(B) $500 + 840x$
(C) $500x$
(D) $750x + 500$

> ✓ **Solution**

As you read this problem, you can underline key words and write out important information. You should use abbreviations for the sake of time. For instructional purposes, though, everything is written out here using complete words. For example:

$$\$500 = \text{security deposit}$$

$$\$750 = \text{monthly rent}$$

$$\$40 + \$50 = \$90 \text{ for total monthly utilities}$$

To rent the apartment for x months, Katie will need to pay the $500 security deposit one time. Then, she will need to pay $750 in rent each month plus $90 in utilities each month for a total of $840 each month.

So the correct answer is choice (B) because there is a flat fee of $500 plus the $840 per month, varying with how many months she rents. Writing this out, rather than doing it in your head, makes this a much easier problem to solve. If you happen to be taking a digital version of the test, you will have scrap paper provided that you can use.

Tactic 2: Minimize Careless Errors by Writing Out Your Work.

Students often dismiss careless errors as ones that should not concern them in their preparation. However, if you make careless mistakes in your practice, you will likely make them on the real PSAT. Although it may be nice to focus your preparation on learning to solve the most challenging questions elegantly, realize that a couple of careless errors on easier problems may be more detrimental than having conceptual difficulties on a challenging question.

Here is a problem where careless errors can be avoided with careful writing on the provided scrap paper.

> **Example**

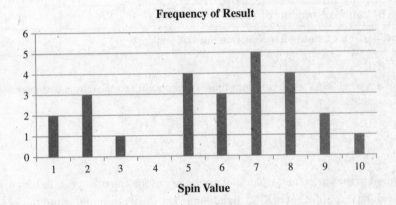

A board game has a circular wheel evenly divided into ten segments, each with a numerical value between 1 and 10. For the spins recorded in the above graph, what is the mean value of a spin, rounded to the nearest hundredth?

✓ **Solution**

If you try to do this in your head, you will likely make a careless mistake. You need to use this formula:

$$\text{Mean} = \frac{\text{Sum of Values}}{\text{Total Number of Values}}$$

The sum of all of the responses is:

$$2(1) + 3(2) + 1(3) + 0(4) + 4(5) + 3(6) + 5(7) + 4(8) + 2(9) + 1(10) = 144$$

The total number of responses is:

$$2 + 3 + 1 + 0 + 4 + 3 + 5 + 4 + 2 + 1 = 25$$

Calculate the mean:

$$144 \div 25 = 5.76$$

Tactic 3: Patiently Visualize What the Parts of an Algebraic Expression Signify.

The PSAT will have questions that require you to interpret algebraic expressions. For many questions, it is helpful to look at the answer choices before solving to see where the question is headed. On questions like these, it is advisable to "look before you leap." The incorrect answers here will likely be very persuasive. So use writing to visualize what the parts of the algebraic expression signify before you evaluate the answer choices. Although this takes more time up front, it will probably save you time in the long run. Here is an example of the kind of problem that applies to this approach.

> Example

A book warehouse has an inventory of books, I, that is modeled by the equation $I = 42,500 - 600w$, where w represents the number of weeks that have gone by after the beginning of the year. What do the numbers 42,500 and 600 represent in the equation?

(A) The average book inventory throughout the year is 42,500. The number of books at the end of the year is 600.
(B) The book inventory in the warehouse at the end of the year is 42,500. The number of weeks that it takes for the book inventory to be gone is 600.
(C) The initial monetary investment in the book warehouse is 42,500. The weekly revenue from outside book sales is 600.
(D) The warehouse book inventory at the beginning of the year is 42,500. The number of books removed from the warehouse each week is 600.

> Solution

Start by rewriting the provided equation:

$$I = 42,500 - 600w$$

Next, try plugging in different values for w to see how these impact the inventory, I.

When 0 weeks have gone by, w is 0. So the inventory is 42,500. This means that at the beginning of the year, the inventory is 42,500.

At the beginning of week 1, the initial inventory is still 42,500. At the end of week 1, though, 600 books have been subtracted from the inventory. After 2 weeks go by, the original inventory goes down by 1,200. So a pattern emerges—the 600 in the equation represents the amount by which the book inventory decreases each week. The correct answer is choice (D).

If you just jumped into the answer choices without thinking this question through and making some notes, it would have been quite easy to become trapped by a persuasive answer and overthink the question.

Tactic 4: Plug in the Answer Choices.

One of the most tried-and-true PSAT Math strategies is to plug the answers into an equation, starting with a middle value, like choice (B) or choice (C). Why? That way you will need to try only a maximum of two or three choices instead of potentially all four. The choices are almost certainly going to be in numerical order. So if the first value you choose is too large, you will know which choices to try next. Here is an example of where this technique can save you time.

> **Example**

What is a possible value of x that satisfies the equation below?

$$-(x-3)^2 = -25$$

(A) 6
(B) 8
(C) 10
(D) 12

✓ **Solution**

If you write all of this, it will make for a relatively long, messy calculation. If you work backward from the choices, you will arrive at the answer with ease. Start with choice (C), where $x = 10$, because it is a middle value among your choices:

$$-(10-3)^2 = -25$$
$$-49 \neq -25$$

So choice (C) doesn't work. If you try a larger value, like 12, the difference between the answers will be even larger. So try choice (B) next, where $x = 8$:

$$-(8-3)^2 = -25$$
$$-(5)^2 = -25$$

Since $x = 8$ is true, the correct answer is choice (B). It is unlikely that some of the later, more challenging questions will permit this sort of backsolving. However, this method can save you time on earlier questions, giving you more time to work through the difficult questions.

Tactic 5: Plug in Numbers to Solve Certain Types of Problems More Easily.

A common situation where plugging in numbers can be helpful is when the problem provides a variable within a possible range. In this case, you can pick a number within the given range and plug it in to see the value of the expression. Here is an example.

> **Example**

Assuming that x is not equal to zero, what is the value of the following expression?

$$\frac{1}{4}\left(\frac{(2x)^3}{(3x)^3}\right)$$

Student-Produced Response Question: Write Your Answer_____

✓ **Solution**

Perhaps you see that you can cancel out the x^3 from the top and bottom. If you don't make that intellectual leap, plugging in a value can make things much easier and more concrete. Based on the question, any number that is not equal to zero would work for x. This provides you with infinite options to try for x. Instead of trying a really large number or a fraction, how about plugging in 1 for x? It is not equal to zero, so it is a valid input. It is easy to work with since it will remain 1 when cubed:

$$\frac{1}{4}\left(\frac{(2x)^3}{(3x)^3}\right) =$$

$$\frac{1}{4}\left(\frac{(2\cdot1)^3}{(3\cdot1)^3}\right) =$$

$$\frac{1}{4}\left(\frac{8}{27}\right) =$$

$$\frac{8}{108} = \frac{2}{27}$$

The answer is $\frac{2}{27}$.

Tactic 6: Isolate a Constant in Order to Find Its Value.

If a question asks you to find the value of a constant, simplify the expression so you can isolate the constant and determine its value.

❯ Example

In the equation that follows, a is a constant:

$$(2 - 3x)(x^2 + 4x - 5) = -3x^3 - 10x^2 + ax - 10$$

Given that this equation is true for all values of x, what is the value of the constant a?

(A) -3
(B) 15
(C) 23
(D) 30

✓ Solution

Solve this by first expanding the left-hand side of the equation:

$$(2 - 3x)(x^2 + 4x - 5)$$

Multiply and distribute:

$$2x^2 + 8x - 10 - 3x^3 - 12x^2 + 15x$$

Combine like terms:

$$-3x^3 - 10x^2 + 23x - 10$$

Now that the left-hand side has been simplified, rewrite the original problem to see what matches up to the constant a:

$$-3x^3 - 10x^2 + 23x - 10 = -3x^3 - 10x^2 + ax - 10$$

After looking at this, it becomes clear that 23 corresponds to the constant a. Therefore, choice (C) is the correct answer. Whenever you encounter a problem involving constants, don't worry about solving for multiple variables—just isolate the constant.

Tactic 7: Use the Provided Formulas on Geometry and Trigonometry Problems.

Not many problems use geometry and trigonometry on the PSAT. Because of this, it is easy to forget that the PSAT provides you with several extremely helpful formulas. Although it would be best if you didn't have to look because you have the formulas memorized, here are the provided formulas in case you need them.

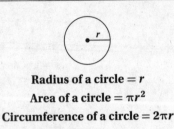

Radius of a circle = r
Area of a circle = πr^2
Circumference of a circle = $2\pi r$

Area of a rectangle = length × width = lw

Area of a triangle = $\frac{1}{2}$ × base × height = $\frac{1}{2}bh$

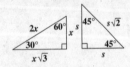

Pythagorean theorem: $a^2 + b^2 = c^2$

Special right triangles: 30-60-90 and 45-45-90

Volume of a box = length × width × height = lwh

Volume of a cylinder = $\pi r^2 h$

Volume of a sphere = $\frac{4}{3}\pi r^3$

Volume of a cone = $\frac{1}{3}\pi r^2 h$

Volume of a pyramid = $\frac{1}{3}$ × length × width × height = $\frac{1}{3}lwh$

Key Facts:

- A circle has 360 degrees.
- There are 2π radians in a circle.
- There are 180 degrees in a triangle.

The following example is the sort of problem where referring to the formulas can make a big difference.

> **Example**

The area of a sector of a circle represents 20% of the area of the entire circle. What is the central angle that corresponds to this sector in degrees?

(A) 72°
(B) 90°
(C) 120°
(D) 180°

✓ **Solution**

A provided fact is key to solving this:

"A circle has 360 degrees."

If a sector is taking up 20% of the circle, it is also taking up 20% of the degrees in the center of that circle. Since a circle has 360 degrees, the sector is taking up:

$$(0.20)(360°) = 72°$$

The answer is choice (A).

Tactic 8: Use Proportions and Canceling to Solve Unit Conversion Problems.

Converting among different types of units—such as mass measurements, currency conversion rates, and length measurements—is a major component of the PSAT. You can do unit conversions in several ways.

If you are doing a relatively straightforward conversion between just two units, you can set up a proportion or do simple multiplication. Here is an example.

TIP

Many students learn the process for unit conversions in chemistry or other science classes.

> **Example**

A cook needs to measure $3\frac{1}{2}$ cups of flour for a recipe, but he has only a tablespoon available to measure the flour. Given that there are 16 tablespoons in 1 cup, how many tablespoons of flour will the cook need for the recipe?

(A) 32 tablespoons
(B) 56 tablespoons
(C) 64 tablespoons
(D) 73 tablespoons

✓ **Solution**

Option 1: Set up a proportion. There are 16 tablespoons in 1 cup, and the cook needs 3.5 cups. So set up a proportion that has the tablespoons to cup ratio on either side:

$$\frac{16 \text{ tablespoons}}{1 \text{ cup}} = \frac{x \text{ tablespoons}}{3.5 \text{ cups}}$$

Cross multiply to solve for x:

$$3.5 \times 16 \text{ tablespoons} = 56 \text{ tablespoons}$$

The correct answer is choice (B), 56 tablespoons.

Option 2: If you are comfortable enough with conversions, you could simply jump to the last step of the above calculations and multiply 3.5 cups by 16 tablespoons to get the same result.

If you are doing a more intricate conversion that involves three or more units, you can set it up in the same way you probably learned to do unit conversions in your science classes. This method may have been called *dimensional analysis* or the *unit-factor method*. Here is an example.

> Example

If John traveled 20 miles in a straight line from his original destination, approximately how many meters is he from his original destination given that there are 1.609 kilometers in a mile and 1,000 meters in a kilometer?

(A) 32.18
(B) 12,430
(C) 24,154
(D) 32,180

✓ Solution

Write this out in an organized way where you can see which units should be canceled:

$$20 \text{ miles} \times \frac{1.609 \text{ kilometers}}{1 \text{ mile}} \times \frac{1,000 \text{ meters}}{1 \text{ kilometer}} =$$

$$20 \text{ miles} \times \frac{1.609 \text{ kilometers}}{1 \text{ mile}} \times \frac{1,000 \text{ meters}}{1 \text{ kilometer}} =$$

$$20 \times 1.609 \times 1,000 \text{ meters} \approx 32,180 \text{ meters}$$

The miles and kilometers cancel, so 20 miles approximately equals 32,180 meters, choice (D).

Tactic 9: Use Estimation When Applicable to Save Time.

Don't be overly reliant on estimation, but use it when it can help avoid a longer calculation. Here is an example.

> Example

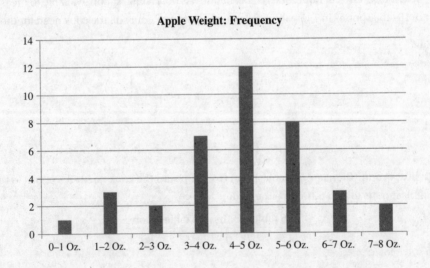

The chart above shows the distribution of individual apple weights that a customer at an apple-picking orchard placed into his bag. Which of the following could be the median weight of the 38 apples in his bag?

(A) 4.6 oz.
(B) 5.1 oz.
(C) 5.4 oz.
(D) 5.7 oz.

✓ Solution

The median of a set of numbers is the middle value when the values are arranged from least to greatest. Although you could come up with sample values and do a laborious calculation, there is no need. The choices have only one possibility that is in the range between 4 and 5 ounces. Since the 4–5 oz. column clearly contains the median value based on a simple eyeball estimation, you can pick choice (A) and move on to the next question.

Another time when estimation is useful is when the numbers in the problem can be rounded to numbers that are easier to manipulate.

❭ Example

Annie initially has $1,997 in her checking account. After shopping for her friend's birthday, the amount of money in her checking account decreases by $603. To the nearest whole number, by what percentage has the amount in her checking account decreased?

(A) 25 percent
(B) 30 percent
(C) 35 percent
(D) 40 percent

✓ Solution

Instead of using the numbers 1,997 and 603, estimate and use numbers that are easier to manipulate: 2,000 for 1,997 and 600 for 603. Use these numbers to estimate the percentage change in the amount of money in her checking account:

$$\frac{\text{Part}}{\text{Whole}} \times 100 = \text{Percentage}$$

$$\frac{600}{2,000} \times 100 =$$

$$\frac{6}{20} \times 100 =$$

$$\frac{3}{10} \times 100 = 30\%$$

This corresponds to choice (B).

Tactic 10: Don't Let Unusual Concepts Intimidate You.

You will be presented with concepts and situations on the PSAT Math that may intimidate you due to their unfamiliarity. Don't respond by quickly giving up because you were never officially taught the concept. Instead, use your intuition and reasoning to think through the problems. Your job is to get the right answer, not to explain your thought process to someone else. If you can devise a clever way to work through the problem, go with it. Remember that the PSAT is designed to assess your general mathematical thinking skills, not your memorization of formulas.

> ### Example

When measuring temperature, the equation to convert degrees Celsius, C, to degrees Fahrenheit, F, is $\frac{9}{5}C + 32 = F$. For the same actual temperature, what is the range of degrees Fahrenheit for which the given number is greater than the given number of degrees Celsius?

(A) $F < -78$

(B) $F > -40$

(C) $F < 26$

(D) $F > 30$

> ### ✓ Solution

Although this problem seems as though you may need to incorporate outside knowledge from chemistry, everything you need to figure it out is right in front of you. First paraphrase what the question is asking: "For what temperatures will F be bigger than C?" To determine this, find a value for C and F that is identical. Why? Because if you know the point at which the values are equal to one another, you can then test values greater than or less than that value to determine the direction of the inequality sign.

Let x equal the value for which C and F are the same. Plug it into the equation and solve:

$$\frac{9}{5}C + 32 = F$$

$$\frac{9}{5}x + 32 = x$$

$$32 = -\frac{4}{5}x$$

$$x = -40$$

Since C and F are equivalent at -40 degrees, plug in a simple number for F to see if the expression should be $F > -40$ or $F < -40$. Try 0 for F since it is easy to plug in:

$$\frac{9}{5}C + 32 = F$$

$$\frac{9}{5}C + 32 = 0$$

$$\frac{9}{5}C = -32$$

$$C \approx -17.8$$

From this, you can see that when the F value is 0, it is greater than the value of C, which is a negative number. So the values for which F are greater than the values of C when both numbers represent the actual temperatures are $F > -40$, making the answer choice (B).

TIP

Keep in mind that the PSAT/NMSQT is for students starting their junior year. If you have taken Algebra 1, Geometry, and some Algebra 2, you should have covered all the concepts you will see on test day. Use the "Math Review" chapter to go over anything you do not remember.

Alternatively, you can use an algebraic approach. Since the answers are in terms of F, first solve for C in terms of F:

$$\frac{9}{5}C + 32 = F$$

$$\frac{9}{5}C = F - 32$$

$$C = \frac{5}{9}(F - 32)$$

Then you can make $F > C$ and solve the inequality:

$$F > \frac{5}{9}(F - 32)$$

$$F > \frac{5}{9}F - \left(\frac{5}{9}\right)32$$

$$\frac{4}{9}F > -\left(\frac{5}{9}\right)32$$

$$F > -\left(\frac{9}{4}\right) \times \left(\frac{5}{9}\right) \times 32$$

$$F > -\frac{5}{4} \times 32$$

$$F > -40$$

If you did not realize the algebraic approaches to solving the problem, an alternative would be to take the time to test out the different answers by trying sample values from their ranges to see what would make them true. This approach can work, but it may take you more time than if you can recognize an algebraic solution.

Tactic 11: Approach the Questions Like a Puzzle, Not Like a Typical School Math Problem.

Challenging school math questions often require long calculations and cover tough concepts. The PSAT Math Test questions will not be difficult in these ways. In contrast, the tough questions will involve the patient and creative mindset needed to solve puzzles. Many of the PSAT Math problems can be solved using intuition, trying out sample values, and using the given diagrams. These approaches are not what you would find in a math textbook, yet they often work. Why? Because the PSAT Math Test has generally more *elegant* problems involving pattern recognition than the cut-and-dried problems found on typical school math tests. When you try to do a Sudoku puzzle, a jigsaw puzzle, or a challenging video game, you succeed by setting up the puzzle well instead of going full-speed ahead and doing unnecessary steps. The same applies to answering tough PSAT Math questions.

> Example

Consider a set of 25 different numbers. If two numbers are added to the set, one that is larger than the current median of the set and one that is smaller than the current median of the set, which of the following quantities about the set MUST NOT change?

(A) Range
(B) Mean
(C) Mode
(D) Median

✓ Solution

On a problem like this, try visualizing what will happen by making up some sample values. Suppose you have a simple set of numbers, something like this:

$$\{1, 1, 2, 3, 4, 5, 6, 7, 8, 9, 10, 11, 12, 13, 14, 15, 16, 17, 18, 19, 20, 21, 22, 23, 24\}$$

The range of the set is 23, which is the difference between the smallest value (1) and the largest value (24).

The mean for this set is all of the above numbers added together and then divided by 25.

The mode is 1 since it appears the most frequently.

The median is 12 since it is the middle value when the numbers are placed in order from smallest to largest.

If you can come up with even one set of values that will make one of these quantities change, that answer is out as a possibility.

If you add −5 and 100 to the set, the range of the set will become much larger—it will be 105. So choice (A) is not correct.

If you add 2 and 1,000 to the set, the mean will change because the average will shift significantly upward. So choice (B) is not correct.

If you add 7 and 17 to the set, it will have 3 different modes instead of just having 1 as the only mode. So choice (C) is not correct.

Choice (D) is correct. As long as you add any number less than 12 and any number greater than 12, the median will remain the same because 12 will still be in the middle of the set of numbers when they are all placed in order from smallest to largest.

You could also solve this more intuitively if you have a solid understanding of the concept of the median of a set. When given a particular median, if you add one number greater than and one number less than the median, the median will not change since it will remain in the very middle of the set.

Tactic 12: Don't Jump to an Answer Too Quickly.

Unlike in traditional math tests where the incorrect answers are often just random numbers, the answers on the PSAT are designed to reflect the errors students can make when solving the problems. Simply because an answer is on your calculator is no guarantee that it is correct. For example, in math class you typically solve for x and the answer is a given solution. On the PSAT, however, the question may be asking for the value of an expression, like $-2x^2 - x$.

If you have absolutely no idea what the correct answer is to a question, then guess. There is no penalty for guessing. The PSAT does not consistently favor one answer choice letter over another. So before you take the test, choose a letter at random. When you have to guess an answer, just use that letter. Choosing a particular letter ahead of time and always using it when you are blindly guessing will help you avoid wasting time during the test deciding which letter to pick.

> **Example**

What is/are the real number value(s) of x in this equation?

$$x = \sqrt{2x + 15}$$

(A) -3 only

(B) 5 only

(C) -3 and 5

(D) Cannot determine based on the given information.

✓ **Solution**

Although this looks fairly easy to solve, more is here than meets the eye. You have to be careful that what seems to be a solution actually is a solution. Start by squaring both sides and determining the potential values for x:

$$x = \sqrt{2x + 15}$$
$$x^2 = 2x + 15$$
$$0 = x^2 - 2x - 15$$
$$0 = (x + 3)(x - 5)$$

So if $(x + 3) = 0$ or if $(x - 5) = 0$, the entire expression equals 0. That means -3 can be a solution since you can set $(x + 3)$ equal to 0 and solve for x:

$$(x + 3) = 0$$

Subtract 3 from both sides:

$$x = -3$$

You can do the same procedure for $(x - 5)$:

$$(x - 5) = 0$$

Add 5 to both sides:

$$x = 5$$

So it appears that both -3 and 5 work as solutions since they both cause $(x + 3)(x - 5)$ to equal 0. When you try these in the original equation, however, only 5 works. Why? Because -3 cannot be the principal square root of 9 since -3 cannot equal the positive square root of a number. So -3 is an "extraneous solution," making choice (B) the answer.

Tactic 13: Know the Student-Produced Response Question Rules.

On the PSAT Math Test, approximately 20–25% of the questions are student-produced response questions. Here are some key things to know about these types of problems.

- It is possible that a question could have more than one correct answer. Enter just one correct answer.
- Long decimal answers that continue past the five spots allowed for gridding can be rounded up or shortened as long as you use all of the spaces. You can also express a decimal answer as a fraction. For example, you can write $\frac{7}{9}$ as 7/9, 0.777, 0.778, .7777, or .7778.
- You don't need to reduce fractions. For example, since $\frac{2}{3}$, $\frac{4}{6}$, and $\frac{6}{9}$ are equivalent, any of them will work as an answer.

⟩ Example

What is the value of x if $(3x + 2) - (5x - 6) = -4$?

✓ Solution

On a problem like this, the math is not too difficult. The challenge is to avoid making a careless error because of confusing a negative sign or incorrectly adding numbers. This is especially important on a student-produced response question since you will not have four multiple choices to help you detect a major miscalculation. Avoid making careless mistakes by writing out all of your steps. Start by writing the original equation:

$$(3x + 2) - (5x - 6) = -4$$

Remove the parentheses around $(3x + 2)$ and distribute the -1 through the $(5x - 6)$:

$$3x + 2 - 5x + 6 = -4$$

Check that you distributed the negative sign correctly. Then combine like terms:

$$-2x + 8 = -4$$

Subtract the 8 from both sides:

$$-2x = -12$$

Divide both sides by -2 to solve for x:

$$x = 6$$

You can check your work by plugging in 6 for x into the original equation:

$$(3x + 2) - (5x - 6) = -4$$
$$(3(6) + 2) - (5(6) - 6) = -4$$
$$18 + 2 - 30 + 6 = -4$$
$$-4 = -4$$

It checks out. So the final answer is 6.

Algebra Practice

1. Which ordered pair (x, y) satisfies the pair of equations below?

$$3x + y = -3$$
$$x - 2y = -8$$

   (A) $(2, 4)$
   (B) $(-2, 3)$
   (C) $(-3, 2)$
   (D) $(1, -4)$

2. The United States primarily uses a 12-hour clock with 12-hour periods for the morning (A.M.) and for the afternoon/evening (P.M.). Much of the rest of the world uses a 24-hour clock (e.g., 3:00 P.M. would be expressed as 15 hundred hours). Which of the following inequalities expresses the digits for hours, H, on a 24-hour clock that correspond to the business hours for a restaurant that is open from 7 P.M. until 11 P.M. (Ignore the "hundred" expressed with the hours in the 24-hour clock)?

   (A) $7 \leq H \leq 11$
   (B) $12 \leq H \leq 24$
   (C) $19 \leq H \leq 23$
   (D) $24 \leq H \leq 27$

3. A video arcade charges a set $5 charge to purchase a game card and then charges $0.50 for each video game played. What expression gives the relationship between the number of games played, G, and the total amount of dollars spent using the game card, T?

   (A) $T = 5G - 0.50$
   (B) $T = 4.50G + 5$
   (C) $T = 0.50G - 2.5$
   (D) $T = 0.50G + 5$

4.

Age	Maximum Recommended Heart Rate
50	165
55	160
60	155
65	150

A cardiologist uses the guidelines for maximum recommended heart rate (measured in beats per minute) shown in the table above, which vary based on a patient's age. One of the cardiologist's patients, age 55, wants to start an exercise program. The cardiologist recommends that the patient maintain a heart rate greater than 50% and less than 85% of the maximum recommended heart rate while exercising. Which of the following expressions gives the range in which the patient's heart rate, H, should be during exercise?

   (A) $50 < H < 85$
   (B) $80 < H < 136$
   (C) $85 < H < 160$
   (D) $150 < H < 160$

5. Hannah has only nickels and dimes in her wallet. She has a total of $2.50 and a total of 30 coins. How many nickels does she have?

   (A) 10
   (B) 12
   (C) 15
   (D) 16

6. A two-digit number has a tens place, t, and a units place, u. The digits have the following relationships:

$$t + u = 8$$
$$t = 2 + u$$

   What is the value of the two-digit number given by these two digits?

   (A) 41
   (B) 53
   (C) 63
   (D) 79

7. 18-karat gold has 18 parts gold for 24 total parts metal (the difference comes from the 6 parts that are metals other than gold). 24-karat gold is pure gold. In order to make a piece of jewelry that is 2.4 ounces in weight and is 20-karat gold, how many ounces of 18-karat gold, X, and of 24-karat gold, Y, are needed to make this piece of jewelry?

   (A) $X = 0.4, Y = 0.6$
   (B) $X = 0.9, Y = 1.7$
   (C) $X = 1.2, Y = 1.1$
   (D) $X = 1.6, Y = 0.8$

8. For the equation $3 + 4x - 2 = k + 6x - 2x$, what does the constant k need to equal in order for there to be multiple solutions for x?

   (A) 1
   (B) 2
   (C) 3
   (D) 4

9. What is the value of y in the system of equations below?

   $$16x - 4y = 12$$
   $$8x + 2y = 4$$

   (A) 2
   (B) $\frac{3}{2}$
   (C) $-\frac{1}{2}$
   (D) -4

10. What are the solutions for x and y in the equations below?

    $$-\frac{3}{4}x + 2\left(y - \frac{1}{2}\right) = 3$$
    $$\frac{2}{3}x = 6 - 2y$$

    (A) $x = \frac{24}{17}$, $y = \frac{43}{17}$
    (B) $x = \frac{2}{13}$, $y = \frac{14}{19}$
    (C) $x = -3$, $y = \frac{7}{19}$
    (D) $x = -\frac{4}{11}$, $y = \frac{18}{23}$

11. Electrical engineers use Ohm's law, $V = IR$, to give the relationship among voltage (V), current (I), and resistance (R). Which of the following statements is always true about the relationship among voltage, current, and resistance based on Ohm's law?

    I. If the current increases and the resistance remains the same, the voltage increases.
    II. If the voltage increases, the resistance must increase.
    III. If the resistance increases and the voltage remains the same, the current must decrease.

    (A) I only
    (B) II only
    (C) I and III only
    (D) II and III only

12. What is the graph of the following function?

    $$3 + y = 2 + 3x$$

    (A)
    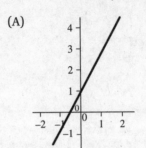

    (B)
    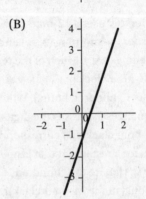

    (C)
    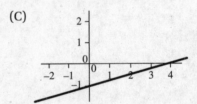

    (D)
    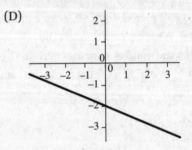

Answer Explanations

1. **(B)** You can use substitution to solve, although elimination could also work.

$$3x + y = -3$$
$$x - 2y = -8$$

Rearrange the second equation to be in terms of y:

$$x - 2y = -8$$
$$x = 2y - 8$$

Substitute into the first equation and solve for y:

$$3x + y = -3$$
$$3(2y - 8) + y = -3$$
$$6y - 24 + y = -3$$
$$7y - 24 = -3$$
$$7y = 21$$
$$y = 3$$

Then plug in 3 for y into the first equation to solve for x:

$$3x + y = -3$$
$$3x + 3 = -3$$
$$3x = -6$$
$$x = -2$$

2. **(C)** Simply add 12 to both 7 and 11 to find the correct range since all of the P.M. times are 12 hours less than the time on a 24-hour clock:

$$12 + 7 = 19 \text{ and } 12 + 11 = 23$$

This makes the range between 19 and 23 hours inclusive, which is expressed as the inequality $19 \leq H \leq 23$.

3. **(D)** There will be a $5 charge no matter how many games are played. So the $5 should be represented as a constant. For each game played, there is an additional $0.50 fee. Since G represents the number of games played, the total cost is $0.50G + 5$ dollars. This can be expressed as $T = 0.50G + 5$. Alternatively, you could make up a number of games played and the total dollars spent. Then find which of the equations gives an identical result.

4. **(B)** Use the table to find the maximum recommended heart rate for a 55-year-old person—160 beats per minute. Then take 50% and 85% of 160 to determine the lower and upper bounds of the recommended heart rate:

$$50\% \text{ of } 160 = 0.50 \times 160 = 80$$
$$85\% \text{ of } 160 = 0.85 \times 160 = 136$$

So the range is between 80 and 136 beats per minute, which is expressed as the inequality $80 < H < 136$.

5. **(A)** Set up a series of two equations. Put everything in terms of cents for sake of simplicity. Use N as the number of nickels and D as the number of dimes:

The total number of coins: $N + D = 30$
The total number of cents: $5N + 10D = 250$

Express D in terms of N based on the first equation:

$$N + D = 30$$
$$D = 30 - N$$

Then, substitute this for D in the second equation:

$$5N + 10D = 250$$
$$5N + 10(30 - N) = 250$$
$$5N + 300 - 10N = 250$$
$$-5N = -50$$
$$N = 10$$

Alternatively, you can solve this by working backward from the answers. Since the total number of cents must be 250, try the different possible values of nickels from the choices to see which one works. You can try choice (B) or choice (C) since they are in the middle. Once you get to choice (A), you will find that if you have 10 nickels, you have 50 cents from nickels. That means there must be 200 cents from dimes, which also means there are 20 dimes. Since 20 dimes and 10 nickels add together to give you 30 coins total, choice (A) is correct.

6. **(B)** Use substitution to solve for t and u:

$$t + u = 8$$
$$t = 2 + u$$

Plug in $2 + u$ for t into the first equation:

$$(2 + u) + u = 8$$
$$2 + 2u = 8$$
$$2u = 6$$
$$u = 3$$

Plug in 3 for u into one of the original equations, and solve for t. This gives 5 in the tens place and 3 in the ones place, making 53 your answer.

Alternatively, you can solve this using elimination.

$$t + u = 8$$
$$t = 2 + u$$

Rearrange the second equation:

$$t = 2 + u$$
$$t - u = 2$$

Then you have this as the set of equations:

$$t + u = 8$$
$$t - u = 2$$

Add the two together to get:

$$2t = 10$$
$$t = 5$$

Then substitute $t = 5$ into the first equation to solve for u:

$$t + u = 8$$
$$5 + u = 8$$
$$u = 3$$

The answer is still 53.

7. **(D)** Set up a system of two equations. One equation models the number of actual gold karats:

$$\frac{18}{24}X + \frac{24}{24}Y = \frac{20}{24} \times 2.4 \rightarrow \frac{3}{4}X + Y = \frac{5}{6} \times 2.4$$

One equation models the weight of the jewelry:

$$X + Y = 2.4$$

You can use either substitution or elimination to solve this system. However, using elimination is better since a Y-term in each equation will

be easily canceled. Start by simplifying the first equation:

$$\frac{3}{4}X + Y = \frac{5}{6} \times 2.4$$
$$\frac{3}{4}X + Y = 2$$

Now subtract it from $X + Y = 2.4$:

$$X + Y = 2.4$$
$$-\left(\frac{3}{4}X + Y = 2\right)$$
$$\frac{1}{4}X = 0.4$$

Then solve for X:

$$\frac{1}{4}X = 0.4$$
$$X = 4 \times 0.4$$
$$X = 1.6$$

Now plug in 1.6 for X into one of the equations to solve for Y. Use $X + Y = 2.4$ since it is simpler:

$$X + Y = 2.4$$
$$1.6 + Y = 2.4$$
$$Y = 0.8$$

So the final answer is $X = 1.6$, $Y = 0.8$.

8. **(A)** Before proceeding too far, simplify the equation by grouping like terms:

$$3 + 4x - 2 = k + 6x - 2x$$
$$1 + 4x = k + 4x$$

So if $k = 1$, both sides of the equations are equivalent to one another. The equation reduces to $x = x$, which has an infinite number of solutions.

9. **(C)** Solve this using elimination by taking the first equation and multiplying it by $\frac{1}{2}$:

$$16x - 4y = 12$$
$$8x + 2y = 4$$

$$8x - 2y = 6$$
$$8x + 2y = 4$$

Subtract the two so we can easily find y:

$$8x - 2y = 6$$
$$-(8x + 2y = 4)$$
$$-4y = 2$$
$$y = -\frac{1}{2}$$

10. **(A)** Start by simplifying both equations:

$$-\frac{3}{4}x + 2\left(y - \frac{1}{2}\right) = 3$$

$$-\frac{3}{4}x + 2y - 1 = 3 \quad \text{and} \quad \frac{2}{3}x = 6 - 2y$$

$$-\frac{3}{4}x + 2y = 4 \qquad\qquad \frac{2}{3}x + 2y = 6$$

Then use elimination to solve:

$$-\frac{3}{4}x + 2y = 4$$

$$-\left(\frac{2}{3}x + 2y = 6\right)$$

$$-\frac{3}{4}x - \frac{2}{3}x = -2$$

$$-\frac{9}{12}x - \frac{8}{12}x = -2$$

$$\frac{-17}{12}x = -2$$

$$x = \frac{24}{17}$$

Since only choice (A) has x equal to $\frac{24}{17}$, you can save time by just picking it as the correct answer.

11. **(C)** Choice I is correct. Increasing current while keeping resistance constant increases the right side of the equation. This means the left side—the voltage—increases as well. Choice III is correct. If the voltage—the left side of the equation—remains the same while the resistance increases, the current must decrease in order for the value on the right side of the equation to remain the same. Choice II is NOT correct. The current could increase without the resistance increasing if the voltage increases.

12. **(B)** Put the equation into slope-intercept form:

$$3 + y = 2 + 3x$$

$$y = 3x - 1$$

This line has a slope of 3 and a y-intercept of -1, which has the following graph:

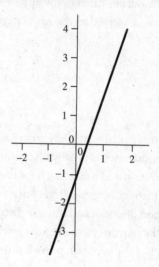

Problem-Solving and Data Analysis Practice

1. A subway map is drawn to scale so that 1 inch on the map corresponds to 2 miles of actual distance on the track. The subway train travels at a constant average rate of 30 miles per hour. How many minutes will a journey on the subway take if the track distance as portrayed on the map is 3 inches?

   (A) 6
   (B) 9
   (C) 12
   (D) 18

2. An electronic reader typically costs $100. However, the price is heavily discounted due to both a coupon and a sale that have the same percent off the regular price. If the price using both the coupon discount and the sale discount is $49, what is the percent off the regular price that the coupon and the sale each provide independently?

   (A) 25%
   (B) 30%
   (C) 35%
   (D) 40%

3. If n percent of 80 is 20, what is n percent of 220?

   (A) 42
   (B) 48
   (C) 55
   (D) 76

4. If 132 men and 168 women are living in a dormitory, what percent of the total dormitory residents are men?

   (A) 28%
   (B) 34%
   (C) 40%
   (D) 44%

5. If 1 Canadian dollar can be exchanged for 0.80 U.S. dollars and vice versa, how many Canadian dollars can a traveler receive in exchange for 120 U.S. dollars?

   (A) 60
   (B) 90
   (C) 150
   (D) 220

6. David is developing a fitness plan and wants to get his weight to a level that will be considered healthy in terms of the body mass index (BMI) calculation. The currently recommended BMI is between 18.6 and 24.9. To calculate BMI using inches and pounds, David takes his weight in pounds and divides it by the square of his height in inches. Then he multiplies the entire result by 703. David is 6 feet, 3 inches tall and currently weighs 260 pounds. To the nearest whole pound, what is the least number of whole pounds he needs to lose in order for his BMI to be within the healthy range?

   (A) 61
   (B) 68
   (C) 75
   (D) 83

7. A marine biologist has conducted research into the population of blue whales over the past few decades. The estimated global blue whale population is plotted against the given year in the graph below:

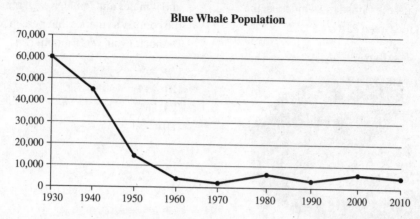

Blue Whale Population

From 1940 until 1970, the best-fit equation for the values of the blue whale population has which general characteristic?

(A) Linear decay

(B) Linear growth

(C) Exponential decay

(D) Exponential growth

8. The graph below gives the current GPA of every one of the 389 students at County High School.

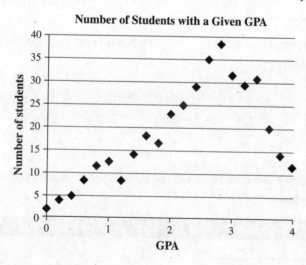

Number of Students with a Given GPA

The school administrators have decided that too much grade inflation occurs at the school. They believe the average GPA is skewed too high by teachers giving too many A's and B's and by not enough students receiving C's, D's, and F's. If the administrators want to ensure that grade inflation is minimized, which of these quantities would be important to bring close to 2.0?

(A) Median only

(B) Mean only

(C) Both mean and median

(D) Neither mean nor median

9. In a recent election in a European country, the political parties divided the vote among the Social Democrats, the Christian Democrats, the Socialists, and the Green Party.

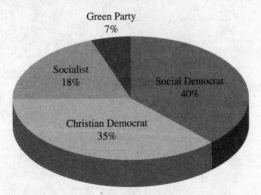

Green Party
7%

Socialist
18%

Social Democrat
40%

Christian Democrat
35%

Percentage of Votes

If women provided 60% of the total votes for the Green, Socialist, and Christian Democrat parties and if males and females each represent 50% of the country's voters, what percent of the Social Democrat vote was from men?

(A) 45%

(B) 49%

(C) 56%

(D) 65%

10. 300 patients at a hospital were categorized based on whether they had high or low cholesterol and on whether they had high or low blood pressure. The results are tabulated in the table below.

	High Cholesterol	Low Cholesterol	Total
High Blood Pressure	40	30	70
Low Blood Pressure	50	180	230
Total	90	210	300

What is the percent chance that one of the 300 patients will have at least one of the conditions—high cholesterol or high blood pressure?

(A) 36%

(B) 40%

(C) 48%

(D) 52%

11. A researcher surveyed several residents in a town about the types of vehicles the residents own. The results are shown in the table below.

	Car	Van	Truck/SUV	Total
Gas	104	31	43	178
Hybrid	10	1	m	n
Electric	6	3	0	9
Total	120	35	45	200

What are the values of m and n in the table above?

(A) $m = 4$ and $n = 8$

(B) $m = 8$ and $n = 26$

(C) $m = 2$ and $n = 13$

(D) Cannot determine based on the given information.

Answer Explanations

1. **(C)** Since 1 inch on the map corresponds to 2 miles of actual distance, double the 3 inches shown on the map to determine that the subway has traveled 6 actual miles. Since the subway is traveling at 30 miles per hour, solve for the number of hours the subway has traveled:

$$\text{Distance} = \text{Rate} \times \text{Time}$$
$$6 = 30 \times \text{Time}$$
$$\text{Time} = \tfrac{1}{5} \text{ hours}$$

   Then multiply $\tfrac{1}{5}$ by 60 minutes to determine how many minutes the train takes to travel 6 miles:

$$\tfrac{1}{5} \times 60 = 12 \text{ minutes}$$

2. **(B)** Since both the coupon and the sale provide the same percent discount, you can set up an equation to determine what you must multiply $100 by in order to end up with a price of $49. Alternatively, you can simply multiply $100 by the same variable twice, which will let you determine the correct percentage:

$$(x)(x)(100) = 49$$
$$100x^2 = 49$$
$$x^2 = \frac{49}{100}$$
$$x^2 = 0.49$$
$$x = \sqrt{0.49}$$
$$x = 0.7$$

   If x equals 0.7, subtract 0.7 from 1 to find the percent discount:

$$1 - 0.7 = 0.3 = 30\%$$

   This means that a 30 percent discount has been applied to the original amount two times.

3. **(C)** Set this up as an equation to determine what n equals. Use the first bit of information in the question:

$$\frac{\text{Part}}{\text{Whole}} \times 100 = \text{Percent}$$
$$\frac{20}{80} \times 100 = n$$
$$\tfrac{1}{4} \times 100 = n$$
$$n = 25\%$$

   Then take 25% of 220:

$$0.25 \times 220 = 55$$

4. **(D)** Since $\frac{\text{Part}}{\text{Whole}} \times 100 = \text{Percent}$, take the number of men and divide it by the total number of residents to determine the percentage of just men:

$$\frac{132}{132 + 168} \times 100 = 44\%$$

5. **(C)** This is easiest to solve using a simple proportion:

$$\frac{1 \text{ Canadian dollar}}{0.80 \text{ U.S. dollars}} = \frac{x}{120}$$

   Cross multiply to find the solution:

$$(1 \text{ Canadian dollar})(120) = (0.80 \text{ U.S. dollars})(x)$$
$$x = \frac{120}{0.80} = 150 \text{ Canadian dollars}$$

6. **(A)** First solve for the weight that David must be in order to have a BMI of 24.9 given his height since this would put the BMI within the appropriate range. Use the wording in the question to set up an equation: "To calculate BMI using inches and pounds, David takes his weight in pounds and divides it by the square of his height in inches. Then he multiplies the entire result by 703." This gives the following BMI equation:

$$\frac{\text{Weight}}{\text{Height}^2} \times 703 = \text{BMI}$$

   Since David is 6 feet, 3 inches tall, his height is $(12 \times 6) + 3 = 75$ inches. Plug in 24.9 for the BMI and 75 for the height into the equation, and solve for the weight:

$$\frac{\text{Weight}}{75^2} \times 703 = 24.9$$
$$\text{Weight} \times 703 = 24.9 \times 75^2$$
$$\text{Weight} = \frac{24.9 \times 75^2}{703}$$
$$\text{Weight} \approx 199$$

   Then subtract the desired weight from David's current weight to determine how many whole pounds he should lose:

$$260 - 199 = 61$$

7. **(C)** Between 1940 and 1970, the blue whale population is decreasing and the function has a substantial curve. So the graph shows exponential decay. Note that if the decay were linear, the graph would have gone down in a straight line.

8. **(C)** The median is the middle value of all the GPAs. If the middle value was much above 2.0, it would be a strong indication that there was grade inflation. The mean is the arithmetic average of the GPAs, so if it was much above 2.0, it would also indicate grade inflation. So both the median and mean should be close to 2.0 in order to minimize grade inflation.

9. **(D)** Women provided 60% of the vote for the 60% of the total votes for the Green, Socialist, and Christian Democrat parties. That means that women provided $0.6 \times 0.6 \times$ total votes $= 36\%$ of the total votes, not including the Social Democrat votes. Since women make up 50% of the country's voters, 14% of the country's total voters are women who voted for the Social Democrats since $50 - 36 = 14$. That means that 26% of the total population of the country are males who voted for the Social Democrats. To determine the percentage of Social Democrat votes from males, take 26 and divide it by the total percentage of 40 and then convert that value to a percent:

$$\frac{26}{40} \times 100 = 65\%$$

10. **(B)** There are 40 patients with both conditions, 50 who have only high cholesterol, and 30 who have only high blood pressure:

$$40 + 50 + 30 = 120$$

Divide 120 by the 300 total to find the percent:

$$\frac{120}{300} \times 100 = 40\%$$

11. **(C)** The value of m must be 2. All of the trucks and SUVs must add up to a total of 45, and there are 43 of the other truck/SUV types: $43 + 2 = 45$. The value of n must be 13. The total of all the different types of vehicles must add up to 200. The numbers in the last column show a total of $178 + 9 = 187$ and $187 + 13 = 200$.

Advanced Math Practice

1. Michele wants to design a floor that will have a length and width that add up to 30 feet. She also wants the area of the floor to be 216 square feet. What will the dimensions of the floor need to be?

   (A) 10 feet by 20 feet
   (B) 12 feet by 18 feet
   (C) 14 feet by 16 feet
   (D) 17 feet by 17 feet

2. $\left(\dfrac{n^2 - n^3}{n^4}\right)^{-2}$ is equivalent to which of the following?

   (A) $\dfrac{n^4}{1 - 2n + n^2}$

   (B) $\dfrac{n}{n^8}$

   (C) $\dfrac{1 - 2n + n^2}{n^2}$

   (D) $\dfrac{n^2}{1 + 4n - n^2}$

3. For the real integers x and y, what must $\dfrac{2x + 2y}{4}$ equal?

   (A) The mode of x and y
   (B) $x^2 + y^2$
   (C) The arithmetic mean of x and y
   (D) The median of $2x$ and $2y$

4. Factor: $16a^2 - 9b^2$

   (A) $(2a + b)(a - b)$
   (B) $(3a + 2b)(6a - 3b)$
   (C) $(4a + 3b)(4a - 3b)$
   (D) $(8a + 3b)(2a - 3b)$

5. What are the two solutions for x in the equation $4x^2 + 8x - 4 = 0$?

   (A) $x = 3\sqrt{2}$ and $x = -4$
   (B) $x = 2\sqrt{3}$ and $x = \sqrt{11} + 13$
   (C) $x = -\sqrt{7}$ and $x = -5$
   (D) $x = -1 - \sqrt{2}$ and $x = \sqrt{2} - 1$

6. Simplify: $x^4 y^2 + x^3 y^5 + xy^6 + 2x^3 y^5$

   (A) $xy(x^4 + 3x^2 y^3 + y^6)$
   (B) $y^2(x^4 + 4x^3 y^4 + y^3)$
   (C) $xy^2(x^3 + 3x^2 y^3 + y^4)$
   (D) $x(x^3 y^2 + x^2 y^5 + y^6 + 2x^4 y^4)$

7. $\dfrac{x}{2} = \dfrac{2(n^0)}{2} - \dfrac{1}{2x}$

   What is the value of x?

   (A) 0
   (B) 1
   (C) 2
   (D) 3

8. What is the sum of $3x^3 + 5x - 3$ and $2x^2 - 4x + 6$?

   (A) $x^2 - 9x + 9$
   (B) $2x^3 + 4x^2 - x$
   (C) $3x^3 - x^2 + 2x + 3$
   (D) $3x^3 + 2x^2 + x + 3$

9. $(25a^4 + 40a^2 b^4 + 16b^8) \div (5a^2 + 4b^4) = ?$

   (A) $5b^4 + 40a^2 b^4 + 5a^2$
   (B) $4b^4 + 5a^2$
   (C) $25a^4 + 8a^2 b^4 + 4a^2$
   (D) 1

10. The formula used by the National Weather Service to calculate wind chill in degrees Fahrenheit is:

$$35.74 + 0.6215 \times T - 35.75 \times \left(V^{(0.16)}\right) + 0.4275 \times T \times \left(V^{(0.16)}\right)$$

T represents the air temperature in degrees Fahrenheit, and V represents the wind velocity in miles per hour.

Which of these is an accurate statement about the relationship between wind chill and temperature?

   I. The relative impact on wind chill of a particular increase in wind speed is more significant at lower wind speeds than at higher wind speeds.

   II. Wind chill has an impact on the relative temperature feeling only at temperatures greater than or equal to 35.75 degrees Fahrenheit.

   III. Wind chill and temperature are inversely related to one another.

   (A) I only
   (B) II only
   (C) I and II only
   (D) II and III only

11. Consider the function below.

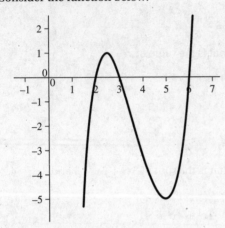

If the function is written as $f(x) = (x - 2) \times A \times (x - 3)$, what is the value of A?

(A) x

(B) $(x + 2)$

(C) $(x - 6)$

(D) $(x - 14)$

12. The function $y = 6x^3 + 19x^2 - 24x + c$ has zeros at the values of $-\frac{1}{2}$, $\frac{4}{3}$, and -4. What is the value of the constant c in this function?

(A) -16

(B) -9

(C) 2

(D) 14

13. The graph of the function below is given by which equation?

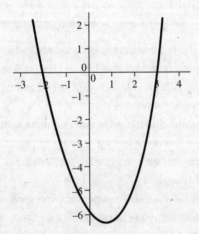

(A) $f(x) = 2x^2 - 2x - 4$

(B) $f(x) = 3x^2 - 6x - 7$

(C) $f(x) = x^2 + x - 3$

(D) $f(x) = x^2 - x - 6$

14. What will happen to the graph of $y = x^2$ in the xy-plane if it is changed to

$$y = (x + 8)^2 + 4?$$

(A) It will shift to the left 8 units and shift up 4 units.

(B) It will shift to the right 8 units and shift up 4 units.

(C) It will shift to the left 8 units and shift down 4 units.

(D) It will shift to the right 8 units and shift down 4 units.

15. Calculating the total cost C, including the sales tax (and no other fees), of a good with an untaxed price of P is given by the expression $C = 1.07P$. How could you calculate the cost of only the sales tax on the good?

(A) P

(B) $0.07P$

(C) $0.13P$

(D) $0.17P$

Answer Explanations

1. **(B)** This is easiest to solve if you work your way backward from the answer choices. The only answer that multiplies to give an area of 216 is choice (B):

$$12 \times 18 = 216$$

If you wanted to solve this algebraically, finding the solution would be much more complicated. This question demonstrates that you should be open to plugging in answers when you anticipate a lengthy calculation. Set up two equations, one equation for the sum of the length and width and one equation for the area:

$$L + W = 30$$
$$L \times W = 216$$

Use substitution to solve:

$$L + W = 30$$
$$L = 30 - W$$

Substitute this in for L in the other equation:

$$L \times W = 216$$
$$(30 - W) \times W = 216$$
$$-W^2 + 30W - 216 = 0$$

This looks rather challenging to solve by factoring, so use the quadratic formula:

$$x = \frac{-b \pm \sqrt{b^2 - 4ac}}{2a}$$
$$x = \frac{-30 \pm \sqrt{30^2 - 4(-1)(-216)}}{2(-1)}$$
$$x = \frac{-30 \pm \sqrt{900 - 864}}{-2}$$
$$x = \frac{-30 \pm \sqrt{36}}{-2}$$
$$x = \frac{-30 \pm 6}{-2}$$
$$x = 15 \pm 3$$
$$x = 12, 18$$

If you plug in 12 as the width, you get 18 as the length. If you plug in 18 as the width, you get 12 as the length:

$$L \times W = 216$$
$$L \times 12 = 216$$
$$L = 18$$
$$L \times W = 216$$
$$L \times 18 = 216$$
$$L = 12$$

So the dimensions are 12 feet by 18 feet, regardless of what you call the length and width.

2. **(A)** Simplify the expression:

$$\left(\frac{n^2 - n^3}{n^4}\right)^{-2} = \left(\frac{n^2}{n^2}\left(\frac{1 - n}{n^2}\right)\right)^{-2}$$

Cancel the n^2 terms on the outside:

$$\left(\frac{\cancel{n^2}}{\cancel{n^2}}\left(\frac{1 - n}{n^2}\right)\right)^{-2} = \left(\frac{1 - n}{n^2}\right)^{-2}$$

Flip the fraction so it has a positive exponent:

$$\left(\frac{1 - n}{n^2}\right)^{-2} = \left(\frac{n^2}{1 - n}\right)^2$$

Square both the numerator and the denominator and simplify:

$$\left(\frac{(n^2)^2}{(1 - n)^2}\right) = \left(\frac{n^4}{(1 - n)(1 - n)}\right) = \frac{n^4}{1 - 2n + n^2}$$

3. **(C)** $\frac{2x + 2y}{4} = \frac{x + y}{2}$, which is the arithmetic mean (simple average) of x and y.

4. **(C)** Both the first term and the second term of the expression are squared terms. So the expression can be restated as the difference of squares, the general form of which is $x^2 - y^2 = (x + y)(x - y)$:

$$16a^2 - 9b^2 =$$
$$(4a)^2 - (3b)^2 = (4a + 3b)(4a - 3b)$$

5. **(D)** Solve by simplifying and completing the square:

$$4x^2 + 8x - 4 = 0$$
$$x^2 + 2x - 1 = 0$$
$$x^2 + 2x = 1$$

Then complete the square by adding 1 to both sides:

$$x^2 + 2x + 1 = 2$$

Then factor the left-hand side:

$$(x + 1)^2 = 2$$

Then take the square root of both sides, remembering to include both the positive and the negative values on the right:

$$x + 1 = \sqrt{2} \text{ and } x + 1 = -\sqrt{2}$$

Solve for x to find the solutions:

$$x = \sqrt{2} - 1 \text{ and } x = -\sqrt{2} - 1$$

Alternatively, you could solve this using the quadratic equation. Start by dividing by 4 to simplify:

$$4x^2 + 8x - 4 = 0$$
$$x^2 + 2x - 1 = 0$$
$$x = \frac{-b \pm \sqrt{b^2 - 4ac}}{2a}$$
$$x = \frac{-2 \pm \sqrt{2^2 - 4(1)(-1)}}{2(1)}$$
$$x = \frac{-2 \pm \sqrt{8}}{2}$$
$$x = \frac{-2 \pm 2\sqrt{2}}{2}$$
$$x = \frac{-1 \pm \sqrt{2}}{1}$$
$$x = -1 \pm \sqrt{2}$$

This is equivalent to the answers $x = \sqrt{2} - 1$ and $x = -\sqrt{2} - 1$.

6. **(C)** Combine like terms, and then factor out what is common to all of the terms:

$$x^4 y^2 + x^3 y^5 + x y^6 + 2x^3 y^5 =$$
$$x^4 y^2 + 3x^3 y^5 + x y^6 =$$
$$x y^2 (x^3 + 3x^2 y^3 + y^4)$$

7. **(B)** This is probably easiest to solve by plugging in the answers. Start with choice (B) or choice (C) as your first attempt since the answers are in order from smallest to largest. (Note that $n^0 = 1$ since anything to the zero power is 1.) If you plug in 1 for x, it works:

$$\frac{x}{2} = \frac{2(n^0)}{2} - \frac{1}{2x}$$
$$\frac{1}{2} = \frac{2(1)}{2} - \frac{1}{2(1)}$$
$$\frac{1}{2} = 1 - \frac{1}{2}$$

You can also solve the problem algebraically, but doing so may take more time:

$$\frac{x}{2} = \frac{2(n^0)}{2} - \frac{1}{2x}$$
$$x = 2(n^0) - \frac{1}{x}$$
$$x = 2 - \frac{1}{x}$$

Multiply by x:

$$x^2 = 2x - 1$$
$$x^2 - 2x + 1 = 0$$
$$(x - 1)(x - 1) = 0$$
$$(x - 1)^2 = 0$$
$$x = 1$$

8. **(D)** Combine the like terms together to find the sum:

$$
\begin{array}{r}
3x^3 + 5x - 3 \\
+ 2x^2 - 4x + 6 \\
\hline
3x^3 + 2x^2 + x + 3
\end{array}
$$

9. **(B)** $(25a^4 + 40a^2b^4 + 16b^8) \div (5a^2 + 4b^4) =$

$$\frac{25a^4 + 40a^2b^4 + 16b^8}{5a^2 + 4b^4} =$$
$$\frac{(5a^2 + 4b^4)(5a^2 + 4b^4)}{5a^2 + 4b^4} =$$
$$5a^2 + 4b^4 = 4b^4 + 5a^2$$

10. **(A)** Choice I is correct. Since the velocity is raised to a fractional exponent, the impact of a certain amount of wind speed increase is more significant at lower wind speeds than at higher wind speeds. Choice II is not correct. Wind chill still has an impact when the temperature is less than 35.75 degrees Fahrenheit since this number is a constant, not a minimal temperature. Choice III is not correct. As temperature increases, the perceived temperature due to wind chill also increases.

11. **(C)** The function intersects the x-axis at $x = 6$, making 6 a zero of the function. Therefore, A can be expressed as $(x - 6)$.

12. **(A)** Plug in one of the zeros for x and plug in the number 0 for y since a zero intersects the x-axis. Remember that the y-value must be 0 for an x-intercept since that indicates where the function intersects the x-axis. Use this to solve for the constant c. Use -4 as that x-value so that you do not have to calculate with fractions:

$$y = 6x^3 + 19x^2 - 24x + c$$
$$0 = 6(-4)^3 + 19(-4)^2 - 24(-4) + c$$
$$0 = 6(-64) + 19(16) + 96 + c$$
$$0 = -384 + 304 + 96 + c$$
$$0 = 16 + c$$
$$-16 = c$$

13. **(D)** Since the parabola has zeros at 3 and -2, it can be written in this way:

$$f(x) = (x - 3)(x + 2)$$

Use FOIL:

$$f(x) = x^2 - x - 6$$

Alternatively, you can set $x = 0$. Then see which of the choices results in a y-value of -6 since this is the y-intercept of the parabola based on the graph. Only choice (D) works:

$$f(x) = x^2 - x - 6$$
$$f(0) = 0^2 - 0 - 6 = -6$$
$$f(0) = -6$$

14. **(A)** When you add a number to the x-value itself, the function shifts to the left by that number of places. When you add a number to the function as a whole, the function shifts upward by that number of places. Since 8 is added to the x-value itself and 4 is added to the function as a whole, the function shifts to the left 8 units and shifts up 4 units.

15. **(B)** The cost of the sales tax on the good is found by subtracting the untaxed price from the total cost:

$$1.07P - P = 0.07P$$

You can also visualize this by plugging in a sample value for the price of the good. A helpful sample value to use with percentages is 100 since it gives easily understood results. If, for example, you suppose that the price of the good is $100, the cost with the sales tax included is $1.07 \times \$100 = \$107$. So the sales tax on the good is $\$107 - \$100 = \$7$. This is equivalent to $0.07 \times \$100 = \$7$.

Geometry and Trigonometry Practice

1. If Alaina wishes to paint all six faces of a rectangular box that has dimensions in feet of $8 \times 4 \times 6$, how many square feet of paint does she need?

   (A) 124
   (B) 168
   (C) 208
   (D) 256

2. If a circle has a radius of 3 units, what is the length in units of the arc on the circle that measures $\frac{\pi}{2}$ radians?

   (A) π
   (B) $\frac{3}{2}\pi$
   (C) $\frac{5}{2}\pi$
   (D) 7π

3. If x represents the diameter of a circle, what is the area of a 60-degree sector of the circle?

   (A) πx^2
   (B) $\frac{\pi x^2}{24}$
   (C) $\frac{\pi x^2}{6}$
   (D) $\frac{\pi x^2}{36}$

4.

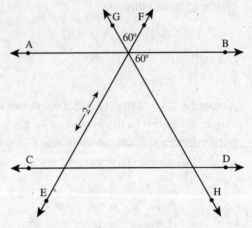

In the above drawing, lines AB and CD are parallel. Lines EF and GH intersect line AB at the same point and with the angle measures as indicated. What is the perimeter of the triangle formed by lines CD, EF, and GH between lines AB and CD?

   (A) 2
   (B) 4
   (C) 6
   (D) 8

5. A cube with edge length x has all of its edges doubled. Suppose the volume of the original cube is V cubic inches. What is the volume of the new cube in terms of the original cube?

   (A) $2V$
   (B) $4V$
   (C) $8V$
   (D) $16V$

6. The sides of a right triangle are 6, $6\sqrt{3}$, and 12. In a triangle similar to this triangle, what is the measure of the triangle's smallest interior angle?

   (A) $10°$
   (B) $30°$
   (C) $40°$
   (D) $45°$

Answer Explanations

1. **(C)** The box is drawn below:

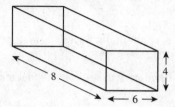

   Add up all of the surface areas of the six faces of the box. Since there are 2 of each face dimension, you can set up your equation as follows:

   $$2((8 \times 4) + (4 \times 6) + (8 \times 6)) = 208$$

2. **(B)** A measure of $\frac{\pi}{2}$ radians corresponds to $\frac{1}{4}$ of the distance around the circle since 2π radians is the entire distance around the circle. First find the circumference of a circle with radius of 3:

   $$2\pi r = 2\pi 3 = 6\pi$$

   Then calculate $\frac{1}{4}$ of the circumference:

   $$\frac{1}{4} \text{ of } 6\pi \text{ is } \frac{3}{2}\pi$$

3. **(B)** A 60-degree sector of the circle is $\frac{60}{360} = \frac{1}{6}$ of the total circle's area since there are 360 degrees in a circle. The area of a circle is calculated using πr^2. Since the diameter of the circle is x, the radius of the circle is half of x: $\frac{x}{2}$. So the area of this circle equals:

   $$\pi r^2 = \pi \left(\frac{x}{2}\right)^2 = \frac{\pi x^2}{4}$$

   Multiply the circle area by $\frac{1}{6}$ to find the area of the sector:

   $$\frac{1}{6} \times \frac{\pi x^2}{4} = \frac{\pi x^2}{24}$$

4. **(C)** Perimeter is the sum of the side measures of the triangle. The internal angles of the triangle formed are all 60 degrees. Since the angles are all congruent, the sides of the triangle are all congruent as well. Thus, the perimeter of the triangle is $2 + 2 + 2 = 6$ units. You can see this more clearly in the diagram below:

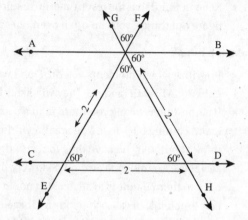

5. **(C)** Each edge of the cube is doubled. So instead of each edge having a length of x, each edge now has a length of $2x$. The volume formula for a cube is $V = x^3$. The original cube has a volume of x^3. The new cube has a volume of $(2x)^3 = 2^3 x^3 = 8x^3$. So the volume of the new cube is 8 times the volume of the original cube, which is $8V$.

6. **(B)** The sides given are a multiple of a special right triangle, the $30°-60°-90°$ triangle that has sides the length of x, $\sqrt{3}\,x$, and $2x$. In this problem, 6 corresponds to the x, $6\sqrt{3}$ corresponds to the $\sqrt{3}\,x$, and 12 corresponds to the $2x$. In this triangle, $30°$ is the smallest angle.

Troubleshooting

Here are some further pointers for common strategy issues.

"I haven't taken enough math yet."

- Most of the PSAT will be from Algebra 1 and Algebra 2. Don't worry about not having taken precalculus yet—just be comfortable using sine, cosine, and tangent.
- Review the key formulas at the beginning of the chapter. If you memorize these, you will feel much more confident.
- Keep in mind that the test primarily requires critical thinking. If you go into the PSAT Math Test ready to figure out things, you can often overcome a lack of advanced training.

"I take too long."

- Prioritize which problems you do. Don't worry about the last question or two on either PSAT Math module. They will likely be more difficult.
- If a question is taking you more than a couple of minutes to solve, consider flagging it and coming back to it. You are not writing off the problem. You will continue to think about it. If you have time to revisit the problem, it will likely seem quite a bit easier the second time around. Skip very difficult problems here and there. Then go back to them if time is available. Do not initially spend too much time on very difficult problems, because you may not have enough time to finish the test. Because the test is graded on a curve, skipping a problem isn't a big deal. However, not finishing the Math Test because of poor time management could be detrimental to scholarship chances if you leave enough problems incomplete. All problems are worth the same number of points. So it is better to get to the later problems and earn a few more points than just get that one tricky question but not have time for other problems you could be capable of solving. At the very least, be certain that you guess on a very difficult problem because there is no guessing penalty on the test.
- Pace yourself—take about 1.5 minutes per question on average. The earlier questions should take less time than this. The later questions should take more time. Keep yourself moving along.

TIP

You only have so much energy to devote to thinking on test day. Focus on solving the problems and not on things like overanalyzing the questions, checking your pace too frequently, and excessively reviewing your work.

"I finish too quickly."

- Consider what would be the most effective use of your extra time. For most people, it will be taking more time the first time through the questions. For some, it may be helpful to start with the most challenging questions later in the test so that you will have a couple of chances to try them—both when you start the test and when you finish. Note: Be sure to try this approach first on a practice test before you try it on the actual test. It is not typically an effective strategy; most students end up rushing through easier questions because they become stuck on the more difficult questions. Another possibility is to use the Desmos calculator to solve the questions in a different way from what you used in your first attempt to be sure you arrived at the correct answer.
- Pace yourself—be sure you are taking enough time on each question, on average about 1.5 minutes a question.

"I have math anxiety."

- The confidence that comes with rigorous practice is the best way to overcome your anxiety. If you work through the problem sets throughout this book, you will be ready for the PSAT.

- Realize that some anxiety is welcome—it can help you stay focused and tune out distractions. It can also help push you to work through a challenging problem. Channel your nervous energy into action instead of letting it paralyze your thought process.

- Keep things in perspective. The Math Test represents half of the test; you can still miss several questions and achieve a top score. The PSAT, although vital for National Merit consideration, is primarily preparation for the SAT. You will have plenty of chances to take the SAT and/or ACT, the tests that colleges use for admissions decisions. All the practice you are doing for the PSAT will directly help you prepare for these later tests as well.

TIP

Don't forget to try the drills in the next chapter, "Advanced Math Drills," for more challenging practice.

7

Advanced Math Drills

The following nine drills represent the most challenging types of math questions you will encounter on the PSAT, helping prepare you to earn National Merit recognition. You can practice all of these or focus on your most challenging question types. The drills as a whole are designed to give you comprehensive coverage of the variety of questions you may face on test day. The passages are arranged by topic and type of question:

- Algebra Drill 1
- Algebra Drill 2
- Problem-Solving and Data Analysis Drill 1
- Problem-Solving and Data Analysis Drill 2
- Advanced Math Drill 1
- Advanced Math Drill 2
- Geometry and Trigonometry Drill
- Free-Response Problems Drill
- Mixed Drill

To practice these passages under timed conditions, take about 15 minutes per drill. Answer explanations for each drill appear at the end of the chapter.

Algebra

Algebra Drill 1

1. What is the value of x in the following equation?

$$-\frac{3}{8}x + \frac{5}{16}x - \frac{1}{2}x = \frac{18}{32}$$

   (A) 1
   (B) -1
   (C) 3
   (D) $\frac{117}{8}$

2. What is the value of a in the following equation?

$$\frac{(3a-4)}{5} = \frac{(3a-4)}{8}$$

   (A) $\frac{4}{3}$
   (B) 0
   (C) $\frac{28}{9}$
   (D) $\frac{52}{9}$

3. What is the solution with the least possible y-value that satisfies both of the following inequalities?

$$y \geq 2x + 5$$
$$\text{and}$$
$$4 - y \leq x$$

   (A) $\left(\frac{1}{2}, \frac{5}{2}\right)$

   (B) $\left(\frac{1}{3}, \frac{11}{3}\right)$

   (C) $\left(-\frac{1}{2}, 4\right)$

   (D) $\left(-\frac{1}{3}, \frac{13}{3}\right)$

4. If $|3x - 1| = 4$, what are all of the possible value(s) of x?

   I. -1

   II. $\frac{5}{3}$

   III. 1

   (A) II only
   (B) III only
   (C) I and II only
   (D) All of the above

5. What is the value of x?

$$\frac{3}{2}x - \frac{2}{3} = \frac{x}{6} - \frac{10}{27}$$

   (A) $-\frac{7}{9}$

   (B) $\frac{2}{9}$

   (C) $\frac{17}{54}$

   (D) $\frac{9}{2}$

6. The graph of each equation in the system below is a line in the xy-plane.

$$y = 6x - 2$$
$$-6 = 12x - 2y$$

   What must be true about these two lines?

   (A) The lines are parallel.
   (B) The lines are perpendicular.
   (C) The lines intersect at $\left(\frac{3}{2}, 7\right)$.
   (D) The lines are the same.

7. Towns A and B are 200 miles apart. Caitlin starts driving from Town A to Town B at 3 P.M. at a rate of 30 miles per hour. Hannah starts driving from Town B to Town A at 4 P.M. on the same day at a rate of 40 miles per hour. At what time will they meet (to the nearest minute)?

   (A) 3:42 P.M.
   (B) 5:29 P.M.
   (C) 6:26 P.M.
   (D) 7:32 P.M.

8. A person can ride a roller coaster at an amusement park if he or she is between 36 and 72 inches tall. Which of the following inequalities models all possible values of permitted heights in inches for the ride?

   (A) $|x - 36| < 72$
   (B) $|x - 38| < 34$
   (C) $|x - 30| < 42$
   (D) $|x - 54| < 18$

9. A line in the xy-plane has a slope of $\frac{3}{5}$ and passes through the origin. Which of the following is a point on the line?

   (A) $(15, 10)$
   (B) $(3, 5)$
   (C) $\left(0, \frac{3}{5}\right)$
   (D) $(10, 6)$

10. A salesperson earns a commission (C) on the number of phone plans sold (x) if the value of C is positive. (There is no penalty or cost to the salesperson for a negative value of C; simply no commission is paid.) The amount of commission in dollars is modeled by this equation:

    $$C = 50x + 25(x - 100) - 2{,}000$$

    What is the least number of phone plans that the salesperson must sell in order to earn a commission?

    (A) 60
    (B) 61
    (C) 75
    (D) 100

Algebra Drill 2

1. If the volume of a pyramid is given by the formula $V = \frac{1}{3} lwh$, where V is the volume, l is the length, w is the width, and h is the height, what is the width of the pyramid in terms of the other variables?

   (A) $\frac{V}{3lh}$
   (B) $\frac{3V}{lw}$
   (C) $\frac{3V}{lh}$
   (D) $\frac{lh}{3V}$

2. What is the negative solution to the following equation, rounded to one decimal place?

   $$18x - \frac{21}{x} = \frac{2x}{3} + 12$$

   (A) 1.5
   (B) -0.8
   (C) -0.6
   (D) -1.5

3. An employee at a company has the following rules for days off from work:

   - Employees are granted 30 flex days paid time off in a year for non-weekend and holiday days.
   - Sick days with a doctor's note count as half a flex day.
   - Personal days count as a full flex day.

   If an employee wants to use at least half of the flex days but less than $\frac{5}{6}$ of them, what inequality would express the total number of sick days, S, and personal days, P, he or she could take in a year?

   (A) $\frac{1}{2} \leq \frac{1}{2}S + P < \frac{5}{6}$
   (B) $15 \leq \frac{1}{2}S + P < 25$
   (C) $15 \leq 2S + P < 25$
   (D) $15 \leq S + 2P < 30$

4. If $g(x) = 9x + 2$, what does $g(-4x)$ equal?

   (A) $-36x - 8$

   (B) $-36x + 2$

   (C) $5x + 2$

   (D) $-36x^2 + 2$

5. A carpenter charges a \$40 initial fee for an in-home visit and \$60 for each half hour worked. Which inequality models the total fee, F, for H hours worked where $H > 0$?

   (A) $F(H) = 40 + 30H$

   (B) $F(H) = 40 + 60H$

   (C) $F(H) = 40 + 120H$

   (D) $F(H) = 60 + 40H$

6. What are the values of x and y in the following equations?

   $$0.75x - 0.1y = 1.2$$
   $$2.6x + 3.4y = 15.4$$

   (A) $x = 1, y = -4.5$

   (B) $x = 2, y = 3$

   (C) $x = 3, y = 10.5$

   (D) $x = 4, y = 18$

7. If $\frac{m}{n} = -3$, what does $-2\frac{n}{m}$ equal?

   (A) -6

   (B) $\frac{2}{3}$

   (C) $\frac{3}{2}$

   (D) 6

8. If Equation A is defined by $y = \frac{2}{3}x - 4$ and if Equation B is defined by $3y = 2x + 3$, what must be done to Equation B so that the system of both Equation A and Equation B will have infinitely many solutions?

   (A) Add 9 to the right side

   (B) Subtract 5 from the right side

   (C) Subtract 7 from the right side

   (D) Subtract 15 from the right side

9. At 1:00 P.M., a blimp and a hot-air balloon are above the cities of Springfield and Washington, respectively. The two cities are 300 miles apart horizontally. The blimp is moving from Springfield to Washington at a horizontal speed of 10 miles per hour; the balloon is moving from Washington to Springfield at a horizontal speed of 200 miles per hour. The blimp starts at an altitude of 5,000 feet and is descending at a rate of 5 feet per minute; the balloon starts at an altitude of 500 feet and is ascending at a rate of 4 feet per minute. At what time will the blimp and balloon be at the same altitude, to the nearest minute?

   (A) 6:20 P.M.

   (B) 7:20 P.M.

   (C) 8:20 P.M.

   (D) 9:20 P.M.

10. Rosa's metabolism is 65 calories per hour when resting and 300 calories per hour when exercising. If Rosa wants to burn more than 2,000 calories per day, what is the range of hours, H, she should spend exercising, calculated to the nearest tenth, assuming that she is either resting or exercising at any time in a given day?

   (A) $24 > H > 1.9$

   (B) $24 > H > 2.4$

   (C) $24 > H > 6.7$

   (D) $24 > H > 22.1$

Problem-Solving and Data Analysis

Problem-Solving and Data Analysis Drill 1

1. In an animal shelter consisting of only dogs and cats, the ratio of dogs to cats is 3 to 1. If there are 360 animals in the shelter, how many dogs must be present?

    (A) 90
    (B) 120
    (C) 270
    (D) 300

2. A reporter finds that on average, a particular politician receives 14 seconds of applause out of every minute of a speech. If the politician were to give a speech for exactly two hours, how many minutes of the speech would be devoted to applause?

    (A) 14
    (B) 28
    (C) 37
    (D) 1,680

3. Whole milk has 3.5% fat content. If you used equal amounts of 1% and 2% milk, how many total gallons of the combined milk would you use to equal the fat content in exactly 1 gallon of whole milk?

    (A) $\frac{1}{200}$
    (B) $\frac{1}{2}$
    (C) $1\frac{1}{6}$
    (D) $2\frac{1}{3}$

4. Katie is interested in running a marathon, which is 26.2 miles long. She just finished a 5-kilometer race, and she wants to see how many 5K races she would have to complete in order to equal a full marathon. Given that there are approximately 0.62 miles in 1 kilometer, how many complete 5K races would Katie have to finish to go at least the distance of a marathon?

    (A) 6
    (B) 8
    (C) 9
    (D) 10

5. At the beginning of the year, 1 U.S. dollar can be exchanged for 0.9 euros, and 1 Canadian dollar can be exchanged for 0.7 U.S. dollars. If someone wants to convert 100 Canadian dollars to euros at these exchange rates and assuming that there are no transaction fees, how many euros would the person have after the conversion?

    (A) 63
    (B) 78
    (C) 129
    (D) 158

6. **Spread of a Computer Virus**

Day	Number of Computers Infected
1	101
2	110
3	200
4	1,100
5	10,100

    The table above gives the number of computers infected with a virus. Which of the following functions models the number of computers infected, $C(d)$, after d days?

    (A) $C(d) = 10^{2d} + 10(d - 1) + 1$
    (B) $C(d) = 100 + 10^d$
    (C) $C(d) = 100 + 10(d - 1) + 1$
    (D) $C(d) = 100 + 10^{(d - 1)}$

7. Light travels at approximately 3.00×10^8 meters per second. When the planet Jupiter is at its closest point to Earth, it is 588 million kilometers away. When Earth and Jupiter are this close, approximately how many minutes does light reflected off of Jupiter take to reach Earth?

    (A) 3 minutes
    (B) 33 minutes
    (C) 58 minutes
    (D) 18 minutes

8.

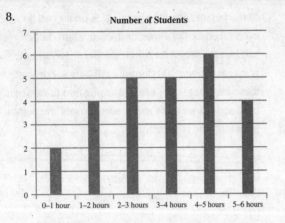

A group of 26 teenagers was asked about their daily smartphone usage. What was the median range of hours that this group used smartphones each day?

(A) Between 1 and 2
(B) Between 2 and 3
(C) Between 3 and 4
(D) Between 4 and 5

9.

	Finished Summer Reading	Did Not Complete Summer Reading	
Mrs. Smith's Class	21	8	29
Mr. Walker's Class	14	17	31
	35	25	

Given that the average of Mrs. Smith's and Mr. Walker's classes together represents the average enrollment in each English class at the school and that there are a total of 14 English classes, how many total students are enrolled in English classes at the school, assuming that students are enrolled in exactly one English class?

(A) 280
(B) 420
(C) 560
(D) 840

10. Bob deposits x dollars into his savings account on January 1, 2023, and the account grows at a constant annual rate of 3%, compounded annually. Assuming that Bob makes no deposits or withdrawals and that there are no account fees or other charges, what will be the amount of dollars in his account on January 1, 2025?

(A) $0.06x$
(B) $1.06x$
(C) $1.0609x$
(D) $1.092727x$

Problem-Solving and Data Analysis Drill 2

1. A student writes a double-spaced typed paper using Times New Roman 12-point font. He finds that each page contains an average of 240 words. If the student changes to Comic Sans 12-point font, each page contains an average of only 170 words. If the student is required to write a 10-page double-spaced report, how many fewer words would he be required to write if the teacher accepts Comic Sans 12-point font instead of Times New Roman 12-point font?

(A) 70
(B) 170
(C) 700
(D) 1,700

2. On a map of a rectangular fenced-in area, the drawing of the enclosed area has a surface area of 20 square inches. If one side of the fenced-in area drawing is 4 inches long and the key of the map indicates that for every 1 inch drawn on the map there are 6 feet in actual distance, what is the perimeter of the actual fence, assuming there are no gaps or gates?

(A) 18 ft
(B) 108 ft
(C) 120 ft
(D) 720 ft

3. John's performance on his first test was only 60%. His performance increased by 20% on the next test, and it increased an additional 25% on the third test. What did John earn on the third test, to the nearest whole percent?

    (A) 72%
    (B) 75%
    (C) 90%
    (D) 105%

4. Linda's 15-gallon car tank has only 2 gallons left when she pulls into a gas station. She wants to purchase only the gas she will need to drive 240 miles and still have 1 gallon remaining. Her car gets 28 miles to the gallon. How many gallons should Linda purchase, to the nearest tenth of a gallon?

    (A) 6.6 gallons
    (B) 7.6 gallons
    (C) 8.6 gallons
    (D) 9.6 gallons

5.

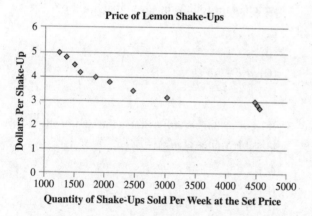

    If you were to graph dollars per shake-up along the x-axis and quantity of shake-ups sold per week at the set price on the y-axis, which of the following would be a property of the function between the values of 3 and 5 dollars?

    (A) It would be a decreasing exponential function.
    (B) It would be an increasing exponential function.
    (C) It would be a decreasing linear function.
    (D) It would be an increasing linear function.

6. A pastry chef has a recipe that calls for 3 tablespoons of vanilla extract for a cake. The chef has misplaced his tablespoon and has only a teaspoon available—there are 3 teaspoons for each tablespoon. If the chef is making a total of 2 cakes, how many teaspoons of vanilla extract should he use?

    (A) 3
    (B) 6
    (C) 12
    (D) 18

7.

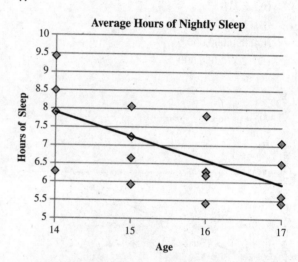

    A scientist surveys 16 randomly selected teenage students, recording their ages and their average number of hours of nightly sleep.

    If x represents the age and y represents the average hours of sleep, which of the following gives the equation of the best-fit line for the survey results?

    (A) $y = -0.6x + 7.8$
    (B) $y = 0.8x + 7.8$
    (C) $y = -0.6x + 16.2$
    (D) $y = -1.9x + 16.2$

8. A particular black hole has a density of 1.0×10^6 kg/m³. A physicist is conducting a thought experiment in which she would like to approximate how much she would weigh if she had the density of a black hole rather than her current weight of 150 pounds, assuming her volume remained the same. Given that her overall body density is approximately 990 kg/m³ and that there are approximately 2.2 pounds in a kilogram, approximately how many pounds would she weigh in her thought experiment?

(A) 2,178
(B) 151,500
(C) 990,000,000
(D) 2,178,000,000

9.

Average Daily Caloric Consumption

What choice most closely approximates the slope of the best-fit line of the graph above?

(A) $-\dfrac{1}{10}$
(B) $\dfrac{3}{50}$
(C) $\dfrac{1}{5}$
(D) $\dfrac{50}{3}$

10. A copyeditor takes 3 minutes to edit each page of a book that is p pages long. Which of the following expressions gives the total number of <u>hours</u> that the copyeditor would take to edit the book?

(A) $\dfrac{p}{20}$
(B) $3p + 60$
(C) $\dfrac{p}{60}$
(D) $60 - 3p$

Advanced Math

Advanced Math Drill 1

1. A cubic function would be most appropriate when modeling which of the following mathematical relationships?

(A) A sphere's volume and its radius
(B) A circle's circumference and its diameter
(C) A triangle's area and its height
(D) A cube's edge length and its total surface area

2. $\dfrac{a^3 - b^3 + 2a^2b - 2ab^2 + ab^2 - ba^2}{a^2 - b^2}$ equals which of the following, given that $a \neq \pm b$?

(A) $a + b$
(B) $a - b$
(C) $a^2b - ab^2$
(D) $a^2 + b^2$

3. If $-5m^5 + 3m^3 = 2m^7$, what is the sum of all possible values of m^2?

(A) -2.5
(B) 0
(C) 0.5
(D) 2.5

4. Solve for x: $\frac{1}{2}x^2 + \frac{1}{4}x - \frac{1}{8} = 0$

   (A) $\frac{1}{2}(-1 \pm \sqrt{3})$

   (B) $\frac{1}{2}(-1 \pm \sqrt{5})$

   (C) $\frac{1}{4}(-1 \pm \sqrt{3})$

   (D) $\frac{1}{4}(-1 \pm \sqrt{5})$

5. What is/are the solution(s) to the following equation?

   $$a + 4 = \sqrt{a^2 - 2}$$

   (A) $-\frac{9}{4}$

   (B) $\frac{9}{4}$

   (C) $\frac{-7}{4}$ and $\frac{9}{4}$

   (D) No solutions

6. How many distinct zeros does the function $f(x) = (x - 3)(x + 7)(x - 3)$ have?

   (A) 0

   (B) 1

   (C) 2

   (D) 3

7. Consider the function $f(x) = x^2 + 2$. What operation could be performed on the right-hand side of the equation to expand the range to include negative values?

   (A) Add 5

   (B) Add -2

   (C) Subtract 3

   (D) Subtract 1

8. What is the vertex of the parabola $(y - 4)^2 = 17(x + 2)$?

   (A) $(-2, 4)$

   (B) $(2, -4)$

   (C) $(-4, 2)$

   (D) $(4, -2)$

9. The root mean squared speed of a molecule, v_{rms}, is calculated using the formula $v_{\text{rms}} = \sqrt{\frac{3RT}{M}}$, where R is a gas constant, T is the temperature, and M is the molecular mass. The molecular mass of substance A is most likely to be less than the molecular mass of substance B if the temperature and v_{rms} of substance A compare in which ways to those of substance B?

   (A) Greater v_{rms} and lower temperature

   (B) Lower v_{rms} and greater temperature

   (C) Lower v_{rms} and equal temperature

   (D) Cannot be determined

10. Two different stock portfolios, A and B, have had no new deposits or withdrawals over a ten-year period and had the same initial amount in the account. If stock portfolio A has grown at an annual rate of $x\%$, if stock portfolio B has grown at an annual rate of $y\%$, and if $x > y$, what would represent the ratio of the value of portfolio A over that of portfolio B at the end of the ten-year period?

   (A) $\left(\dfrac{1 + \frac{x}{100}}{1 + \frac{y}{100}}\right)^{10}$

   (B) $\left(\dfrac{x}{y}\right)^{10}$

   (C) $10\left(\dfrac{x}{y}\right)$

   (D) $\left(\dfrac{1 - \frac{x}{100}}{1 - \frac{y}{100}}\right)^{10}$

Advanced Math Drill 2

1. A car and a truck are initially 180 miles apart and are driving toward each other on a straight road when an observer measures their respective speeds. The car is driving at a constant speed of x miles per hour, and the truck is going twice this speed. If the car and the truck meet each other after three hours of driving, what is the speed of the truck?

   (A) 20 mph
   (B) 30 mph
   (C) 40 mph
   (D) 60 mph

2. The formula for the area of a trapezoid is $\frac{B_1 + B_2}{2} \times H$, where B_1 and B_2 are the bases of the trapezoid and H is its height. If the mean of the bases of the trapezoid is twice the height and if the area of the trapezoid is 72 square inches, what is the trapezoid's height in inches?

   (A) 6
   (B) $6\sqrt{2}$
   (C) 24
   (D) 36

3. $2m^{-2} - 4m^{-3}$ is equivalent to which of the following?

   (A) $\frac{2m - 1}{4m^3}$

   (B) $\frac{-2}{m^5}$

   (C) $\frac{2m - 4}{m^3}$

   (D) $-2m^2 + 4m^3$

4. $(2y^4 + 3x^6) + (5x^6 + 3y^4)$ is equivalent to which of the following?

   (A) $5y^4 + 8x^6$
   (B) $7y^4 + 6x^6$
   (C) $13y^4 x^6$
   (D) $5y^8 + 8x^{12}$

5. Which of the following is equivalent to the expression $\frac{2x^2 - 12x + 18}{3(x-3)^3}$?

   (A) $\frac{x^2 + 9}{x - 3}$

   (B) $\frac{2(x + 3)}{3(x - 3)^2}$

   (C) $\frac{2(x - 6)}{(x - 3)}$

   (D) $\frac{2}{3(x - 3)}$

6. What are the solutions to $21x^2 = 15x + 18$?

   (A) $\frac{5 \pm \sqrt{193}}{14}$

   (B) $\frac{15 \pm \sqrt{1527}}{14}$

   (C) $\frac{5 \pm \sqrt{67}}{14}$

   (D) No real solutions

7. The supply for a given item at a varying price p (in dollars) is given by the equation $s(p) = 3p + 6p^2$. The demand for the same item at a varying price p is given by the equation $d(p) = 156 - 12p$. At what price are the supply and the demand for the item equivalent?

   (A) $3.50
   (B) $4
   (C) $6.50
   (D) $12

8. If x and y are variables and if c is a nonzero constant, which of the following choices would not necessarily have a y-intercept when graphed?

   I. $x = c$
   II. $y = -c$
   III. $y = cx$

   (A) I only
   (B) I and II only
   (C) II and III only
   (D) None of the above

9.

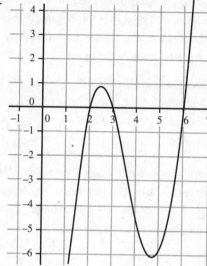

Which of the following equations represents the function graphed above?

(A) $x^3 + 11x^2 + 36x + 36$
(B) $x^3 - 11x^2 + 36x - 36$
(C) $x^3 + x^2 - 24x + 36$
(D) $x^2 - 5x + 6$

10. The formula for annual compounded interest is $A = P\left(1 + \frac{r}{n}\right)^{nt}$, where P is the initial amount invested, A is the future value of the initial amount, r is the annual interest rate expressed as a decimal, n is the number of times the investment is compounded each year, and t is the number of years the amount is invested. If an initial investment, P, is compounded once every 12 months, which expression is equivalent to the future value of the investment if its interest rate is 5% and if the money is invested for exactly 1 year?

(A) $0.05P$
(B) $0.5P$
(C) $1.05P$
(D) $1.50P$

Geometry and Trigonometry Drill

1. A right circular cylinder has a volume of $30x$ cubic feet, and a cube has a volume of $21x$ cubic feet. What is the sum of the volumes of a cone with the same height and radius as the cylinder and of a pyramid with the same length, width, and height of the cube?

(A) $7x$ cubic feet
(B) $10x$ cubic feet
(C) $17x$ cubic feet
(D) $51x$ cubic feet

2. Andrew rides his bike 20 miles directly north and then 15 miles directly to the east. How many miles would he travel if he could fly directly from his starting point to his ending point?

(A) 25
(B) 31
(C) 35
(D) 625

3. In a right triangle with legs of length a and b, what is the value of the hypotenuse of the triangle?

(A) $\sqrt{a + b}$
(B) $\sqrt{a^2 - b^2}$
(C) $\sqrt{a^2 + b^2}$
(D) $a^2 + b^2$

4. A rectangle has side lengths of 6 inches and 8 inches. What is the length of the diagonal of the rectangle?

(A) 9 inches
(B) 10 inches
(C) 12 inches
(D) 13 inches

5. What would be the measure, in radians, of an arc on a circle if the measure of the arc in degrees was 270?

   (A) $\dfrac{2\pi}{3}$

   (B) $\dfrac{3\pi}{2}$

   (C) 270π

   (D) $\dfrac{48,600}{\pi}$

6.

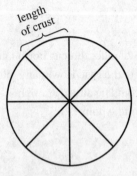

A circular pizza has a radius of 8 inches. If the pizza is cut into 8 equal sectors as shown in the drawing above, what is the length of the crust on the edge of each piece, rounded to two decimal places?

   (A) 0.13 inches
   (B) 0.79 inches
   (C) 3.74 inches
   (D) 6.28 inches

7.

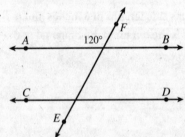

In the above drawing, lines AB and CD are parallel, and line EF is a transversal. How many angles made from the given lines measure 60 degrees?

   (A) 1
   (B) 2
   (C) 4
   (D) 6

8. A four-sided figure has three interior angles of the same measure and the other interior angle measuring 120 degrees. What is the measure of the smallest interior angle in the figure?

   (A) 40 degrees
   (B) 50 degrees
   (C) 65 degrees
   (D) 80 degrees

9. In two similar isosceles triangles, triangle A has two sides each of length 5 and one side of length 7. Triangle B has exactly one side of length 28. What is the perimeter of triangle B?

   (A) 17
   (B) 20
   (C) 38
   (D) 68

10. Triangle XYZ has a right angle for angle Y and has side lengths of 24 for XY and 26 for XZ. For a triangle that is similar to XYZ, what would be the value of the tangent of its smallest angle?

   (A) $\dfrac{5}{12}$

   (B) $\dfrac{5}{13}$

   (C) $\dfrac{12}{13}$

   (D) $\dfrac{12}{5}$

Free-Response Problems Drill

1. A circle has the equation $x^2 + y^2 = 36$. What is the shortest distance in units from the origin to a point on the circle?

2. Jamie can run $\dfrac{3}{2}k$ miles in the time that Matt takes to run k miles. If Jamie and Matt run for the same amount of time and their combined mileage is 10 miles, how many miles did Jamie run?

3. What is the product of all solutions to $(x + 2)^2 = (2x - 3)^2$?

4. If $a^4 - 2a^3 + 2a^2 + ma + 2$ has $(a + 1)$ as a factor, what is the value of the constant m?

5. What will be the new slope of the line $y = 2x + 3$ after it is translated 3 units to the right and 2 units down?

Mixed Drill

1. What is the value of x in the following equation?

$$15x + \frac{1}{2} = -5\left(x - \frac{5}{2}\right)$$

(A) $-\frac{3}{20}$

(B) $-\frac{13}{20}$

(C) $\frac{3}{5}$

(D) $\frac{3}{10}$

2. If $f(x) = 7x + 3$ and $g(x) = 2 \times 2$, what is the value of $f(g(1))$?

(A) 10
(B) 13
(C) 17
(D) 21

3. What is the value of the constant c in the equation below?

$$(x - 6)(x - 10) = (x - 8)^2 + c$$

(A) −4
(B) 0
(C) 4
(D) 16

4.

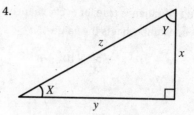

Which trigonometric expression would give the value of angle X?

(A) $\sin^{-1}\left(\frac{x}{z}\right)$

(B) $\cos^{-1}\left(\frac{x}{z}\right)$

(C) $\sin\left(\frac{x}{z}\right)$

(D) $\sin^{-1}\left(\frac{y}{z}\right)$

5. The ideal gas equation is $PV = nRT$, where P is the pressure, V is the volume, n is the number of moles, R is the gas constant, and T is the temperature. According to the equation, the volume of a gas is inversely related to

(A) the number of moles.
(B) gas constant.
(C) temperature.
(D) none of the above.

6. In physics, the mirror equation is $\frac{1}{f} = \frac{1}{d_o} + \frac{1}{d_i}$, where f represents the mirror's focal length, d_o is the distance of an object from the mirror, and d_i is the distance of the image from the mirror. Which expression gives d_o in terms of focal length and image distance?

(A) $\dfrac{1}{\frac{1}{f} + \frac{1}{d_i}}$

(B) $\frac{1}{f} - \frac{1}{d_i}$

(C) $\dfrac{1}{\frac{1}{d_i} - \frac{1}{f}}$

(D) $\dfrac{1}{\frac{1}{f} - \frac{1}{d_i}}$

7. If the following equation is true for every value of x and if a is a constant, what is the value of a?

$$(x+4)(x^2 + ax + 2) = x^3 + x^2 - 10x + 8$$

(A) -10

(B) -3

(C) -2

(D) 1

8. $\left(6y^3 + \frac{1}{2}y - \frac{2}{3}\right) - \left(4y^3 - y^2 + \frac{1}{2}y + \frac{1}{6}\right) = ?$

(A) $2y^3 + y^2 + y + \frac{5}{6}$

(B) $2y^3 - y^2 + y - \frac{1}{2}$

(C) $2y^3 - \frac{1}{2}y - \frac{1}{2}$

(D) $2y^3 + y^2 - \frac{5}{6}$

9. If the slope of line A is $-\frac{x}{y}$, where x and y are positive numbers, what is the slope of a line that is perpendicular to A?

(A) $-\frac{x}{y}$

(B) $-\frac{y}{x}$

(C) $-\frac{x}{y}$

(D) $\frac{y}{x}$

10. The formula for the surface area of a sphere is $A = 4\pi r^2$. If the volume of sphere A is 8 times the volume of sphere B, what is the ratio of the surface area of sphere A to that of sphere B?

(A) 1:2

(B) 2:1

(C) 4:1

(D) 8:1

Answer Explanations

Algebra Drill 1

1. **(B)** To add all of these fractions, you need a common denominator. The least common denominator for the three fractions is 16. However, because the other side has a denominator of 32, let's use 32 for ease. To convert $-\frac{3}{8}x$ to a fraction with a denominator of 32, multiply both the numerator and the denominator by 4. Thus, $-\frac{3}{8}x$ becomes $-\frac{12}{32}x$. Similarly, $\frac{5}{16}x$ becomes $\frac{10}{32}x$ after multiplying both the numerator and denominator by 2. Finally, $-\frac{1}{2}x$ becomes $-\frac{16}{32}x$ after multiplying both the numerator and denominator by 16. Therefore, we're left with:

$$-\frac{12}{32}x + \frac{10}{32}x - \frac{16}{32}x = \frac{18}{32}$$

Combining like terms gives:

$$-\frac{18}{32}x = \frac{18}{32}$$

To isolate x, divide both sides by $-\frac{18}{32}$. Dividing by a fraction is the same as multiplying by its reciprocal, so you're left with:

$$x = \left(\frac{18}{32}\right) \times \left(\frac{-32}{18}\right) = -1$$

So $x = -1$, or choice (B).

2. **(A)** Let's cross multiply here:

$$8(3a - 4) = 5(3a - 4)$$

Next we need to distribute both the 8 and the 5:

$$24a - 32 = 15a - 20$$

Combine both a terms by subtracting $15a$ from both sides:

$$9a - 32 = -20$$

Combine the constants by adding 32 to both sides:

$$9a = 12$$

Finally, solve for a by dividing both sides by 9. So $a = \frac{12}{9} = \frac{4}{3}$, choice (A).

Alternatively, realize that $3a - 4 = 0$ because if we plug in x for $3a - 4$, $\frac{x}{5} = \frac{x}{8}$, meaning $8x = 5x$. Therefore, x must be zero.

3. **(D)** First, get the second inequality in the same form as the first. To do this, subtract 4 from both sides of the second inequality:

$$-y \le x - 4$$

Then divide by -1, remembering to flip the inequality since you're dividing by a negative:

$$y \ge -x + 4$$

If you graph these two inequalities, you'll see that the point where the lines intersect is the solution that they share that has the lowest y-value.

We can use this knowledge to set both inequalities equal to one another and solve:

$$2x + 5 = -x + 4$$

To solve for x, add an x to both sides to get all of the x-terms on the left. Subtract 5 from both sides to get all constants on the right:

$$3x = -1$$

Dividing by 3 tells us that $x = -\frac{1}{3}$. That's enough to narrow it down to choice (D).

However, if we wanted to know the y-value, we could plug the x-value into the equation for either of the two lines:

$$y = -x + 4 = -\left(-\frac{1}{3}\right) + 4 = \frac{1}{3} + \frac{12}{3} = \frac{13}{3}$$

This also agrees with choice (D).

Alternatively, you can plug in the values of the answers and see which set works for both equations.

4. **(C)** Recall that absolute value can be thought of as the distance of something from the origin. So if the absolute value of something is 4, it is 4 units away from the origin in either direction. This means that it can be either 4 or −4. Therefore, to solve for the values of x, we can set what's inside the absolute value equal to both 4 and −4 and solve. Setting it equal to 4 gives:

$$3x - 1 = 4$$

Adding 1 to both sides results in:

$$3x = 5$$

Dividing both sides by 3 gives us our first solution:

$$x = \frac{5}{3}$$

Next, set the inside of the absolute value sign equal to −4:

$$3x - 1 = -4$$

Adding 1 to both sides gives:

$$3x = -3$$

Dividing by 3 gives us our second solution:

$$x = -1$$

Therefore, there are two solutions, I and II, choice (C).

5. **(B)** To combine the x-terms, you need a common denominator, 6. To combine the constant terms, you also need a common denominator, 27:

$$\frac{9}{6}x - \frac{18}{27} = \frac{1}{6}x - \frac{10}{27}$$

To get all x-terms on the left, subtract $\frac{1}{6}x$ from both sides:

$$\frac{8}{6}x - \frac{18}{27} = -\frac{10}{27}$$

Next, add $\frac{18}{27}$ to both sides to get all constants on the right:

$$\frac{8}{6}x = \frac{8}{27}$$

Finally, divide both sides by $\frac{8}{6}$ (which is the same thing as multiplying both sides by $\frac{6}{8}$) to solve for x:

$$x = \frac{8(6)}{27(8)} = \frac{48}{216} = \frac{2}{9}$$

This matches choice (B).

6. **(A)** Let's get the second equation in $y = mx + b$ form. First, let's get the y-terms on the left by adding $2y$ to both sides:

$$2y - 6 = 12x$$

Next we need to bring the constant to the right side by adding 6 to both sides:

$$2y = 12x + 6$$

Finally, divide both sides by 2:

$$y = 6x + 3$$

Comparing the two lines shows they have the same slope but different y-intercepts. Therefore, they are parallel lines, choice (A).

If their slopes had been negative reciprocals of one another, they would have been perpendicular lines.

If the lines had had different slopes, they would have intersected at exactly one point.

If they had had the same slope and the same y-intercept, then they would have been the same line.

7. **(C)** The women will meet when their positions are equal, so we need to come up with equations to model each of their positions. First, notice that Caitlin leaves a full hour before Hannah. In that first hour, she'll travel 30 miles since she's traveling at 30 mph. Therefore, the women start out 170 miles apart at 4:00 P.M.

Let's say that Caitlin starts at position 0, while Hannah starts at position 170. Caitlin is moving toward 170, so she's moving in the positive direction at 30 mph. Keeping in mind that distance = rate × time, Caitlin's position, s, can then be described as:

$$s = 0 + 30t = 30t$$

On the other hand, Hannah is traveling from position 170 toward position 0, so she's traveling in the negative direction. Therefore, her position can be described as:

$$s = 170 - 40t$$

In order to solve for t, we must set the women's positions equal to one another:

$$30t = 170 - 40t$$

Adding $40t$ to both sides results in:

$$70t = 170$$

Dividing by 70 tells us:

$$t = 2.429$$

Because our rates were in miles per hour, this time is in hours. Therefore, it takes the women two full hours and a fraction of a third hour, so they meet sometime between 6 and 7. This is enough information to narrow down the solution to choice (C).

To find the exact time, we can figure out how many minutes 0.429 hours is by multiplying 0.429 hours by 60 minutes/hour. $0.429(60) = 25.74$ minutes. Therefore, Caitlin and Hannah meet 2 hours and 26 minutes after the time Hannah started traveling, 4:00 P.M. So the women arrive at the same place at 6:26 P.M.

8. **(D)** Recognize that those who are allowed to ride are the ones who aren't too far in either direction from the mean of the permitted heights. If you take the mean height of the constraints, you get:

$$\frac{36 + 72}{2} = 54$$

$72 - 54 = 18$ and $36 - 54 = -18$. Therefore, anyone who is less than 18 units away from 54 is allowed to ride, which is what choice (D) says.

If you didn't recognize this, you could use the process of elimination. You could pick heights that aren't allowed to ride. If you plug in a height that isn't allowed to ride but the inequality is still true, then you'd know that you could eliminate the choice. For instance:

Choice (A): $|35 - 36| = 1$. Since 1 is less than 72, we can rule out this answer choice.

Choice (B): $|35 - 38| = 3$. Since 3 is less than 34, we can rule out this answer choice as well.

Choice (C): $|35 - 30| = 5$. Since 5 is less than 42, we're left with choice (D).

9. **(D)** The answer choices are all positive, so let's come up with some of the positive points on the line. The line has a slope of $\frac{3}{5}$ and passes through the origin (thus has a y-intercept of 0). So the equation for the line is:

$$y = \frac{3}{5}x$$

The line starts at the origin and goes up 3 units and to the right 5 units. So (5, 3) is a point. From there, the line goes up 3 more units and to the right 5 more units, so (10, 6) is also a point, which is choice (D).

Alternatively, you could have used the process of elimination by plugging in the x-coordinates of the answer choices to get the y-coordinate at that value of x.

10. **(B)** In order for the commission to be positive, change the expression to an inequality where the commission will be positive and solve for x:

$$C = 50x + 25(x - 100) - 2{,}000 \boxed{?}$$
$$0 < 50x + 25(x - 100) - 2{,}000 \boxed{?}$$
$$0 < 50x + 25x - 2{,}500 - 2{,}000 \boxed{?}$$
$$0 < 75x - 4{,}500 \boxed{?}$$
$$4{,}500 < 75x \boxed{?}$$
$$60 < x$$

Since the salesperson cannot sell a partial phone plan, the least number of phone plans must be the first integer greater than 60, which is 61.

Algebra Drill 2

1. **(C)** This problem is simply asking you to isolate the w variable. To begin, let's move the constant to the left side of the equation by dividing both sides by $\frac{1}{3}$.

Dividing by $\frac{1}{3}$ is the same as multiplying by 3. (Remember that dividing by a fraction is the same as multiplying by its reciprocal.) So we're left with:

$$3V = lwh$$

Next, let's divide both sides by l:

$$\frac{3V}{l} = wh$$

The final step is to divide both sides by h, giving us our final answer:

$$\frac{3V}{lh} = w$$

This is choice (C).

2. **(B)** First, we need to get the x out of the denominator by multiplying both sides of the equation by x:

$$18x^2 - 21 = \frac{2x^2}{3} + 12x$$

We have two x^2-terms to combine. So we need a common denominator, which is 3:

$$\frac{54x^2}{3} - 21 = \frac{2x^2}{3} + 12x$$

This is a quadratic equation since the highest degree of the terms is 2. We bring all terms to the same side so that we can eventually use the quadratic formula:

$$\frac{52x^2}{3} - 12x - 21 = 0$$

Recall the quadratic formula for a quadratic equation of the form $ax^2 + bx + c$:

$$x = \frac{-b \pm \sqrt{b^2 - 4ac}}{2a}$$

Filling in our values for a, b, and c gives:

$$x = \frac{12 \pm \sqrt{(-12)^2 - 4\left(\frac{52}{3}\right)(-21)}}{2\left(\frac{52}{3}\right)}$$

$$x = \frac{12 \pm \sqrt{1600}}{\left(\frac{104}{3}\right)} = \frac{12 \pm 40}{\left(\frac{104}{3}\right)}$$

So $x = \frac{3}{2}$ or $x = -\frac{21}{26}$.

We're looking only for the negative value of x, so we only care about the second value. This second value can also be expressed as -0.8077. Rounded to one decimal place, we get choice (B).

3. **(B)** First, figure out what $\frac{1}{2}$ and $\frac{5}{6}$ of 30 are so that you know what range of flex days an employee wants to take:

$$\frac{1}{2}(30) = 15 \text{ and } \frac{5}{6}(30) = 25$$

So the employee wants to take at least 15 days but fewer than 25 days. If we consider F to be the number of flex days taken, this can be expressed as:

$$15 \le F < 25$$

Now we need an expression for flex days using sick days, S, and personal days, P. A sick day counts as half of a flex day, and a personal day counts as a total flex day. So the number of flex days used will be represented by:

$$\frac{1}{2}S + P = F$$

We can plug in this expression for F in our previous inequality:

$$15 \le \frac{1}{2}S + P < 25$$

This is choice (B).

4. **(B)** For this question, we simply plug in $-4x$ for every x in the original function:

$$g(-4x) = 9(-4x) + 2 = -36x + 2$$

This answer matches choice (B).

5. **(C)** The carpenter charges a flat fee of $40, so our equation will have a constant of 40. The carpenter also charges $60 for each half hour worked. Therefore, the carpenter charges $120 for each hour, H, worked. Therefore, the carpenter's total fee for working H hours is:

$$F(H) = 40 + 120H$$

This is answer (C).

6. **(B)** Let's use elimination to get rid of the y-terms. Start by multiplying the first equation by 34: $34(0.75x - 0.1y = 1.2)$. This results in:

$$25.5x - 3.4y = 40.8$$

Now we can add this new equation to the second equation to eliminate the y-terms:

$$\begin{array}{r} 25.5x - 3.4y = 40.8 \\ + \quad 2.6x + 3.4y = 15.4 \\ \hline 28.1x = 56.2 \end{array}$$

Dividing by 28.1 tells us that $x = 2$. This is enough to narrow the answer down to choice (B). However, let's solve for y just for practice:

$$2.6(2) + 3.4y = 15.4$$

$$5.2 + 3.4y = 15.4$$

Subtract 5.2 from both sides and then divide by 3.4 to learn that $y = 3$.

7. **(B)** If $\frac{m}{n} = -\frac{3}{1}$, then $\frac{n}{m} = -\frac{1}{3}$. Therefore, $-2\left(\frac{n}{m}\right) = -2\left(-\frac{1}{3}\right) = \frac{2}{3}$, which is choice (B).

8. **(D)** First, you must consider how two lines could have infinitely many solutions. The answer is that they need to have the same slope and the same y-intercept. In other words, they are the same line when graphed.

Let's start by rewriting Equation B in slope-intercept form by dividing both sides by 3:

$$y = \frac{2}{3}x + 1$$

The equations already have the same slope. However, they also need to have the same y-intercept: -4.

Let's subtract 5 from the right side of Equation B so that it matches Equation A:

$$y = \frac{2}{3}x - 4$$

However, we want to know what we need to change about the *original* Equation B. Therefore, we want to get Equation B back in its original form to see what changed. We can do this by multiplying both sides by 3:

$$3\left(y = \frac{2}{3}x - 4\right) \text{ becomes } 3y = 2x - 12$$

Now we can see that from Equation B to this final equation, we subtracted 15 from the right side to change the y-intercept from $+3$ to -12. This matches choice (D).

9. **(D)** Don't get confused by all of the unnecessary information here! We want to know when the hot-air balloon and the blimp will be at the same altitude. Since altitude deals with only vertical movement, we only care about their vertical movements. The balloon and blimp will be at the same altitude when their vertical positions are equal.

Start with some notation. Let's say that traveling up is in the positive direction. So the balloon is traveling in the positive direction. Let's also say that traveling down is in the negative direction. So the blimp is traveling in the negative direction.

Remember that distance = rate × time.

The blimp's position can be defined as $s = 5{,}000 - 5t$.

The balloon's position can be described as $s = 500 + 4t$.

The blimp and balloon will be at the same altitude when their positions are equal. So we can set the two expressions equal to one another:

$$5{,}000 - 5t = 500 + 4t$$

Add $5t$ to both sides while subtracting 500 from both sides:

$$4{,}500 = 9t$$

Dividing by 9 tells us that $t = 500$.

Because our rates were in feet/minute, our time is in minutes. Let's divide by 60 to convert this to hours:

$$\frac{500}{60} = 8.333$$

So it takes 8 hours and $\frac{1}{3}$ of the 9th hour. One-third of an hour is 20 minutes since $\frac{1}{3}(60) = 20$. So it takes 8 hours and 20 minutes. Since the balloon and blimp started moving toward one another at 1:00 P.M., they'll meet at 9:20 P.M., which is choice (D).

10. **(A)** Let's first set up an inequality that models this situation. Rosa wants to burn more than 2,000 calories, so we can represent this as 2,000 < calories.

Next we need to come up with an expression that represents the number of calories Rosa burns. Rosa is either burning 65 calories per hour by resting or burning 300 calories per hour while exercising. Let's call H the number of hours she spends exercising. Since there are 24 hours in a day and she's not exercising for the rest of the hours outside of H, the hours spent resting will be $24 - H$.

Therefore, the number of calories Rosa burns can be expressed as:

$$2,000 < 300H + 65(24 - H)$$

Now we solve for H. First, distribute the 65:

$$2,000 < 300H + 1560 - 65H$$

Combine like terms:

$$2,000 < 235H + 1560$$

Subtract 1,560 from both sides:

$$440 < 235H$$

Divide both sides by 235:

$$1.87 < H$$

This means that Rosa has to work out for at least 1.9 hours. She can't work out more than 24 hours per day since there are only 24 hours in a day. So the correct answer is (A).

Problem-Solving and Data Analysis Drill 1

1. **(C)** Let's use the variable d to represent the number of dogs in the shelter and the variable c to represent the number of cats. If the ratio of dogs to cats is 3:1, then there are 3 times as many dogs as cats:

$$d = 3c$$

If there are 360 animals in the shelter:

$$d + c = 360$$

We want to know the number of dogs present. So let's solve the first equation for c in terms of d and plug this into the second equation. Dividing by 3 tells us:

$$\frac{1}{3}d = c$$

Plugging this into the second equation results in:

$$d + \frac{1}{3}d = 360$$

Combining like terms gives:

$$\frac{4}{3}d = 360$$

We can divide both sides by $\frac{4}{3}$ (in other words, multiply both sides by $\frac{3}{4}$) to learn that $d = 270$, which is answer choice (C).

Alternatively, you can solve this as a ratio problem:

$$\frac{d}{c} = \frac{3}{1}$$

As a fraction of the whole, the number of dogs can be expressed as $d = \frac{3}{(3 + 1)} = \frac{3}{4}$ of the total. Then take $\frac{3}{4}$ of the total number of animals to find the number of dogs:

$$\frac{3}{4} \times 360 = 270$$

2. **(B)** Let's set up a proportion for this problem. The politician receives 14 seconds of applause for every minute of a speech. We want our units to be the same, so let's call that minute 60 seconds. We can model this part of our proportion as $\frac{14}{60}$.

We want to know how many minutes of applause he'll get for 2 hours of speech. Since we want our answer in minutes, let's call 2 hours 120 minutes. We want applause on top again. Therefore, this side of the proportion can be modeled by $\frac{x}{120}$, where x represents the number of minutes of applause the politician will receive in 120 minutes.

You can then set both sides of the proportion equal to one another:

$$\frac{14}{60} = \frac{x}{120}$$

Next, cross multiply:

$$14(120) = 60x$$
$$1{,}680 = 60x$$

Dividing by 60 gives us $x = 28$, choice (B).

3. **(D)** A gallon of whole milk would have 3.5% of a gallon of fat, or 0.035 gallons. If we mix 1% milk and 2% milk in equal parts, we will essentially have 1.5% milk since the fat content will be the average of the two fat contents.

Therefore, the whole milk has $\frac{0.035}{0.015} = 2.333$ times the amount of fat of the 1% and 2% mixture. You would need 2.333 times the amount of milk of the mixture to have the same quantity of fat as in 1 gallon of whole milk. Because 0.333 can be represented as $\frac{1}{3}$, the answer is choice (D).

Alternatively, take the combined average of the lower-fat milks:

$$\frac{1+2}{2} = 1.5$$

Then using x as the number of gallons needed of the combined milks, you can set up this equation:

$$1.5x = 3.5$$

Then solve for x to get $2\frac{1}{3}$.

4. **(C)** Let's first convert the marathon distance to kilometers:

$$26.2 \text{ miles} \times \frac{1 \text{ kilometer}}{0.62 \text{ miles}} = 42.26 \text{ kilometers}$$

If Katie has to run 42.26 km and if she's doing it 5 km at a time, she would need to run:

$$\frac{42.26}{5} = 8.45 \text{ races}$$

Therefore, she would need to run a minimum of 9 whole races to run the distance of a marathon.

Alternatively, you could have done dimensional analysis for the last step, canceling out units that you don't want and leaving only the units that you do want. Katie wants to go 42.26 km, and she's running 5 km/race. Cancel out kilometers, so that we're left with number of races:

$$42.26 \text{ kilometers} \times \frac{1 \text{ race}}{5 \text{ kilometers}} = 8.45 \text{ races}$$

We again need to round up to 9 so that Katie runs the full marathon distance.

5. **(A)** Let's use dimensional analysis, canceling out the units that we don't want and leaving the units that we do want (euros). In the dimensional analysis, let CAD mean Canadian dollars, let USD mean U.S. dollars, and let EUR mean euros:

$$100 \text{ CAD} \times \frac{0.7 \text{ USD}}{1 \text{ CAD}} \times \frac{0.9 \text{ EUR}}{1 \text{ USD}} = 63 \text{ EUR}$$

The correct answer is choice (A).

6. **(D)** The easiest way to approach a problem like this is to test some points with each equation to see which equation works.

Choice (A):

$$C(1) = 10^{2(1)} + 10(1-1) + 1 = 100 + 1 = 101$$

So the equation works for day 1. Let's see if it works with day 2:

$$C(2) = 10^{2(2)} + 10(2-1) + 1 = 10{,}000 + 10 + 1$$
$$= 10{,}011$$

This doesn't match the number for day 2, so we can rule out choice (A).

Choice (B):

$$C(1) = 100 + 10^1 = 100 + 10 = 110$$

This isn't the right number for day 1, so we can rule out choice (B).

Choice (C):

$$C(1) = 100 + 10(1-1) + 1 = 100 + 1 = 101$$

This works, so let's try $C(2)$:

$$C(2) = 100 + 10(2-1) + 1 = 100 + 10 + 1 = 111$$

This doesn't work, so we can rule out choice (C).

Choice (D):

$$C(1) = 100 + 10^{1-1} = 100 + 1 = 101$$
$$C(2) = 100 + 10^{2-1} = 100 + 10 = 110$$
$$C(3) = 100 + 10^{3-1} = 100 + 100 = 200$$
$$C(4) = 100 + 10^{4-1} = 100 + 1,000 = 1,100$$
$$C(5) = 100 + 10^{5-1} = 100 + 10,000 = 10,100$$

Obviously, choice (D) is the correct answer.

7. **(B)** Let's first convert 588 million kilometers to meters:

$$588,000,000 \text{ kilometers} \times \frac{1,000 \text{ meters}}{\text{kilometer}}$$
$$= 588,000,000,000 \text{ meters}$$

Because distance = rate × time, it follows that $t = \frac{d}{r}$. Therefore, the t in seconds is given by the following expression:

$$t = \frac{588,000,000,000}{3.00 \times 10^8} = 1,960 \text{ seconds}$$

Because there are 60 seconds in every minute,

$$1,960 \text{ sec} \times \frac{1 \text{ min}}{60 \text{ sec}} = 32.67 \text{ min}$$

This answer rounds to 33 minutes, which is choice (B).

8. **(C)** Since the total number of responses was 26, the median response will be the mean of the 13th and 14th terms.

Terms 1–2 were 0–1 hours.

Terms 3–6 were 1–2 hours.

Terms 7–11 were 2–3 hours.

Terms 12–16 were 3–4 hours.

Therefore, the 13th and 14th terms were both 3–4 hours, which is choice (C).

9. **(B)** Every student in each class either did or did not complete summer reading. So the total number of students enrolled in Mrs. Smith's class is 29, and the total number enrolled in Mr. Walker's class is 31. The average number of students enrolled in the two classes is:

$$\frac{29 + 31}{2} = 30$$

We can assume that each of the 14 English classes has, on average, 30 people. Therefore, the total number enrolled in English classes would be:

$$14(30) = 420$$

The correct answer is choice (B).

10. **(C)** To determine a 3% increase of an original amount of x, add 3% to the original amount:

$$x + 0.03x = 1.03x$$

You can save time if you recognize that you can simply multiply x by 1.03 to determine the total of x plus 3% interest. The amount in the account is compounded twice because the money stays in the account for 2 years. So, multiply x by 1.03 twice:

$$x \cdot 1.03 \cdot 1.03 = 1.0609x$$

Problem-Solving and Data Analysis Drill 2

1. **(C)** First, figure out the number of words that each report would have. We know the number of words per page. So if we multiply this by the number of pages, the pages unit will cancel from the top and bottom. This will leave us with the number of words. If the student uses Times New Roman, he will write:

$$240(10) = 2,400 \text{ words}$$

However, if he uses Comic Sans, he will write only:

$$170(10) = 1,700 \text{ words}$$

We want to know how many fewer words he will write in the second situation.

$$2,400 - 1,700 = 700 \text{ words}$$

So choice (C) is correct.

2. **(B)** The area of a rectangle is given by the formula $A = lw$, where l is length and w is width. If the length of the drawing is 4 inches, we know from dividing both sides of our area equation by the length that:

$$w = \frac{A}{l} = \frac{20}{4} = 5 \text{ inches}$$

The key tells us that each inch on the map represents 6 feet. We can multiply 4 inches by 6 feet/inch to tell us that the length is 24 feet. Similarly, we can multiply the 5-inch width by 6 feet/inch to tell us that the width is 30 feet.

Alternatively, you could have solved for actual distance by setting up a proportion. For the length, the proportion might look something like:

$$\frac{1''}{6'} = \frac{4''}{x'}$$

Cross multiplying gives you:

$$1x = (4)(6)$$

So $x = 24$.

The question wants to know the perimeter of the fence. Perimeter of a rectangle is given by the formula $P = 2l + 2w$. Plugging our dimensions into the formula tells us:

$$P = 2(24) + 2(30) = 48 + 60 = 108$$

The correct answer is choice (B).

3. **(C)** If John's performance increased by 20%, then he performed at 120% of his original performance. 120% can be expressed in decimal form as 1.2, and we can find 120% of his original score of 60 by multiplying the two:

$$1.2(60) = 72$$

So John got a 72% on his second test. His performance then increased another 25%, so his third test performance was 125%, or 1.25, of test 2. Therefore, John's third score was:

$$1.25(72) = 90\%$$

The answer is choice (C).

Alternatively, you could have found John's second score by finding 20% of 60 and adding that to 60:

$$\text{Test 2} = 60 + (0.2)(60) = 60 + 12 = 72$$

Then you could have found the third score by finding 25% of 72 and adding that to 72:

$$\text{Test 3} = 72 + (0.25)(72) = 72 + 18 = 90$$

4. **(B)** If you were told that you had to travel 50 miles and that your car got 10 miles/gallon, you may intuitively see that you need 5 gallons of gas. You get that by dividing 50/10. Following this logic, we can get the number of gallons of gas Linda needs to travel 240 miles by dividing 240 by 28:

$$240 \div 28 = 8.57 \text{ gallons}$$

If this doesn't quite make sense, you could also do dimensional analysis to cancel out the units you don't want. You want to cancel out miles and end up with gallons:

$$240 \text{ miles} \times \frac{1 \text{ gallon}}{28 \text{ miles}} = 8.57 \text{ gallons}$$

Linda also wants to have 1 gallon left, so she'll want to have 9.57 gallons in her tank when she starts out. Linda already has 2 gallons in her tank, so she needs to buy $9.57 - 2 = 7.57$ gallons, or 7.6 rounded to the nearest tenth. This matches choice (B).

5. **(A)** We can see from the negative slope that as the quantity of shake-ups increases, price decreases. Therefore, we know that the function will be decreasing, eliminating choices (B) and (D). We can also see that the slope isn't constant. Therefore, it can't be linear, as in choice (C). The graph starts off fairly steep and then it becomes less steep, consistent with exponential decay, as in choice (A).

6. **(D)** This is an easy question to overthink. There are 3 teaspoons in each tablespoon. So multiply $3 \times 3 \times 2$ to get the 18 total teaspoons needed for the 2 cakes.

7. **(C)** An equation of a line is given by $y = mx + b$, where m is the slope and b is the y-intercept. The formula for slope is calculated by finding the rise over the run, which is illustrated by this formula:

$$m = \frac{\Delta y}{\Delta x} = \frac{y_2 - y_1}{x_2 - x_1}$$

Plug in values for the endpoints:

$$m = \frac{5.9 - 7.8}{17 - 14} = \frac{-1.9}{3} = -0.633$$

Thus, the slope is approximately -0.6, so we can rule out choices (B) and (D).

Next, we need to determine the y-intercept b. To do this, we can plug a particular point on the line into the equation and solve for b. For instance, $(14, 7.8)$ appears to be a point on the line. Plugging these values into the equation gives:

$$7.8 = -0.6(14) + b$$

So $7.8 = -8.4 + b$.

Adding 8.4 to both sides gives $16.2 = b$. Therefore, choice (C) must be correct.

With this graph, you cannot find the y-intercept, b, just by looking at the where the line crosses the y-axis. On this graph, the y-axis crosses the x-axis at 14, not at 0. However, the y-intercept is, by definition, the value of y when the value of x equals 0.

8. **(B)** Divide 1.0×10^6 kg/m³ by 990 kg/m³ to determine the multiple by which her weight will increase. Her weight will be 1,010 times greater. Then multiply 1,010 by 150 pounds to get 151,500 pounds.

9. **(B)** We can rule out choice (A) because the slope is clearly positive. Use the slope formula:

$$m = \frac{\Delta y}{\Delta x} = \frac{y_2 - y_1}{x_2 - x_1}$$

Plug in the values for the approximate endpoints of the line of best fit to get:

$$m = \frac{300 - 150}{5,000 - 2,500} = \frac{150}{2,500} = \frac{3}{50}$$

The answer is choice (B).

10. **(A)** First, figure out what fraction of one hour 3 minutes is:

3 minutes $\times$ (1 hour / 60 minutes) $= \frac{1}{20}$ hour. If he takes $\frac{1}{20}$ of an hour per page, multiplying by p, the number of pages, will tell you the total time taken in hours:

$$\frac{1}{20} \times p = \frac{p}{20}, \text{ Choice (A)}$$

Advanced Math Drill 1

1. **(A)** A cubic function has a variable raised to the third degree or, in terms of geometry, has 3 dimensions. Therefore, we need a shape that is 3-dimensional. This rules out choices (B) and (C).

Choice (D) may be tempting because a cube is 3-dimensional. However, surface area is actually only 2 dimensions, so this wouldn't be a cubic function.

Choice (A) is correct because volume of a sphere varies proportionally to the cube of its radius. Volume is always in 3 dimensions, hence the reason its units are always in cubic units.

Alternatively, you could have written out all of the relationships depicted in the answer choices.

The volume of a sphere is given by the formula $V = \frac{4}{3}\pi r^3$, which is a cubic function since the radius variable has degree 3. So choice (A) is correct.

The formula for a circle's circumference is $C = 2\pi r = \pi d$, where d represents diameter. This is a linear relationship between d and C, making choice (B) incorrect.

A triangle's area is $A = \frac{1}{2}bh$. This isn't a cubic function, so choice (C) can't be correct.

A cube's surface area is given by the formula $SA = 6x^2$, where x represents the length of each side of the cube. Again, this isn't a cubic function since the degree of x is only 2, so choice (D) is incorrect.

2. **(A)** From all of the answer choices, we can see that the whole denominator cancels out somehow. Let's use polynomial long division to figure out an equivalent expression for our original fraction. Before we use long division, let's first combine like terms in the numerator so that the long division isn't as complicated:

$$a^3 - b^3 + 2a^2b - 2ab^2 + ab^2 - ba^2 = a^3 - b^3 + a^2b - ab^2$$

Now do polynomial long division:

$$
\begin{array}{r}
a + b \\
a^2 - b^2 \overline{)\, a^3 - b^3 + a^2b - ab^2} \\
\underline{-(a^3 - ab^2)} \\
-b^3 + a^2b \\
\underline{-(-b^3 + a^2b)} \\
0
\end{array}
$$

Thus, our original fraction is equal to $a + b$, which is choice (A).

Alternatively, you could have simplified directly by factoring. Since $a^3 - b^3 = (a - b)(a^2 + ab + b^2)$, we can rewrite the numerator:

$a^3 - b^3 + 2a^2b - 2ab^2 + ab^2 - ba^2 = a^3 - b^3 + a^2b$
$- ab^2 = (a - b)(a^2 + ab + b^2) + a^2b - ab^2$

Notice that $a^2b - ab^2 = ab(a - b)$, so our numerator becomes:

$(a - b)(a^2 + ab + b^2) + a^2b - ab^2 = (a - b)(a^2 + ab + b^2) + ab(a - b) = (a - b)(a^2 + ab + b^2 + ab)$
$= (a - b)(a^2 + 2ab + b^2) = (a - b)(a + b)^2$

Thus, our original fraction can be rewritten as $\dfrac{(a - b)(a + b)^2}{a^2 - b^2}$. Since our denominator is a difference of squares, it can be rewritten as $a^2 - b^2 = (a + b)(a - b)$. Our entire expression becomes:

$$\frac{(a - b)(a + b)^2}{a^2 - b^2} = \frac{(a - b)(a + b)^2}{(a - b)(a + b)} = a + b$$

Choice (A) is correct.

3. **(C)** We can solve for all possible values of m^2 by subtracting $2m^7$ from both sides, factoring the left side, and setting the left side equal to 0:

$$-5m^5 + 3m^3 - 2m^7 = 0$$

First, factor out $-m^3$:

$$-m^3(5m^2 - 3 + 2m^4) = 0$$

Rearrange the polynomial inside the parentheses so that the terms are decreasing in degree for easier factoring:

$$-m^3(2m^4 + 5m^2 - 3) = 0.$$

Next factor the inside:

$$-m^3(2m^4 + 5m^2 - 3) = -m^3(m^2 + 3)(2m^2 - 1) = 0$$

Now set each factor equal to 0 to solve for possible values of m^2:

$$-m^3 = 0$$

Dividing both sides by $-m$ tells you that $m^2 = 0$, so this is one possible value.

$$m^2 + 3 = 0$$

Subtracting 3 from both sides gives $m^2 = -3$. However, you can't square a number and get a negative, so this solution is extraneous.

$$2m^2 - 1 = 0$$

Add 1 to both sides and divide by 2:

$$m^2 = \frac{1}{2}$$

This is another possible value. Therefore, the two possible values of m^2 are 0 and 0.5. Thus, their sum is 0.5, which is choice (C).

4. **(D)** First, multiply by 8 to avoid dealing with fractions:

$$4x^2 + 2x - 1 = 0$$

Next, use the quadratic formula:

$$x = \frac{-b \pm \sqrt{b^2 - 4ac}}{2a} = \frac{-2 \pm \sqrt{2^2 - 4(4)(-1)}}{2(4)}$$
$$= \frac{-2 \pm \sqrt{4 + 16}}{8} = \frac{-2 \pm \sqrt{20}}{8} = -\frac{2}{8} \pm \frac{2\sqrt{5}}{8} = -\frac{1}{4} \pm \frac{\sqrt{5}}{4}$$

This still doesn't match any of the answer choices. All of the answer choices have a fraction factored out of them. We can factor $\frac{1}{4}$ out of our expression to get the answer:

$$\frac{1}{4}\left(-1 \pm \sqrt{5}\right)$$

Choice (D) is correct.

5. **(A)** Get rid of the square root by squaring both sides. Squaring the right side simply gets rid of the square root, but be careful to FOIL the left side:

$$a^2 + 8a + 16 = a^2 - 2$$

Subtract a^2 from both sides:

$$8a + 16 = -2$$

Next, subtract 16 from both sides:

$$8a = -18$$

Solve for a by dividing by 8:

$$a = -\frac{18}{8} = -\frac{9}{4}$$

This is choice (A).

Note that squaring equations can lead to extraneous answers. In this case, we don't get any extraneous solutions. However, you should get in the habit of checking your solutions by plugging them back into the original equation to ensure that your solution is truly a solution to the original.

6. **(C)** The zeros of a factored polynomial can be found by setting each distinct factor equal to 0 and solving for x. Here there are only 2 distinct factors, $(x - 3)$ and $(x + 7)$. So there will only be 2, choice (C).

$$x - 3 = 0$$
$$x = 3$$
$$x + 7 = 0$$
$$x = -7$$

Note: Although $x - 3$ occurs twice as a factor, this still corresponds to only one zero. We say that 3 is a zero of multiplicity 2 since its corresponding factor occurs twice.

7. **(C)** This function is a parabola. It opens upward because the coefficient in front of x^2 is positive. (In this case, the coefficient of x^2 is 1.) The function has a y-intercept of 2. Therefore, the range is $[2, \infty)$. In order for the range to include negative numbers, the new function either needs to open downward or have a negative y-intercept. In order for it to open downward, you would multiply the right side by a negative number, but this isn't a choice.

The only choice that works is subtracting 3, which would make the y-intercept negative. The y-intercept of the new function would be -1 because $2 - 3 = -1$. The range of the new function would be expanded to $[-1, \infty)$.

8. **(A)** This equation is probably a bit different from the equations of the parabolas that you're used to seeing. To get it into standard form, we need to solve for x instead of the y as we usually do:

$$\frac{1}{17}(y - 4)^2 - 2 = x$$

This is a parabola rotated 90 degrees clockwise. The standard form can be represented by the equation:

$$x = a(y - k)^2 + h$$

Therefore, in this problem, $k = 4$ and $h = -2$. So (h, k) is $(-2, 4)$, as shown in choice (A). Parabola problems like this may not be on the PSAT, but it is included here so that you will be as prepared as possible.

9. **(A)** The relationship is easiest to see if you solve for M first. First, square both sides:

$$(v_{rms})^2 = \frac{3RT}{M}$$

Multiply both sides by M to get M out of the denominator:

$$M(v_{rms})^2 = 3RT$$

Now isolate M:

$$M = \frac{3RT}{(v_{rms})^2}$$

We can now consider how we can lower M. First, M is directly proportional to T. So decreasing T will decrease M. Further, M is inversely proportional to the square of v_{rms}. So increasing v_{rms} will decrease M because you will be dividing by a larger number. Therefore, choice (A) is correct.

10. **(A)** None of the answer choices has a percentage in it, so convert the percentage to a decimal by dividing by 100:

$$x\% = \frac{x}{100} \text{ and } y\% = \frac{y}{100}$$

Suppose P is the initial amount deposited into each portfolio. If portfolio A grows at a rate of $x\%$ yearly, the value after 1 year will be given by the expression:

$$P + \frac{x}{100}P = \left(1 + \frac{x}{100}\right)P$$

The following year, the amount of money in portfolio A again increases by $x\%$. Therefore, the value after the second year will be given by the following expression:

$$\left(1 + \frac{x}{100}\right)\left[\left(1 + \frac{x}{100}\right)P\right] = \left(1 + \frac{x}{100}\right)\left(1 + \frac{x}{100}\right)P$$
$$\text{or } \left(1 + \frac{x}{100}\right)^2 P$$

The third year, the interest will be compounded on the previous value. Therefore, the value will be:

$$\left(1 + \frac{x}{100}\right)^2\left(1 + \frac{x}{100}\right)P \text{ or } \left(1 + \frac{x}{100}\right)^3 P$$

The value after n years is given by:

$$\left(1 + \frac{x}{100}\right)^n P$$

So after 10 years, the value of portfolio A will be $\left(1 + \frac{x}{100}\right)^{10} P$.

Repeat the thought process for portfolio B to arrive at the conclusion that the value of portfolio B after 10 years will be

$$\left(1 + \frac{y}{100}\right)^{10} P$$

since both portfolios A and B start out with the same amount initially, P. Therefore, the ratio of the value of portfolio A to the value of portfolio B is:

$$\frac{\left(1 + \frac{x}{100}\right)^{10} P}{\left(1 + \frac{y}{100}\right)^{10} P} \text{ or } \left(\frac{1 + \frac{x}{100}}{1 + \frac{y}{100}}\right)^{10}$$

This matches choice (A).

Advanced Math Drill 2

1. **(C)** We will use the formula $d = rt$, where d is distance, r is rate, and t is time. Let's define the car's initial position, s, as $s = 0$ and the truck's initial position as $s = 180$.

   The car's position at time t will be its initial position (0) plus the distance it has traveled in that time. We are told that the car's rate r is x, so the distance the car travels in time t is xt. Since the car starts at an initial position of 0, its position at time t will be expressed as $s = xt + 0 = xt$.

   The truck starts at position $s = 180$ and travels toward the 0 position. So the truck's position at time t will be expressed as 180 minus the distance it has traveled in time t. Its speed is twice the speed of the car, or $2x$. So the truck's position at time t will be expressed as $s = 180 - 2xt$.

   They meet where their positions are equal. So set the two equations equal to one another to solve for x:

   $$xt = 180 - 2xt$$

   We know that the vehicles meet after 3 hours, so we can plug in 3 for t:

   $$3x = 180 - 6x$$

   Adding $6x$ to both sides gives:

   $$9x = 180$$

Dividing both sides by 9 results in $x = 20$.

However, before selecting choice (A), make sure to finish the problem.

The question asks you what speed the truck is going. The truck has a speed of $2x$. So its speed is $2(20) = 40$, which is choice (C).

2. **(A)** This problem mentions the "mean of the bases." Notice that $\frac{B_1 + B_2}{2}$, the first part of the area formula, is another way of saying the mean of the bases. Since the mean of the bases is twice the height, we can replace this part of the formula with $2H$:

   $$A = \frac{B_1 + B_2}{2} H = 2H \times H = 2H^2$$

   The area is 72, so plug this in for A and solve for H:

   $$72 = 2H^2$$

   Divide by 2:

   $$36 = H^2$$

   Take the square root of both sides to arrive at the answer $6 = H$, which is choice (A).

3. **(C)** If the negative exponent is in the numerator, it can send whatever is being raised to that exponent to the denominator, but be careful here. In both terms, only the m is being raised to the negative exponents, so the constants stay in the numerator:

   $$2m^{-2} - 4m^{-3} = \frac{2}{m^2} - \frac{4}{m^3}$$

   However, this doesn't match an answer choice. Based on the answer choices, it looks like we may need to add the two fractions together to get just one fraction overall. To add the two fractions, we need a common denominator. If you multiplied the first fraction by $\frac{m}{m}$, both terms would have a denominator of m^3:

   $$\frac{2}{m^2} - \frac{4}{m^3} = \frac{2m}{m^3} - \frac{4}{m^3}$$

   Now that they have a common denominator, you can add the two fractions together:

   $$\frac{2m}{m^3} - \frac{4}{m^3} = \frac{2m - 4}{m^3}$$

   Choice (C) is correct.

4. **(A)** Since there's nothing to distribute, you can just drop the parentheses and combine like terms:

$$2y^4 + 3x^6 + 5x^6 + 3y^4 = 5y^4 + 8x^6$$

The correct answer is choice (A).

5. **(D)** Look at the answer choices. All of the choices indicate that at least one $(x - 3)$ factor cancels out, so divide the numerator by $(x - 3)$:

$$\begin{array}{r} 2x - 6 \\ x - 3 \overline{)2x^2 - 12x + 18} \\ -\underline{(2x^2 - 6x)} \\ -6x + 18 \\ -\underline{(-6x + 18)} \\ 0 \end{array}$$

So the expression can be rewritten as:

$$\frac{(x - 3)(2x - 6)}{3(x - 3)^3}$$

You can cancel an $(x - 3)$ term from the top and bottom:

$$\frac{(2x - 6)}{3(x - 3)^2}$$

The number 2 can be factored out of the numerator:

$$\frac{2(x - 3)}{3(x - 3)^2}$$

Another $(x - 3)$ term cancels:

$$\frac{2}{3(x - 3)}$$

This is choice (D).

Alternatively, you could have factored the numerator directly:

$$2x^2 - 12x + 18 = 2(x^2 - 6x + 9) = 2(x - 3)^2$$

Then you could have canceled out the $(x - 3)^2$ term from the denominator.

6. **(A)** To find the solutions, subtract $15x$ and 18 from both sides to get everything on the left side:

$$21x^2 - 15x - 18 = 0$$

Next, factor out a 3 to make the quadratic equation a bit simpler:

$$3(7x^2 - 5x - 6) = 0$$

Divide both sides by 3:

$$7x^2 - 5x - 6 = 0$$

Notice that the answer choices look similar in structure to the quadratic formula $x = \frac{-b \pm \sqrt{b^2 - 4ac}}{2a}$. This suggests that we try to factor our quadratic equation using the quadratic formula. Letting $a = 7$, $b = -5$, and $c = -6$ in the quadratic formula above, we get choice (A).

7. **(B)** Find where the supply and demand are equivalent by setting the two equations equal to one another and solving for p:

$$3p + 6p^2 = 156 - 12p$$

Subtract 156 and add $12p$ to both sides:

$$15p + 6p^2 - 156 = 0$$

Rearrange the equation to get it in $ax^2 + bx + c$ form while simultaneously factoring out a 3:

$$3(2p^2 + 5p - 52) = 0$$

Divide both sides by 3:

$$2p^2 + 5p - 52 = 0$$

Factor to get:

$$(2p + 13)(p - 4) = 0$$

Set each factor equal to 0 and solve for p to get the two possible values of p:

$$2p + 13 = 0 \text{ so } p = -\frac{13}{2}$$

$$p - 4 = 0 \text{ so } p = 4$$

In this situation, p must be positive since it represents the price of the item, which can't be negative. Therefore, p equals only 4, choice (B).

Alternatively, if you didn't recognize that the quadratic equation could be factored, you could have used the quadratic formula:

$$x = \frac{-5 \pm \sqrt{5^2 - 4(2)(-52)}}{2(2)} = \frac{-5 \pm \sqrt{441}}{4} = \frac{-5 \pm 21}{4}$$

$$x = 4 \text{ or } x = -\frac{13}{2}$$

8. **(A)** Look at each option to see whether it is an answer.

Option I: $x = c$ is a vertical line at c. The line will cross the y-axis only if $c = 0$. Since we are told that c is a nonzero constant, this equation does not have a y-intercept.

Option II: $y = -c$ is a horizontal line at the $-c$ value. The line will cross the y-axis at $-c$. This option, therefore, must have a y-intercept.

Option III: $y = cx$ is a line with slope c. Note that when $x = 0$, $y = c(0) = 0$. So the line has a y-intercept at 0.

Thus, only option I is true, which is choice (A).

9. **(B)** The function has zeros at 2, 3, and 6. We can use this to find the factors of the function.

If $x = 2$, $x - 2 = 0$. So $(x - 2)$ is a factor.

If $x = 3$, $x - 3 = 0$. So $(x - 3)$ is a factor.

If $x = 6$, $x - 6 = 0$. So $(x - 6)$ is a factor.

Therefore, the function can be rewritten as $y = (x - 2)(x - 3)(x - 6)$. All of the answer choices are in their unfactored forms, so use FOIL. Start by using FOIL with the first two factors:

$$y = (x^2 - 5x + 6)(x - 6)$$

Then multiply the remaining factors:

$$y = x^3 - 11x^2 + 36x - 36$$

This matches choice (B).

10. **(C)** First, let's identify all of the givens.

Since we're not provided a value for P, we will leave it as is in the formula.

We're also given that the interest is compounded once every 12 months. In other words, it's compounded once every year. Since n is the number of times the investment is compounded yearly, $n = 1$.

We're also told that the investment rate is 5%. Because r is the interest rate expressed as a decimal, $r = \frac{5}{100} = 0.05$.

We want to know A after 1 year, so $t = 1$.

Now plug everything into the equation:

$$A = P\left(1 + \frac{0.05}{1}\right)^{(1)(1)} = P(1.05) = 1.05P$$

Choice (C) is the answer.

Geometry and Trigonometry Drill

1. **(C)** Let's do this one in two parts. First, we have a right cylinder with a volume of $30x$. We form a cone with the same height and radius as that cylinder. The formula for the volume of a cylinder is $V = \pi r^2 h$, while the formula for the volume of a cone is $V = \frac{1}{3}\pi r^2 h$.

Notice that the volume of a cone is just $\frac{1}{3}$ the volume of a cylinder with the same dimensions. Thus, if the volume of the cylinder is $30x$, the volume of a cone with the same dimensions is $\frac{1}{3}(30x)$ or $10x$.

For the second part of this problem, there's a cube with a volume of $21x$. We have a pyramid with the same length, width, and height as the cube. The formula for the volume of a cube is $V = LWH = L^3$ because the length, width, and height are all the same. The formula for the volume of a pyramid is $V = \frac{1}{3}LWH$.

In this case, the pyramid has the same length, width, and height as the cube, so the volume for the pyramid can be expressed as $V = \frac{1}{3}L^3$.

Notice that in this case, the volume of the pyramid is just $\frac{1}{3}$ of the volume of the cube. The volume of the cube is $21x$, so the volume of the pyramid is $\frac{1}{3}(21x) = 7x$.

The question asked us the sum of the volume of the cone and the pyramid, which can be expressed by:

$$V = V_{\text{cone}} + V_{\text{pyramid}} = 10x + 7x = 17x$$

Choice (C) is correct.

2. **(A)** The length Andrew would fly would simply be the hypotenuse of a right triangle with side lengths of 20 miles and 15 miles. So we can use the Pythagorean theorem, which states that $a^2 + b^2 = c^2$, where a and b represent the sides and c represents the hypotenuse:

$$(20)^2 + (15)^2 = c^2$$
$$400 + 225 = c^2$$
$$c = \sqrt{625} = 25$$

Choice (A) is correct.

Alternatively, you could have saved a bit of time by noticing that this is just a variation of a 3-4-5 triangle:

$$15 = 3(5) \text{ and } 20 = 4(5)$$

Thus, the hypotenuse will be 5(5) or 25.

3. **(C)** In a right triangle, we can use the Pythagorean theorem to solve for an unknown hypotenuse. $a^2 + b^2 = c^2$ where a and b are the 2 shorter legs and c is the hypotenuse. To solve for c, you take the square root of both sides:

$$c = \sqrt{a^2 + b^2}$$

This matches choice (C).

4. **(B)** You can use the Pythagorean theorem to calculate the length of the diagonal of this rectangle since you know the two side lengths of 6 and 8:

$$6^2 + 8^2 = 10^2$$

Alternatively, you could recognize that 6-8-10 is a multiple of the Pythagorean triple 3-4-5, thus saving you the trouble of calculating using the Pythagorean theorem.

5. **(B)** To convert degrees to radians, simply multiply the number of degrees by $\frac{\pi}{180}$:

$$270\left(\frac{\pi}{180}\right) = \frac{3\pi}{2}$$

Choice (B) is the answer.

Alternatively, you could have realized that 270 degrees is $\frac{3}{4}$ of a circle. A circle is 2π radians, so 270 degrees corresponds to:

$$\frac{3}{4}(2\pi) = \frac{6\pi}{4} = \frac{3\pi}{2} \text{ radians}$$

Note: Radians may or may not be a topic tested on the PSAT. It is definitely something that could be on the SAT. So this problem was included here to prepare you.

6. **(D)** To find the length of the crust, we want to find $\frac{1}{8}$ of the total crust measure. The total crust measure is the circumference of a circle with radius 8. So the crust of one piece is $\frac{1}{8}C$. Because $C = 2\pi r$, the measure we're looking for is:

$$\frac{1}{8}2\pi r = \frac{\pi r}{4} = \frac{8\pi}{4} = 2\pi$$

Note that 2(3.14) = 6.28, or choice (D).

7. **(C)** The angle next to the 120-degree angle on line AB is 60 degrees because two angles on a given line (supplementary angles) must add up to 180 degrees.

The angle directly opposite that first 60-degree angle must also be 60 degrees, because angles opposite one another (called vertical angles) are equal. Furthermore, that vertical angle is along line EF with the 120-degree angle. So the sum of these supplementary angles must also be 180 degrees, making the vertical angle 60 degrees.

Because lines AB and CD are parallel and line EF is a transversal, opposite interior angles are also congruent. Therefore, the acute angle along line CD is also 60 degrees.

Because that angle is 60 degrees, the acute angle across from it (also along line CD) is also 60 degrees since angles opposite one another (vertical angles) must be congruent.

8. **(D)** The internal angles of a quadrilateral add up to 360 degrees. Since one angle is 120 degrees, the other angles will add up to $360 - 120 = 240$ degrees. Since the other angles are all congruent, divide 240 by 3 to get 80 degrees as the measure of the other angles. 80 degrees therefore is the measure of the smallest interior angle.

9. **(D)** Similar triangles have similar side lengths, meaning that the side lengths vary in fixed proportions. We know that triangle B has exactly one side length of 28. Since exactly one side of triangle A has length 7, this is $28 \div 7 = 4$ times the side length of the unique side in triangle A. Thus, the two shorter sides in triangle B will also be 4 times the side length of the shorter sides in triangle A. Since the two other sides of triangle A have length 5, triangle B has two sides of length 4(5) = 20 and one side of length of 28.

This could have also been determined using a proportion:

$$\frac{28}{7} = \frac{x}{5}$$

Cross multiplication yields:

$$(28)(5) = 7x$$
$$140 = 7x$$

Dividing both sides by 7 tells us that $20 = x$.

Here we need to be careful. Notice that choice (B) is 20, so you may be tempted to pick choice (B). However, the question is asking us for the perimeter of the triangle rather than for the unknown side length.

The perimeter is $20 + 20 + 28 = 68$, choice (D).

An alternative approach would have been to recognize that the perimeters of similar triangles will vary in the same proportion as the side lengths. We know that triangle B has sides 4 times longer than those of triangle A, so triangle B will also have a perimeter 4 times that of triangle A.

Triangle A has a perimeter of $5 + 5 + 7 = 17$.

Triangle B therefore has a perimeter of $4(17) = 68$.

10. **(A)** We can solve for the unknown side using the Pythagorean theorem:

$$a^2 + b^2 = c^2$$

It follows that

$$b = \sqrt{c^2 - a^2} = \sqrt{26^2 - 24^2} = \sqrt{676 - 576} = \sqrt{100} = 10$$

Similar triangles have the same trigonometric ratios because the similar sides simplify to their lowest multiples.

The smallest angle in this triangle is angle X, as it is across from the shortest side length.

Therefore, a similar triangle will have a tangent of $\frac{\text{opposite}}{\text{adjacent}} = \frac{10}{24}$, which simplifies to $\frac{5}{12}$, choice (A).

Alternatively, you could have saved yourself some time by noticing that this is just a multiple of a 5-12-13 Pythagorean triple. The two known sides are $2(12) = 24$ and $2(13) = 26$. The only side length we were missing was the 5 side, which has a measure of:

$$2(5) = 10$$

Free-Response Problems Drill

1. **(6)** A circle has the formula $(x - h)^2 + (y - k)^2 = r^2$, where (h, k) provides the coordinates for the center of the circle and r is the radius of the circle. This circle, therefore, has a center at $(0, 0)$, otherwise known as the origin. It has a radius of 6. Therefore, a line from the origin to any point on the circle has a distance of 6 units.

2. **(6)** Jamie runs $\frac{3}{2}k$ miles in the time that Matt runs k miles. Their combined distance is 10 miles, so create an equation to show this situation:

$$\frac{3}{2}k + k = 10$$

Get a common denominator so you can add like terms:

$$\frac{3}{2}k + \frac{2}{2}k = 10$$

$$\frac{5}{2}k = 10$$

To solve for k, divide both sides by $\frac{5}{2}$. This is the same as multiplying both sides by the reciprocal, $\frac{2}{5}$:

$$k = 10\left(\frac{2}{5}\right) = \frac{20}{5} = 4$$

However, the question asks how much Jamie runs, so you need to plug this value into $\frac{3}{2}k$:

$$\frac{3}{2}(4) = \frac{12}{2} = 6$$

So Jamie will run 6 miles.

3. $\left(\frac{5}{3}\right)$ Both sides of the equation are squared:

$$(x + 2)(x + 2) = (2x - 3)(2x - 3)$$

If you FOIL both sides:

$$x^2 + 4x + 4 = 4x^2 - 12x + 9$$

To find the solutions, you want to get everything on one side. Moving all terms on the left-hand side to the right side of the equation by subtracting gives:

$$0 = 3x^2 - 16x + 5$$

If you don't see that it can be factored as $(3x-1)(x-5)$, then use the quadratic formula:

$$x = \frac{-b \pm \sqrt{b^2 - 4ac}}{2a} = \frac{16 \pm \sqrt{(-16)^2 - 4(3)(5)}}{2(3)}$$

$$= \frac{16 \pm \sqrt{196}}{6} = \frac{16 \pm 14}{6}$$

Therefore, $x = \frac{1}{3}$ or $x = 5$.

The question asks for the product of all of the solutions, so the answer is

$$5\left(\frac{1}{3}\right) = \frac{5}{3}$$

4. **(7)** If $a+1$ is a factor, it will divide evenly into the polynomial without a remainder. You can do polynomial long division or synthetic division. We will show the steps for long division:

$$
\begin{array}{r}
a^3 - 3a^2 + 5a + (m-5) \\
a+1\overline{)a^4 - 2a^3 + 2a^2 + ma + 2} \\
\underline{-(a^4 + a^3)} \\
-3a^3 + 2a^2 + ma + 2 \\
\underline{-(-3a^3 - 3a^2)} \\
5a^2 + ma + 2 \\
\underline{-(5a^2 + 5a)} \\
(m-5)a + 2 \\
\underline{-((m-5)a + (m-5))} \\
2 - (m-5)
\end{array}
$$

In order for there to be no remainder, $2 - (m-5)$ must be equal to 0. Set it equal to 0 and solve for m:

$$2 - (m-5) = 0$$

Distribute the negative sign:

$$2 - m + 5 = 0$$

Combine like terms on the right:

$$7 - m = 0$$

Adding m to both sides solves for m:

$$7 = m$$

5. **(2)** Translating the line will merely shift it to the right and down. It will not affect the slope. Therefore, the slope will still be 2. Picture moving a line down and to the right on a graph. Does the slope change? No, so the slope remains the same.

Mixed Drill

1. **(C)** First, distribute the -5:

$$15x + \frac{1}{2} = -5x + \frac{25}{2}$$

Now we want to get all of the x-terms on one side and all of the constant terms on the other side. Let's start by adding $5x$ to both sides:

$$20x + \frac{1}{2} = \frac{25}{2}$$

Now all of the x-terms are on the left, so we want all constant terms on the right. Let's subtract $\frac{1}{2}$ from both sides:

$$20x = \frac{24}{2} = 12$$

Dividing both sides by 20 will isolate the x:

$$x = \frac{12}{20}$$

This simplifies to $x = \frac{3}{5}$, which is choice (C).

2. **(C)** Work inside out by first solving for $g(1)$:

$$g(x) = 2 \times 2 \rightarrow g(1) = 2(1)^2 = 2$$

Then put 2 in for x in the $f(x)$:

$$f(x) = 7x + 3 \rightarrow f(2) = 7(2) + 3 = 17$$

3. **(A)** Use FOIL on both sides to get:

$$x^2 - 16x + 60 = x^2 - 16x + 64 + c$$

The coefficients of like terms of both sides of the equation must equal one another. The coefficients of the x^2-terms and of the x-terms are already equal on both sides. However, the constant terms must equal one another as well:

$$60 = 64 + c$$

Subtract 64 from both sides:

$$-4 = c$$

Choice (A) is correct.

4. **(A)** Here we're looking for an angle measure, so we need an inverse trigonometry function. Let's go through the answer choices.

Choice (A) works because sine is the value of the opposite side over the hypotenuse. Side x is opposite of angle X, and side z is the hypotenuse. Thus, $\sin^{-1}\left(\frac{x}{z}\right)$ would provide the measure of angle X.

Choice (B) doesn't work because side x is opposite of angle X rather than adjacent, so we don't want to use $\cos^{-1}$.

Choice (C) won't work because we want an inverse trigonometry function rather than a trigonometry function. The output of an inverse trigonometry function is an angle. In contrast, the output of a trigonometry function is the ratio of two sides of a right triangle.

Choice (D) doesn't work because side y is adjacent to angle X, so $\sin^{-1}$ is not the appropriate inverse trigonometry function to use.

5. **(D)** Solve for V:

$$V = \frac{nRT}{P}$$

Recall that, in general, y is directly proportional to x if $y = cx$ for some constant c, and y is inversely proportional if $y = \frac{c}{x}$. In our case, we are told that R is the gas constant, so we can think of this as our constant. So V is directly proportional to n and T. If you increased either of these variables, V would also increase. V is inversely proportional only to P, which isn't an answer choice. So choice (D) is the correct answer.

6. **(D)** First, isolate $\frac{1}{d_o}$ by subtracting $\frac{1}{d_i}$ from both sides of the equation:

$$\frac{1}{f} - \frac{1}{d_i} = \frac{1}{d_o}$$

We want to find d_o, so we need the reciprocal of $\frac{1}{d_o}$, which is d_o. To find the reciprocal, simply take 1 over both sides:

$$\frac{1}{\frac{1}{f} - \frac{1}{d_i}} = d_o$$

The answer is choice (D).

7. **(B)** First, use FOIL for the left side of the equation:

$$x^3 + ax^2 + 2x + 4x^2 + 4ax + 8$$

Next, combine like terms:

$$x^3 + (a+4)x^2 + (2+4a)x + 8$$

We know that this has to equal the right side of the original equation:

$$x^3 + (a+4)x^2 + (2+4a)x + 8 = x^3 + x^2 - 10x + 8$$

The coefficients of the like terms on both sides of the equation must equal one another. The coefficients on the x^3-terms are already equal and the constants are equal. So we need to worry about only the x^2-terms and the x-terms. Set the coefficients on the x^2-terms equal to one another:

$$a + 4 = 1$$

Subtracting 4 from both sides reveals that $a = -3$, which is choice (B).

We also could have set the coefficients of the x-terms equal to each other to solve for a:

$$2 + 4a = -10$$

Subtracting 2 from both sides and then dividing by 4 gives $a = -3$ as well.

8. **(D)** Distribute the negative sign:

$$\left(6y^3 + \frac{1}{2}y - \frac{2}{3}\right) - \left(4y^3 - y^2 + \frac{1}{2}y + \frac{1}{6}\right)$$
$$= 6y^3 + \frac{1}{2}y - \frac{2}{3} - 4y^3 + y^2 - \frac{1}{2}y - \frac{1}{6}$$

Next combine like terms:

$$6y^3 + \frac{1}{2}y - \frac{2}{3} - 4y^3 + y^2 - \frac{1}{2}y - \frac{1}{6} = 2y^3 + y^2 - \frac{5}{6}$$

This matches choice (D).

9. **(D)** A line perpendicular to line A has a slope that is the negative reciprocal of $-\frac{x}{y}$. The negative reciprocal is $-\left(-\frac{y}{x}\right)$, or $\frac{y}{x}$.

10. **(C)** We're given that $V_A = 8V_B$. From the formula for the volume of a sphere $\left(V = \frac{4}{3}\pi r^3\right)$, it follows that $\frac{4}{3}\pi r_A^3 = 8\left(\frac{4}{3}\pi r_B^3\right)$. The $\frac{4}{3}\pi$ term cancels out on both sides, leaving us with $r_A^3 = 8r_B^3$. Taking the cube root of both sides gives $r_A = 2r_B$. Thus, the radius of sphere A is twice the radius of sphere B. We ultimately want to find the ratio of the surface areas, so consider the surface areas of the two spheres:

$$SA_A = 4\pi r_A^2 = 4\pi(2r_B)^2 = 4\pi(4r_B^2)$$

and

$$SA_B = 4\pi r_B^2$$

To find the ratio of the surface area of sphere A to the surface area of sphere B, we divide the surface area of sphere A by the surface area of sphere B:

$$\frac{SA_A}{SA_B} = \frac{4\pi\left(4r_B^2\right)}{4\pi r_B^2}$$

We can cancel a 4π and an r_B^2 out of both the numerator and the denominator, which leaves us with $\frac{SA_A}{SA_B} = 4$.

Thus, the ratio of the surface area of sphere A to sphere B is $\frac{4}{1}$ or 4:1, which is choice (C).

Adaptive Practice Test

Adaptive PSAT Practice Test Overview

You are about to take an PSAT Adaptive Practice Test. This will simulate the section-adaptive format of the Digital PSAT. Depending on your performance on the first module of each section, you will have a more difficult or less difficult second module of each section. (In order to maximize your potential practice material, there are no overlapping questions in any of the modules—i.e., if you do Reading and Writing Module 2B, for example, you can still go back and try Reading and Writing Module 2A for a later practice exercise.) The format of the test is outlined in the table below. You can use a calculator throughout the Math section; you may want to have the Desmos. com calculator available on a computer or tablet, since that calculator will be embedded in the Math sections. Good luck!

PSAT Module	Format
Reading and Writing Module 1	32 Minutes, 27 Questions, Standard Difficulty Score the module after completion to determine whether you do 2A or 2B.
Reading and Writing Module 2A or 2B	32 Minutes, 27 Questions, Adaptive Difficulty If you get 17 or fewer questions correct, do the less challenging Module 2A. If you get 18 or more questions correct, do the more challenging Module 2B.
Break—10 Minutes	
Math Module 1	35 Minutes, 22 Questions, Standard Difficulty Score the module after completion to determine whether you do 2A or 2B
Math Module 2A or 2B	35 Minutes, 22 Questions, Adaptive Difficulty If you get 13 or fewer questions correct, do the less challenging Module 2A. If you get 14 or more questions correct, do the more challenging Module 2B.

ANSWER SHEET
Adaptive Practice Test

Section 1, Module 1: Reading and Writing

1. _____	10. _____	19. _____
2. _____	11. _____	20. _____
3. _____	12. _____	21. _____
4. _____	13. _____	22. _____
5. _____	14. _____	23. _____
6. _____	15. _____	24. _____
7. _____	16. _____	25. _____
8. _____	17. _____	26. _____
9. _____	18. _____	27. _____

ANSWER SHEET
Adaptive Practice Test

Section 1, Module 2A or 2B: Reading and Writing

1. _____	10. _____	19. _____
2. _____	11. _____	20. _____
3. _____	12. _____	21. _____
4. _____	13. _____	22. _____
5. _____	14. _____	23. _____
6. _____	15. _____	24. _____
7. _____	16. _____	25. _____
8. _____	17. _____	26. _____
9. _____	18. _____	27. _____

ANSWER SHEET
Adaptive Practice Test

Section 2, Module 1: Math

1. _____		12. _____
2. _____		13. _____
3. _____		14. _____
4. _____		15. _____
5. _____		16. _____
6. _____		17. _____
7. _____		18. _____
8. _____		19. _____
9. _____		20. _____
10. _____		21. _____
11. _____		22. _____

ANSWER SHEET
Adaptive Practice Test

Section 2, Module 2A or 2B: Math

1. _____

2. _____

3. _____

4. _____

5. _____

6. _____

7. _____

8. _____

9. _____

10. _____

11. _____

12. _____

13. _____

14. _____

15. _____

16. _____

17. _____

18. _____

19. _____

20. _____

21. _____

22. _____

Adaptive Practice Test

Section 1, Module 1: Reading and Writing

32 MINUTES, 27 QUESTIONS

DIRECTIONS ∨

You will be tested on a variety of important reading and writing skills. Each question has one or more passages, possibly including a graph or table. Carefully read each passage and question and choose the best answer to the question based on the passage(s).

Every question in this section is multiple-choice with four possible answers. Each question has only one best answer.

Though not the first to utilize encryption, Roman emperor Julius Caesar is perhaps the most notable early adopter. A man of many secrets, Caesar would send messages to his generals in which the letters of the alphabet had been shifted a set number of places (A becomes D, B becomes E, and so forth). The recipient of the message would be alerted to the cipher in advance and would thus _____ the message upon delivery. The Caesar Shift was simplistic by today's standards, but in an era in which very few could read in the first place, the encryption was effective.

1

Which choice completes the text with the most logical and precise word or phrase?

- (A) decode
- (B) compose
- (C) imagine
- (D) write

David had just turned fourteen when, walking back from school, he heard the pathetic whimper. The puppy was small—obviously malnourished and feeble—and much too young to be away from its mother. David removed his jacket and <u>coddled</u> the pup against his chest as he walked briskly back to the Hardings, rehearsing what he might say. To his surprise, Mr. Harding's only requests were that David keep the frail animal in his own room.

2

As used in the text, the word *coddled* most nearly means

- (A) spoiled.
- (B) humored.
- (C) cosseted.
- (D) indulged.

Regrettably, because of the second scribe's large and unwieldy penmanship, the poem's last ten lines or so would not fit on the parchment leaf and are thus lost to history. We are instead left with the compellingly _____ ending (roughly translated): "The white wood rang / Grimly as they hacked each other's shields / Until the linden slats grew lean and splintered / Broken by blades . . ."

3

Which choice completes the text with the most logical and precise word or phrase?

- (A) conclusive
- (B) shocking
- (C) ecstatic
- (D) ambiguous

Into the early 20th century, color cameras themselves remained somewhat _____; this owed largely to the logistical complexities of exposing three separate individually filtered plates on the same subject. One design used a system of prisms and mirrors to split the lens image through three internal filters, which in turn exposed three plates simultaneously.

4

Which choice completes the text with the most logical and precise word or phrase?

- (A) unsightly
- (B) unwieldy
- (C) expensive
- (D) precise

The following text is from President Ronald Reagan's 1981 speech to Congress.

Almost 8 million Americans are out of work. These are people who want to be productive. But as the months go by, despair dominates their lives. The threats of layoff and unemployment hang over other millions, and all who work are frustrated by their inability to keep up with inflation.

One worker in a Midwest city put it to me this way: He said, "I'm bringing home more dollars than I ever believed I could possibly earn, but I seem to be getting worse off." And he is. Not only have hourly earnings of the American worker, after adjusting for inflation, declined 5 percent over the past 5 years, but in these 5 years, federal personal taxes for the average family have increased 67 percent.

5

The underlined quotation in the text primarily serves to

- (A) give concrete statistics.
- (B) provide anecdotal evidence.
- (C) separate fact from opinion.
- (D) acknowledge likely objections.

The following text is adapted from James Bronterre O'Brien's 1885 work *The Rise, Progress, and Phases of Human Slavery: How it Came into the World and How it Shall be Made to Go Out.*

And seeing that the [slaves'] owners could have valued them as property only on account of their labor, the idea of their roving about in famished gangs, is an idea that would be as novel and as difficult of explanation to them as (to borrow an illustration from Locke) the peculiar flavor of a pine-apple would be novel and indescribable to one who had never tasted that particular fruit.

6

Which choice best states the function of the underlined phrase in the text as a whole?

(A) To metaphorically describe how unfamiliar an idea would be to a group

(B) To demonstrate the luxurious decadence that the upper classes embraced

(C) To underscore the lack of nutritious foodstuffs for impoverished groups

(D) To suggest that modern readers have no way to conceive of past injustice

Text 1 is from Benjamin Franklin's 1771 autobiography. Text 2 is from Booker T. Washington's 1901 autobiography.

Text 1

I have ever had pleasure in obtaining any little anecdotes of my ancestors. You may remember the inquiries I made among the remains of my relations when you were with me in England, and the journey I undertook for that purpose. Imagining it may be equally agreeable to you to know the circumstances of my life, many of which you are yet unacquainted with, and . . . I sit down to write them for you.

Text 2

Of my ancestry I know almost nothing. In the slave quarters, and even later, I heard whispered conversations . . . of the tortures which the slaves, including, no doubt, my ancestors on my mother's side, suffered in the middle passage of the slave ship while being conveyed from Africa to America. I have been unsuccessful in securing any information that would throw any accurate light upon the history of my family beyond my mother.

7

It is reasonable to conclude that Booker T. Washington would very much like to have had the opportunity to do which of the following things that Benjamin Franklin spoke about in Text 1?

(A) Obtain anecdotes about his ancestors

(B) Take time to write a memoir

(C) Have a relationship with his children

(D) Relive his life

It is hard to imagine what life would be like without the contributions engineers have already made. They have not just helped us to survive, be healthy, explore, and move around better but they have also made life more enjoyable through advances in areas such as communications, computing, and sports. Computer engineers, for example, have helped develop devices and software that we can use to make and share documents and home videos, listen to our favorite music, and talk with co-workers, friends, and family members across the globe. In sports, different engineers have made systems and devices that provide us with better, safer equipment, communications that enable teams to interact better and games to be televised, and environments and infrastructure that improve the playing and watching of games.

8

Which choice best states the main purpose of the text?

- (A) To make the reader feel that engineering is an accessible career
- (B) To show how human life would go extinct without engineers
- (C) To highlight the contributions of computer and sport engineers
- (D) To give examples of how engineers' contributions are used in daily life

If one were to set out to form a nation based on democratic principles, there would be essentially two paths to take: presidential or parliamentary. Both hold their own in terms of advantages and disadvantages, and both possess the endorsement of great prosperous nations. Parliamentary is the far more common order, but many attribute its prevalence to the legacy of the British Empire rather than to its superiority.

9

The author states that a possible reason for the more widespread practice of parliamentary rather than presidential democracy is

- (A) majority rule.
- (B) historical inheritance.
- (C) legislative-executive unity.
- (D) centralized authority.

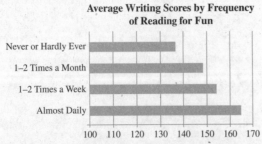

Average Writing Scores by Frequency of Reading for Fun

Note: Writing score range from 0–300, and students surveyed nationwide.
Source: U.S. Department of Eduction, National Center for Eduction Statistics

Those who read for fun more often have higher writing scores—in fact, those who read daily for fun outperform those who never or hardly ever read daily by approximately _____

10

Which choice most effectively uses data from the chart to complete the example?

- (A) 10 points on national writing tests.
- (B) 30 points on national writing tests.
- (C) 60 points on national writing tests.
- (D) 120 points on national writing tests.

"Monadnock in Early Spring" is an early 1900s poem by Amy Lowell. In the poem, the speaker alludes to Mount Monadnock's impressive size relative to the other features of the landscape: _____

11

Which quotation from "Monadnock in Early Spring" most effectively illustrates the claim?

(A) "Cloud-topped and splendid, dominating all / The little lesser hills which compass thee,"

(B) "Thou standest, bright with April's buoyancy, / Yet holding Winter in some shaded wall / Of stern, steep rock";

(C) "and startled by the call / Of Spring, thy trees flush with expectancy / And cast a cloud of crimson, silently,"

(D) "Above thy snowy crevices where fall / Pale shrivelled oak leaves, / while the snow beneath / Melts at their phantom touch."

Lab technicians are able to pinpoint the best antibiotic by measuring the *zone of inhibition* on the microorganism growth plate. The zone with the largest diameter typically signifies that it will be the best at fighting the infection. Prescribing an antibiotic that tests positive for the inhibition of growth or completely stops the growth of the microorganism will hopefully help the patient heal faster and experience fewer side effects.

12

Which choice most effectively uses information from the graph and text to complete the physician's statement?

(A) Vancomycin.

(B) Ciprofloxacin.

(C) Amoxicillin.

(D) *Staphylococcus.*

Antibiotic Tested	*E. coli* Zone of Inhibition	*S. aureus* Zone of Inhibition
Vancomycin	0 mm	20 mm
Ciprofloxacin	17 mm	16 mm
Amoxicillin	10 mm	15 mm

Figure 1 Zone of inhibition measurements to determine the effectiveness of certain antibiotics against the microorganisms *E. coli* and *S. aureus.*

A physician uses this information to conclude that for a patient with an *E. coli* infection (who was not allergic to any antibiotics and had no other illnesses) would be most effectively treated by the following antibiotic: _____

Prior to arranging meetings on behalf of his company, a marketing assistant uses his home kitchen to prepare a packed lunch for his daughter. A graphic designer spends hours a day on her personal PC creating eye-catching brand logos without ever stepping foot outside her apartment. A major shift in a workforce evermore reliant on technology is the increasing number of employees who find themselves _____

13

Which choice most logically completes the text?

- (A) working in supervisory positions.
- (B) increasingly highly compensated for their efforts.
- (C) reliant on education to advance their careers.
- (D) staying at home during the workday.

Most people do not consider the effect on society in general when asking their doctor for antibiotics. However, they do want to know about any side effects to themselves personally. There can be grave personal consequences to strict antibiotic regimes, especially when patients are in a hospital on a very strong dosage. The problem with antibiotics is that they do not necessarily target one specific bacteria. While some will target certain classes, _____

14

Which choice most logically completes the text?

- (A) some attack only selected microorganisms.
- (B) others will cause allergic reactions.
- (C) many simply kill indiscriminately.
- (D) most bacteria are unaffected by treatment.

The bat species whose diet doesn't consist of insects are frugivores, carnivores, or hematophagous. It is the latter bloodsuckers who attract the most attention. The ecological roles of bats _____ not end with pest control.

15

Which choice completes the text so that it conforms to the conventions of Standard English?

- (A) do
- (B) does
- (C) don't
- (D) do's

The ban on foie gras was passed by _____ in an omnibus bill despite the opposition of the city's mayor.

16

Which choice completes the text so that it conforms to the conventions of Standard English?

- (A) Chicago's City Council
- (B) Chicagos City Council
- (C) Chicagos' Cities Council
- (D) Chicagos Cities Council

MODULE 1

1   **1**

Look through the glass and you'll see that, like a correctional lens, these imperfections distort the images that pass through them. _____ windows were often made using a technique called "glassblowing."

17

Which choice completes the text so that it conforms to the conventions of Standard English?

- (A) Well, into the 19th century, glass
- (B) Well, into the 19th century glass
- (C) Well into the 19th century glass
- (D) Well into the 19th century, glass

Described by playwright Bernard Shaw as _____ their lingering influences have coexisted and even comingled in drama for more than a century now.

18

Which choice completes the text so that it conforms to the conventions of Standard English?

- (A) "the giants of the theatre of our time,"
- (B) the giant's of the theatre of our time,
- (C) the giants' of the theatre of our time,
- (D) 'the giants of the theatre of our time,'

The University of Missouri at Columbia—boasting the number one journalism department in the nation according to *The Huffington Post*—offers more than 30 interest areas, incorporating an intensive liberal arts education along with hands-on experience in media labs and internships for academic credit. Ohio _____ three campus publications plus a broadcasting outlet for students to gain professional experience before graduation, not to mention OU's Institute for International Journalism, which offers opportunities for reporting abroad.

19

Which choice completes the text so that it conforms to the conventions of Standard English?

- (A) University also having, a journalism department ranked in the top ten nation-wide offers
- (B) University also having a journalism department ranked in the top ten nation-wide offers
- (C) University, also having a journalism department, ranked in the top ten, nationwide, offers
- (D) University, also having a journalism department ranked in the top ten nation-wide, offers

While our own ancestors were battling drought on the coasts of the African subcontinent, _____ where the Neanderthals developed the tools of flint and bone that have today come to characterize the so-called Mousterian culture of the early Stone Age.

20

Which choice completes the text so that it conforms to the conventions of Standard English?

(A) the icebound north of modern Eurasia experienced the spread of the evolutionarily distinct species *Homo neanderthalensis*,

(B) the evolutionarily distinct species *Homo neanderthalensis* had spread to the icebound north of modern Eurasia,

(C) the species *Homo neanderthalensis*, being evolutionarily distinct, found itself spread to modern Eurasia in the north icebound,

(D) the north icebound of modern Eurasia experience evolutionarily distinct species spread of the *Homo neanderthalensis*,

---

Strindberg mocked and attacked Ibsen's most successful and enduring play, *A Doll's House*, in a short story of the same title and claimed that his ongoing hostilities with Ibsen had cost him his "wife, children, fortune, and career." Ibsen, meanwhile, somewhat more _____ a portrait of Strindberg in his study where he worked, naming it *Madness Incipient.*

21

Which choice completes the text so that it conforms to the conventions of Standard English?

(A) soberly—though no less venomously—kept

(B) soberly; though no less venomously kept

(C) soberly though no less—venomously kept

(D) soberly: though no less venomously, kept

Quite simply, the days of print-only newsrooms are past. Now, one doesn't wait until the 6 p.m. broadcast to hear what's happening around the world, _____ does one grab the newspaper on Sunday morning for breaking news.

22

Which choice completes the text with the most logical transition?

(A) while

(B) because

(C) for

(D) nor

Alongside the Watson-Crick "Double Helix" and Einstein's "Equation of General Relativity," the Periodic Table of Elements is among the most important and instantly recognizable features of modern science. _____ the table as we know it today emerged just 150 years ago, the story of its conceptual evolution goes all the way back to Ancient Greece, when Aristotle proposed that all mass is composed of a mixture of simple elements.

23

Which choice completes the text with the most logical transition?

- (A) While
- (B) Since
- (C) Given
- (D) If

C. *diff* is just one example of how the overuse of antibiotics can harm individuals. Within hospitals, it is a serious issue. This does not mean that we should cease using antibiotics. _____ the lack of antibiotics would kill far more people than C. *diff* likely ever will.

24

Which choice completes the text with the most logical transition?

- (A) However,
- (B) As a result,
- (C) In fact,
- (D) Due to this,

It is said that Benjamin Franklin suggested the use of foxfire (bioluminescent fungi) as a viable light source on an early variety of submarine, _____ it would consume considerably less oxygen than the combustion reactions of candle or lamplight.

25

Which choice completes the text with the most logical transition?

- (A) but
- (B) previously
- (C) as
- (D) while

ADAPTIVE PRACTICE TEST

A student has recently started watching movies from Studio Ghibli and wants to learn more about its creator. The student writes down these notes:

- Studio Ghibli was founded by Hayoa Miyazaki, Isoa Takahata, and Toshio Suzuki.
- Hayoa Miyazaki is the animator, director, producer, screenwriter, author, and manga artist.
- The movies appeal to those who are young at heart and enjoy unique storytelling.
- *Spirited Away*, released in 2001 by the studio, has received an Oscar award and is the highest-grossing film in Japanese history.
- Studio Ghibli is sometimes referred to as "Japan's Disney."

26

The student wishes to write an essay in which he emphasizes the critical acclaim that the work of Studio Ghibli has received. Which choice most effectively uses relevant information from the notes to accomplish this goal?

(A) The teamwork of Miyazaki, Takahata, and Suzuki was critical to the success of Studio Ghibli.

(B) The film *Spirited Away* was recognized for its excellence by receiving an Oscar award in 2001.

(C) Young people are the target audience of the works of Studio Ghibli—they particularly enjoy the unique storytelling that its films offer.

(D) Many observers note the similarities between the films of Studio Ghibli and that of the Disney corporation.

When researching a topic, a student has taken the following notes:

- Bonanza farms were large and incredibly profitable farms on the Great Plains in the 1800s.
- The reapers by Cyrus McCormick and steel plows by John Deere contributed to these farms.
- Another development that supported the development of these farms was displacement of Native Americans onto reservations, thereby opening of huge tracts of land to American settlers.
- The laying of railroad tracks also greatly helped these farmers, as they could now easily bring supplies to their farms and ship their crops East.
- The bonanza farm era continued until the Panic of 1873 and the Great Drought of the 1880s.

27

The student wants to highlight how changes to national transportation infrastructure positively impacted the development of bonanza farms. Which choice most effectively uses relevant information from the notes to accomplish this goal?

(A) The profits of bonanza farms in the 1800s were without historical precedent.

(B) New railroad tracks enabled bonanza farmers to both obtain supplies from and sell goods to faraway regions.

(C) Ultimately, bonanza farms were doomed to failure because of the economic developments of the late 1800s.

(D) Without the displacement of Native Americans onto reservations, bonanza farmers would not have had the land they wanted to create their large farms.

ANSWER KEY
Adaptive Practice Test

Section 1, Module 1: Reading and Writing

1. **A**	10. **B**	19. **D**
2. **C**	11. **A**	20. **B**
3. **D**	12. **B**	21. **A**
4. **B**	13. **D**	22. **D**
5. **B**	14. **C**	23. **A**
6. **A**	15. **A**	24. **C**
7. **A**	16. **A**	25. **C**
8. **D**	17. **D**	26. **B**
9. **B**	18. **A**	27. **B**

Total Correct Answers: _____ / 27

Did you get 17 or fewer questions correct? If so, move to Reading and Writing Module 2A on page 336.

Did you get 18 or more questions correct? If so, move to Reading and Writing Module 2B on page 348.

ADAPTIVE PRACTICE TEST

Section 1, Module 2A: Reading and Writing

32 MINUTES, 27 QUESTIONS

DIRECTIONS ⌄

You will be tested on a variety of important reading and writing skills. Each question has one or more passages, possibly including a graph or table. Carefully read each passage and question and choose the best answer to the question based on the passage(s).

Every question in this section is multiple-choice with four possible answers. Each question has only one best answer.

Will's parents knew he was a very smart child. He mastered concepts in school much more quickly than other students. However, his grades did not reflect his intelligence. His _____ nature was his downfall as he never completed his homework assignments on time. Perfect test scores were not enough to compensate for missing assignments.

1

Which choice completes the text with the most logical and precise word or phrase?

(A) lackadaisical

(B) drowsy

(C) moronic

(D) passionate

There are a number of more indirect, ecologically-oriented ways in which the microbiome confers protection to its host. Abundant colonization of our bodies by benign microorganisms, for example, inhibits the overgrowth of more dangerous ones through the sheer depletion of microbial nutrients. This notion of ecological balance has been of particular interest to scientists studying the microbiome, as it hinges upon both the variable diversity of species that colonize an individual as well as factors that affect the dynamism of a microbiotic population.

2

As used in the text, the word *hinges* most closely means

(A) fulcrums.

(B) analyzes.

(C) depends.

(D) joints.

The following text is from Jane Austen's 1814 novel Mansfield Park. *The novel's protagonist, Fanny Price, returns home after many years of living with her wealthy relatives at Mansfield Park.*

Her disappointment in her mother was greater: there she had hoped much, and found almost nothing. Every flattering scheme of being of consequence to her soon fell to the ground. Mrs. Price was not unkind; but, instead of gaining on her affection and confidence, and becoming more and more dear, her daughter never met with greater kindness from her than on the first day of her arrival. The <u>instinct of nature</u> was soon satisfied, and Mrs. Price's attachment had no other source. Her heart and her time were already quite full; she had neither leisure nor affection to bestow on Fanny. Her daughters never had been much to her. She was fond of her sons, especially of William, but Betsey was the first of her girls whom she had ever much regarded.

3

As used in the text, the phrase *instinct of nature* most nearly means

- (A) desire for survival.
- (B) maternal feeling.
- (C) thirst for acceptance.
- (D) sense of justice.

From "The New Colossus," by Emma Lazarus in 1883, engraved on the Statue of Liberty—one of the first things that new immigrants to the United States would see if they arrived by boat.

Give me your tired, your poor,

Your huddled masses <u>yearning</u> to breathe free,

The wretched refuse of your teeming shore.

Send these, the homeless, tempest-tost to me,

I lift my lamp beside the golden door!

4

As used in the text, what does the word "yearning" most nearly mean?

- (A) Crafting
- (B) Enabling
- (C) Desiring
- (D) Trusting

According to the United States Department of Labor, the 2021 median pay for veterinarians was approximately $100,000 annually, with the top ten percent _____ more than $165,000.

5

Which choice completes the text with the most logical and precise word or phrase?

(A) using

(B) discovering

(C) earning

(D) writing

The following text is from a 1981 speech to Congress by President Ronald Reagan.

Can we, who man the ship of state, deny it is somewhat out of control? Our national debt is approaching $1 trillion. A few weeks ago I called such a figure, a trillion dollars, incomprehensible, and I've been trying ever since to think of a way to illustrate how big a trillion really is. And the best I could come up with is that if you had a stack of thousand dollar bills in your hand only 4 inches high, you'd be a millionaire. A trillion dollars would be a stack of thousand-dollar bills 67 miles high. The interest on the public debt this year we know will be over $90 billion, and unless we change the proposed spending for the fiscal year beginning October 1st, we'll add another almost $80 billion to the debt.

6

The primary function of the text is to

(A) share relevant first-hand observations.

(B) concretely illustrate the severity of a problem.

(C) verbalize the incomprehensible complexity of a concept.

(D) highlight the widespread interest in a particular solution.

1   MODULE 2   1

Text 1

According to Darwin's theory of evolution, all organisms arise and develop through the process of natural selection, or small functional inheritances that boost one's ability to compete and survive in the wild. When small genetic mutations occur and prove beneficial, they are passed on to offspring, allowing a slow evolution to occur while the less competitive organism dies out. Eventually, Darwin argues, these mutations accumulate and form an entirely new organism.

Text 2

Without having a grasp of Gregor Mendel's work on heredity, Darwin couldn't anticipate modern discoveries within genetics such as genetic drift. Darwin himself acknowledged that his theory would encounter challenges if any complex organ were to be found which could not possibly have been formed by successive, slight modifications. With modern advancements in molecular biology and biochemistry, these "irreducibly complex systems" are not only known to exist, but are, in fact, very prevalent on the cellular level.

7

Which of the following best describes the relationship between the two texts?

(A) Both texts agree on the infallibility of an evolutionary theory.

(B) Text 1 anticipates and addresses an objection presented by Text 2.

(C) Text 2 explains the historical influence of one biologist on another, bolstering Text 1's argument.

(D) Text 2 highlights a shortcoming in the theory presented in Text 1.

Ecologically, organic farming is designed to promote and enhance biodiversity, so it must combine scientific knowledge and technologies to stimulate naturally occurring biological processes. For instance, organic farming uses pyrethrin, a natural pesticide found in the chrysanthemum flower, to deter pests, and potassium bicarbonate to control disease and suppress unruly weeds. Furthermore, where conventional farming focuses on mass production of each individual crop, organic farming encourages polyculture, or multiple crops being raised in the same space.

8

Based on the passage, when compared to a non-organic farm field, an organic farm field will most likely be more

(A) productive.

(B) diverse.

(C) mature.

(D) centralized.

The following text is from Charles Dickens's 1861 novel Great Expectations. *In it, Pip, a poor orphan who is cared for by his sister and her husband, meets the young girl who will become the lifetime object of his affections while simultaneously becoming aware of his lowly position in the caste system.*

My uncle Pumblechook, who kept a cornchandler's shop in the high-street of the town, took me to the large old, dismal house, which had all its windows barred. For miles round everybody had heard of Miss Havisham as an immensely rich and grim lady who led a life of seclusion; and everybody soon knew that Mr. Pumblechook had been commissioned to bring her a boy.

9

The text primarily serves to explain

- (A) why Pip wanted to be a gentleman.
- (B) why Miss Havisham desired companionship.
- (C) how Pip came to be at Miss Havisham's.
- (D) how Pip came to fall in love with Estella.

The infamous *four-letter words* are almost exclusively descended from the Germanic components of English. Even without an expertise in linguistics, one might sense this simply by the way they sound—phonically, most profanity in English is composed of short, terse syllables, and rounds off abruptly with a hard consonant.

10

A newly formed profane English word with which of the following suffixes would most effectively illustrate the author's claim?

- (A) -lah
- (B) -ock
- (C) -soo
- (D) -aly

A state is considering increasing the payment it provides to unemployed workers from $300 a week to $500 a week. An economist hypothesizes that this change in policy will discourage unemployed citizens from seeking out work since they will receive increased funds from unemployment.

11

Which finding, if true, would most undermine the economist's hypothesis?

(A) Observation that in a similar state that when unemployment benefits were doubled, there was no change in those seeking unemployment

(B) Data demonstrating that a 50 percent increase in unemployment benefits in a neighboring state resulted in a 100 percent increase in those seeking unemployment

(C) Analysis of economic statistics showing a strong correlation between an increase in unemployment benefits and a decreased willingness to work

(D) Results from a voluntary survey of 300 people in a particular city showing that respondents would be unwilling to let an increase in unemployment benefits affect their decision about whether to seek out benefits

Population Structure

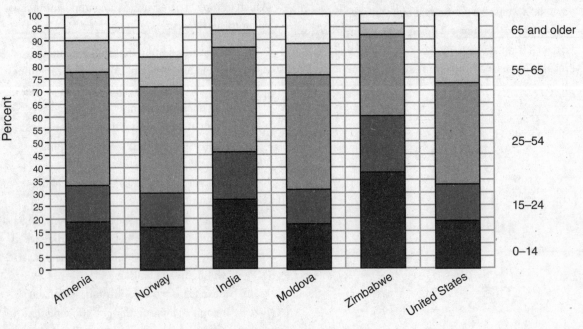

Country
(Cia.gov)

An examination of the age demographics with respect to a country's population structure can offer important insights. A sociologist claims that with respect to the countries of Armenia, India, Moldova, Zimbabwe, and the United States, Norway stands out in a unique way.

_____

12

Which choice most effectively uses data from the table to complete the example?

(A) Norway has the greatest percentage of people age 65 and older.

(B) Norway has the best health care for older adults.

(C) Most Norwegians choose not to have children.

(D) Norway will soon feel the economic effects of its low birth rate.

1   MODULE 2   1

Folklorists—regardless of their focus within the wide, interdisciplinary field of folklore—often use a similar approach and methodology, called *ethnographic fieldwork*. This means the folklorist's job is not confined to a desk, a university, or a museum; instead, _____ often in exciting, real-world settings in the expressive realms of festival, narrative, faith, art, architecture, and food, among others.

13

Which choice most logically completes the text?

(A) the occupation is dull and monotonous.

(B) the work is participatory and engaging.

(C) the field is abstract and complex,

(D) the career is highly compensated,

The weeks-long displays of fireworks around the 4th of July are not sustainable for veterans, pets, or the environment. To truly allow those affected by fireworks peace, it may seem like a harmless option to get rid of fireworks, but this too would have its own consequences. Those who cherish this practice would feel an attack on their patriotic rights, others would be saddened about the end of a tradition, and the remaining would simply continue lighting fireworks. The answer does not seem to be to eradicate fireworks—they do not need to disappear from the night sky—but perhaps their colors, sounds, magic, and consequences _____

14

Which choice most logically completes the text?

(A) could be limited to just that one night in early July.

(B) should be made less polluting through scientific research.

(C) could be banned for both private and public usage.

(D) might be enjoyed by those celebrating the birth of the nation.

In the third grade, my teacher, Mrs. Wabash, asked the class to spend ten minutes sketching our homes, specifically the exterior of our houses as they appeared to passersby. This prelude was part of a larger exercise that I _____

15

Which choice completes the text so that it conforms to the conventions of Standard English?

(A) have long since forgotten.

(B) had since long forgot.

(C) has long since forgotten.

(D) forgot since long.

In ancient times past, the subtle beauty and architectural refinement of the monument _____ uncontested. Now, conventional opinions are more mixed on the topic.

16

Which choice completes the text so that it conforms to the conventions of Standard English?

- (A) is
- (B) are
- (C) was
- (D) were

From contracts to design to construction, the architect is there, _____ never done. It is indeed an occupation that encompasses nearly every field of work—engineering, mathematics, marketing, administration, customer service, law, and public safety are all needed in successful architecture.

17

Which choice completes the text so that it conforms to the conventions of Standard English?

- (A) there job
- (B) their job
- (C) our job
- (D) they're job

The revolutionary theory of the four bodily humors (i.e., the idea that disease results from a physical imbalance in the bodily "humors") _____ popularized in 400 B.C.E. in ancient Greece and has been a major obstacle to scientific advancement ever since.

18

Which choice completes the text so that it conforms to the conventions of Standard English?

- (A) had
- (B) have
- (C) was
- (D) were

The replication crisis does not mean that psychology is necessarily _____ refrain from running down a rabbit hole of follow-up studies and making grand claims about human nature based on a single study.

19

Which choice completes the text so that it conforms to the conventions of Standard English?

- (A) unreliable, it would, however, be wise to
- (B) unreliable. It would however be wise to
- (C) unreliable; it would, however, be wise to
- (D) unreliable, it would however be wise to

1   MODULE 2   1

I have had a warning lamp flashing on my car dashboard for the past month. At the oil change, my car _____ brake fluid checked. I want to be sure I won't have a serious problem with the car that could have been easily prevented.

20

Which choice completes the text so that it conforms to the conventions of Standard English?

(A) need their

(B) needs their

(C) need its

(D) needs its

More than 300 years ago, the idea was quite _____ gravitational force toward one another with a force proportional to the product of the two masses and inversely proportional to the square of the distance between them.

21

Which choice completes the text so that it conforms to the conventions of Standard English?

(A) revolutionary: two objects, regardless of their mass, exert

(B) revolutionary, two objects regardless of their mass, exert

(C) revolutionary—two objects regardless of their mass, exert

(D) revolutionary; two objects, regardless of their mass exert

My very educated mother just served us nine pizzas is a sentence that may not mean much to young students anymore. However, to people of an older generation this sentence is almost universally recognized as a mnemonic device used to aid children in remembering the planets of our solar system. The sentence has changed recently, not because serving nine pizzas is against school lunch health standards, _____ the planets themselves have changed.

22

Which choice completes the text with the most logical transition?

(A) and since

(B) but because

(C) for a result

(D) and

ADAPTIVE PRACTICE TEST

Schrödinger won the Nobel Prize in Physics in 1933 for his work in quantum mechanics, _____ he is most remembered for a theoretical experiment he proposed two years later.

23

Which choice completes the text with the most logical transition?

- Ⓐ but
- Ⓑ for
- Ⓒ since
- Ⓓ and

Assessment signifies what we value in the classroom and how we assign that value. _____ to stop testing a subject is to see it all but disappear from the curriculum.

24

Which choice completes the text with the most logical transition?

- Ⓐ In other words,
- Ⓑ However,
- Ⓒ In contrast,
- Ⓓ Henceforth,

After being tasked with writing an essay about Jane Austen, a student has taken the following notes:

- Jane Austen was an English novelist who wrote books from 1811 to 1815.
- She published several novels during her lifetime: *Pride and Prejudice*, *Sense and Sensibility*, *Emma*, and *Mansfield Park*.
- Her books centered around women's dependence on marriage for social and economic standing.
- Jane Austen acquired most of her fame after her death when her nephew published *A Memoir of Jane Austen*.
- *Pride and Prejudice* follows a woman who refuses to follow societal norms, turning down suitors even though the financial gain would be of benefit to her family.

25

The student wants to cite an example of the impact that a posthumous publication had on her reputation. Based on the notes, which of the following of Austen's works should the student cite in order to accomplish this goal?

- Ⓐ *Pride and Prejudice*
- Ⓑ *Sense and Sensibility*
- Ⓒ *Emma*
- Ⓓ *A Memoir of Jane Austen*

While researching a topic, a student has taken the following notes:

- Spider mites tend to live on house plants.
- They spin silk webs on the underside of the plants.
- Damage comes from the spider mites puncturing the leaves to feed.
- If a plant is infested, clean the webs off and treat it with insecticide.
- The best treatment is prevention—keep the soil wet because spider mites cannot survive in highly moist environments.

26

The student wants to highlight information about spider mites for an audience particularly concerned with averting spider mite infestations. Which choice most effectively uses relevant information from the notes to accomplish this goal?

- (A) Because spider mites tend to live on house plants, it is important to be aware that they can be found primarily on the underside of such plants.
- (B) Insecticide is the optimal way to prevent a spider mite infestation, since the insecticide will kill the spider mites without killing the plants themselves.
- (C) Spider mite infestations are a major threat to plants, since they puncture the leaves to eat, leaving plants unable to create their own food from photosynthesis.
- (D) The best thing one can do to keep spider mites away from plants is to keep the plant soil wet, because spiders cannot survive in a highly wet environment.

While researching a topic, a student has taken the following notes:

- Creating a stained-glass window masterpiece is a very difficult process that includes many phases.
- In addition to designing the entire piece to be aesthetically pleasing, the artist also must consider the weight of the pieces and the structural integrity of the overall design.
- Pieces that are poorly designed may buckle and fall after being installed in a wall.
- In addition to the design aspect, artists must deal with safety concerns. Artists routinely suffer minor lacerations from their glass work, but also need to worry about chemical poisoning from soldering fumes, lead came, and patina chemicals.

27

The student wants to outline a possible worst-case scenario as far as the potential health impact on someone who crafts stained glass. Which choice most effectively uses relevant information from the notes to accomplish this goal?

- (A) A stained-glass artist faces the possibility of chemical poisoning.
- (B) Those who live in buildings with stained glass could see the fragile windows shatter.
- (C) The challenges of creating stained glass often intimidate those who consider taking on such a project.
- (D) While stained glass is difficult to make, its beauty makes the work well worth the effort.

MODULE 2

Section 1, Module 2B: Reading and Writing

32 MINUTES, 27 QUESTIONS

DIRECTIONS ∨

You will be tested on a variety of important reading and writing skills. Each question has one or more passages, possibly including a graph or table. Carefully read each passage and question and choose the best answer to the question based on the passage(s).

Every question in this section is multiple-choice with four possible answers. Each question has only one best answer.

After living in a single dorm room as an under-graduate, I had found his apartment listed under the enticing entry "Looking for One Roommate, Cheap Rent for the Quiet and Introverted," and _____ the adventure of graduate school and a roommate who preferred books to parties.

1

Which choice completes the text with the most appropriate word?

(A) accepted

(B) excepted

(C) inspected

(D) respected

In 1862, Ralph Waldo Emerson delivered the excerpt below as part of a lecture called "American Civiliza-tion" at the Smithsonian Institution in Washington, D.C.

At this moment in America the aspects of political society absorb attention. In every house, from Canada to the Gulf, the children ask the serious father—"What is the news of the war today? and when will there be better times?" The boys have no new clothes, no gifts, no journeys; the girls must go without new bonnets; boys and girls find their education, this year, less liberal and complete. All the little hopes that heretofore made the year pleasant are deferred. The state of the country fills us with anxiety and <u>stern</u> duties.

2

As used in the text, the word *stern* most nearly means

(A) playful.

(B) terrifying.

(C) serious.

(D) pointless.

There are few biochemical compounds as familiar to us as hemoglobin, and as the primary transporter of oxygen in our blood, the <u>celebrity</u> of this curious little compound is not without just cause. Vital to almost every known vertebrate, hemoglobin appears within the very first week of embryogenesis, and while its role may not change throughout development, its molecular structure undergoes a series of significant transformations.

A German patent clerk, Albert Einstein, turned Newtonian Mechanics on its head and developed the Theory of Relativity and the notion of space-time. In the 1920s, women studying photographic plates of various star systems took measurements that Edwin Hubble used to demonstrate that the universe is not static at all, but is expanding in all directions, no matter where you might be; this became known as Hubble's Law. Hubble's constant—the rate at which the universe is expanding—is currently estimated to be 21 km/s per one million light-years from Earth. This ushered in the notion of the Big Bang as the <u>singular</u> beginning of an expanding space-time and everything in it.

Spanning more than 1,500 miles, the border between Canada and the United States has been called the longest undefended international boundary in the world. This is true to some extent, in that neither the U.S. nor Canada maintains a military presence at the border. <u>But as anyone who has crossed from one side of Niagara Falls to the other knows, civilian law enforcement is present and accounted for at checkpoints on both sides of the boundary, where entrants are monitored, and customs laws administered.</u> Partly because of our cultural similarities and partly because of the remarkable amiability of our diplomatic relations over the past 150 years, it can sometimes seem almost as though the distinction between Canada and the United States is more of one of policy than one of practice.

3

As used in the text, the word "celebrity" most nearly means

- (A) notoriety.
- (B) disreputability.
- (C) personage.
- (D) festivity.

4

As used in the text, what does the word "singular" most nearly mean?

- (A) Odd
- (B) Unattached
- (C) Definitive
- (D) Lonely

5

Which choice best states the function of the underlined sentence in the text as a whole?

- (A) To analyze the economic consequences of international borders on global commerce
- (B) To explain the details of the security screenings that people who cross the U.S.-Canadian border must undergo
- (C) To give evidence of the continual border hostility that the U.S. and Canada have had since the war of 1812
- (D) To clarify that although the U.S. and Canada have friendly relations, they are still clearly two different countries

ADAPTIVE PRACTICE TEST

For better or for worse, our culture of *germophobia* was hard won by its proponents. From the time it was first proposed in the sixteenth century, the germ theory of disease faced three hundred years' worth of influential naysayers, and it was not until the late 1800s that the theory began to gain the pervasive public vindication it enjoys today. However, an emerging body of research indicates that we have been perhaps overzealous in our crusade to eradicate the germs that live within us.

6

Which choice best states the main purpose of the text?

(A) To articulate that while society has now embraced germ theory, taking the theory too far may be detrimental

(B) To argue that germophobia has continued to be a major obstacle to scientific progress

(C) To point out the shortcomings of germ theory by presenting the valid concerns of germophobics

(D) To present the many ways that germ theory has concrete applications to everyday life

Text 1

I saw you from across the room, and I knew immediately. My pulse began to race; I started to sweat; I could barely breathe. From the first moment that I laid eyes on you, I was convinced that you were the one. On our first date, the chemistry was obvious. We laughed and smiled and held hands and talked for hours. I couldn't sleep or eat or even pay attention at work. I just had to be with you.

Text 2

Within one-fifth of a second, your physical appearance and body language caused an excessive release of dopamine in my brain creating feelings of excitement and happiness. We made eye contact for 8.2 seconds; your pheromones were indistinguishable from my mother's. Then, your voice triggered my brain mechanism for generating long-term attachment. Once vasopressin and oxytocin reached my receptors, I knew that I could never be without you.

7

The different perspectives represented by the first and second texts are generally described as what, respectively?

(A) Ethical, scientific

(B) Trivial, important

(C) Authentic, misguided

(D) Subjective, objective

MODULE 2

1   **1**

Text 1

If you have a driver's license, I expect that you are aware that this is the process by which one registers as an organ donor (at least in most states). Yet, it may surprise you that only 40 percent of American adults have registered; that's only two out of every five. This statistic is particularly jarring when it is contrasted with another: 95 percent of Americans strongly support organ donation (according to a 2005 Gallup poll). That is every nineteen out of twenty people, which is a figure that positively dwarfs the number who have registered.

Text 2

Contrary to tabloid sensationalism, no organ donor has ever been declared dead prematurely; donors are subject to more post-mortem testing than non-donors just to ensure that this scenario never occurs. Thus, you are far more likely to be buried alive as a non-donor than to be declared dead as a donor.

The third step of glycolysis involves the hormonally controlled phosphorylation of fructose-6-phosphate into fructose-1, 6-bisphosphate. When glucose is abundant, pancreatic insulin induces the forward glycolytic catalysis of this reaction, allowing the production of fructose-1, 6-bisphosphate, which in turn is cleaved into glyceraldehyde-3-phosphate and dihydroxyacetone phosphate. When glucose is scarce, pancreatic glucagon blocks glycolysis, and induces the gluconeogenic production of fructose-6-phosphate, which is subsequently isomerized into glucose-6-phosphate, and released into the blood.

8

The argument presented in Text 2 could be best used to explain which portion of Text 1?

- (A) That the driver's license is the primary way by which one can register to become an organ donor
- (B) That premature burial is a major safety concern for most American adults
- (C) That most states record one's willingness to become an organ donor through official government documents
- (D) That 95 percent of Americans support organ donation, while only 40 percent are registered as organ donors

9

According to the text, bodily regulation of glucose levels is best described as

- (A) artificial.
- (B) dynamic.
- (C) arbitrary.
- (D) static.

The following is an excerpt from Jane Austen's Mansfield Park *(1814). The novel's protagonist, Fanny Price, returns home after many years of living with her wealthy relatives at Mansfield Park.*

William was gone: and the home he had left her in was—Fanny could not conceal it from herself—in almost every respect the very reverse of what she could have wished. . . . On her father, her confidence had not been sanguine, but he was more negligent of his family, his habits were worse, and his manners coarser, than she had been prepared for.

He did not want abilities; but he had no curiosity, and no information beyond his profession; he read only the newspaper and the navy-list; he talked only of the dockyard, the harbor, Spithead, and the Motherbank; he swore and he drank, he was dirty and gross. She had never been able to recall anything approaching to tenderness in his former treatment of herself. There had remained only a general impression of roughness and loudness; and now he scarcely ever noticed her.

A biologist attempts to determine the cause of evolutionary divergence among the populations of a frog found in the Amazonian rain forest. Based on her observations, the biologist supports the *riverine barrier* hypothesis, claiming that dispersion across opposite riverbanks is responsible for the observed differences in the frogs. She notes that the width, depth, and water speed of the rivers form an obstacle that makes it extremely challenging for the frogs to cross.

10

The text characterizes Fanny's father's intellectual interests as

- (A) relevant and interesting.
- (B) coarse and joking.
- (C) overly pragmatic.
- (D) arrogantly erudite.

11

Which finding, if true, would most undermine the biologist's hypothesis?

- (A) Discovery of increased industrial pollutants in one branch of the Amazon River system
- (B) Presence of fish and snakes that prey on this species of frog in large portions of the river
- (C) Observation of present-day mating of this frog by specimens from opposite riverbanks
- (D) The popularity of tourist activities in the river system, including cruises and fishing expeditions

Number of Universities Offering Folklore Degrees / Concentrations

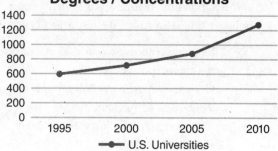

— U.S. Universities

12

A social scientist would like to make a statement to demonstrate the increasing interest in folklore scholarship. Which statement would be best supported by the information in the graph?

(A) If the number of universities offering folklore degrees and concentrations increases between 2010 and 2015 at the same rate as it did between 2000 and 2005, there will be approximately 2,000 schools in 2015 that offer such programs.

(B) If the number of universities offering folklore degrees and concentrations increases between 2010 and 2015 at the same rate as it did between 1995 and 2005, there will be approximately 1,800 schools in 2015 that offer such programs.

(C) If the number of universities offering folklore degrees and concentrations increases between 2010 and 2015 at the same rate as it did between 2005 and 2010, there will be approximately 1,700 schools in 2015 that offer such programs.

(D) If the number of universities offering folklore degrees and concentrations increases at the same rate between 2010 and 2015 as it did between 1995 and 2010, there will be approximately 1,400 schools in 2015 that offer such programs.

In 1918, the American Federation of Labor discussed the possible ramifications of labor uprisings and revolts in Europe as the end of World War 1 approached. A historian claims that the American Federation of Labor was concerned about a potential imbalance in international power relationships were a peace treaty to be immediately agreed to in the year 1918.

13

Which quotation from the American Federation of Labor Records best illustrates the historian's claim?

(A) "The direct objective of our [American] government in 'establishing a better understanding' with the Bolsheviki is not to encourage them either in their home or their foreign policy but solely to delay and restrict their approach to Germany and above all to encourage their efforts to revolutionize the peoples of Central Europe."

(B) "Entirely independently of German victories, brutal German peace terms, Bolshevik surrenders, or other events, the Stockholm movement grows without … interruption."

(C) "A general European movement would almost certainly spread to England. Nor could it fail to have an effect on Chicago, New York, San Francisco, and other foreign industrial centrals in this country."

(D) "Even if—in the midst of such a crisis— the German government were overthrown and the war brought to an end, Germany would keep a very large part of the advantages she has won."

1   MODULE 2   1

The primary problem with deriving major amounts of dietary sugar directly from fructose rather than from starch lies in the fact that the degradation of fructose—which, upon entry into the cell, is split immediately into dihydroxyacetone phosphate and glyceraldehyde—completely bypasses the first four steps of glycolysis, including the most critical regulatory reaction in the entire process. Thus, how our bodies handle the usage of fructose is utterly dissociated from the hormonal controls of insulin and glucagon, which, over time, invariably predisposes one to obesity, diabetes mellitus, and a host of other dangerous metabolic disorders. The long-term consumption of fructose will lead to _____

14

Which choice most logically completes the text?

(A) an increasingly well-regulated hormonal balance.

(B) a significant increase in neurotoxins in the blood supply.

(C) a greater likelihood of developing health ailments.

(D) no significant changes to bodily processes.

Those who live in climates prone to ice will be all too familiar with the feeling of not being able to control their car when it hits a large patch of ice. When the wheels lock up, no matter which direction the steering wheel is turned, the car will continue in the same direction, and the force from braking will only be applied in the opposite direction that the car is sliding. Locked wheels lead to slipping, which is uncontrollable. Anti-lock braking attempts to prevent slipping, therefore

_____

15

Which choice most logically completes the text?

(A) maximizing the possibility of an accident.

(B) allowing a more controlled stop.

(C) improving a car's fuel economy.

(D) enhancing automobile acceleration.

Colonel Sartoris, or "Sarty," is trapped in a world stricken by fear, grief, and misery. _____ father, Sarty is continually faced with the paradox of detesting the man who raised him, while also feeling an inherent fidelity to him.

16

Which choice completes the text so that it conforms to the conventions of Standard English?

(A) While physically similar and often volatile like his

(B) While physically similar, and often, volatile, like his

(C) While physically similar, and often volatile like his

(D) While physically similar and often, volatile like his

When the skin and the natural flora are compromised and not strong enough to fight off the attack, the body's second line of _____

17

Which choice completes the text so that it conforms to the conventions of Standard English?

(A) defense—the innate immune system—kicks in.

(B) defense—the innate immune system, kicks in.

(C) defense the innate immune system—kicks in.

(D) defense the innate immune system; kicks in.

Though we can only speculate on its use among preliterate peoples, some historical anthropologists have suggested that the bullroarer's ubiquity across the world's ancient cultures suggests that _____ primary function must have been practical rather than ritual.

18

Which choice completes the text so that it conforms to the conventions of Standard English?

(A) its

(B) it's

(C) its'

(D) their

Once completely oblivious of the damages to the environment caused by pollution, waste, and overpopulation, the world _____ to look seriously upon the depletion of our natural resources. Whether we scrutinize the harmful exhaust gases that pollute our air—carbon dioxide, sulfur dioxide, ammonia, among others—or turn to deforestation and chemical effluents, the situation is clearly out of control.

19

Which choice completes the text so that it conforms to the conventions of Standard English?

(A) had now began

(B) has now began

(C) has now begun

(D) have now begun

Technology and its _____ on all areas of the job market are tedious subjects for the student and young professional.

20

Which choice completes the text so that it conforms to the conventions of Standard English?

(A) endless affects

(B) endless effects

(C) endlessly affects

(D) endlessly effects

1   MODULE 2   1

Because emission spectra are unique to each element and constant throughout the universe, scientists are able to attach a spectrometer to a telescope, locate a celestial body, and

_____

21

Which choice completes the text so that it conforms to the conventions of Standard English?

(A) determine, the chemical composition of that body simply, by comparing the resulting spectrum to those of known compounds on Earth.

(B) determine the chemical composition, of that body simply by comparing, the resulting spectrum to those of known compounds on Earth.

(C) determine the chemical composition of that body simply by comparing the resulting spectrum to those of known compounds on Earth.

(D) determine the chemical composition of that body, simply by comparing the resulting spectrum to those of known, compounds on Earth.

A commitment to an education in environmental engineering does not go unrewarded. The median annual income is recorded at well over $80,000, and the outlook is promising. Tightening federal regulations _____ expected to only stimulate the need for environmental engineers over the next decade.

22

Which choice completes the text so that it conforms to the conventions of Standard English?

(A) to meet environmental safe standards and for the purpose of the cleaning of contaminated sites are

(B) to meet environmentally safe standards and clean up contaminated sites are

(C) in order to meet environmentally safe standards and in order to clean up contaminated sites are

(D) to meeting environmentally safe standards and cleaning up contaminated sites were

Here are three easy ways that we ballet dancers can improve bone mineral density. First, we're athletes. Ensure you are eating enough to fuel a professional athlete. Focus on foods high in calcium and vitamin D. It's not all dairy—seeds, canned fish, beans, lentils, almonds, and leafy greens are also great choices. _____ get your vitamin D level checked. Vitamin D is needed for calcium absorption and almost 42 percent of adults are deficient. Third, go outside. We spend a lot of time in the studio, but sun exposure is a great way to get some more vitamin D. On a break, head outside, roll up your tights and enjoy a little bit of sun.

23

Which choice completes the text with the most logical transition?

(A) Nonetheless,

(B) Second,

(C) In contrast,

(D) Finally,

Dark matter—unobserved material inferred to exist by its quantifiable gravitational effect on visible galaxies—is estimated to comprise roughly 27 percent of the universe by density. Visible atoms, _____ , constitute less than 5 percent.

24

Which choice completes the text with the most logical transition?

(A) meanwhile

(B) as a result

(C) due to this fact

(D) precisely

Some will contend that the true problem of retrosynthesis lies not in the end-products, but rather in the byproducts and novel synthetic intermediates required to artificially reproduce biochemical compounds. It must be acknowledged that this is indeed a valid concern. The design of stable synthetic intermediates not found in nature has at times led to unforeseen consequences. Methylenedioxymethamphetamine, _____ is a dangerous and highly concerning drug of abuse among youth.

25

Which choice completes the text with the most logical transition?

(A) on the other hand,

(B) in contrast,

(C) for example,

(D) due to this,

1   MODULE 2   1

While researching a topic, a student has taken the following notes:

- The origin of the Lunar New Year can be traced back to 3,500 years ago.
- It is theorized to have started during the Shang Dynasty (1600–1046 B.C.E.) where people held sacrificial ceremonies to honor gods and ancestors.
- The date of the Lunar New Year—fixed during the Han Dynasty—is the first day of the first month in the Chinese lunar calendar.
- The myth of the beast Nian and its fear of red and loud noises are thought to be the origin of setting off firecrackers and decorating with red for the festival.
- All the history may not be known, but the traditions surrounding this event are highly celebrated and continued through families.

26

The student wants to explain the establishment of when the Lunar New Year is celebrated. Which choice most effectively uses relevant information from the notes to accomplish this goal?

(A) While the Lunar New Year originated in the Shang Dynasty 3,500 years ago, the date of the Lunar New Year celebration was established during the Han Dynasty.

(B) The Lunar New Year has established many traditional rituals, like setting off firecrackers and decorating using the color red.

(C) Historians have little knowledge about the origin of the Lunar New Year calendar, preventing the statement of even generalizations about the topic.

(D) The ancient sacrificial practices that originated in the Shang Dynasty continue in their original forms with the modern-day rituals associated with the Lunar New Year celebration.

While researching a topic, a student has taken the following notes:

- In the United States, people who have been detained by the police have a right to swiftly appear before the court to determine whether the detention is valid.
- This right is known as the writ of "habeas corpus," a Latin phrase that translates as "you should have the body."
- This right prevents people who are being detained from disappearing into a jail or prison without due process of the law.
- Habeas corpus was first set as a right in the Magna Carta, one of the founding documents of the English systems of laws.
- This right today is an important check on the power of police and governments.

27

The student wants to suggest a possible negative consequence of not having a policy requiring habeas corpus in place. Which choice most effectively uses relevant information from the notes to accomplish this goal?

(A) If the right of habeas corpus were suspended, prisons and jails would be overrun with criminals in an unsafe and unsanitary manner.

(B) While some may want to remove the right to habeas corpus, they should keep in mind what the Magna Carta says about human dignity.

(C) Without the right of habeas corpus, those who are detained could disappear into jail without a proper legal process.

(D) If the United States removed the right to habeas corpus, other countries, like England, may follow its moral lead.

Section 2, Module 1: Math

35 MINUTES, 22 QUESTIONS

- All expressions and variables use real numbers.
- All figures are drawn to scale.
- Every figure lies in a plane.
- The domain of given functions is the set of all real numbers for which the corresponding value of the function is real.

For **multiple-choice questions**, solve the problem and pick the correct answer from the provided choices. Each multiple-choice question has only one correct answer.

For **student-produced response questions**, solve each problem and enter your answer following these guidelines:

- If you find **more than one correct answer**, enter just one answer.
- You can enter up to five characters for a **positive** answer and up to six characters (this includes the negative sign) for a **negative** answer.
- If your answer is a **fraction** that does not fit in the given spaces, enter the decimal equivalent instead.
- If your answer is a **decimal** that does not fit in the given spaces, enter it by stopping at or rounding up at the fourth digit.
- If your answer is a **mixed number** $\left(\text{like } 4\frac{1}{2}\right)$, enter it as an improper fraction (9/2) or its decimal equivalent (4.5).
- Do not enter **symbols** like a comma, dollar sign, or percent sign.

Examples

Answer	Acceptable Entries	Unacceptable Entries That Will Receive Zero Credit
4.5	4.5 4.50 9/2	41/2 4 1/2
$\frac{8}{9}$	8/9 .8888 .8889 0.888 0.889	0.8 .88 0.88 0.89
$-\frac{1}{9}$	−1/9 −.1111 −0.111	−.11 −0.11

2   **MODULE 1**   **2**

ADAPTIVE PRACTICE TEST

REFERENCE ⌄

Radius of a circle = r
Area of a circle = πr^2
Circumference of a circle = $2\pi r$

Area of a rectangle = length × width = lw

Area of a triangle = $\frac{1}{2}$ × base × height = $\frac{1}{2}bh$

Pythagorean theorem: $a^2 + b^2 = c^2$

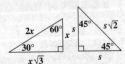

Special right triangles: 30-60-90 and 45-45-90

Volume of a box = length × width × height = lwh

Volume of a cylinder = $\pi r^2 h$

Volume of a sphere = $\frac{4}{3}\pi r^3$

Volume of a cone = $\frac{1}{3}\pi r^2 h$

Volume of a pyramid =
$\frac{1}{3}$ length × width × height = $\frac{1}{3}lwh$

Key Facts:

- A circle has 360 degrees.
- There are 2π radians in a circle.
- There are 180 degrees in a triangle.

1

$$3x + 2 = \frac{4}{3}x$$

What is the value of x in the above equation?

(A) $-\frac{6}{5}$

(B) $-\frac{2}{3}$

(C) $\frac{1}{4}$

(D) $\frac{5}{6}$

2

A roller coaster requires riders to be at least 48 inches tall. Given that there are approximately 2.54 centimeters in an inch, how tall must a rider be to the nearest whole <u>centimeter</u> to ride the roller coaster?

3

A bus is traveling at a constant rate of 50 miles per hour. At this rate, how far will the bus travel in $3\frac{1}{4}$ hours?

(A) 150 miles

(B) 160 miles

(C) 162.5 miles

(D) 175.5 miles

4

Which of the following is a solution to the equation below?

$$(x - 3)^2 - 81 = 0$$

(A) 12

(B) 11

(C) 9

(D) 8

5

A typist has already typed 3,500 words of a document. How many total words, $W(t)$, of the document will he have typed if he can type 70 words per minute and types for an additional t minutes?

Ⓐ $W(t) = 3,500t$

Ⓑ $W(t) = 70t - 3,500$

Ⓒ $W(t) = 3,500t + 70$

Ⓓ $W(t) = 3,500 + 70t$

6

$6a^2 + 8ab - 4ac$ is equivalent to which of the following expressions?

Ⓐ $a(3a + 4b + 2c)$

Ⓑ $2a(3a + 4b - 2c)$

Ⓒ $4a(a + b - 2c)$

Ⓓ $2a(3a - 4b + 2c)$

7

The expression $\left(\frac{2}{3}x + 1\right)\left(\frac{3}{4}x - 1\right) = ?$

Ⓐ $\frac{1}{6}x^2 - \frac{1}{3}x + 1$

Ⓑ $\frac{1}{4}x^2 + \frac{1}{12}x - 4$

Ⓒ $\frac{1}{2}x^2 + \frac{1}{12}x - 1$

Ⓓ $x^2 + \frac{1}{4}x - 1$

8

In the isosceles trapezoid above, what is the measure of the smallest interior angle?

9

If $\frac{x}{4} = \frac{1}{2}$, then $\frac{4(x-3)}{(-12)}$ equals which of the following?

Ⓐ $\frac{1}{16}$

Ⓑ $\frac{1}{12}$

Ⓒ $\frac{1}{6}$

Ⓓ $\frac{1}{3}$

10

On a particular college campus, there are two men for every three women. If the total number of men and women on campus is equal to 4,000, how many more women are there on campus than men?

┌─────────────┐
│   │
│ _____ │
└─────────────┘

11

When $x > 0$, which of these expressions is equivalent to $\frac{1}{\frac{1}{2x}} + \frac{3}{\frac{6}{4x}}$?

Ⓐ $4x$

Ⓑ $7x$

Ⓒ $\frac{1}{2}x - 4$

Ⓓ $x^2 - 12$

12

A coffee shop recorded data on the types of beverages ordered by its patrons in a given month. Each patron visited only once during the month and purchased only one beverage, and the four listed beverages are the only ones sold at this coffee shop.

	Cappuccino	Espresso	Latte	Americano	Total
Females under 18	230	125	325	170	850
Males under 18	170	185	240	220	815
Females age 18 and older	425	328	530	290	1,573
Males age 18 and older	350	429	477	313	1,569
Total	1,175	1,067	1,572	993	4,807

What (approximate) percentage of the drinks purchased at the coffee shop in the given month were espresso beverages?

(A) 11%

(B) 17%

(C) 22%

(D) 36%

13

At what point in the xy-plane will the functions $y = 4x - 3$ and $y = -\frac{1}{2}x + 2$ intersect?

(A) $\left(2, -\frac{2}{3}\right)$

(B) $\left(-\frac{3}{4}, \frac{5}{6}\right)$

(C) $\left(\frac{10}{9}, \frac{13}{9}\right)$

(D) $\left(1, \frac{3}{7}\right)$

14

David has two quarters (25 cents each) for every five dimes (10 cents each) in his change dish, with no other coins present. If he has a total of $2 in coins in the dish, how many total coins does he have?

15

The value of money is affected by the inflation rate—the higher the inflation rate, the less valuable money will become over time. The rate of inflation is calculated using the formula below, in which CPI represents the Consumer Price Index, a measure of the average of a typical basket of consumer goods and services (where goods and services are weighted relative to how often they are purchased by a normal consumer):

$$\frac{\text{This Year's CPI} - \text{Last Year's CPI}}{\text{Last Year's CPI}} \times 100$$

The current rate of inflation would *definitely* be zero if the CPI a year ago equaled which of the following?

(A) The CPI a year from now
(B) This year's CPI
(C) Zero
(D) 100

16

A line has the equation $y - 4x = 5$. What is the slope of a line that is perpendicular to this line?

(A) -4
(B) $-\frac{1}{4}$
(C) $\frac{5}{4}$
(D) 4

17

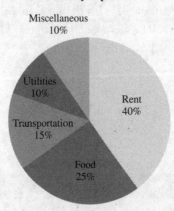

Monthly Expenses

The percentages of Anita's monthly expenses are portrayed in the above chart. If Anita spent $600 on rent, what was the total of her other expenses for the month?

(A) $600

(B) $900

(C) $1200

(D) $1400

18

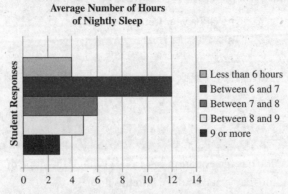

Average Number of Hours of Nightly Sleep

In the above histogram, the distribution of the number of hours of sleep per night as self-reported by thirty students is recorded. Which of the following values would be equal for the above set of values?

(A) Mean and median

(B) Mode and mean

(C) Median and mode

(D) Mean and range

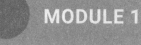

2   **MODULE 1**   **2**

19

An equilateral triangle has a side length of 6 centimeters. What is the area of the equilateral triangle?

(A) 4

(B) $3\sqrt{2}$

(C) $9\sqrt{3}$

(D) $12\sqrt{3}$

20

A wall's width is two-thirds that of its length. If paint to be used to cover the entire wall costs \$12 per gallon, and one gallon of paint will cover 60 square feet, what expression gives the cost in dollars of the paint (assuming one can purchase partial and full gallons) to cover such a wall that is L feet long?

(A) $\text{Cost} = L^2$

(B) $\text{Cost} = \frac{1}{5}L^2$

(C) $\text{Cost} = \frac{2}{15}L^2$

(D) $\text{Cost} = \frac{3}{64}L^2$

21

An animal shelter can house only cats and dogs. Each dog requires 2 cups of food and three treats a day, while each cat requires 1 cup of food a day and 2 treats a day. If the shelter has a total of 400 cups of food and 500 treats a day, what expressions portray the full scope of the number of c cats and d dogs the shelter could potentially house?

(A) $2d - c \leq 400$ and $3d + c < 500$

(B) $2d + c \leq 400$ and $3d + 2c \leq 500$

(C) $4d + c < 400$ and $d + c < 500$

(D) $2d + 2c \leq 400$ and $2d + 3c \leq 500$

22

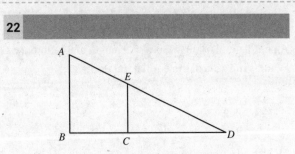

Note: Figure not drawn to scale

In the figure above, both angles *ABC* and *ECD* are 90
degrees. If the area of triangle *ECD* is 20 square inches,
the length of *EC* is 4 inches, and the length of *BC* is 8
inches, what is the area of triangle *ABD*?

Ⓐ   32.4 square inches

Ⓑ   64.8 square inches

Ⓒ   320 square inches

Ⓓ   640 square inches

ANSWER KEY
Adaptive Practice Test

Section 2, Math Module 1

1.	**A**	12.	**C**
2.	**122**	13.	**C**
3.	**C**	14.	**14**
4.	**A**	15.	**B**
5.	**D**	16.	**B**
6.	**B**	17.	**B**
7.	**C**	18.	**C**
8.	**75**	19.	**C**
9.	**D**	20.	**C**
10.	**800**	21.	**B**
11.	**A**	22.	**B**

Total Correct Answers: _____ / 22

Did you get 13 or fewer questions correct? If so, move to Math Module 2A on page 372.

Did you get 14 or more questions correct? If so, move to Math Module 2B on page 381.

Section 2, Module 2A: Math

35 MINUTES, 22 QUESTIONS

- All expressions and variables use real numbers.
- All figures are drawn to scale.
- Every figure lies in a plane.
- The domain of given functions is the set of all real numbers for which the corresponding value of the function is real.

For **multiple-choice questions**, solve the problem and pick the correct answer from the provided choices. Each multiple-choice question has only one correct answer.

For **student-produced response questions**, solve each problem and enter your answer following these guidelines:

- If you find **more than one correct answer**, enter just one answer.
- You can enter up to five characters for a **positive** answer and up to six characters (this includes the negative sign) for a **negative** answer.
- If your answer is a **fraction** that does not fit in the given space, enter the decimal equivalent instead.
- If your answer is a **decimal** that does not fit in the given space, enter it by stopping at or rounding up at the fourth digit.
- If your answer is a mixed number $\left(\text{like } 4\frac{1}{2}\right)$, enter it as an improper fraction (9/2) or its decimal equivalent (4.5).
- Do not enter symbols like a comma, dollar sign, or percent sign.

Examples

Answer	Acceptable Entries	Unacceptable Entries That Will Receive Zero Credit
4.5	4.5 4.50 9/2	41/2 4 1/2
$\frac{8}{9}$	8/9 .8888 .8889 0.888 0.889	0.8 .88 0.88 0.89
$-\frac{1}{9}$	−1/9 −.1111 −0.111	−.11 −0.11

1

A bicyclist's distance in miles from her starting point can be modeled by the function $d(x) = 16x$, in which x is given in hours. What does the number 16 represent in this function?

- (A) Her constant speed
- (B) Her varying speed
- (C) Her constant acceleration
- (D) Her varying acceleration

2

$3x\left(\frac{1}{3}x - 5\right)$ is equivalent to which of the following expressions?

- (A) $3x^2 - 30x$
- (B) $6x^2 - 5x$
- (C) $x^2 + 15x$
- (D) $x^2 - 15x$

3

If a line has a slope of 3 and intersects the point (1, 8), what is the y-intercept of the line?

- (A) 5
- (B) 3
- (C) -1
- (D) -3

4

The following chart tabulates the breakfast items ordered at Sam's Breakfast Dine-In & Drive-Thru on a particular Monday.

	Egg Sandwich	Cinnamon Roll	Breakfast Burrito	Chicken and Waffles	Totals
Dine-in	73	40	68	110	291
Drive-through	94	26	89	75	284
Totals	167	66	157	185	575

What is the best estimation of the probability that a randomly selected item sold from the drive-through that Monday is a breakfast burrito?

(A)   0.28

(B)   0.31

(C)   0.36

(D)   0.43

5

$$\frac{n+3}{2} = 5$$

What is the value of n in the above equation?

6

A school day at Washington High School is seven and a half hours long. How many <u>minutes</u> long is this school day?

7

What represents the range of values of x in this inequality?

$$-3(x+4) > 2x$$

(A) $x < -\dfrac{12}{5}$

(B) $x \leq -\dfrac{1}{3}$

(C) $x > \dfrac{7}{8}$

(D) $x \geq 3\dfrac{1}{2}$

8

A retailer sells certain numbers of shirts of the following price ranges during a particular day:

Number of Shirts Sold	Price Range
12	$0 <$ Price $< \$10$
15	$\$10 \leq$ Price $< \$15$
10	$\$15 \leq$ Price $< \$20$
21	$\$20 \leq$ Price $< \$25$
7	$\$25 \leq$ Price

Which of the following is justifiable from the given table?

(A) The range of prices is $25.

(B) The mean price is between $15 and $20.

(C) The median price is between $15 and $20.

(D) None of the above.

9

$9a^2 - 81b^2$ is equivalent to which of the following expressions?

(A) $(3a + 3b)(3a - 3b)$

(B) $3(a - b)(a + 3b)$

(C) $9(a + 3b)(a - 3b)$

(D) $9(a - 3b)(a - b)$

10

For how many points in the xy-plane will the functions $y = 4x$ and $2y = 8x - 5$ intersect?

- (A) Infinitely many
- (B) 2
- (C) 1
- (D) None

11

$\frac{1}{3}x + 2\left(\frac{x}{6} + 3\right)$ is equivalent to which of the following expressions?

- (A) $\frac{2}{3}x + 6$
- (B) $x + 3$
- (C) $\frac{4}{6}x + 2$
- (D) $3x + 6$

12

A polling company surveys 1,000 randomly selected senior citizens in the state of Connecticut. The senior citizens surveyed are representative of the typical demographics of senior citizens in the state. There are approximately 3.6 million residents in Connecticut, and approximately 14% of these residents are senior citizens. If 23% of the survey respondents indicated they planned on supporting a new tax regulation, what is the best estimate for how many senior citizens in the state as a whole would support the tax regulation?

- (A) 83,000
- (B) 98,000
- (C) 116,000
- (D) 828,000

13

A circle has a radius of 4 inches. One sector of the circle has a central angle measure of 60 degrees. What is the area of this sector of the circle in square inches?

(A) $\frac{\pi}{4}$

(B) 2π

(C) $\frac{8\pi}{3}$

(D) $\frac{15\pi}{2}$

14

If $-\frac{2}{3}x = \frac{1}{6}$, then $\frac{-\left(\frac{3}{2}\right)}{x}$ is equivalent to which of the following?

(A) $\frac{2}{3}$

(B) 6

(C) -3

(D) $\frac{8}{3}$

15

A customer orders food to be delivered from a restaurant. The cost of the food, including tax, is c. The total price, t, the customer pays upon delivery is given by the equation $t = 1.2c + 2$, which accounts for the cost of the food, a 20% tip on the food, and a $2 delivery fee. The restaurant doubles its delivery fee, and in response, the customer halves the percent of tip he pays. Which of the following expressions would represent the new total price the customer pays for food of cost c delivered from the restaurant?

(A) $1.2c + 2$
(B) $1.1c + 4$
(C) $0.6c + 4$
(D) $1.4c + 2$

16

At a city park, there are three dogs that weigh an average of 40 pounds each, and three cats. If two of the cats weigh 25 pounds each, what must the weight (in pounds) of the third cat be if the average weight of all six of these animals in the park is 30 pounds?

17

The costs of packages of generic brand soda, G, and name brand soda, N, at a grocery store are directly proportional to each other. If the relationship between the two is modeled by the equation $N = 2G$, where 2 represents the constant of proportionality, which of the following statements would be true?

Ⓐ The name brand soda is twice as expensive as the generic soda.

Ⓑ The name brand soda is half as expensive as the generic soda.

Ⓒ The prices of the generic and name brand sodas are equivalent.

Ⓓ The average number of packages sold of the generic brand soda is twice that of the name brand.

18

If 3 A's equal 2 B's, and 3 C's equal one B, how many C's will there be for each A?

Ⓐ 1

Ⓑ 2

Ⓒ 3

Ⓓ 6

2 ◆ MODULE 2 ◆ 2

19

If a square has a diagonal that measures $3\sqrt{2}$ units, what is the square's perimeter in units?

20

A business starts a social media account at the beginning of the year, beginning with 100 followers. With each month that passes, the number of followers increases by 5%, compounding on the previous month's total number of followers. Which would best represent the relationship between months and the number of followers?

Ⓐ An exponentially increasing relationship
Ⓑ An exponentially decreasing relationship
Ⓒ A linear relationship, with the line of the relationship having a constant slope
Ⓓ A linear relationship, with the line of the relationship having a positive, changing slope

---

21

The vertex form of parabola f is given by the function $f(x) = x^2 + 3$. The function $g(x)$ is given by the equation $g(x) = -f(x) + 2$. If the vertex of $f(x)$ is point (a, b), what is the vertex of $g(x)$ in terms of a and b?

Ⓐ $(a, b + 2)$
Ⓑ $(-a, -b + 4)$
Ⓒ $(2a, b - 2)$
Ⓓ $(a, b - 4)$

22

Consider a rectangular prism with a height of A, a length of B, and a width of C. The volume of how many pyramids of the same length and width of this prism, but half its height, could fit into the prism (i.e., just the volume of the pyramids, not the entire pyramids themselves)?

2 ◆ MODULE 2 ◆ 2

Section 2, Module 2B: Math

35 MINUTES, 22 QUESTIONS

1

What are the solution(s) to the following equation?

$$5x^2 - 15x + 10 = 0$$

(A) 0

(B) 1, 2

(C) 1, 4

(D) 2, 5

2

At what x-values would the function $y = x(x - 5)(x + 2)$ intersect the x-axis?

(A) -10

(B) 0, 3, 12

(C) 2, -5

(D) 0, 5, -2

3

The function f is given by $f(x) = 2 - |x - 4|$. For what value of x does the function f achieve its maximum value?

(A) 2

(B) 4

(C) 5

(D) 6

4

If $(x^2)^{\frac{1}{5}} + \sqrt[5]{32x^2} = ax^{\frac{2}{5}}$ for all values of x, what is the value of a?

(A) 0

(B) 3

(C) 5

(D) 16

5

What is the x-coordinate of the minimum of the parabola with the equation $y + 17 = 6x^2 + 12x$?

- (A) -1
- (B) 0
- (C) 2
- (D) 3

6

Given that (x, y) is a solution to the following system of equations, what is the sum of x and y?

$$2x - y = 3$$

$$4y = 6x$$

7

Given that $x \neq 0$, find the value of $\left(\dfrac{2x^4 + 3(2x^2)^2}{x^4} \right)^2.$

8

If $-16 - 6x + x^2 = x^2 - abx - 8b$, where a and b are constants, what is the value of a?

- (A) -6
- (B) -2
- (C) 1
- (D) 3

2 ◆ MODULE 2 ◆ **2**

9

The table below gives the results of a survey of a randomly selected sample of 400 fifteen- and sixteen-year-olds. Each respondent selected the method of electronic communication that he or she used the most.

Primary Method of Electronic Communication

	Texting	E-mail	Video Chatting	Other	Total
15-year-olds	110	20	40	30	200
16-year-olds	85	45	30	40	200
Total	195	x	70	70	400

The table omitted the value for x in the bottom row. Based on the structure of the table, what should its value be?

- Ⓐ 24
- Ⓑ 38
- Ⓒ 57
- Ⓓ 65

10

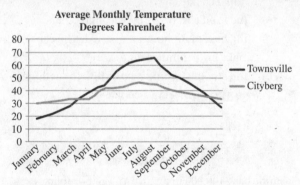

The average monthly temperatures for the cities of Townsville and Cityberg were recorded in the last calendar year. Based on the graph, which statement is true?

- Ⓐ The temperature on a randomly selected day in Townsville will be greater than the temperature on a randomly selected day in Cityberg.
- Ⓑ The temperature on a randomly selected day in Cityberg will be greater than the temperature on a randomly selected day in Townsville.
- Ⓒ The average monthly temperature in Townsville was greater than the average monthly temperature in Cityberg for the majority of the year.
- Ⓓ The average monthly temperature in Cityberg was greater than the average monthly temperature in Townsville for the majority of the year.

11

If the sale price on a coat is $72, and the original price of the coat was $90, what is the percent discount from this sale?

(A) 14%

(B) 20%

(C) 26%

(D) 80%

12

A chef is making cookies from scratch. He requires a set period of time to gather the ingredients and get everything set up to make the cookies, and then needs a set period of time to make each individual cookie. If c represents the total number of cookies he is making, and t represents the total amount of time it takes to make c cookies, what is the meaning of the 20 in this equation: $t = 20 + 10c$?

(A) How much time it takes to make each individual cookie

(B) The fixed cost of the cookie ingredients

(C) The maximum number of cookies he can make in 10 minutes time

(D) The amount of time it takes him to set things up prior to making a cookie

13

Jasmine has $100,000 in an investment portfolio, divided among only the categories of stocks, bonds, and cash. She has twice as much invested in stocks as she does in bonds, and three times as much invested in bonds as she has in cash. What percent of her portfolio is invested in bonds?

(A) 22%

(B) 27%

(C) 30%

(D) 44%

2 ◆ MODULE 2 ◆ 2

14

John and Mary had a gardening business. On a Monday, Mary weeded 3 lawns an hour for x hours and John weeded 2 lawns an hour for y hours. What is the total number of lawns they weeded all together on that Monday?

(A) $3xy$

(B) $6xy$

(C) $3x + 2y$

(D) $3(x + y)$

15

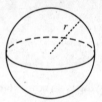

Which of the following expressions would be equivalent to the diameter of the sphere portrayed above, with a radius of r and volume V?

(A) $2\sqrt[3]{\dfrac{3V}{4\pi}}$

(B) πr^3

(C) $4\sqrt{\dfrac{2r^3}{3}}$

(D) $\dfrac{4\,V^3}{3\,r^2}$

16

Caitlin opens a checking account to set aside spending money for vacations. Each month she puts the same dollar amount, $50, in the account. Unfortunately, she does not expect to be able to take a vacation at any point in the foreseeable future. What would best describe the relationship between the number of months and the total amount of money in the account?

(A) A linear relationship, with the line of the relationship having a negative slope

(B) A linear relationship, with the line of the relationship having a positive slope

(C) An exponentially increasing relationship

(D) An inverse exponential relationship

17

Which of the following is an equivalent form of
$$\frac{(7x - 7)(7x + 7)}{7}?$$

(A) $x^2 - 1$

(B) $49x^2 + 7$

(C) $7(x^2 - 1)$

(D) $\frac{(x^2 - 7)}{7}$

2   ◆ MODULE 2 ◆   2

18

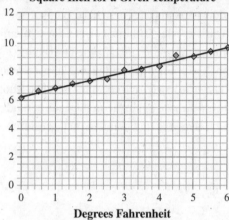

Refrigerant ABC: Pressure in Pounds per Square Inch for a Given Temperature

Degrees Fahrenheit

◆ Pressure in Pounds per Square Inch
— Linear (Pressure in Pounds per Square Inch)

A refrigerant manufacturer recorded the pressure associated with certain temperatures in a refrigerator using its new refrigerant, ABC. What would best approximate the equation of the best-fit line portrayed by the data in this graph, using P for pressure and T for temperature (using the same units as portrayed in the graph)?

Ⓐ $P = 0.5T + 6.5$
Ⓑ $P = T + 6.5$
Ⓒ $P = 0.5T - 3$
Ⓓ $P = 7T + 5$

19

A certain cube has edges of length L inches, surface area of A square inches, and volume of B cubic inches. For what value of L would $A = B$?

_____

20

John is taking a rowboat both up and down a 16 km length of a river. A constant current of 1 km/hr makes his trip downstream faster than his trip upstream because he is moving with the current downstream and fighting against the current when traveling upstream. If a round-trip journey took him a total of 4 hours and if he rowed at a constant pace the whole time, what is the rate in km/hr, to the nearest tenth, at which John is rowing independent of the current?

Ⓐ 7.3

Ⓑ 8.1

Ⓒ 8.9

Ⓓ 9.7

2 ◆ MODULE 2 ◆ 2

21

A currency conversion store at an airport in New York City posts the following conversion rate table:

Currency Type	Currency per 1 U.S. Dollar
U.S. dollar	1.00
Euro	0.90
Indian rupee	68.01
South African rand	16.17
Japanese yen	116.36
Australian dollar	1.41

The conversion store charges 1 percent of the amount converted, plus a $2 flat fee for each total transaction (including multiple-currency exchanges, so long as they take place in a single visit to the store. The fee is assessed *in addition* to the 1 percent conversion fee).

Suppose a customer wanted to see the conversion rate, before doing a transaction with any associated charges or fees, of U.S. dollars to Australian dollars. What is the conversion rate of U.S. dollars to one Australian dollar to the nearest hundredth?

[_____]

22

Consider the function $f(x) = 2x - 3$. What is the range of the absolute value of this function?

- (A) $y < -3$
- (B) $y \leq 0$
- (C) $y \geq 0$
- (D) $y > 5$

ANSWER KEY
Adaptive Practice Test

Score whichever module you completed: 2A or 2B.

Reading and Writing Module 2A

1. A	10. B	19. C
2. C	11. A	20. D
3. B	12. A	21. A
4. C	13. B	22. B
5. C	14. A	23. A
6. B	15. A	24. A
7. D	16. D	25. D
8. B	17. B	26. D
9. C	18. C	27. A

Total: ____ / 27

Reading and Writing Module 2B

1. A	10. C	19. C
2. C	11. C	20. B
3. A	12. C	21. C
4. C	13. D	22. B
5. D	14. C	23. B
6. A	15. B	24. A
7. D	16. A	25. C
8. D	17. A	26. A
9. B	18. A	27. C

Total: ____ / 27

ANSWER KEY
Adaptive Practice Test

Score whichever module you completed: 2A or 2B.

Math Module 2A

1.	**A**	12.	**C**
2.	**D**	13.	**C**
3.	**A**	14.	**B**
4.	**B**	15.	**B**
5.	**7**	16.	**10**
6.	**450**	17.	**A**
7.	**A**	18.	**B**
8.	**C**	19.	**12**
9.	**C**	20.	**A**
10.	**D**	21.	**D**
11.	**A**	22.	**6**

Total: _____ / 22

Math Module 2B

1.	**B**	12.	**D**
2.	**D**	13.	**C**
3.	**B**	14.	**C**
4.	**B**	15.	**A**
5.	**A**	16.	**B**
6.	**15**	17.	**C**
7.	**196**	18.	**A**
8.	**D**	19.	**6**
9.	**D**	20.	**B**
10.	**C**	21.	**0.71**
11.	**B**	22.	**C**

Total: _____ / 22

Adaptive Digital PSAT Score Estimator

This streamlined guide will give you an approximation of the score you would earn on the Digital PSAT. On the actual Digital PSAT, there will be some small but important differences in how the test will be scored. First, there will be 2 experimental questions in each module that will be omitted. You will almost certainly be unable to determine which questions are experimental, so just do your best on every single question. In this guide, we are making every question count to simplify your estimation. Second, the Digital PSAT will utilize "Item Response Theory" in its scoring. Certain questions may have more weight on your performance than others. The latest information about the precise scoring guidelines can be found at *collegeboard.org*

Be sure you look at the correct chart depending on whether you did Module 2A or 2B for each section.

Reading and Writing Scoring Charts

Use this table if you did **Reading and Writing Modules 1 and 2A**.

Tally the number of correct answers from the entire Reading and Writing section (out of 54) to find your Reading and Writing section score. Since you would have to miss at least 10 questions to move to Module 2A, the table ends at a maximum of 44 questions correct.

Number of Correct Reading and Writing Questions (Out of 54)	Reading and Writing Test Score (Out of 760)	Number of Correct Reading and Writing Questions (Out of 54)	Reading and Writing Test Score (Out of 760)
0	160	28	440
1	170	29	450
2	180	30	460
3	190	31	470
4	200	32	480
5	210	33	490
6	220	34	500
7	230	35	510
8	240	36	520
9	250	37	530
10	260	38	540
11	270	39	550
12	280	40	570
13	290	41	580
14	300	42	590
15	310	43	600
16	320	44	610
17	330		
18	340		
19	350		
20	360		
21	370		
22	380		
23	390		
24	400		
25	410		
26	420		
27	430		

Use this table if you did Reading and Writing **Modules 1 and 2B.**

Tally the number of correct answers from the entire Reading and Writing section (out of 54) to find your Reading and Writing section score. Since you would need to answer at least 18 questions on the first module correctly to do Module 2, the table starts at 18 questions correct as the minimum.

Number of Correct Reading and Writing Questions (Out of 54)	Reading and Writing Test Score (Out of 760)
18	410
19	420
20	430
21	440
22	450
23	460
24	470
25	480
26	490
27	500
28	510
29	520
30	530
31	540
32	550
33	560
34	570
35	580
36	590
37	600
38	610
39	620
40	630
41	640
42	650
43	660
44	670
45	680
46	690
47	700
48	710
49	720
50	730
51	740
52	750
53	760
54	760

Math Scoring Charts

Use this table if you did Math **Modules 1 and 2A**.

Tally the number of correct answers from the entire Math section (out of 44) to find your Math section score. Since you would have to miss at least 9 questions to move to Module 2A, the table ends at a maximum of 35 questions correct.

Number of Correct Math Questions (Out of 44)	Math Section Score (Out of 760)
0	160
1	180
2	190
3	200
4	210
5	240
6	260
7	280
8	300
9	310
10	320
11	340
12	350
13	360
14	370
15	390
16	400
17	410
18	420
19	440
20	450
21	460
22	470
23	480
24	490
25	500
26	510
27	520
28	530
29	540
30	550
31	560
32	570
33	580
34	590
35	610

Use this table if you did **Math Modules 1 and 2B**.

Tally the number of correct answers from the entire Math section (out of 44) to find your Math section score. Since you would need to answer at least 14 questions on the first module correctly to do Module 2, the table starts at 14 questions correct as the minimum.

Number of Correct Math Questions (Out of 44)	Math Section Score (Out of 760)
14	410
15	420
16	440
17	450
18	470
19	480
20	490
21	510
22	520
23	530
24	540
25	550
26	570
27	580
28	590
29	600
30	610
31	630
32	640
33	650
34	660
35	670
36	680
37	690
38	700
39	710
40	720
41	730
42	740
43	750
44	760

Add the Reading and Writing section score and the Math section score to find your approximate total PSAT test score:

_____ Reading and Writing section score +

_____ Math section score =

_____ **Total Approximate PSAT Test Score (between 320 and 1520)**

Approximate your testing percentiles (1st–99th) using this chart:

Total Score	Section Score	Total Percentile	Reading and Writing Percentile	Math Percentile
1520	760	99+	99+	99
1420	710	98	98	96
1320	660	94	94	91
1220	610	86	86	84
1120	560	74	73	75
1020	510	59	57	61
920	460	41	40	42
820	410	25	24	27
720	360	11	11	15
620	310	3	3	5
520	260	1	1	1
420	210	1	1	1
320	160	1	1	1

Scoring data approximations based on information at *collegeboard.org*

Answer Explanations

Section 1: Reading and Writing Module 1

1. **(A)** Because the text is focused on encryption, it makes the most sense to say that a recipient of an encoded message would "decode" it. It is not choice (B) or (D) because the recipient would not create a response but would instead decipher it. It is not choice (C) because the recipient would want the literal meaning of the message.

2. **(C)** *Cosseted* makes the most sense here since one of its definitions is "to cuddle or caress lovingly." Choices (A), (B), and (D) can be eliminated because, although they are ways David may treat the dog, they are not reflective of his hugging the animal to his chest.

3. **(D)** The transliterated text presented in the text shows that there is not a clear ending to the story, making *ambiguous* the best option. The other choices would all indicate much more decisive outcomes.

4. **(B)** The color cameras are described as being cumbersome and challenging to use, which aligns with "unwieldy." While the cameras were larger than ones used today, the text does not support calling them "unsightly" or ugly. No mention is directly made of their expense. Also, since the cameras were less advanced than ones used today, it is highly unlikely that they would be "precise."

5. **(B)** In the text, Reagan quotes an American worker to illustrate the incongruity of the hourly wage. Since *anecdotal* means an "account based on personal story or experience," (B) is accurate. These lines specifically do not contain *statistics* or address a counterargument. Moreover, choice (C) is wrong because rather than separating them, Reagan uses facts directly after the quote to support the personal testimony.

6. **(A)** The author here is saying that it would be as difficult to explain the concept of "roving about in famished gangs" to enslaved people as it would be to explain the taste of pineapple to someone who had never tried it before. This best fits with choice (A). Choice (B) is incorrect as the author is not explaining an upper class lifestyle. Choice (C) is incorrect as he is not describing what people are actually eating (or not eating). Choice (D) is incorrect as he is not trying to talk to modern readers.

7. **(A)** In Text 1, Franklin mentions "obtaining little anecdotes" about his ancestors. The consistent theme in Washington's text is a thirst to know his roots. The ability to obtain such anecdotes would assist him in his quest for knowledge, so choice (A) is the correct answer. Choice (B) is flawed in that Washington is already writing an autobiography, or memoir. Washington makes no reference to children, as in choice (C), or to wishing to relive his life, as in choice (D).

8. **(D)** Text 4 discusses the contributions engineers have made to making life more enjoyable, specifically in the daily areas of "communications, computing, and sports." Hence, (D) is right. The author is not discussing engineering specifically as a career, ruling out (A). (C) is incorrect because the author is considering how engineers from varying fields have impacted communications and sports, rather than focusing on two types of engineers. Choice (B) is tempting, but the author's purpose is to show how entirely engineers have impacted certain aspects of daily life, not to illustrate how human life would go extinct without them.

9. **(B)** The text states that the prevalence of parliamentary rule is connected to "the legacy of the British Empire," so the answer is (B). Choice (A) is an aspect of presidential rule. (C) and (D), although features of a parliamentary system, are not stated as reasons for its popularity.

10. **(B)** Analyze the chart for this question. You are comparing the writing scores of those who read for fun "almost daily" with the scores of those who read "never or hardly ever daily." The difference in points between these two groups is approximately 30.

11. **(A)** The question asks you to find a quote that illustrates that Mount Monadnock has an impressive size relative to the other features of the

landscape. Choice (A) states that the mountain is "dominating all the little lesser hills which compass thee," indicating that it is indeed of an impressive size compared to the features surrounding it. The other options do not compare the mountain to the size of the features around it.

12. **(B)** The text states that the "zone with the largest diameter typically signifies that it will be the best at fighting infection." Under the *E. coli* column (2nd column), ciprofloxacin has the largest diameter at 17 mm. It would therefore be the most effective antibiotic in this particular instance, as in choice (B). Vancomycin would be the most effective medication against *S. aureus,* not against *E. coli.* Amoxicillin is the second most effective. Not only is there no data on *Staphylococcus*, but it also is actually a bacterial strain and not an antibiotic.

13. **(D)** The previous examples are of workers who are able to work from home, accomplishing home-based tasks during the workday. Therefore, ending the sentence with *staying at home during the workday* would be most logical. The other options do not relate to at-home work.

14. **(C)** The previous sentence states that "The problem with antibiotics is that they do not necessarily target one specific bacteria." Thus, it is logical to illustrate how this could be a potential problem with a strict antibiotic regimen, in that many of the antibiotics will not allow for a targeted treatment of the harmful bacteria but will instead kill many types of bacteria in the body without exception. Choice (A) provides the opposite of the needed meaning. Choice (B) is irrelevant, as allergic reactions are not discussed in the text. Choice (D) is contradicted by the statement that antibiotics can target "certain classes," meaning that at least some forms of bacteria will be eliminated.

15. **(A)** *Do* is numerically consistent with the plural subject "roles." Choice (B), *does*, is singular. Choice (C), *don't*, causes a double negative given the "not" that follows. Choice (D), *do's*, is not a word.

16. **(A)** This is the only choice that shows ownership by the singular city of Chicago of the City Council.

Choices (B) and (D) do not show possession, and choice (C) shows plural possession.

17. **(D)** "Well" is used similar to the word "far" in this context, stating that this is for a great duration of time into the 19th century. A comma is needed after "century" to separate the dependent introductory phrase from the independent clause that follows. Choices (A) and (B) break up the phrase "well into," and choice (C) has no needed pauses.

18. **(A)** This is the only option that puts quotation marks around a direct quote from Bernard Shaw. Choices (B) and (C) have no quotation marks. Choice (D) would work if this phrase were inside another quotation.

19. **(D)** This choice correctly places commas around the parenthetical phrase. Choice (A) has a comma at an awkward point, choice (B) lacks the necessary pauses, and choice (C) is too choppy.

20. **(B)** Mention of the Neanderthals at the beginning of the underlined portion is necessary to make a logical comparison with "our own ancestors." Choices (A) and (D) make illogical comparisons since they compare geographic regions to ancestors. Choice (C) has confusing word order at the end, placing *icebound* such that it literally means that the Neanderthals were icebound. Choice (B) puts things in a logical order and makes a logical comparison of people to Neanderthals.

21. **(A)** The dashes properly set aside a parenthetical phrase. Choice (B) does not work, since a complete sentence does not appear after the semicolon. Choice (C) interrupts the thought right in the middle. Choice (D) uses inconsistent punctuation on either side of the parenthetical phrase.

22. **(D)** The sentence is stating two things that do not happen, so stating "doesn't" in conjunction with *nor* makes sense. Choice (B) shows cause and effect. Choice (C) shows a direct connection between two ideas. Choice (A) shows contrast.

23. **(A)** This is the only option to provide the needed contrast between the relatively recent origin of the periodic table and its ancient inspiration.

24. **(C)** "In fact" leads into the clarification that antibiotics should not be eliminated—the other options would not convey clarification.

25. **(C)** "As" conveys a cause-and-effect relationship between Franklin's suggestion and the reason for his suggestion. The other options do not show a cause-and-effect relationship.

26. **(B)** "Critical acclaim" involves recognition by other professionals, often through awards. The fact that *Spirited Away* received an Oscar would best illustrate its critical acclaim. The other options relate to other information presented in the notes, but not to critical acclaim.

27. **(B)** The student wants to highlight the impact that national transportation infrastructure changes had on helping bonanza farms develop—emphasizing how the railroad tracks connected the farmers to faraway regions would accomplish this goal. The other options do not connect to the development of transportation infrastructure.

Section 1: Reading and Writing Module 2A

1. **(A)** Will never completes his assignments on time, so you can infer that the intended meaning is *lackadaisical*, as in choice (A). (B) refers more to sleepiness than idleness. (C) would indicate that Will was unintelligent, and would not fit the context. (D) is a near antonym to what is needed, since it refers to eagerness and intensity.

2. **(C)** *Depends* works best here since the line refers to ecological balance being contingent on two things. It would be incorrect to say the balance *fulcrums*, *analyzes*, or *joints* on two things.

3. **(B)** The sentence before indicates that Mrs. Price never showed Fanny more kindness than she did on that first day. The sentence after states that "she had neither leisure nor affection to bestow." So, it can be inferred that the "instinct of nature" that had to be satisfied was her *maternal feeling*. It is not related to *survival*, *acceptance*, or *justice*.

4. **(C)** The "tired" and "poor" immigrants would be eager to embrace a new life of freedom, making "desiring" the most logical option. The other options do not signify desire.

5. **(C)** The sentence is providing statistics on how much money veterinarians can make, so *earning* is the most appropriate word. The other options do not describe how much someone's salary would be.

6. **(B)** The best approach to a question like this is to consider the purpose of the text as a whole. Reagan speaks directly to Congress here, providing visuals and empirical evidence of just how bad the current situation is. So, (B) is the only choice that indicates his intention to illustrate severity.

7. **(D)** Text 2 argues that because Darwin did not have a grasp of Mendel's work on heredity, he was unable to anticipate the phenomenon of genetic drift. This would be a shortcoming in the theory presented in Text 1 that Text 2 highlights. It is not (A), because neither text claims that the evolutionary theory presented is infallible. It is not (B), because Text 1 does not address any objection from Text 2. It is not (C), because there was a lack of influence of Mendel on Darwin, causing Darwinian theory to be a problem in the eyes of the author of Text 2.

8. **(B)** According to the author, organic farming "encourages polyculture," so it produces more *diversity*. The text states that conventional farming is more productive and centralized. There is no evidence for (C) either way.

9. **(C)** The selection provides the backstory for how Pip came to the house of Miss Havisham. (A), (B), and (D) all are not presented in this selection.

10. **(B)** *-Ock* is the only option that has a short syllable coupled with a hard consonant ending.

11. **(A)** To *undermine* the hypothesis is to "find a flaw" in it. The economist is arguing that making unemployment benefits more generous will cause fewer people to seek out work. Choice (A) most directly undermines this because it would show that in a similar situation in another state, an increase in unemployment benefits did not result in an increase in unemployment. (B) and (C) would confirm the original hypothesis instead of undermining it. (D) presents a flawed sample of voluntary results that would not be helpful in making a determination on this topic.

12. **(A)** We are asked to find what makes Norway unique with respect to these other countries. The graph does not provide evidence on health care or birth rates, ruling out choices (B), (C), and (D). Additionally, you can confirm (A) by seeing that about 17 percent of the population is made up of those 65 and older. The only country close to this percentage is the United States with about 15 percent of the population being in this category.

13. **(B)** The sentence states that a folklorist's job is not confined to an academic setting of a university or desk, but is instead highly involved in exciting real-world settings. Therefore, calling the work *participatory and engaging* would emphasize the interesting settings in which the field takes place. It is not (A), because the field is described in a more positive way. It is not (C), because the field is described as being more hands-on instead of abstract. It is not (D), because there is no mention of the pay for folklorists.

14. **(A)** The text argues that the "weeks-long" displays of fireworks around July 4th causes difficulties for pets, veterans, and the environment. The author does not suggest eliminating fireworks altogether, because their lighting on July 4th is entrenched in tradition. However, it is most logical to complete the text by stating that instead of having the displays go on for several weeks, they could be limited to a single night—this makes choice (A) the best option. It is not choice (B) because this solution would not address the concerns about noise. It is not choice (C) because this is too extreme based on the qualified statement in the previous sentence. It is not choice (D) because this does not offer a precise solution.

15. **(A)** This option correctly uses the present perfect tense to indicate that the narrator has forgotten this exercise. Choice (B) incorrectly uses *forgot*, choice (C) incorrectly uses *has*, and choice (D) is nonsensical.

16. **(D)** The sentence refers to "ancient times past," making it most logical to use the past tense. Also, the subject is plural with "beauty and . . . refinement," making the past plural word "were" most fitting.

17. **(B)** *Their* shows possession in the third person. Choice (A) is wrong, because *there* is used for places. Choice (C) would be used if the subject had been "we" instead of the "architect," and choice (D) is a contraction meaning "they are."

18. **(C)** "Was" correctly indicates singular past tense. (A) and (B) would need to be used in conjunction with another verb in this context, and (D) is plural.

19. **(C)** Choice (C) provides a semicolon to break up the two independent clauses in the sentence. It also provides commas to surround the word "however," which provides a transition and could be removed from the sentence without making the sentence incomplete. Choices (A) and (D) create run-on sentences by using just use a comma to join two independent clauses. Choice (B) does not surround "however" with the needed punctuation.

20. **(D)** The subject "car" is singular, making "needs" the correct verb. Also, since the pronoun in the underlined selection refers to "car," "its" would be the correct insertion to represent singular possession. Choices (A) and (C) use the incorrect plural verb "need," and choice (B) incorrectly uses "their."

21. **(A)** The colon sets off the clarification that follows, and the commas set aside the nonessential yet descriptive phrase, *regardless of their mass*. Choice (B) causes a run-on sentence. Choices (C) and (D) are both missing needed pauses.

22. **(B)** In this sentence, there is a pattern of, essentially, *not for* this *reason,* but *for* that *reason.* That *but* is necessary because it demonstrates the contrasting relationship that is apparent. And *since, and,* and *for a result* fail to capture that pattern of *not for this, but for that.*

23. **(A)** To determine the correct conjunction to use, analyze the relationship between the two clauses. Here, the second clause contrasts with the first. Essentially, although Schrödinger won the Nobel Prize, he is more famous for something else. "Although," like "but," is a contrasting term. Choice (A) is the correct answer. Choices (B) and

(C) emphasize a causal relationship. Choice (D) is not contrasting but, rather, conjoining.

24. **(A)** Analyze the relationship between this sentence and the previous statement. Essentially, the second sentence is a restatement of the previous sentence. "In other words" serves to introduce a restatement. Choices (B) and (C) create a contrasting relationship that is not apparent here. "Henceforth" is often used chronologically to signify from this point forward.

25. **(D)** *Posthumous* means "after one's death." Since (A) *Memoir of Jane Austen* is described as being published after Austen's death, this is the only logical option. The other works were not described as being published after Austen's death.

26. **(D)** The student's goal is to provide information about spider mites for people who want to avoid spider mite infestations. Choice (D) accomplishes this goal by stating that by keeping plant soil wet, spider mites will keep away from plants. Choices (A) and (C) provide information about spider mites, but do not discuss how to prevent the infestations. Choice (B) focuses on what to do after a spider mite infestation, not on how to prevent it in the first place.

27. **(A)** The answer must both outline a worst-case scenario and do so with respect to the user's health impact. Choice (A) is the only option to focus on the worst-case possibility of a stained-glass artist becoming poisoned. Choice (B) does not focus on the health impact of the person making stained glass. Choices (C) and (D) do not connect to worst-case scenarios.

Reading and Writing Module 2B

1. **(A)** The sentence requires a word that signifies *to undertake* the adventure/*to embrace* the adventure. *Inspected* the adventure and *respected* the adventure do not communicate that meaning. *Excepted* means "excluded," and doesn't suit our purposes. *Accepted* is the best option.

2. **(C)** According to the text, the state of the country induces "stern duties," so *serious* is the correct choice. A country at war would not connect to anything playful. (B) is too negative. Choice (D) would inaccurately indicate that what's at stake is pointless.

3. **(A)** *Notoriety* refers to fame, so it is the correct choice. *Disreputability* is a close synonym, but it is associated with being well known for a bad deed, which makes it incorrect; although the disorders associated with erroneous hemoglobin may be infamous, hemoglobin itself is not. *Personage* refers specifically to a famous person. *Festivity* refers to a celebration.

4. **(C)** In the context of the text, "singular" refers to the type of beginning that the Big Bang was, making "definitive" most appropriate. While the other words can be stand-ins for "singular," they are not consistent with the context of the text.

5. **(D)** The sentences prior to this indicate that there is not much of a border between the U.S. and Canada, given how undefended it is. These lines clarify that the two countries are, in fact, very much independent of one another. Choice (A) would require more information about other countries' borders to provide such an analysis. Choice (B) is incorrect because there is no detail provided about the security screening process. And choice (C) is incorrect, because the essay does not support the idea that there has been continued border hostility between the two countries since the War of 1812.

6. **(A)** The author suggests that we have been too adamant in our germophobia, making (A) correct. There is no evidence for (B). Choice (C) is contradictive because the valid concerns of germophobics would support rather than refute germ theory. Choice (D) would inaccurately indicate that the purpose of this text was to show the everyday instances of germ theory; in fact, this text gives a historical reminiscence of germ theory before positing the argument that the elimination of all germs is not necessarily the best approach to human health.

7. **(D)** The first text is very personal and emotional in its approach to describing love. The second takes a very scientific and factual approach to love. Since the first is not based on principles of

morality, *ethical* is an inaccurate description. (B) takes an opinion on which basis is more significant, assuming an emotional, heartfelt description of love is *trivial* or foolish. (C) indicates that the technical approach is *misguided*. Thus, (D) is the only accurate choice. *Subjective* means "based on personal experience," while *objective* means "based on a representation of facts."

8. **(D)** Text 2 highlights how many people may feel a fear of being declared dead prematurely, which could dissuade them from wanting to be organ donors. This unfounded fear would go a long way in explaining why there would be such a disparity between those who support organ donation—95 percent of Americans—and those who actually registered to be organ donors—just 40 percent. It is not (A) or (C), because there is no focus on the procedure to become an organ donor in Text 2. It is not (B), because Text 1 does not suggest that premature burial is a major safety concern for most adults.

9. **(B)** The text discusses a step of glycolysis and how it works in tandem with the body's current levels of glucose. So, *dynamic*, or in a "state of constant activity and change," is appropriate. *Artificial* means "fake," while *arbitrary* means "random." *Static*, or "unchanging," is the opposite of *dynamic*.

10. **(C)** The text depicts Fanny's father as a man without ambition, curiosity, or knowledge "beyond his profession," making *overly pragmatic* the correct answer. *Pragmatic* means "practical and realistic, uninterested in ideas or theories," so her father's simplemindedness fits this description. She finds him dull rather than interesting as in (A). (B) describes his personality, but not his intellectual interests. And *erudite* means "cultured" or "well-educated," making (D) the opposite of Fanny's description of her father.

11. **(C)** To *undermine* would be to show the flaws with an argument. If present-day frogs mate with one another from across riverbanks, this would hurt the notion that the river poses a barrier to frog mating. It is not (A), because the presence of pollutants in one branch of the Amazon would

not determine whether cross-river mating could occur throughout the river system. It is not (B), because that would add support to the biologist's hypothesis, since predators in the river would present another barrier to the frogs' crossing the river. It is not (D), because tourist activity could also provide a barrier to frog crossing, supporting rather than undermining the hypothesis.

12. **(C)** Between 2005 and 2010, there is a rough increase of about 400 along the *y*-axis. So, if the number of universities offering folklore increases at the same rate as this between 2010 and 2015, there will be approximately 1,700 schools in 2015 that offer such programs. Choices (A), (B), and (D) do not make conclusions supported by the trends in the presented data.

13. **(D)** This quotation best illustrates the historian's claim, because they forecast that if the war were ended prematurely, Germany would keep much of its winnings—this could be reasonably inferred to lead to an imbalance in international power relationships, with Germany more dominant than its counterparts. It is not choice (A) because these lines explore the motivations of the American government. It is not choice (B) because these lines emphasize the concerns the author has about the growth in the Stockholm movement, with no indication that a peace treaty would bring this trend to an end. And it is not choice (C) because these lines forecast potential future consequences of a spreading revolutionary ideology.

14. **(C)** According to the author, consuming your sugars from fructose eventually causes obesity and other health issues. Thus, (C) is correct because it is the only choice that considers the long-term effects of fructose according to the text.

15. **(B)** The text highlights the need to avoid having a car slip when it breaks, preventing an uncontrolled stop. Therefore, choice (B) makes the most sense as it states what the goal of using an antilock braking system would be—namely, to allow a more controlled stop. Choices (A) and (D) would be the opposite of what would be required from a braking system. Choice (C) would be unrelated to safety concerns.

16. **(A)** Keep the entire dependent clause uninterrupted by commas, which is precisely what choice (A) does. The other options make this phrase too choppy.

17. **(A)** *The innate immune system* is a parenthetical phrase: eliminate it, and the sentence still functions acceptably. It can be surrounded with either two commas or two dashes to differentiate it from the main clause. Choices (C) and (D) both neglect the necessary preceding punctuation. Choice (B) starts with a dash, but then uses a comma. It is necessary to be consistent with whichever one (comma or dash) begins the parenthetical phrase.

18. **(A)** *Its* gives the singular possessive adjective needed to refer to "bullroarer" and shows the instrument possessing a "function." Choice (B) is wrong because *it's* means "it is." Choice (C) is wrong because *its'* is always incorrect. Choice (D) is wrong because *their* is plural.

19. **(C)** The sentence that follows indicates that this essay is written from the present-day perspective. Choice (C) correctly uses the present perfect tense, *has now begun*, and is numerically consistent with the singular subject of "world." Choices (A) and (B) improperly use *began* in the perfect tense (*began* is for the past tense), and choice (D) is plural.

20. **(B)** The adjective *endless* is needed to modify the noun *effects*. Also, *affect* is generally a verb, and *effect* is generally a noun. The incorrect options either use the adverb *endlessly* and/or use the verb *affect*.

21. **(C)** No commas are needed in this long, descriptive phrase. The other options are too choppy.

22. **(B)** This choice is the most concise and uses parallel phrasing. Choices (A) and (C) are too wordy. Choice (D) uses "*meeting*," which is incorrect to use in conjunction with "*to*"—one says, "*to meet*" rather than "*to meeting.*"

23. **(B)** This is the only option to be consistent with the numeric listing found elsewhere in the text: "First" and "Third."

24. **(A)** *Meanwhile* provides a logical contrast between the relatively large percentage of dark matter and the relatively small percentage of visible atoms. None of the other options provides a logical contrast.

25. **(C)** The previous sentence makes a broad statement about the unforeseen consequences of synthetic intermediates design, while the final sentence gives a specific elaboration about one of these consequences. Thus, "*for example*" is the only logical possibility.

26. **(A)** The student's goal is to explain the establishment of when the Lunar New Year is celebrated. Choice (A) effectively accomplishes this goal by pointing out that the date was established during the Han Dynasty. It is not choice (B) or (D) because these focus on rituals instead of dates. It is not choice (C) because historians do in fact have knowledge about the origin of the celebration date.

27. **(C)** The student wants to suggest a possible negative consequence of not having habeas corpus in place—the third bullet outlines how this right prevents people from receiving jail sentences without the due process of law. This aligns with choice (C). Choice (A) is a negative consequence but is not supported by the notes, since it is likely that in the absence of habeas corpus, the number of people in prison would increase, not decrease. Choices (B) and (D) do not outline possible negative consequences.

Section 2: Math Module 1

1. **(A)** First, get all x terms on one side by subtracting $3x$ from both sides. To combine the x terms, you need a common denominator, so first convert $3x$ to $\frac{9}{3}x$. After combining the x terms, the equation becomes

   $2 = -\frac{5}{3}x$. Next, solve for x by dividing both sides by $-\frac{5}{3}$ $\left(\text{in other words, multiply both sides by } -\frac{3}{5}\right)$:

   $-\frac{6}{5} = x$, answer (A).

2. **122** You can use the conversion given in the problem (2.54 centimeters per 1 inch) to cancel out the units you don't want (inches),

leaving you with only the units that you do want (centimeters):

$$48\ inches \times \frac{2.54\ centimeters}{1\ inch} =$$

$$121.92\ centimeters \approx 122\ centimeters$$

3. **(C)** Recognize that $d = rt$ where d is distance, r is rate, and t is time. In this problem, $r = 50$ and $t = 3\frac{1}{4} = 3.25$. Use this to solve for distance:

$$d = rt = 50 \times 3.25 = 162.5,\ answer\ (C)$$

Alternatively, you could have done dimensional analysis to cancel out the units you don't want, leaving you only with the units you do want (miles):

$$\frac{50\ miles}{1\ hour} \times 3.25\ hours = 162.5\ miles$$

4. **(A)** First, FOIL the $(x-3)^2$ term in the equation to obtain:

$x^2 - 6y + 9 - 81 = 0$. Then you can combine like terms:

$x^2 - 6y - 72 = 0$. This factors to

$(x-12)(x+6) = 0$. Setting each term equal to 0 tells you that x can either equal 12 or -6. Only 12 is an answer choice, choice (A).

5. **(D)** The typist has already typed 3,500 words, so this will be a constant in the expression. The typist types 70 words per minute, so if he types for t minutes, he will type $70t$ more words. Therefore, the total number of words typed, $W(t)$, will be given by the expression

$$W(t) = 3{,}500 + 70t,\ choice\ (D)$$

6. **(B)** First, begin by factoring out all common factors. $2a$ is a factor of all three terms, so it can be factored out, leaving you with $2a(3a + 4b - 2c)$. Alternatively, you could have redistributed the answer choices to eliminate choices (A), (C), and (D), which respectively equal $3a^2 + 4ab + 2ac$, $4a^2 + 4ab - 8ac$, and $6a^2 - 8ab + 4ac$.

7. **(C)** FOIL this like you'd FOIL any other equation:

$\frac{6}{12}x^2 - \frac{2}{3}x + \frac{3}{4}x - 1$. The coefficient in front of the x^2 can be reduced, giving:

$\frac{1}{2}x^2 - \frac{2}{3}x + \frac{3}{4}x - 1$. To combine the x terms, they need to have a common denominator:

$\frac{1}{2}x^2 - \frac{8}{12}x + \frac{9}{12}x - 1$. Combining these terms gives you $\frac{1}{2}x^2 + \frac{1}{12}x - 1$, or (C).

8. **75** Isosceles trapezoids have two sets of congruent angles, and their interior angles add up to $360°$. Therefore, you know that

$360 = 105 + 105 + x + x$. Combine like terms:

$360 = 210 + 2x$. Subtract 210 from both sides:

$150 = 2x$. Dividing by 2 tells you that $x = 75$. Therefore, the smallest interior angle is $75°$.

9. **(D)** First, solve for x by cross-multiplying:

$2x = 4$. Dividing by 2 tells you that $x = 2$. Next, plug 2 in for x in the expression:

$\frac{4(2-3)}{-12} = \frac{4(-1)}{-12} = \frac{-4}{-12} = \frac{1}{3}$, answer (D)

10. **800** This is a system of equations. If there are 2 men for every 3 women, the ratio is $\frac{m}{w} = \frac{2}{3}$. If there is a total of 4000 students, $m + w = 4000$. To solve this system of equations, solve the first equation for m and plug this into the second equation using substitution. Solving for m, you get $m = \frac{2}{3}w$, so the second equation becomes $\frac{2}{3}w + w = 4000$. Combine like terms: $\frac{5}{3}w = 4000$. Dividing by $\frac{5}{3}$ (the same as multiplying by $\frac{3}{5}$) tells you that $w = 2400$. To figure out how many more women there are than men, you also need to know how many men there are. Plug 2400 in for w in the equation you already solved in terms of m:

$$m = \frac{2}{3}w = \frac{2}{3}(2400) = 1600$$

$w - m = 2400 - 1600 = 800$, so there are 800 more women than men.

11. **(A)** Dividing by a fraction is the same as multiplying by its reciprocal, so $\dfrac{1}{\frac{1}{2x}} = 1 \times \dfrac{2x}{1} = 2x$ and

$\dfrac{3}{\frac{6}{4x}} = 3 \times \dfrac{4x}{6} = \dfrac{12x}{6} = 2x$. Therefore,

$$\dfrac{1}{\frac{1}{2x}} + \dfrac{3}{\frac{6}{4x}} = 2x + 2x = 4x, \text{ answer (A)}$$

12. **(C)** 4807 beverages were purchased, and 1067 of them were espresso. Therefore, the percentage of beverages that was espresso is represented by the expression $\dfrac{1067}{4807} \times 100\% = 22.2\%$, answer (C).

13. **(C)** Notice that both functions give equations of lines. To find the point of intersection, you want to find the point (x, y) that is on both lines. Since (x, y) is on both lines, you can find this common x-value by setting the right sides of both equations equal to one another:

$4x - 3 = -\dfrac{1}{2}x + 2$. Combine like terms by adding $\dfrac{1}{2}x$ to both sides and adding 3 to both sides:

$\dfrac{9}{2}x = 5$. Solve for x by dividing both sides by $\dfrac{9}{2}$ $\left(\text{in other words, multiply both sides by } \dfrac{2}{9}\right)$ to learn that $x = \dfrac{10}{9}$. This is enough to narrow it down to choice (C), but you could solve for y by plugging $\dfrac{10}{9}$ in for x in either equation:

$$y = 4\left(\dfrac{10}{9}\right) - 3 = \dfrac{40}{9} - 3 = \dfrac{40}{9} - \dfrac{27}{9} = \dfrac{13}{9}$$

14. **(14)** For this problem, you need to create a system of equations. First, having 2 quarters for every 5 dimes means that the ratio of quarters to dimes is $\dfrac{q}{d} = \dfrac{2}{5}$.

Next, you need to come up with an expression that represents the value of the coins. Because quarters are worth 25 cents, the number of cents David has from q quarters will be $25q$. Similarly, the number of cents he has from d dimes will be $10d$. Because these expressions are in cents, you need the amount of money he has to also be in cents. There are 100 cents in 1 dollar, so he has 200 cents. Therefore $25q + 10d = 200$. Since $\dfrac{q}{d} = \dfrac{2}{5}$, you have that $q = \dfrac{2}{5}d$. Next, plug this in for q in the second equation:

$25\left(\dfrac{2}{5}d\right) + 10d = 200$. Combine the d terms:

$$20d = 200 \rightarrow d = 10$$

Thus, there are 10 dimes. Plug 10 in for d in the equation that expresses q in terms of d:

$$q = \dfrac{2}{5}d \rightarrow q = \dfrac{2}{5} \times 10 = 4$$

Thus, there are 4 quarters and 10 dimes, giving David 14 coins total.

15. **(B)** In order for the inflation rate, as given by this formula, to equal 0, the numerator of the fraction must equal 0. This will happen if the current year's CPI is equal to the last year's CPI, because subtracting a number from itself will equal 0. This matches answer (B).

16. **(B)** First, get this line in slope-intercept form so that you can easily tell what the slope of this line is. You can do so by adding $4x$ to both sides to get the equation $y = 4x + 5$. The slope of this line is 4. The slope of a line perpendicular to this one will have a slope that is the negative reciprocal of this, $-\dfrac{1}{4}$, which matches (B).

17. **(B)** Anita's $600 rent represented 40% of her expenses, while 60% of her expenses were spent on everything else. You want to figure out what this 60% was, so you can set up a proportion:

$\dfrac{x}{60} = \dfrac{600}{40}$. Next, cross multiply:

$40x = 36{,}000$. Divide both sides by 40 to determine that $x = 900$. Therefore, she spent $900 on everything else, choice (B).

18. **(C)** In this problem, the mean can't easily be figured out because you can't sum together all of the responses without knowing the actual numerical responses (you only know the range of hours for each student). The mode is between 6 and 7 hours, since this was the most frequent response (12 students chose this range). The median in a series of 30 terms is found by arranging them from smallest to largest, then taking the average of the 15th and 16th terms. In this case, the 15th and 16th terms are both between 6 and 7 hours, so the median will be between 6 and 7 hours. Thus, the median and mode are the same, answer (C).

19. **(C)** Recall that the area formula for an equilateral triangle is:

$$Area = \frac{\sqrt{3}}{4}(Side\ Length)^2$$

So, simply plug in 6 for the side length and solve for the area:

$$\frac{\sqrt{3}}{4}(6)^2 = \frac{\sqrt{3} \times 36}{4} = \sqrt{3} \times 9 = 9\sqrt{3}$$

If you forget this formula, you can use the given 30-60-90 triangle ratio to solve.

20. **(C)** You need to come up with an expression for the area of the wall, then recognize that it will cost $12 for every 60 square feet (paint costs $12 per gallon and one gallon covers 60 square feet).

You know that $W = \frac{2}{3}L$ and $A = LW$ since the wall is a rectangle, so plugging in $\frac{2}{3}L$ for W, you get

$$A = L\left(\frac{2}{3}L\right) = \frac{2}{3}L^2.$$

Multiplying the cost/area by the area will cancel area and leave you with cost:

$$\frac{2}{3}L^2 ft^2\left(\frac{12}{60\ ft^2}\right) = \frac{24}{180}L^2 = \frac{2}{15}L^2, \text{ answer (C)}$$

21. **(B)** First, you come up with an expression to represent the amount of food consumed. Each dog consumes 2 cups, so d dogs will consume $2d$ cups of food. Each cat consumes 1 cup of food, so c cats will consume c cups of food. Together, the dogs and cats consume $2d + c$ cups of food. The shelter has 400 cups of food, so $2d + c$ cannot exceed 400. This can be represented by the inequality $2d + c \leq 400$.

Similarly, each dog needs 3 treats daily, so d dogs eat $3d$ treats. Cats eat 2 treats daily, so c cats need $2c$ treats daily. The shelter has 500 treats, so $3d + 2c$ cannot exceed 500:

$3d + 2c \leq 500$. These two equations match answer (B).

22. **(B)** Triangle ECD has an area of 20 and a height of 4. You can plug this into the formula for the area of a triangle $\left(A = \frac{1}{2}bh\right)$ to obtain the base of the triangle, CD.

$20 = \frac{1}{2}b(4) = 2b$. Divide both sides by 2 to get that the base $CD = 10$. Therefore, the base of triangle ABD, BD, is $8 + 10 = 18$. Next, you need to find the height of triangle ABD. You can utilize the fact that these are similar triangles to set up a proportion:

$\frac{AB}{4} = \frac{18}{10}$. Cross multiply: $10AB = 72$. Dividing by 10 tells you that $AB = 7.2$. Plug 7.2 in for the height and 18 in for the base in the area equation:

$$A = \frac{1}{2}(18)(7.2) = 64.8, \text{ answer (B)}$$

Section 2: Math Module 2A

1. **(A)** Distance = (rate) × (time), so $16x$ must represent a rate multiplied by a time.

   You're told that x is the time given in hours, so 16 must represent her rate. *Rate* is another word for speed, so you can narrow it down to choice (A) or choice (B). Because 16 is constant (not changing), the correct answer is choice (A).

2. **(D)** The $3x$ must be distributed to both the $\frac{1}{3}x$ term and the -5 term:

$$3x\left(\frac{1}{3}x - 5\right) = \frac{3}{3}x^2 - 15x$$

   Then, the fraction can be reduced, giving $x^2 - 15x$, choice (D).

3. **(A)** Plug the given slope and point coordinates into the point-slope equation: $y - y_1 = m(x - x_1)$, where m is the slope and (x_1, y_1) are the coordinates of a point on the line. Therefore,

$$y - 8 = 3(x - 1)$$

   Next, distribute the 3:

$$y - 8 = 3x - 3$$

   To get the line in slope-intercept form, add 8 to both sides:

   $y = 3x + 5$. Therefore, the y-intercept is 5, choice (A). You could also plug 3 in for the slope and the point (1, 8) into the line when it is in slope-intercept form: $y = mx + b$. Then you could solve for the y-intercept b.

4. **(B)** The drive-through sold a total of 284 items, and 89 of those were breakfast burritos. Therefore, the probability that a randomly selected item will be a breakfast burrito is given by the expression $\frac{89}{284} = 0.31$, choice (B).

5. **7** Start by multiplying both sides by 2:

$$n + 3 = 10$$

Subtracting 3 from both sides tells you that $n = 7$.

6. **450** You can use the conversion 60 minutes per hour to figure out this problem. Use dimensional analysis to cancel out the units that you don't want (hours) and end up with the units that you do want (minutes):

$$7.5 \text{ hours} \times \frac{60 \text{ min}}{1 \text{ hour}} = 450 \text{ min}$$

7. **(A)** First, isolate what's inside the parentheses by dividing both sides by -3, remembering that dividing by a negative flips the inequality sign.

$x + 4 < -\frac{2}{3}x$. Next, you'll need to subtract x from both sides to get all x terms on the right, but first get a common denominator for the x terms: $\frac{3}{3}x + 4 < -\frac{2}{3}x$, so $4 < -\frac{5}{3}x$. Finally, divide both sides by $-\frac{5}{3}$, which is the same as multiplying both sides by $-\frac{3}{5}$, again remembering to flip the inequality since you are multiplying by a negative number:

$$-\frac{12}{5} > x, \text{ or } x < -\frac{12}{5}, \text{ choice (A)}$$

8. **(C)** Use process of elimination here. You can eliminate choice (A) because you don't know the range: there is no upper limit provided. You only know that the upper limit is over $25.

Choice (B) can also be eliminated because you can't figure out an exact mean without knowing what the prices are. For instance, if the prices in the last row were all well above $25, and thus outliers, the mean would be very skewed.

Choice (C) can be tested. There are $12 + 15 + 10 + 21 + 7 = 65$ terms in this series, so the median term will be the 33rd term (there are 32 terms smaller than this number and 32 terms larger than it). The first row encompasses terms 1–12. The

second row encompasses 13–27, and the third has terms 28–37. Therefore, the 33rd term will fall in this third row, and thus will have a price between $15 and $20. Therefore, choice (C) is correct.

9. **(C)** First, you can factor out a 9:

$$9(a^2 - 9b^2)$$

Something of the form $(x^2 - y^2)$ is a difference of perfect squares and factors to $(x + y)(x - y)$. In this case, $x = a$, while $y = 3b$ since $(3b)^2 = 9b^2$. Therefore, $a^2 - 9b^2 = (a + 3b)(a - 3b)$. Remembering the 9 you previously factored out gives you $9(a + 3b)(a - 3b)$, choice (C).

Alternatively, you could have FOILed all answer choices to see which choice gave you the expression in the question's statement.

10. **(D)** Get the second equation into slope-intercept form so you can see how the two equations relate. In order to accomplish this, divide both sides by 2:

$$y = 4x - 2.5$$

Therefore, both lines have the same slope, but different y-intercepts. This means that they're parallel lines and never intersect, choice (D).

Alternatively, if you don't recognize this right away, you can set the right side of both equations (in slope-intercept form) equal to each other and attempt to solve for x to see where the two lines intersect:

$$4x = 4x - 2.5$$

Subtracting $4x$ from both sides, you have $0 = -2.5$, which is a false statement, so there are no solutions to this equation, and hence no intersection points.

11. **(A)** First, distribute the 2 in the second term:

$$\frac{1}{3}x + \frac{2}{6}x + 6$$

Reduce the second fraction:

$$\frac{1}{3}x + \frac{1}{3}x + 6$$

Combine like terms:

$$\frac{2}{3}x + 6$$

Thus, the answer is choice (A).

12. **(C)** First, you need to know how many senior citizens there are in the state of Connecticut. If 14% of 3.6 million are seniors, then $3,600,000(0.14) = 504,000$ are senior citizens. This also could have been done using a proportion, recognizing that 3.6 million is 100% of the population.

Next, you know that 23% of the survey respondents said that they would support the new tax regulation. Since the question says that those surveyed are representative of the population, it follows that 23% of the senior population would also support the tax regulation. Find 23% of 504,000 by using a proportion (although you could just as easily multiply 504,000 by 0.23 to find the answer).

$$\frac{504,000}{100} = \frac{x}{23}$$

Next, cross-multiply:

$$(504,000)(23) = 100x$$

$$11,592,000 = 100x$$

Dividing by 100 tells you that $x = 115,920$. This most closely matches choice (C).

13. **(C)** First, calculate the area of the circle:

$$\pi r^2 \rightarrow \pi (4)^2 = 16\pi$$

Since the sector has a measure of 60 degrees and a circle has a total of 360 interior degrees, calculate the fraction of the total circle's area that the sector is as follows:

$$16\pi \times \frac{60}{360} \rightarrow 16\pi \times \frac{1}{6} = \frac{16\pi}{6} = \frac{8\pi}{3} \text{ square inches}$$

14. **(B)** Notice that the expression the question is asking about is just the reciprocal of the left side of the first expression. Therefore, it will equal the reciprocal of the right side of the first expression. Because the reciprocal of $\frac{1}{6}$ is 6, the answer is choice (B).

Alternatively, if you do not recognize that it is the reciprocal, you can solve for x in the first equation and then plug this into the second expression:

If $-\frac{2}{3}x = \frac{1}{6}$, then multiplying both sides by $-\frac{3}{2}$ gives $x = \frac{1}{6}\left(\frac{-3}{2}\right) = -\frac{1}{4}$. Plugging this into your expression gives $\dfrac{-\left(\frac{3}{2}\right)}{x} = \dfrac{-\left(\frac{3}{2}\right)}{-\left(\frac{1}{4}\right)} = \left(\frac{3}{2}\right)\left(\frac{4}{1}\right) = 6$.

15. **(B)** The 2 in the original equation is an added constant, so it is the delivery fee. Doubling the delivery fee would make it a constant $4. Thus, you can narrow the answer down to choices (B) and (C) since the delivery fee will be the only constant (the cost of food and tip will depend on c). You can eliminate choice (C) as it is unlikely that the restaurant would allow the customer to pay only 0.6 or 60% of the cost of the food.

If you want to see where the correct answer, choice (B), comes from, you could separate the original equation into $t = c + 0.2c + 2$, where c is the cost of the food, $0.2c$ is the 20% tip, and 2 is the delivery fee.

Thus, if the tip is halved, it will now be 10% of the cost of food, or $0.1c$. If the delivery fee is doubled, it will now be 4 instead of 2. Therefore, the new equation will be $t = c + 0.1c + 4 = 1.1c + 4$, which matches choice (B).

16. **10** The average of their weight would be the total weight of all six animals divided by 6:

$$\frac{d_1 + d_2 + d_3 + c_1 + c_2 + c_3}{6}$$

where d_i represents the weight of dog i, and c_i represents the weight of cat i. You are told that the three dogs weigh an average of 40 pounds each, so $\dfrac{d_1 + d_2 + d_3}{3} = 40$ and thus the three dogs' combined weigh $d_1 + d_2 + d_3 = 3(40) = 120$. Also, you know two cats each weigh 25 pounds, so $c_1 = 25 = c_2$.

Thus, the average weight of the six animals is

$$\frac{d_1 + d_2 + d_3 + c_1 + c_2 + c_3}{6} = \frac{120 + 25 + 25 + c_3}{6}$$

$$= \frac{170 + c_3}{6}$$

You are told that the average weight is 30 pounds, and you want to find the weight of the third cat, so you set your above expression equal to 30 and solve for c_3:

$$\frac{170 + c_3}{6} = 30$$

First, multiply by 6:

$170 + c_3 = 180$. Next, subtract 170 from both sides:

$c_3 = 10$. Therefore, the cat of unknown weight weighs 10 pounds.

17. **(A)** You can determine the answer by assigning particular values to G. For instance, suppose the generic brand soda costs \$1 (i.e., $G = 1$). Since $N = 2G$, it follows that $N = 2(1) = 2$. Thus, the name brand soda is twice as expensive as the generic brand. Similarly, trying other values for G, you always multiply G by 2 to find N, so N is always twice the cost of G, or choice (A).

18. **(B)** Take this step by step. You are told that 3 A's equal 2 B's, or $3A = 2B$, and 3 C's equal one B, or $3C = 1B$. You want to know how many C's there will be if you have just one A. You don't know the relationship between A and C right away, but you do know how A is related to B and how C is related to B. You can, therefore, use these relationships with B to find the relationship between A and C. Since you want to know how many C's there are for one A, you should first find out how B relates to one A. Since $3A = 2B$, it follows that $A = \frac{2}{3}B$. But, you also know $3C = B$, so plugging this expression in for B in your previous equation, you obtain $A = \frac{2}{3}B = \frac{2}{3}(3C) = 2C$. Thus, 2 C's equal one A, which corresponds to choice (B).

19. **12** A diagonal of a square cuts that square into two 45-45-90 triangles. If the diagonal of the square (the hypotenuse of the triangles) has a length of $3\sqrt{2}$, then that square will have side lengths of 3. This is because a 45-45-90 triangle has legs of length x and a hypotenuse of length $x\sqrt{2}$. (This relationship is given on the formula sheet at provided in the Math section.)

Therefore, the perimeter of the square will be $4l = 4(3) = 12$.

Alternatively, if you don't recognize this special triangle, you know that this is a square, so the two sides of the triangle will have the same length l. Using the Pythagorean theorem, $l^2 + l^2 = (3\sqrt{2})^2$, so $2l^2 = 18$. Dividing by 2 gives $l^2 = 9$, so $l = 3$.

20. **(A)** Calculate the number of followers in the first few months and see if you can find a pattern.

In the beginning, or month 0, there are 100 followers.

After month 1, the number of followers increases by 5%, so there are now

$$1.05(100) = 105 \text{ followers}$$

After month 2, the number of followers increases by 5% again, giving $1.05(105)$ followers.

Since $105 = 1.05(100)$ based on your calculation in the previous month, you can substitute this expression in for 105 to get that the number of followers is $1.05(1.05(100))$, or $(1.05)^2 (100)$ followers.

Similarly, you get that the number of followers in month 3 is $(1.05)^3(100)$. Continuing in this manner, a pattern emerges, giving you a formula for the number of followers in month n: $(1.05)^n(100)$. This is an exponential relationship between months and number of followers since the months variable is the exponent in your function. Also, the number of followers increases each month, so this is an exponentially increasing relationship. This matches choice (A).

21. **(D)** Note that in general, the vertex form of a parabola is given by $(x - h)^2 + k$, where (h, k) is the vertex of the parabola. You are told that the vertex form of parabola f is $f(x) = x^2 + 3$, which can be rewritten as $f(x) = (x - 0)^2 + 3$. Thus, the vertex of f is $(0, 3) = (a, b)$. Now, you want to know how the vertex of $g(x)$ compares to (a, b). Note that $g(x) = -f(x) + 2 = -(x^2 + 3) + 2 = -x^2 - 3 + 2 = x^2 - 1$. Thus, the vertex of g is $(0, -1) = (a, -1)$. So, you just need to determine how b compares to -1. Since $b = 3$ and $-1 = 3 - 4 = b - 4$, it follows that the vertex of g is $(a, b - 4)$ when written in terms of a and b, which matches choice (D).

Alternatively, you can think about what is happening in terms of transformations. Suppose (a, b) is the vertex of f. Then $-f(x)$ reflects f across the x-axis, so the vertex (a, b) becomes $(a, -b)$ when reflected. Then $g(x) = -f(x) + 2$ shifts $-f(x)$ up vertically by 2, so the vertex of $g(x)$ is

$(a, -b + 2)$. Note that this is not an answer choice. However, the vertex of f is $(0, 3)$ since f shifts the parabola x^2 up 3 units. Thus, $b = 3$. So the vertex of g is $(a, -b + 2) = (a, -3 + 2) = (a, -1)$. Plugging 3 in for b in the answer choices, you see that choice (D) is the only choice that results in vertex $(a, -1)$.

22. **6** You are given the formula for the volume of a rectangular prism, $V_r = lwh$, at the beginning of the Math section. In this problem, your rectangular prism has height A, length B, and width C, so the formula becomes $V_r = BCA$. You want to know how many pyramids with the same length and width of the prism, but half of its height, can fit into the prism. You are also given the formula for the volume of a pyramid, $V_p = \frac{1}{3}lwh$, at the beginning of the Math section. Since the pyramids have the same length and width as the prism, $l = B$ and $w = C$. The height is half of the prism, so $h = \frac{A}{2}$. Thus, each pyramid has volume $V_p = \frac{1}{3}BC\left(\frac{A}{2}\right) = \frac{1}{6}BCA$. Note that $\frac{1}{6}BCA = \frac{1}{6}V_r$. Therefore, since $V_p = \frac{1}{6}V_r$, it follows that $6V_p = V_r$. In other words, you can fit the volume of pyramids into the rectangular prism.

Math Module 2B

1. **(B)** First, factor a 5 out:

   $5(x^2 - 3x + 2) = 0$. Dividing both sides by 5 leaves you with $x^2 - 3x + 2 = 0$. This can be factored as $(x - 2)(x - 1) = 0$. Set each factor to 0 to solve for possible x-values: $x - 2 = 0$, so $x = 2$ or $x - 1 = 0$, so $x = 1$. Therefore, the answer is (B). Alternatively, you could have used the quadratic formula to solve for possible x-values.

2. **(D)** A function intersects the x-axis at its roots where $y = 0$: this will occur when any of these three factors equals 0. Set each factor equal to 0 to determine the x-values.

   $x = 0$.

   $x - 5 = 0$, so $x = 5$.

   $x + 2 = 0$, so $x = -2$.

   Therefore, the three x-values are 0, 5, and -2, answer (D).

3. **(B)** Notice that the function is 2 minus the absolute value of something. The absolute value of something must always be greater than or equal to 0, so either $f(x) = 2 - 0 = 2$ or $f(x)$ equals 2 minus some positive number. But, this second case will result in a value that is less than 2. (Convince yourself of this. For instance, if the absolute value is 1, then $f(x) = 2 - 1 = 1$.) Therefore, the maximum value of f is 2. So, to find where this maximum will occur, you need to determine which x-values give $|x - 4| = 0$. This occurs when $x - 4 = 0$. Thus, $x = 4$, which is choice (B).

   Alternatively, you could have plugged the potential x-values in to determine which gave the maximum value for $f(x)$.

4. **(B)** You need to try to simplify the left side of the equation a bit to get it in the same form as the right side.

   When an exponent is raised to another exponent, you multiply those exponents, so $(x^2)^{\frac{1}{5}} = x^{\frac{2}{5}}$.

   Also, $\sqrt[5]{32x^2}$ can be broken up into $\sqrt[5]{32} \cdot \sqrt[5]{x^2}$. Since $\sqrt[5]{32} = 2$, the expression can be further simplified:

   $\sqrt[5]{32} \cdot \sqrt[5]{x^2} = 2x^{\frac{2}{5}}$. Therefore, the left side of the equation simplifies to $x^{\frac{2}{5}} + 2x^{\frac{2}{5}}$. You can then combine like terms:

   $x^{\frac{2}{5}} + 2x^{\frac{2}{5}} = 3x^{\frac{2}{5}}$. If $3x^{\frac{2}{5}} = ax^{\frac{2}{5}}$, then it follows from dividing both sides by $x^{\frac{2}{5}}$ that $a = 3$, answer (B).

5. **(A)** First, get the equation into standard form by subtracting 17 from both sides: $y = 6x^2 + 12x - 17$. When a parabola is in standard form, $y = ax^2 + bx + c$, the axis of symmetry is given by the equation $x = -\frac{b}{2a}$. Because the axis of symmetry passes through the vertex and this parabola opens up, the x-value that gives the axis of symmetry will also give the x-coordinate of the vertex. The y- and x-values of the vertex give the minimum value and its location on the parabola, respectively, so you want to know the x-value of the vertex to solve this problem.

In this case, $a = 6$ and $b = 12$, so $x = -\frac{b}{2a} = -\frac{12}{2(6)} = -\frac{12}{12} = -1$. This corresponds to answer (A).

Alternatively, have graphed the parabola using Desmos to visualize the minimum point of the parabola. Just be sure to find the x-coordinate.

6. **15** Solve the second equation for y to solve this system of equations using substitution.

$y = \frac{6}{4}x = \frac{3}{2}x$. Next, plug $\frac{3}{2}x$ in for y in the first equation:

$2x - \frac{3}{2}x = 3$. In order to combine the x terms, you need a common denominator:

$\frac{4}{2}x - \frac{3}{2}x = \frac{1}{2}x$, so our equation becomes $\frac{1}{2}x = 3$. Dividing both sides by $\frac{1}{2}$ tells you that $x = 6$. Next, plug in 6 for x in the equation that you already solved for y:

$y = \frac{3}{2}x = \frac{3}{2}(6) = \frac{18}{2} = 9$. Since $x = 6$ and $y = 9$, their sum is $6 + 9$, or 15.

7. **196** First, simplify the second term in the numerator:

$3(2x^2)^2 = 3(4x^4) = 12x^4$, so our entire expression becomes

$\left(\frac{2x^4 + 3(2x^2)^2}{x^4}\right)^2 = \left(\frac{2x^4 + 12x^4}{x^4}\right)^2$. The x^4

terms of the numerator can be combined:

$\left(\frac{2x^4 + 12x^4}{x^4}\right)^2 = \left(\frac{14x^4}{x^4}\right)^2$. The x^4 in

the numerator cancels with the x^4 in the denominator:

$\left(\frac{14x^4}{x^4}\right)^2 = (14)^2 = 196$, so the answer is 196.

8. **(D)** The different terms on the two sides of the equation equal each other. So, $-16 = -8b$, $-6x = -abx$, and $x^2 = x^2$. Why? This occurs because the constants must equal each other, the terms with an x must equal each other, and the terms with an x^2 must equal one another. Since $-16 = -8b$, $b = 2$. Plug in 2 for b in the second equation and cancel out the $-x$ to solve for a:

$-6x = -abx \rightarrow 6 = a \cdot 2 \rightarrow a = 3$

9. **(D)** Look at the bottom row. There are a total of 400 individuals, and each selected one type of communication that they preferred, so the first four numbers in the bottom row must add up to 400:

$195 + x + 70 + 70 = 400$. Combine like terms on the left side of the equation.

$335 + x = 400$. Subtract 335 from both sides to isolate x:

$x = 65$, answer (D).

Alternatively, you could have added up the first two terms in the email column to obtain x: $20 + 45 = 65$.

10. **(C)** From the graph, you can tell that the average monthly temperature in Townsville is greater than that in Cityberg for April, May, June, July, August, September, October, and November, or 8 months. This excessive temperature is sufficient to outweigh the lesser average that Townsville is in the remaining four months to make its average monthly temperature greater than that of Cityberg. Therefore, choice (C) is correct. (A) and (B) are incorrect because the graph doesn't tell you anything about the temperature on any random day. (D) is incorrect because the average temperature in Cityberg is only greater for January, February, March, and December.

11. **(B)** This question is asking you what percent the discount is of 90. First, you need to know what the discount is, which you can get by subtracting the new price from the original price: $90 - 72 = 18$. Then, you can figure out what percentage 18 is of 90 by setting up a proportion, recognizing that 90 will represent 100% of the quantity:

$\frac{x}{100} = \frac{18}{90}$. Next, cross multiply.

$90x = 1800$. Dividing by 90 yields $x = 20$, so $18 is 20% of $90, answer (B).

12. **(D)** In this equation, the 20 is a constant. Therefore, this is a constant amount of time required that isn't dependent on the number of cookies he makes. Therefore, this is the amount of time he requires to get the ingredients and set things up, which matches choice (D).

13. **(C)** Create a system of equations. First, you know that she has \$100,000 invested among the three categories, so if s, b, and c represent the amount of money in stocks, bonds, and cash, respectively, then $s + b + c = 100{,}000$.

She has invested twice as much in stocks as in bonds, so $s = 2b$.

She has invested three times as much in bonds as in cash, so $b = 3c$.

The question asks how much money is invested in bonds, so you want to get s and c in terms of b, plug these expressions into the first equation, and solve for b. The second equation is already solved for s in terms of b, but you need to solve the third equation for c in terms of b:

$\frac{1}{3}b = c$. Next, plug these expressions in for s and c in the first equation:

$s + b + c = 2b + b + \frac{1}{3}b = 100{,}000$. You can combine like terms to get $\frac{10}{3}b = 100{,}000$. Divide both sides by $\frac{10}{3}$ to get $b = 30{,}000$. The question asks what percent is invested in bonds, so find what fraction 30,000 is of 100,000, and multiply that number by 100%:

$\frac{30{,}000}{100{,}000} \times 100\% = 30\%$, answer (C).

Alternatively, you can figure out the ratio of the investments:

Cash: Bonds: Stocks $= 1 : 3 : 6$

The total of the numbers in this ratio is $1 + 3 + 6 = 10$.

Therefore, as fractions of the whole, the investments are $\frac{1}{10}$, $\frac{3}{10}$, and $\frac{6}{10}$.

The bonds are $\frac{3}{10}$, which translates to 30%.

14. **(C)** Mary would weed a total of $3x$ lawns since she weeded 3 lawns an hour for x hours. John would weed a total of $2y$ lawns since he weeded 2 lawns an hour for y hours. So, the total they weeded that day would be $3x + 2y$ lawns.

15. **(A)** The volume of a sphere is given by the formula $V = \frac{4}{3}\pi r^3$. The diameter is twice the radius, so you can solve for the radius and multiply by 2. To solve for r, first divide both sides by $\frac{4}{3}\pi$:

$\frac{3V}{4\pi} = r^3$. To solve for r, take the cube root of both sides:

$\sqrt[3]{\frac{3V}{4\pi}} = r$. Multiply this by 2 to get an expression for the diameter:

$d = 2\sqrt[3]{\frac{3V}{4\pi}}$, answer (A).

16. **(B)** Each month, she adds \$50, so the function will have a constant slope of 50. Because the slope is constant, the function is linear. The slope is positive 50, so the answer is (B). You know that the slope will be positive because the two variables are directly proportional: as time goes on, the amount of money in the account increases.

17. **(C)** First, you can factor a 7 out of both factors of the numerator:

$\frac{7(x-1) \cdot 7(x+1)}{7}$. One 7 in the numerator will cancel out with the 7 in the denominator, leaving you with $7(x-1)(x+1)$. Next, FOIL the terms in the parentheses to get $7(x^2 - 1)$, answer (C).

18. **(A)** The y-intercept of the function is somewhere between positive 6 and 8, so you can eliminate choices (C) and (D). Next, find the approximate slope. You can use any two points on the line of best fit, such as the endpoints:

$m = \frac{y_2 - y_1}{x_2 - x_1} = \frac{9.6 - 6.5}{6 - 0} = \frac{3.1}{6} \approx 0.5$, so the answer is (A). The line has a slope of 0.5 and a y-intercept of 6.5.

19. **6** A cube has six sides, so its surface area is given by the formula $SA = 6L^2$. The volume of a cube is given by the formula $V = L^3$. Set these two equations equal to one another:

$6L^2 = L^3$. You can divide both sides by L^2 to obtain that $6 = L$.